Meta-Communication for Reflective Online Conversations:

Models for Distance Education

Ugur Demiray
Anadolu University, Turkey

Gulsun Kurubacak
Anadolu University, Turkey

T. Volkan Yuzer
Anadolu University, Turkey

Information Science
REFERENCE

Published in the United States of America by
Information Science Reference (an imprint of IGI Global)
701 E. Chocolate Avenue
Hershey PA 17033
Tel: 717-533-8845
Fax: 717-533-8661
E-mail: cust@igi-global.com
Web site: http://www.igi-global.com

Library of Congress Cataloging-in-Publication Data

Meta-communication for reflective online conversations: models for distance education / Ugur Demiray, Gulsun Kurubacak, and T. Volkan Yuzer, editors.
p. cm.
Includes bibliographical references and index.
Summary: "This book discusses the potential of meta-communication models for building and managing reflective online conversations among distance learners, offering models for meta-communication, distance education, and reflective online conversations"--Provided by publisher.
ISBN 978-1-61350-071-2 (hardcover) -- ISBN 978-1-61350-072-9 (ebook) -- ISBN 978-1-61350-073-6 (print & perpetual access) 1. Distance education--Computer-assisted instruction. 2. Communication in education. 3. Interaction analysis in education. I. Demiray, Ugur. II. Kurubacak, Gulsun, 1964- III. Yuzer, T. Volkan, 1972-
LC5803.C65M48 2012
371.19--dc23

2011026555

British Cataloguing in Publication Data
A Cataloguing in Publication record for this book is available from the British Library.

Editorial Advisory Board

Table of Contents

Section 2
Dynamic Models of Meta-Communication and Reflective Conversations

Section 3
Designing Online Messages for Reflections

Foreword

We all have hang-ups about using certain words because we find their meaning vague. For me *'meta'* is such a word. Attempts to define it, for example: *'a prefix meaning between, with, after, behind, over, about, reversely'* or *'a concept which is an abstraction from another concept, used to complete or add to the latter'* do not help much.

It gets better when you look up *'meta-communication'*. Lexicographers can be ponderous but this definition does illuminate the subject: *'communication that indicates how verbal information should be interpreted; stimuli surrounding the verbal communication that also have meaning, which may or may not be congruent with that of or support the verbal talk. It may support or contradict verbal communication; Communication which is implicit and not expressed in words'*.

The authors of these chapters have accepted a challenge. Online communication is mostly through the written word, so how can non-verbal communication help us interpret it? Emoticons are hardly the answer. I prefer people to make their emotions clear in their writing and do not want to be told what feelings the words are meant to evoke in me.

The inclusion of the words 'reflective' and 'conversation' in the title does nothing to lessen the challenge facing the authors. Reflection is a vital element of learning but in some terms, such as 'reflective practice', it has become a cliché. Conversation theory is an important and difficult branch of learning science, yet we now use 'conversation' simply as a trendy synonym for 'discussion'. Surprisingly, there is no reference to conversation theory in the book, which reminds us how geographically fragmented research on educational technology has become. Although there are contributions from Australia, India, Saudi Arabia, and Thailand, this book mainly reflects work from Turkey and the US. How would scholars from Western Europe have tackled these issues?

The final challenge to the contributors is the sub-title 'models for distance education'. Are they attempting to apply the traditional models of distance education to a new technology or to replace those traditional models with something new?

How do the authors address these multiple challenges and what does the book have to tell us?

Its first lesson is that there is no magic instructional medium and probably never will be. Online learning is merely the latest manifestation of our tendency to invest unreasonable expectations in new technologies. Each new communication medium is hailed for its transformational impact on the human intellect. Yet while McLuhan was correct that each medium brings a new message, we should not exaggerate the change it brings. Online conversations are unlikely, in and of themselves, to lead students to the holy grails of critical thinking, objective reasoning, and constructivist learning. It all depends on how they are fostered. Similarly, we can hardly expect the theory of distance education to usher in a new era of digital democracy.

Professor Demiray and his colleagues tackle these issues in the first chapter of the book. One of the advantages of online courses is that those who develop them pay more attention to instructional design than they would for a classroom course, and therefore include specific strategies for achieving the learning objectives that they value. Since an online discussion among students does not automatically yield anything valuable, the authors explore some techniques for leading them to participate in useful ways.

Some of the later authors refute implausible assumptions about online conversations. Why should we expect online teaching to mute the sub-conscious racist and sexist attitudes of the individuals who write the courses – or make these same individuals more likely to challenge similar prejudices in students' work? Surely the answer is to place online learning within the older tradition of distance education where quality and balance is achieved by having courses developed by teams with diverse viewpoints and having student assignments reviewed by tutors specially trained for this function? The graduate who told me, with a blend of satisfaction and frustration, that after studying at the UK Open University he could not see less than six sides to any question, gave me one of my proudest moments as head of that institution. Inculcating the fundamental academic habit of systematic scepticism does not depend on particular learning media but on how teachers use them.

One chapter finds that online learning expanded the intellectual horizons of female students in Saudi Arabia. Even the limited access to Internet resources allowed in that country gave women a new appreciation of the diversity of views that people hold, not least within their own student group. This gave them more mental independence, just as the ability to study from home and on their own schedules allowed them more physical autonomy. This is the heart of the meta-communication inherent in online teaching. By placing teaching and learning in the ordered chaos of the Internet and by bringing some of the principles of distance education to bear on the design and delivery of teaching, we create, in the words of the earlier definition 'stimuli surrounding the verbal communication that also have meaning'.

The virtue of this book, like Professor Demiray's earlier collection of studies on e-learning across Europe, is that it exposes and explores the challenges of working at the frontiers of practice. Not everything is rosy. An interesting contribution about an attempt by four countries (Indonesia, Laos, Philippines, and Thailand) to develop a joint graduate course is candid about the difficulties of connectivity, low participation, hierarchy, language, and timidity that dogged the project. Other contributions reflect the enthusiasm of novelty. Academics are prepared to work hard to foster reflective online conversations, and it is both churlish and too early to ask questions about the economic sustainability of their approaches.

I commend this book for illustrating the considerable diversity of expectations and practice of online learning. All readers who are involved in e-learning will find much here that they can juxtapose with their own experience in building better practices for the future.

John Daniel
President & CEO, Commonwealth of Learning, Canada

Sir John Daniel *became President of Commonwealth of Learning in 2004 after gaining wide international experience in universities and the United Nations system. He obtained his full-time university education in Metallurgy at Oxford and Paris and later demonstrated his commitment to lifelong learning by taking 25 years to complete a part-time Master's degree in Educational Technology at Concordia University. However, the internship for that programme, which took him to the UK Open University in 1972, was a life-changing experience. He saw the future of higher education and wanted to be part of it. This quest took him on an international odyssey with appointments at the Télé-université (Directeur des Études, 1973-77), Athabasca University (Vice-President for Learning Services, 1978-80), Concordia University (Vice-Rector, Academic, 1980-84),*

Laurentian University (President, 1984-90), the UK Open University (Vice-Chancellor, 1990-2001) and UNESCO (Assistant Director-General for Education, 2001-04). His non-executive appointments have included the presidencies of the International Council for Open and Distance Education, the Canadian Association for Distance Education, and the Canadian Society for the Study of Higher Education. He also served as Vice-President of the International Baccalaureate Organisation. Among Sir John's 290 publications are his books Mega-Universities and Knowledge Media: Technology Strategies for Higher Education (Kogan Page, 1996) and Mega-Schools, Technology and Teachers: Achieving Education for All (Routledge, 2010). He was knighted by Queen Elizabeth for services to higher education in 1994 and holds over 30 honorary doctorates, fellowships and professorships from universities and professional bodies in 16 countries. He is a citizen of Canada and the UK.

Preface

The main purpose of this book is to discuss meta-communication for reflective online conversations to provide digital people with models for distance education. The unique approach of the publication brings together meta-communication, distance education, and models as well as reflective online conversations at the same time.

This book, consisting of 17 chapters, is divided into four sections: Meta-communicative knowledge building and online communications, dynamic models of meta-communication and reflective conversations, designing online messages for reflections, and meta-communicative assessments and reflective communication skills.

Chapter 1 focuses on how online discussion has become one of the most effective teaching tools in recent years in terms of its power to promote students' critical thinking skills in educational contexts. This chapter aims at presenting an overview of recently conducted research studies on critical thinking and online discussions, explaining online discussion as a pedagogical vehicle for maximizing language learning and teaching, identifying problems related to online discussions as well as some suggested solutions, describing application activities that promote critical thinking skills, illustrating how language teachers and learners can use meta-communication in creating successful online discussions, and stressing the importance of the teacher's role in designing an effective online discussion environment for students.

Chapter 2 focuses on how to build a dynamic theoretical background of distance education as *a source of meta-communication,* and how this affects the use of online learning for reflective meaning making to construct a knowledge society. Based on the main purpose of this study, the virtual world can provide online learners with an interactive milieu for problem solving, critical thinking, and personalized/group discussion, multimedia presentation of global resources, connectivity, and visualization of social aspects of discussion and communication. In this context, distance education can respond to concerns and issues to create digital self-representations through a communication theory and learning theory together. Furthermore, discussing the main features of the cross-cultural implications of reflective conversations can construct a very powerful paradigm shift to establish public interests encompassing the reflections of every aspect of social networking with the enthusiasms, persuasions, as well as judgments.

Chapter 3 takes a contrary view of the "meta" aspect of meta-communication (where meta is defined as "behind" or "beneath") in the online multicultural teacher education classroom, arguing that such communication inhibits learning about (content) and through (pedagogy) sociopolitically-located multicultural teacher education by enabling e-racism, e-classism, and e-sexism to operate in largely covert manners in the distance education context. Accordingly, this chapter contends that digital meta-communication on issues of race/ethnicity, socioeconomic class, and sex/gender needs to be "de-meta-ed" or made explicit in order for the kind of liberatory reflective conversation on these topics to occur that is foundational to the adequate preparation of PK-12 teachers to effectively educate all students.

Chapter 4 is based on the online conversation that transpired among faculty members of higher educational institutions from four Southeast Asian countries who were in the process of designing a proposed regional graduate program on natural resources knowledge management. Knowledge management is synonymous to the sharing and reuse of intellectual capital. In other words knowledge management is engaged in what Habermas calls the *communicative act*. This communicative act being the subject of the online conversation has transformed the online discussion for the proposed program into meta communication, i.e., communication on communication or discourse (online discussion threads) on knowledge management (communication). The researchers documented the online conversation to test the efficacy of the platform used. In the process, however, they have uncovered certain oppressive factors peculiar to this setting that hindered the communicative act (i.e., knowledge management) and meta-communication (i.e., the online conversation) itself.

Chapter 5 describes a meta-communication model and illustrates its applicability. The model integrates previous discursive approaches to reflective practice and extends them with additional relevant concepts. The concepts of the meta-communication model are mainly based on Avatar Manager and Student Reflective Conversations pedagogical theory. By means of case examples, this chapter also illustrates how the model can be used for making meaning in experiential and theoretical based online educational courses and collective sense-making, i.e. the articulation and contesting the meaning and relevance of ideas. This chapter argues that the model provides a way for systematically and meaningfully structuring and organizing meta-level conversations in virtual classroom. The use of reflective pedagogies has long been considered critical to facilitating meaningful learning through experientially based curricula; however, the use of such methods has not been extensively explored as implemented in virtual environments. The study reviewed utilizes a combination of survey research and individual interviews to examine student perceptions of the meaningful learning which occurred as a result of their participation in two Web-based courses that utilized reflective pedagogies. One course focuses on topics related to service-learning and the second on placement-based internships. Both were instructed using online coursework based in reflective pedagogies to compliment on-site placements within local communities. Thus, created software of Meta-Communication Model applicable for using in virtual education process and in virtual research collaboration works at Astrakhan State University (Russian Federation) and at All Armenian Internet University (Australian Federation and Republic of Armenia) for the development of avatars has significant potential to enhance realism, automation capability, and effectiveness across a variety of training environments.

Chapter 6 ensures that the discipline of science is accessible to all individuals. By many organizations this has been termed “Science for All,” and those who promote this idea also advocate the connection to science literacy. Teaching science in the online environment has been one way to offer science content to many different individuals who do not necessarily need to be in the same location. Discourse in the science classroom is framed under situated cognition theory, whereby interactions between individuals are part of the normal culture of the classroom. For science knowledge to be adequately constructed by a student, these interactions must be meaningful ones. This is especially important in an online science course where typically learning occurs through interactions between the students and the instructor, the students with one another, and within the individual themselves. As part of these online interactions, good reflective practice includes the different forms of feedback and the quality of this feedback. However, even with quality reflective interactions, there are barriers to science concept construction in an online environment. These barriers are discussed, and future research directions are suggested based on this review.

Chapter 7 includes information about communication patterns and organizational discourse at an online university, which utilizes a mentoring model to educate students. The mentoring approach involves the assignment of individual students to work one-to-one with a faculty mentor for each course of the degree or certificate program in which the student is enrolled. To address the types of communication inherent in this virtual education model, a mentor, a doctoral dissertation committee member, and a student shed light on their experiences of communication at the university. These diverse prospective serve as a meta-communication model can be implemented to enhance the effectiveness of discourse at other institutions-particularly those seeking to implement a one-to-one mentoring approach.

Chapter 8 focuses on knowledge building through interactivity, social engagement, and communication technologies in a distance learning environment. Emphasis is placed on online collaboration and community building to encourage collaborative learning and ultimately knowledge acquisition. Theoretical constructs surrounding social constructivism and practical application to instruction are provided to the reader to enhance a distance learning course using meta-communication strategies. Sharing knowledge through collaboration and community using distance learning tools is an important component of today's 21st century education. Distance learning is growing in educational institutions worldwide, and instructors are developing enhanced teaching strategies focused on incorporating meta-communication that engages and empowers students in their quest for understanding.

Chapter 9 addresses the evolving strategies that have been used in the deployment of publicly viewable assignments used on asynchronous message boards for freshman and sophomore writing classes since 1997 through the consortium WashingtonOnline (WAOL), which consists of 32 community colleges in Washington State. Asynchronous message boards provide a critical space for university students to learn collaboratively, support each other, and develop critical thinking skills in freshman and sophomore composition and research writing classes. How asynchronous message board assignments - icebreakers, discussion questions, summaries, reading analyses, lead-up assignments (research topic proposals, source evaluations, outlines, and drafts), and cumulative projects - all work towards building reflective online conversations and deep learning.

Chapter 10 is based on the claim that the metaphors used as a new and powerful tool in different sciences, especially including Information Systems and a number of sociological disciplines such as linguistics, education, and sociology, can be used for the implementation and sustainability of the components of meta-communication for distance education. The meta-communication aims to move the intercultural components of metaphors to the distance education and its applications. Thereby, metaphors serve to the basic mission of distance education creating cross-cultural educational environments. In order to use metaphors with the meaning put forward by this claim, restructuring of metaphors with the contemporary metaphor theory, use of metaphors in computer systems and user interfaces, the intersection of metaphors and meta-communication, and finally, the power of metaphors in digital meta-communication for distance education are discussed below.

Chapter 11 builds on the insights of educators regarding the relationship between culture and online learning. In this chapter, the author sheds light on the ways in which culture has a significant influence on online education and vice versa. The chapter is based on primary data drawn from undergraduate female students' responses regarding how online education is changing their learning culture and how their culture is influencing online education. Sixty undergraduate Saudi female students participated in the survey in order to identify how using the Internet, online education, and online discussion forums is challenging cultural norms. The literature in the field of online and distance education is also explored to help answer these questions. Students indicated that online education helped them to challenge some cultural norms, enhance their learning culture, and improve their communication skills.

Chapter 12 explores the technology perceptions and preparedness of pre-service and in-service teachers from three different countries. Twenty-one students in the Republic of Korea, twelve students in the United Arab Emirates, and thirty-five students in the United States of America were virtually connected through the BlackBoard communication system. They participated in weekly online discussion forums for six weeks and shared how well prepared they felt about using technology in their content areas and how they would effectively use technology in their future classrooms. This study can serve as a good model for facilitating a global conversation and supporting a reflective online conversation across geographic distances and cultural barriers.

Chapter 13 discusses some common points of Distance Education and photography in the context of meta- communication. Distance Education is a system. Therefore, it has a peculiar structure like all other systems; it is composed for heterogeneous student masses, but is accounted as having an individualistic quality. Distance Education is an intact system with no room for discrepancy, hesitation, disagreement, intellectual fantasies, et cetera. It perfectly represents the humanistic tradition in postmodern times. Distance Education is a meta–communication problem. Everything can be taught by Distance Education, because there are innumerous programs ranging from business administration to literature. But to what extent can it be taught? There are the heteronyms of this problem such as Polanyi's "tacit knowledge" or Hegel's / Agamben's Eleusinian Mystery.

Chapter 14 focuses on defining assessment in the context of technology enhanced learning, analyzes global trends regarding assessment of students by using technology, discusses possible technology supported assessment, offers useful strategies for teachers to use technology for assessment, and predicts the future of technology supported assessments in different educational contexts. Educators at any stage of their career or dealing with any discipline of knowledge are required to delve into number of tasks like presenting and constructing assessment tasks, making valid judgments of the student progress in learning, facilitating the provision of feedback, and supporting the production and delivery of marks/grades to assess their students. Assessing students is a cumbersome task, and technologies offer a number of possibilities and opportunities for educators to make this task more enjoyable and meaningful.

Chapter 15 acknowledges knowledge as a mental activity is to define external factors which have a direct impact on the content of e-learning, which is a sort of distance learning at the same time. By this way, this study also tries to contribute to the exactness of such a learning act. Initially the study focuses on the concept of knowledge; after defining the nature, types, and features of knowledge, communicational conformation of mass media is emphasized in the chapter. Then, within the dialectic context of mind and tool, types of mass media interactions, linear and bidirectional interactions are investigated. Consequently, within the reference of previous chapters, construction of knowledge through mass media as a type of learning is discussed in the final part. In conclusion, some suggestions relating to external factors to be refrained for the sake of exactness of e-learning are made.

Chapter 16 examines the role of digital poster sessions in contemporary online conferences and highlights some basic production-quality issues in the creation of digital posters. In recent years, pre-recorded digital poster sessions have become more widely used as parts of real-time face-to-face conferences and as complements to online conferences and colloquiums. The multimedia-enriched building of various types of digital poster sessions offers high potential for conference organizers to be more inclusive of a variety of topics, and it helps conference participants gain more value from the shared synchronous time and virtual experiences.

Chapter 17 discusses and examines online learning in distance education context. It seeks to argue how learners cope up with online education and becomes successful online learners. Further, while learning through online mode, how does communication skills assist them to prevent barriers in their learning activities? A critical reflection on communication skills of online learners are summarized and highlighted. The online learners' reactions and responses are mentioned in many occasions in this chapter which are documented in a few case studies available at different journals and Web portals.

One of the ways which distance education is capable of reaching online learners is the basis and method of meta-communication. Therefore, it is important to understand how to design reflective online conversations and how to implement a diverse milieu for prospective online learners so that they are able to transfer their information, knowledge, and learning from theoretical forms to real life experiences. The chapter author(s) explain these issues and subjects with the models they build. Not only the frameworks, but also the case studies can be used for explaining the online transformative ideas radically. Finally, this book gathers professionals from across disciplines, from all levels of education and from multicultural communities to design and implement lifelong learning practices with meta-communicative models which encourage high-quality reflective online conversations for the entire global society in distance education.

Ugur Demiray
Anadolu University, Turkey

Gulsun Kurubacak
Anadolu University, Turkey

T. Volkan Yuzer
Anadolu University, Turkey

Acknowledgment

We have many individuals to thank for their impressive on the book. First, we would like to praise the people at IGI Global; Jan Travers, Christine Bufton, and Emily Golesh, as well as Hannah Abelbeck, our editors, provided framework for the revision; they also suggested areas that could be strengthened and were invaluable in shaping the book. They helped make critical decisions about the transformative structure of the book, and provided useful feedback on stylistic issues.

We would also to express our appreciations to the Editorial Advisory Board (EAB) members. The EAB members helped on the book included, Shalin Hai-Jew, Santosh Panda, Alexander G. Flor, Christine Clark, Melanie Shaw, Mary Beth Klinger, Teresa L. Coffman, Vardan Mkrttchian, H. Prentice Baptiste, Mustafa Yunus Eryaman, Pradeep Kumar Misra, Amani Hamdan, Dele Braimoh, and Figen Kilic. The excellent advice from these people helped shape the book.

We would particularly like to thank all of the authors of the individual chapters for their excellent contributions. Special mention in this regard must go to Murat Hismanoglu, Sibel Hismanoglu, Christine Clark, Gwen Stowers, Alexander G. Flor, Narong Sompong, Vardan Mkrttchian, Jennifer J. Neakrase, H. Prentice Baptiste, Ashley N. Ryan, Elsa Q. Villa, Melanie Shaw, Susan Stillman, Gayle M. Cicero, David Cross, Dennis Lessard, Mary Beth Klinger, Teresa L. Coffman, Shalin Hai-Jew, Mehmet Firat, Isil Kabakci Yurdakul, Amani Hamdan, Kay Kyeongju Seo, Aimee deNoyelles, Simber Atay, Pradeep Kumar Misra, Nurdan Oncel Taskiran, Recep Yilmaz, and Satya Sundar Sethy.

The final words of thanks belong to our families and parents separately: Ugur Demiray would like to thank to his wife Dr. Emine Demiray and his daughter Gokce Demiray. Gulsun Kurubacak would like to thank to her parents Öznur Kurubacak-Cemalettin Kurubacak. Volkan Yuzer would like to thank his wife Saliha Yuzer and his son Ozan Yuzer as well as his parents Bahriye Yuzer-Dr. Ali Fuat Yuzer and his brother M. Erkan Yuzer. They deserve thanks for their enthusiasm, appreciation, help, and love. Their pride in our accomplishments makes it even more rewarding to be the editors.

Ugur Demiray
Anadolu University, Turkey

Gulsun Kurubacak
Anadolu University, Turkey

T. Volkan Yuzer
Anadolu University, Turkey

Section 1
Meta Communicative Knowledge Building and Online Communications

Chapter 1
Promoting Critical Thinking Skills in Language Education through Online Discussions

Ugur Demiray
Anadolu University, Turkey

Murat Hismanoglu
European University of Lefke, Turkey

Sibel Hismanoglu
European University of Lefke, Turkey

ABSTRACT

Online discussion has become one of the most effective teaching tools in recent years in terms of its power to promote students' critical thinking skills in educational contexts. This chapter aims at presenting an overview of recently conducted research studies on critical thinking and online discussions, explaining online discussion as a pedagogical vehicle for maximizing language learning and teaching, identifying problems related to online discussions, as well as some suggested solutions, describing application activities that promote critical thinking skills, illustrating how language teachers and learners can use meta-communication in creating successful online discussions, and stressing the importance of the teacher's role in designing an effective online discussion environment for students.

INTRODUCTION

Learning via discussions or conversations is a crucial aspect of teaching and learning, especially in higher education contexts. Modern communication technologies enable discussions to be conducted online as well as in the classroom. These discussions may constitute a part of a totally online distance education class or be deployed as a supplement to a traditional face-to-face class (Maurino, 2006). In an online context, the discussions can be either synchronous or asynchronous. Synchronous discussions involve that the participants of the discussion all meet at the same time to talk about the issue at hand, whereas asynchronous

DOI: 10.4018/978-1-61350-071-2.ch001

discussions are discussions that students can join at any time (Benson, 2003).

From a social constructivist viewpoint, online discussions provide opportunities for students to form meanings together and infuse new knowledge into their prior experiences (Rourke & Anderson, 2002). Online discussions can constitute a platform for students and teachers to communicate in a social context with no boundaries of time and distance, enhancing students' critical thinking and assisting students in reflecting on their ideas (Brooks & Jeong, 2006; Hew & Cheung, 2008; Wang, 2008).

Despite being employed as a powerful pedagogical tool for maximizing students' critical thinking skills, online discussions have given rise to the emergence of several problems such as inadequate critical analysis of peers' ideas (Rourke & Anderson, 2002), limited student involvement (Hewitt, 2005) and lack of motivation, commitment, and time, and failure to interact powerfully (Brooks & Jeong, 2006). To overcome some of these problems, a variety of facilitation strategies, mostly concentrating on the teacher as facilitator or moderator, have been described in the literature (Anderson, Rourke, Garrison, & Archer, 2001). Tutors and teachers play a pivotal role in online discussion contexts. However, their domination may give rise to a teacher-centered discussion, suppressing students' active involvement (Rovai, 2007).

The aim of this chapter is to give an overview of recently conducted research studies on critical thinking and online discussions, expound online discussion as a pedagogical tool for enhancing language learning and teaching, describe problems relevant to online discussions as well as some suggested solutions, describe application activities that enhance critical thinking skills, exemplify how language teachers and learners can utilize meta-communication in creating effective online discussions and emphasize the prominence of the teacher's role in creating an ideal online discussion environment for students.

DEFINING CRITICAL THINKING

The term critical thinking has been defined by a number of researchers. According to Angelo (1995:6), critical thinking is "the intentional application of rational, higher order thinking skills, such as analysis, synthesis, problem recognition and problem solving, inference, and evaluation". Scriven & Paul (1996) defined critical thinking as "the intellectually disciplined process of actively and skillfully conceptualizing, applying, analyzing, synthesizing, and/or evaluating information gathered from, or generated by, observation, experience, reflection, reasoning, or communication, as a guide to belief and action". Facione (1998) described 6 main skills of critical thinking self-regulation, interpretation, analysis, inference, explanation and evaluation as exhibited in Figure 1.

Facione (1998) categorized these 6 main skills of critical thinking from the experts' consensus concerning critical thinking and the optimal critical thinker in the APA Delphi Report, Critical Thinking: A Statement of Expert Consensus for Purposes of Educational, 1992. As a consequence, Facione (1998:12) stressed that "critical thinking is the process of purposeful, self-regulatory judgment. This process reasoned consideration to evidence, context, conceptualizations, methods, and criteria."

From a practical prospect, Haskins (2006:2) stated that critical thinking is "a process by which we use our knowledge and intelligence to effectively arrive at the most reasonable and justifiable positions on issues, and which endeavors to identify and overcome the numerous hindrances to rational thinking."

In the light of the definitions given above, a critical thinker, according to Birjandi & Bagherkazemi (2010:137), is someone who among other characteristics:

- has a strong inclination to notice the prominence of good thinking;
- describes problems and concentrates on related topics and issues;

Figure 1. Core critical thinking skills (Source: Facione, P. A. (1998))

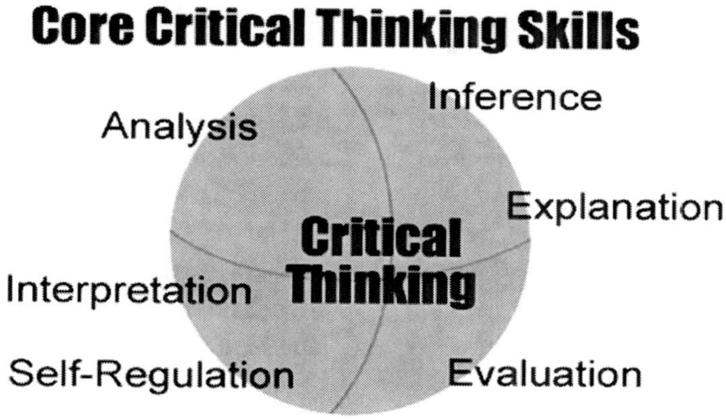

- differentiates between logical and illogical inferences;
- postpones judgments and decisions in the absence adequate proof;
- comprehends the difference between logical reasoning and rationalizing;
- knows that one's comprehension is restricted and that there are degrees of belief;
- distinguishes between facts, views and suppositions;
- watches out for authoritarian effects and specious assertions;
- predicts the results of alternative actions.

RESEARCH ON CRITICAL THINKING AND ONLINE DISCUSSIONS

Critical Thinking

In recent years, a number of researchers have focused on critical thinking in their studies. In the following section, some prominent studies carried out in this field will be described. Sahinel (2001) aimed to develop the integrated language skills (reading, writing, listening, and speaking) in Turkish through critical thinking. He conducted his research at the fifth grade level and employed a variety of tools (e.g., achievement tests, attitude scales, interviews, journals, observations and questionnaires) to investigate the effect of the treatment on the experimental group. The research unearthed helpful outcomes for the experimental group both on the enhancement of critical thinking skills and the integrated language skills.

Akinoglu (2001) conducted a study to test the impact of science instruction based on critical thinking skills on learning among 4th grade primary school students. Akinoglu detected significant differences in the results in favor of the experimental group. As for the implications for further research, he assigned the researchers the task of finding out the challenges in relation to the enhancement of critical thinking by drawing their attention to the examination of school, teacher, classroom, and student characteristics.

Sahbat (2002) examined the impact of the attitudes of religious culture and ethics teachers on the promotion of students' critical thinking skills in three public secondary schools and one private secondary school in Istanbul in the 2001-2002 academic year. The results of the research showed that there was such effect on students' critical thinking skills and that, for most of the students, it was difficult to reject to the ideas stressed by teachers. Moreover, most of the students viewed teachers as lecturers who communicate knowledge and regarded the opinions of their teachers as valid and trusted them. Besides this, the students considered factors other than themselves such as school administration, inspectors and the curriculum as impediments to the enhancement of critical thinking skills.

Irfaner (2002) in his case study on the application of the elements of critical thinking in a freshman English course on writing at Bilkent University asked the question what the teacher involved in the study viewed the elements of critical thinking to be according to students' written performance. The results of the study showed that the teacher did not stress continually the same elements of critical thinking; instead, with each assignment she concentrated on different critical thinking skills. Moreover, Irfaner recommended for future research the examination of differences between experienced and novice teachers in the department according to their comprehension of elements of critical thinking.

Dayıoglu (2003) investigated the critical thinking levels of the students attending the English Preparatory School of Hacettepe University in 2002-2003 Academic Year. She also utilized Watson-Glaser Appraisal Test as an instrument to gather data from her sample. The findings of the study indicated a significant difference in favor of the science students who had been accepted to the university with their scores from numerical type questions as opposed to the students in social sciences.

Osana and Seymour (2004) examined the impact of the deployment of a rubric for evaluating arguments and statistical reasoning on enhancing critical thinking in pre-service teachers. The researchers implemented a cognitive apprenticeship model, which consisted of three phases, namely, modeling, coaching, and scaffolding and fading. The rubric, which was developed to measure students' conceptions and use of proof, notions about research and its applicability in assessing complex social problems, and ability to view alternative perspectives proved to develop the ability of participant student teachers to focus on conceptions of evidence when judging complicated matters. The results also unearthed that the participants made progress in making distinctions between evidence quality and evidence type in evaluating the essence of ill-structured problems.

Halvorsen (2005) conducted a study to help teachers who are interested in promoting and encouraging critical thought in their foreign language classrooms. The researcher defined the concept critical thinking and expounded why it was important, relevant, and highly applicable to the EFL/ESL teaching context. Following that, two basic elements teachers engaged in this topic should bear in mind were taken into account. The majority of this article, however, focuses on an analysis of some classroom techniques that teachers in any situation can commence to utilize almost immediately. Techniques which help students to focus on the extralinguistic world around them and which teachers deploy even with restricted resources were also stressed in this study.

Mecit (2006) studied the impact of 7E learning cycle model as an inquiry-based learning on the enhancement of the fifth grade students' critical thinking skills. She utilized experimental design in her research by assigning one class of a science teacher to control group, while assigning another class of the same teacher to the experimental group. While the students in the control group were instructed with traditional method, those in the experimental group were instructed with 7E learning cycle model. The Cornell Critical Thinking Skills Test Series as pre-test and post-test were administered to students both in the control and experimental groups by the researcher. The findings of the research indicated that the students in the experimental group achieved significantly better than those in the control group.

Cubukçu (2006) aimed to determine the disposition of critical thinking of the teacher candidates who were in the faculty of education at Eskişehir Osmangazi University. According to the findings of this research, age, the high school they graduated, university exam entrance point type, the programs they were attending, income level and social activities were influential on candidates' thinking potential-capacity and their thinking skills as different variables.

Alagözlü (2006) stressed that learners should be taught how to think rather than what to think and that judging, reasoning, problem solving, decision making are vital for successful academic and social lives. She also stated that, in a rote-memorization based educational system as in Turkey, learners should be taught to express their own thoughts and to judge the ideas prior to making a decision and solving the problems. Moreover, some classroom applications such as statements, scenarios, situations, literary texts, and graphic organizers to improve critical reading in ELT were presented in the article.

Rear (2010) utilized a systematic approach towards promoting the critical thinking skills of students having relatively low linguistic abilities. The researcher conducted a program by employing a categorization of skills drawn up by Facione (1990) to design a course based around debates of social issues. The conducted program took students via a six-stage process, exhibiting them how to expound the essence of a problem, collect and arrange suitable data, evaluate the worth of that data, examine the data to draw conclusions, state those conclusions overtly in the form of a debate, and lastly evaluate their performance for future enhancement.

Online Discussions and Critical Thinking

In the literature, a number of researchers studied online discussions with respect to critical thinking. Yang, Newby & Bill (2005) examined the effects of employing Socratic questioning to develop students' critical thinking (CT) skills in asynchronous discussion forums (ADF) in university-level distance learning courses. The findings of the study revealed that teaching and modeling of Socratic questioning assisted students in displaying a higher level of CT skills and those students maintained their CT skills after being exposed to and modeling of Socratic questioning in the ADF.

Mandernach (2006) studied the theoretical basis of critical thinking in higher education, stressed empirically-based strategies for infusing online instructional supplements to develop critical thinking, presented techniques for creating instructional opportunities beyond the restrictions of traditional class time, and made practical suggestions for the modern deployment of critical thinking strategies through online resources.

Varaki (2006) investigated whether web-based instruction can successfully enhance students' critical thinking skills or not. The researcher also described the teaching strategies and instructional designs that can enhance critical thinking in an online learning context. The results of the study showed that web-based instruction can be a powerful tool for fostering critical thinking when delivered on an instructional design specifically designed for web-based instruction.

Athinarayanan (2006) conducted a research study on a group of four subject students to examine the usage of online discussion in helping them to stimulate critical thinking. The result showed that online discussion is a beneficial learning device in stimulating students to "speak" and exchange their opinions. It helped problem solving exercises to take place regardless of the space of time and place, which provided students with more flexibility and opportunity to analyze and post mind-provoking messages. Moreover, this study indicated that students often post and read online messages since these messages are stored online while classroom discussions are not recorded. Hence, it was revealed in this study that online discussion board can be a beneficial learning device for teaching and learning because of presenting limitless information for students to analyze and post quality messages.

Debela & Fang (2006) studied how discussions can utilized to enhance critical thinking in a number of English as a Second Language (ESL) courses offered by Marshall University's Graduate School of Education and Professional Development (GSEPD) program. At the end of the semester, a qualitative survey was designed to identify the powerfulness of such discussions, and the chances for improvement. The survey was sent to 21 students who were elementary and secondary school teachers in West Virginia. Out of 21 students, 15 of them responded to the three questions asked in the survey. Almost all the respondents stressed that discussion was beneficial in developing learning and critical thinking. Most students boosted the engagement of an online instructor in the *online discussion*, and faculty members' engaging in these discussions function as helpers in the enhancement of critical thinking skills.

Baglione & Nastanski (2007) examined the theoretical benefits of online discussion groups and the survey results from 122 experienced faculty members to reveal (a) how many faculty members prefer the online environment and (b) the relationship of this preference to their evaluation of the superiority of online discussion. The results of the study showed that half of the faculties who teach online and on-ground prefer teaching in both contexts and those three quarters of those educators believe the online context paves the way for more substantive discussion.

Cheong & Cheung (2008) studied lower secondary school students' critical thinking in an asynchronous online discussion context. The results of the study unearthed that the students in this age group merely minimally displayed critical thinking skills during the online discussion. Nevertheless, investigation into students' perception of online discussion exhibited positive attitudes. In this study, some enhanced scaffolding strategies for online discussion participants and guides on developing good questions were suggested to develop critical thinking skills in this context.

Bai (2009) investigated whether the use of the practical inquiry model as discourse guide paved the way for students' critical thinking in online discussion or not. The results of the study revealed that the inquiry model increased students' awareness of critical thinking and that assisted them in engaging in reflection and higher-order thinking when responding online.

Arend (2009) investigated how asynchronous discussions within online courses affected critical thinking among students. In this study, *online discussions* were related to higher levels of critical thinking. However, qualitative data showed that how discussions are utilized and facilitated is crucial for fostering critical thinking. It was stressed in the study that online discussions aim at creating a space and time for informal, open-ended thinking to occur. Moreover, it was reported that critical thinking is best stimulated among students when a more consistent emphasis is made on the discussions, and when teacher facilitation is less frequent but more purposeful.

Gao, Wang, Sun (2009) proposed a new model of productive online discussion relying on a brief review of research literature on online discussion. When compared to former discussion models, the new model presented a more systematic and detailed foundation to comprehend how learning takes place via online discussion. Dependent on the new model, the researchers suggested several directions for research on promoting the quality of online discussion and learning.

Alexander, Commander, Greenberg, Ward (2010) investigated the effect of a four-questions technique utilized to develop critical thinking *in online discussions*. Students in a graduate educational psychology course took part in three online asynchronous discussions in reaction to case studies. Before the second discussion only, students responded to questions developed to stimulate critical thinking via the four-questions technique of analyzing, reflecting, applying, and questioning. The researchers evaluated evidence of critical thinking by rating students' comments in an online discussion with The Washington State University Critical and Integrative Thinking Scale. The results of the study showed that the four-question technique was powerful for developing critical thinking in online discussions.

ONLINE DISCUSSION AS A PEDAGOGICAL VEHICLE FOR MAXIMIZING LANGUAGE LEARNING AND TEACHING

Online discussion can be utilized as a pedagogical vehicle for enhancing language learning and teaching. Before using online discussion in the foreign language classroom, the language teacher should make links between the online discussion and the course aims, objectives and assessment activities clear to students, establish a warm, stress free, non-threatening virtual classroom environment, explain online discussion netiquette, divide students into groups consisting of 4-6 members, design discussion questions, explain how students will respond to discussion questions, decide who will control discussion topics, model how to give feedback, signal start and end days for discussions, and explain his role as a facilitator. Raleigh (2000) summarizes the benefits of using online discussions in the classroom as seen in the following:

- *Sharing knowledge.* Every student has a unique set of experiences and learning. Sharing individual "expertise" via online discussions creates improvement for others and assists the student expert in explaining his/her own knowledge related to the subject.
- *Reflecting on ideas.* Reflection assists students in explaining concepts and masters the information-to-knowledge process. Taking part in an online discussion, the process of writing can help that reflection process. Furthermore, students who are passive in class actively join the online discussions.
- *Improving critical thinking.* Because students communicate with their peers and with the teacher via the activities deployed in online discussions, they often must compare, contrast, analyze, synthesize, and evaluate. Hence, they have the chance to develop their critical thinking skills.

Kilpin (2002) lists the benefits of using online discussions in the foreign language classroom as follows:

- teachers are offered an 'educational model' in comprehending and discussing concepts – they display the suitable level of academic language and analytical skills students can learn to follow.
- development of the students' comprehension of course concepts is noticeable via the posts they make.
- students learning off-campus have a context in which to communicate with other students, thus enhancing a community of those registered in the course. Thus, distant students or those restricted by work or family engagements can interact with their contemporaries and live a part of the intellectual terrain normally denied by restricting time or distance factors.
- having access to a team of specialists' views and methods to course material, students can pose technical questions relevant to terminology or homework
- unrestricted space to further extend appealing discussion from lessons; provides students the opportunity to think deeply and critically in relation to the concepts they are learning in the course.
- creates a space for shy or introvert students to make contribution towards an academic discussion.

- cooperative teaching style avoids social signs privileging male students.

In Baglione and Nastanski's (2007) viewpoint, the online context stimulates, facilitates debate and, when faculty members create netiquette rules, requires students to prove their views and admit that others have done so as well. It may have a more powerful, more dynamic discussion, compared to the traditional classroom. Since the discussion is recorded, the faculty member can reflectively assess each participant's contribution and, relying on these transcripts, feedback to the student can be enhanced when compared to the traditional classroom. The transcript helps to ensure that all students take part in the discussion equally and that the discussion is substantive and makes contribution to the group's knowledge. This compares positively to the traditional context, where content is promoted to memory. Lessons are rarely videotaped. When they are videotaped, evaluation relies on the spoken words, which can be heard multiple times by the time-consuming process of rewinding. Evaluations are then dependent on content and delivery style. This is naturally problem causing and rarely employed, as compared to the online transcript.

PROBLEMS RELATED TO ONLINE DISCUSSIONS AND SUGGESTED SOLUTIONS

Research has described several problems relevant to online discussions, such as limited student participation (Hewitt, 2005); inadequate critical analysis of peers' ideas (Rourke & Anderson, 2002); and lack of motivation, commitment, and time, and failure to communicate effectively (Brooks & Jeong, 2006). To solve some of these problems, a number of facilitation strategies, mostly concentrating on the teacher as facilitator or moderator, have been identified in the literature (Anderson, Rourke, Garrison, & Archer, 2001). More specifically, in online discussions, students sometimes encounter problems that may lead to stress anxiety and decrease their motivation to participate such as (Plumpton, 2009):

- Not knowing what to say
- Saying too much
- Not everyone is participating in discussion and group work
- Nobody is saying anything

In the following section, we will present some tips suggested by Plumpton (2009) for overcoming these problems.

Problem 1: Not Knowing What to Say

Students sometimes have difficulty in contributing to online discussions due to not being able to think of anything to say or feeling shy and uncomfortable. When being unsure about what they can contribute, students can make use of one or more of the tips below to solve this problem.

- Students can try to find other people's postings that they agree with, and say so. They can give their own examples.
- Students can look for postings that provide them with ideas they hadn't considered before, or that get them considering something, and respond to the posting to make the author aware of the fact that they have learned something.
- Students can pose a question about something they don't fully comprehend, and hopefully, someone will help students out. Students should not be anxious about posing 'irrelevant' questions, there will probably be others having the same question and students will be doing them a favor by posing those questions.
- If someone poses a question students wished to pose, students should help them

feel more relaxed by stating they would like to know the answer too.

- If someone asks about something that students consider they know a little about, students should answer their posting.
- If someone poses a question that students can't help with but no-one seems to be responding, students can at least display their thoughtfulness and maybe recommend other sources of help.

Problem 2: Saying Too Much

Some students post too many messages to their discussion forums. If students feel that they have confused their peers with their postings, they can hold back a bit and stimulate other classmates to join the discussion by:

- emailing individual classmates to recommend something they can contribute
- waiting a day or so before giving response to questions asked by the teacher or other classmates, to view if someone else will give response to it
- exhibiting them welcome responses to their postings with terminating messages like "What do other people think"
- asking for help from classmates about something they feel less confident about so people can view that they don't know everything

Problem 3: Not Everyone Is Participating in Discussion

When some students in the course do not take part in online discussion, this situation can be demotivating. In most online discussions, there may be one or two students rarely or never joining for certain reasons – the negative effect of personal circumstances, shyness, illness, or a deliberate decision. If students are joining an online discussion or working with their peers on an assignment, and they have made their contributions, it is comprehensible if they feel stressed when waiting for others to contribute. The tips below can be utilized to solve these issues:

- students can do what they can do to stimulate their peers to take part in the discussion. They can email them privately to learn when they expect to join or whether they have decided not to. Students should accept their reasons and apologies with good grace.
- students can focus on some other aspects of the course while they are waiting for others to take part in the discussion
- students can organize online group work so that people who are behind can do some of the later tasks
- if some classmates don't take part in the discussion and don't give response to their enquiries, students should admit that they will have to manage without them, and they should not spend time or emotional energy waiting for them or worrying about their lack of involvement. Students should not compromise their ability to keep to the activity or assignment schedule, and they should not finish their work on time.
- students try to make the discussions so appealing that they will motivate the others to participating. The chances are that they are reading the discussions.
- students should attempt to be responsive to classmates who may be attempting to catch up with a discussion or online group project that is already half-completed – it is difficult for them to participate when other classmates have done much of the work. Students should suggest what support they can.

Problem 4: Nobody Is Saying Anything

In an online discussion, if no student posts anything for a while, it may become difficult to break the silence, and no student becomes willing to be the first to contribute. At this point, someone should be brave and break the spiral as soon as they notice what is happening. The following tips can be employed by students to solve this problem.

- posting a question that gives rise to a response, for instance: "Can anyone clarify what the author is really saying in the section that commences...", and responding if anyone answers them
- arranging with another classmate to get a debate going – taking sides on an issue and arguing it actively, which stimulates the rest of the group to take sides
- commencing a new thread in the discussion about something basic to the course, for instance, how this discussion will serve to doing the next assignment

APPLICATION IDEAS FOR ONLINE DISCUSSIONS

The language teacher can make use of case scenarios, brainstorming, role-playing, reaction postings, expand course content and extend in-class discussions so as to create online discussions in the foreign language classroom that promote students' critical thinking skills. In case scenarios, students can be put into small groups or work in large groups to respond to cases that assist them in applying theories and concepts included in class or in readings. In brainstorming, students can employ the online discussion format to brainstorm ideas on a topic as a pre-class or post-class activity.

In role-playing, in small groups, students can each take on roles and design scenarios around course content. In reaction postings, students can react to posted readings, assigned readings, or web sites. Moreover, discussion questions relevant to the course textbook can establish the foundation for discussion. In expand course content, students may read various articles and post summaries or find suitable web resources and post links. Moreover, students may react to their peers' postings (Raleigh, 2000).

SUCCESSFUL ONLINE DISCUSSIONS AND META-COMMUNICATION

Meta-communication is communication about communication. For instance, in an online discussion environment, when a student posts a message with a seemingly sarcastic comment and then puts a smiley at the end, this smiley communicates about his communication; it indicates that the message should not be taken literally since the student is trying to be humorous. The smiley is a meta-message; it is a message about a message. At this point, all emoticons, such as:-) "happy",:-("sad",:-/ "perplexed", O.o "confused" are called meta-communication because they communicate about communication. Students can employ keyboard symbols to exhibit the gestures and facial expressions that normally convey messages in a face-to-face discussion. Moreover, they can use some acronyms like (BTW= By the way, MHO= My Humble Opinion, ASAP= as soon as possible, R= regarding, TBDL= to be discussed later, TM= tomorrow, TWYT= that's what you think) to save typing time (Demiray, 2009).

Meta-communication is something that is beyond communication and all foreign language learners and teachers should always be aware of its existence. It is important to keep in mind that the meta-communication which accompanies any message is very forceful. In online discussions, students make use of these clues to help them to better understand what their teacher or peers mean, but more prominently, they often get the real meaning from the meta-communication rather than from the words themselves, especially when what they are saying contradicts with what they are implicating (Demiray, 2009). If, for example, the student totally disagrees with his classmate about the best L2 pronunciation teaching technique in the group discussion, the student can display this by making use of larger fonts, capital letters, or bold fonts in his writing.

All the grammatical symbols that foreign language learners and teachers utilize to describe syntactic structures in English have meta-communicational elements. To illustrate, every teacher or student of English knows the symbols and their meanings as presented in Table 1.

In online discussion environments, students can use these grammatical symbols to respond to some specific questions on English syntax. If, for instance, students are asked to discuss word order in English and Turkish, students can indicate that English is a SVO language, whereas Turkish is a SOV language. This means that while the subject comes the first, the verb comes the second and the object comes the last in English, the subject comes the first, the object comes the second and the verb comes the last in Turkish. It can be stated that SVO and SOV are meta-messages because they are messages about a message.

All the phonetic symbols, such as /θ, æ, ε, ð, w, ŋ/ that foreign language learners and teachers use to refer to consonants and vowels in English have meta-communicational elements. In English, while the symbol /θ/ refers to a voiceless, inter-dental, fricative sound, the symbol /ð/ refers to a voiced, inter-dental, fricative sound. The symbol /ŋ/ indicates a voiced, velar, nasal sound. The symbol /w/ denotes a voiced, bilabial, semi-vowel. The symbol /æ/ refers to a half-open, front, unrounded, lax vowel. The symbol /ε/ indicates a half-open, mid front, unrounded, lax vowel. It can be stressed that /θ, æ, ε, ð, w, ŋ/ refer to meta-communication since they communicate about communication.

In online discussion environments, students can use these phonetic symbols to respond to some specific questions on English phonetics. If, for instance, students are asked to discuss why inter-dental sounds in English are problem-causing for Turkish EFL learners, students can use /θ/ and /ð/ symbols rather than the phrase inter-dental sounds to respond to this specific question. They can indicate that /θ/ and /ð/ are problem-causing for Turkish EFL learners since they are non-existent in the sound system of the Turkish language.

As a result, meta-communication plays an important role in creating successful online discussion environments. At this point, foreign language teachers should be familiar with commonly used emoticons, keyboard symbols, acronyms, grammatical and phonetic symbols. They should introduce them to their students before conducting discussions in virtual environments.

THE TEACHER'S ROLE IN DESIGNING AN EFFECTIVE ONLINE DISCUSSION ENVIRONMENT

A number of researchers (e.g., Berge & Muilenburg 2000; Burstall, 2000; Knowlton & Knowlton 2001; Love 2002; Blignaut & Trollip 2003; Demiray

Table 1. Symbols and their meanings

Symbol	Meaning
S	sentence, subject
V	verb
O	object
N	noun
ADJ	adjective
ADV	adverb
Pr	Pronoun
P	preposition
NP	noun phrase
VP	verb phrase
ADJP	adjective phrase
ADVP	adverbial phrase
PP	prepositional phrase

2010, Li 2003; Mazzolini & Maddison 2003; Wickstrom 2003) have focused on the role of the teacher in online discussion recently. However, these researchers have not agreed on the most suitable strategy for involvement yet. One school of thought emphasizes that teachers play a key role in the success of an online discussion (Demiray 2010, Moller 1998; Figallo 1998; Knowlton & Knowlton 2001; Love 2002; Blignaut & Trollip 2003). The teacher works for promoting the level of discussion to a higher level (Figallo, 1998).

The other school of thought stresses that teachers should encourage students to generate their own knowledge (Burstall, 2000; Li, 2003; Mazzolini & Maddison, 2003). These researchers have indicated that peer messages are more powerful than teacher messages at provoking discussion and that teacher presence can affect the dialogue in a negative way (Li, 2003; Mazzolini & Maddison, 2003). Hence, it can be inferred that the teacher's more active involvement may not be crucial for lower level subject areas since there is no need to pose higher level questions. Nevertheless, the teacher may need to be engaged more so as to correct misconceptions that advance early on in the learning process.

The language teacher aiming at developing successful online discussions should attribute importance to giving clear directions to students, providing feedback (teacher feedback and peer feedback), promoting motivation, establishing clear expectations as to how to use online discussions, organization of discussion and question types to be utilized (Al-Shalchi, 2009). In the following section, different roles of the language teacher will be explained in detail.

Giving Clear Directions to Students

The language teacher should give students directions that are easy, to the point and do not lead to any perplexity in their mind (Rose & Smith, 2007). The teacher should clearly state whether the discussion will be synchronous or asynchronous. If it is a synchronous discussion, the students should know where and when to meet, and if it is asynchronous, the students should know if they must address a deadline for answering the questions posted (Al-Shalchi, 2009).

Providing Feedback

Research has revealed that the quality of student discussion responses can be maximized via the employment of constructive feedback that is immediate, logical, and ongoing (Ertmer & Stepich, 2004). Nevertheless, to attain this level of feedback in online courses, teachers must spend a considerable amount of time and effort on virtual environments. To put it differently, to meet students' needs for prompt and ongoing feedback, the teacher should be online almost continually (Dunlap, 2005), which is a recommendation that is not only impractical but also irrelevant to the types of autonomous, self-directed learning being enhanced via online courses (Dunlap & Grabinger, 2003).

One possible solution is for instructors to stress the importance of peer feedback as an online language teaching strategy, requiring students to give feedback to their classmates while simultaneously stimulating greater levels of interaction. Based on the way in which the peer feedback process is shaped, teachers could be spared from assessing large numbers of student postings, however, still give ample instances of formative and summative feedback. Students, on the other hand, would still receive the feedback they need in order to evaluate their progress in the online environment (Ertmer, Richardson, Belland, Camin, Connolly, Coulthard, Lei & Mong, 2007).

According to Corgan, Hammer, Margolies, & Crossley (2004), the employment of peer feedback in an online learning context provides a plethora of advantages including: maximizing the timeliness of feedback, offering new learning opportunities for both givers and receivers of feedback, humanizing the learning context, and constructing community. As Richardson & Swan (2003) state, by asking students to give constructive feedback to their peers, language teachers stimulate them to take part in each other's learning and hence students can achieve higher comprehension and appreciation for their peers' experiences and perspectives. Ertmer et al. (2007) emphasize that if employed powerfully, both teacher and peer feedback have the power to maximize the quality of discourse, and hence the quality of learning in the online learning context.

Promoting Motivation

Zhang, Koehler, Spatariu (2009) indicate that comprehending and promoting students' motivation to create quality postings is prominent for researchers and teachers who examine the enhancement of critical reasoning skills in online discussions. As Rovai (2007) states, the first component of the course design strategy is to create motivation for students to take part in productive discussions. Although some students will have the related intrinsic motivation to join productive discussions at the start of the course, others will not. Hence, the teacher must present a measure of extrinsic motivation (i.e., motivation induced by external factors) for students to take part in dialog. At this juncture, as *Rovai (2003)* suggests, grading course discussions can motivate students to greater involvement in online discussions and have the additional benefit of maximizing sense of community. Rovai (2007) states that motivation is increased when the student expects specific outcomes from an activity, these outcomes are strikingly valued, and activity is perceived as doable and that the teacher plays a crucial role in maintaining and sustaining students' motivational levels by planning structures and paving the way for interpersonal events. Siribaddana (2002) states that teachers can motivate students to greater participation in online discussions by:

- maximizing the suitability of a discussion towards the participants' professional and personal lives.
- giving constructive feedback to the postings made by a student promptly and stimulating more involvement via the feedback that the teachers give.
- building the discussions to a certain extent where it can show students the correct way without deviating to different areas or else would enable them to comprehend the meaning of being involved in such guided interactions.
- utilizing social contracts or group contracts as a tool for encouraging students to attain a set objectives via participation in *the online discussions*.
- designing evaluation criteria for the online participation while providing the clarity in the discussion for the students to independently interact.
- making the students take part in the process of deciding which discussions would be beneficial and which would not be so.
- deploying rational structures and concept maps to encourage the students to join online discussion forums.

Establishing Clear Expectations as to How to Use Online Discussions

Setting up overt expectations is crucial to help students avoid potential confusion and/or anxiety and gives rise to maximized learner satisfaction in online discussions. At the beginning of class, teachers can set up a general expectation about how much time students should expect to allocate to course work per week.

Thus, students can judge whether they can fulfill the requirements with their available time resources. Moreover, students are less likely to feel frustrated or surprised later on when they see how much time they have to invest in the class (Zhang, 2010).

Teachers should clearly state how often a student should contribute to a weekly discussion. They should inform students of the quality issue. For instance, the teacher can suggest to students saying:

"When responding to a discussion topic or speculating on a classmates' posting, clearly express your point of view first, then foster your speculation or response with information from course readings, personal experiences, and other sources."

Students should be informed of when and how they should contact the teacher to ask questions or receive teacher feedback.

The teacher should always closely monitor the classroom and make explanation when needed. Teachers should also provide clear expectations for students related to assignments. They should clearly state when and where to submit an assignment, how long a paper is expected to be, whether a paper requires a specific writing style (such as APA or MLA), what kind of and how many sources they should use, and more (Zhang, 2010).

Organization of Discussion

Organizing discussions plays a key role in establishing a suitable online environment for students. In Zhu & Kaplan's (2006) viewpoint, to organize online discussions effectively, language teachers should identify clear goals for discussions, organize online discussions in terms of topic and category, set up clear expectations for evaluating student performance in online discussions, identify a clear start time and end time for synchronous discussions, develop questions for discussion ahead of time, summarize the main points students should have learned.

Question Types

The type of question posted in an online discussion serves to determine whether there will be student participant or not (Akin & Neil, 2007). MacKnight (2000) emphasized that questions which concentrate on the basics of thought and reasoning make up the basis of critical thinking.

The teacher is responsible for supporting students and coaching of learning by modeling questioning techniques that enhance critical thinking. One such questioning technique is the employment of Socratic questioning. Table 2 below shows examples of questions for exploring ideas and statements in depth.

Lastly, teachers who aim to increase the effect of online discussions on the enhancement of critical thinking are suggested to undertake the role of facilitator (Cheng & Yeh, 2000; Chiu, 2004; Huang, 2001; Rheingold, 1998; Salmon, 2002). The term, though being frequently employed, seems to be open to various interpretations. Rheingold (1998) views the facilitator as an online host. Kao and Chen (2003) incorporate such activities as supporting, suggesting, interpreting, linking, limiting, emphasizing, evaluating and timing. However, Walker (2004) adopts challenging and probing as the most powerful ways to prompt students' further explanation and expression of their thinking.

FUTURE RESEARCH DIRECTIONS

In future studies, meta-communicational elements used by online EFL learners can be compared and contrasted with meta-communicational elements utilized by traditional EFL learners. Studies that focus on observation of meta-communicational elements in virtual environments can also be conducted in the future to reveal whether there is a correlation between meta-communicational elements and EFL learners' ability to make successful online discussions. Further research is also required to investigate whether there is a significant relationship between students' personality and meta-communicational elements that they use in online discussions.

Table 2. Socratic questioning techniques

Six types of questions (that Socrates asked his pupils)			
1	Questions for clarification	A	What do you mean by ?
		B	Could you put it another way?
2	Questions that probe assumptions	A	What are you assuming?
		B	Is this always the case? Why do you think the assumption holds here?
3	Questions that probe reasons and evidence	A	What would be an example?
		B	Could you explain your reasons to us?
4	Questions that probe questions about the questions	A	To answer this question, What questions would we have to answer first?
		B	Does this question ask us to evaluate something?
5	Questions that probe implications and consequences	A	What are you implying by that?
		B	What effect would that have?
6	Questions about viewpoints or perspectives	A	Can anyone see this another way?
		B	What would someone who disagrees say?

(Extracted from Cheong & Cheung 2008)

CONCLUSION

Online discussions play a crucial role in foreign language learning and teaching despite certain problems. Keller (2000) states that online discussions enhance active learning and critical thinking, create a learning environment within which every student has an equal chance to contribute whether they are extroverted or introverted, provide learners with the opportunity to view the topic from a variety of perspectives because of being open-ended and non-linear, allow time for thinking and reflection since students can join at any time, foster the improvement of literature research skills and establish a platform where students can compare their work to the standards set by the best contributors. Online discussions, as Baglione & Nastanski (2007) stress, provide "a technologically-rich environment for developing virtual learning communities in which students can develop strong analytic and critical thinking skills based on inherent time, reflection, and distribution advantages".

Online discussions promote learners' abilities to think critically about their knowledge, their actions, and their beliefs. To put it differently, it is through online discussions that learners can have the opportunity to "ask appropriate questions, gather relevant information, efficiently and creatively sort through this information, reason logically from this information, and come to reliable and trustworthy conclusions about the world to live and act successfully in it" (Schafersman, 1991:2). The language teacher can deploy case scenarios, brainstorming, role-playing, reaction postings, expand course content and extend in-class discussions so as to generate online discussions in the foreign language classroom that enhance students' critical thinking skills.

In conclusion, online discussions are powerful pedagogical and technological tools offering new opportunities for language teachers and learners beyond traditional classroom context. All language teachers should employ online discussions in their teaching either as a part of a totally online distance language education class or a supplement to a traditional face-to face class to provide students with a motivating, interesting and rich environment that contributes to the enhancement of critical thinking skills.

REFERENCES

Akin, L., & Neil, D. (2007). CREST+ model: Writing effective online discussion questions. *Journal of Online Learning and Teaching, 3*(2). Retrieved April 18, 2010, from http://jolt.merlot.org/ vol3no2/ akin.htm

Akinoglu, O. (2001). *The effect of critical thinking focussed science teaching on learning output.* Unpublished doctoral dissertation. Hacettepe Universitesi, Ankara.

Al-Shalchi, O. N. (2009). The effectiveness and development of online discussions. *Journal of Online Learning and Teaching, 5*(1), 104–108.

Alagözlü, N. (2006). Some Discourse-based suggestions that boost critical thinking skills in ELT classes. *Ankara University Tomer Language Journal, 133,* 60–75.

Alexander, M., Commander, N., Greenberg, D., & Ward, T. (2010). Using the four-questions technique to enhance critical thinking in online discussions. *Journal of Online Learning and Teaching, 6*(2), 409–415.

Anderson, T., Rourke, L., Garrison, D. R., & Archer, W. (2001). Assessing teaching presence in a computer conferencing environment. *Journal of Asynchronous Learning Networks, 5*(2), 1–17.

Angelo, T. A. (1995). Beginning the dialogue: Thoughts on promoting critical thinking: Classroom assessment for critical thinking. *Teaching of Psychology, 22*(1), 6–7. doi:10.1207/s15328023top2201_1

Arend, B. (2009). Encouraging critical thinking in online threaded discussions. *The Journal of Educators Online, 6*(1), 1–23.

Athinarayanan, J. (2006). Promoting critical thinking skills using online discussion board. Retrieved October 19, 2010, from http://digitallearning.in/ dlasia/ 2007/ fullpapers/ jaya-sunway-%20 malaysia.pdf

Baglione, S., & Nastanski, M. (2007). The superiority of online discussion: Faculty perceptions. *The Quarterly Review of Distance Education, 8*(2), 139–150.

Bai, H. (2009). Facilitating students' critical thinking in online discussion: An instructor's experience. *Journal of Interactive Online Learning, 8*(2), 156–164.

Benson, A. D. (2003). Assessing participant learning in online environment. *New Directions for Adult and Continuing Education, 100,* 69–78. doi:10.1002/ace.120

Berge, Z., & Muilenburg, L. (2000). Designing discussion questions for online, adult learning. *Educational Technology,* (Sept-Oct): 53–56.

Birjandi, P., & Bagherkazemi, M. (2010). The relationship between Iranian EFL teachers' critical thinking ability and their professional success. *English Language Teaching, 3*(2), 135–145.

Blignaut, S., & Trollip, S. R. (2003). Developing a taxonomy of faculty participation in asynchronous learning environments – An exploratory investigation. *Computers & Education, 41,* 149–171. doi:10.1016/S0360-1315(03)00033-2

Brooks, D., & Jeong, A. (2006). The effects of pre-structuring discussion threads on group interaction and group performance in computer-supported collaborative argumentation. *Distance Education, 27*(3), 371–390. doi:10.1080/01587910600940448

Burstall, J. (2000). Learning communities for social change in forums on the web. *Australian Journal of Adult Learning, 40*(1), 33–52.

Cheng, Y. Y., & Yeh, Y. C. (2000). The effects of critical thinking instruction for college students. *Social Science Quarterly, 2*(1), 127–142.

Cheong, C., & Cheung, W. (2008). Online discussion and critical thinking skills: A case study in a Singapore secondary school. *Australasian Journal of Educational Technology*, *24*(5), 556–573.

Chiu, Y. C. (2004). *EFL faculty's role in developing EFL students' critical thinking through online interactions in Taiwan*. Paper presented at the 16th Annual ED-MEDIA 2004 World Conference on Educational Multimedia: Hypermedia & Telecommunications Conference, Lugano, Switzerland, June 21–26, 2004.

Corgan, R., Hammer, V., Margolies, M., & Crossley, C. (2004). Making your online course successful. *Business Education Forum*, *58*(3), 51–53.

Cubukçu, Z. (2006). Critical thinking dispositions of the Turkish teacher candidates. *The Turkish Online Journal of Educational Technology*, *5*(4). Retrieved October 10, 2010, from http://www.tojet.net/ articles/ 544.htm

Dayioglu, S. (2003). *A descriptive study on the critical thinking levels of the students at the unit of English preparatory school at Hacettepe University.* Unpublished Master thesis. Middle East Technical University, Ankara.

Debela, N., & Fang, B. (2006). *Using discussions to promote critical thinking in an online environment*. Retrieved October 5, 2010, from http://www.iiisci.org/ journal/ CV$/ sci/ pdfs/ E183SL.pdf

Demiray, U. (2010). Meta communication concept and knowledge building process in distance education: From point of meta cognitive structural collaborated model. In Volkan Yuzer, T., & Kurubacak, G. (Eds.), *Transformative learning and online education: Aesthetics, dimensions and concepts* (pp. 65–88). Hershey, PA: IGI Global. doi:10.4018/978-1-61520-985-9.ch005

Dunlap, J. C. (2005). Workload reduction in online courses: Getting some shuteye. *Performance Improvement*, *44*(5), 18–25. doi:10.1002/pfi.4140440507

Dunlap, J. C., & Grabinger, S. (2003). Preparing students for lifelong learning: A review of instructional methodologies. *Performance Improvement Quarterly*, *16*(2), 6–25. doi:10.1111/j.1937-8327.2003.tb00276.x

Ertmer, P. A., Richardson, J. C., Belland, B., Camin, D., & Connolly, P. Coulthard, et al. (2007). Using peer feedback to enhance the quality of student online postings: An exploratory study. *Journal of Computer-Mediated Communication*, *12*(2). Retrieved September 15, 2010, from http://jcmc.indiana.edu/ vol12/ issue2/ ertmer.html

Ertmer, P. A., & Stepich, D. A. (2004). *Examining the relationship between higher-order learning and students' perceived sense of community in an online learning environment.* Paper presented at the 10th Australian World Wide Web Conference, Gold Coast, Australia.

Facione, P. (1990). *Critical thinking: A statement of expert consensus – The Delphi report. California.* California: Academic Press.

Facione, P. A. (1998). *Critical thinking: What it is and why it counts*. California: Academy Press.

Figallo, C. (1998). *Hosting Web communities: Building relationships, increasing customer loyalty, and maintaining a competitive edge*. New York, NY: Wiley.

Gao, F., Wang, C., & Sun, Y. (2009). A new model of productive online discussion and its implications for research and instruction. *Journal of Educational Technology Development and Exchange*, *2*(1), 65–78.

Halvorsen, A. (2005). Incorporating critical thinking skills development into ESL/EFL courses. *The Internet TESL Journal*, *11*(3), 1-4. Retrieved September 10, 2010, from http://iteslj.org/ Techniques/ Halvorsen- CriticalThinking.html

Haskins, G. R. (2006). *A practical guide to critical thinking*. Retrieved September 22, 2010, from http://www.skepdic.com/essays/haskins.pdf

Hew, K. F., & Cheung, W. S. (2008). Attracting student participation in asynchronous online discussions: A case study of peer facilitation. *Computers & Education*, *51*(3), 1111–1124. doi:10.1016/j.compedu.2007.11.002

Hewitt, J. (2005). Toward an understanding of how threads die in asynchronous computer conferences. *Journal of the Learning Sciences*, *14*(4), 567–589. doi:10.1207/s15327809jls1404_4

Huang, W. T. (2001). *The impact of online small group facilitators' scaffolding on students' critical thinking development*. Unpublished Master's thesis, National Tunghua University, Hualien.

Irfaner, S. (2002). *Implementation of the components of critical thinking in an English 101 course in the first year English program at Bilkent University*. Unpublished master thesis. Bilkent University, Ankara.

Kao, T. C., & Chen, Y. F. (2003). *Group dynamics interactive skills in asynchronous small group discussion online*. Paper presented at the International Conference of Distance Education, National Taiwan University, and Taipei, Taiwan.

Keller, M. (2000). *Online discussions can improve student learning*. Retrieved September 10, 2010 from http://online.adelaide.edu.au/ LearnIT.nsf/ URLs/ On-line_discussions

Kilpin, C. (2002). The advantages and disadvantages of university online discussion boards. In *Proceedings of the IADIS International Conference WWW/Internet 2002, ICWI 2002,* Lisbon, Portugal.

Knowlton, D. S., & Knowlton, H. M. (2001). The context and content of online discussions: Making cyber-discussions viable for the secondary school curriculum. *American Secondary Education*, *29*(4), 38–52.

Li, Q. (2003). Would we teach without technology? A professor's experience of teaching mathematics education incorporating the internet. *Educational Research*, *45*(1), 61–77. doi:10.1080/0013188032000086127

Love, K. (2002). Mapping online discussion in senior English. *Journal of Adolescent & Adult Literacy*, *45*(5), 382–396.

MacKnight, C. (2000). Teaching critical thinking through online discussions. *EDUCAUSE Quarterly*, *4*, 38–41.

Mandernach, B. J. (2006). Thinking critically about critical thinking: Integrating online tools to promote critical thinking. *InSight: A Collection of Faculty Scholarship, 1*, 41-50.

Maurino, P. S. M. (2006). Looking for critical thinking in online threaded discussions. *E-Journal of Instructional Science and Technology*, *9*(2), 1–18.

Mazzolini, M., & Maddison, S. (2003). Sage, guide or ghost? The effect of instructor intervention on student participation in online discussion forums. *Computers & Education*, *40*, 237–253. doi:10.1016/S0360-1315(02)00129-X

Mecit, O. (2006). *The effect of 7E learning cycle model on the improvement of fifth grade students' critical thinking skills*. Unpublished dissertation. Middle East Technical University, Ankara.

Moller, L. (1998). Designing communities of learners for asynchronous distance education. *Educational Technology Research and Development*, *46*(4), 115–122. doi:10.1007/BF02299678

Osana, H. P., & Seymour, J. R. (2004). Critical thinking in preservice teachers: A rubric for evaluating argumentation and statistical reasoning. *Educational Research and Evaluation*, *10*(4-6), 473–493. doi:10.1080/13803610512331383529

Plumpton, B. (2009). *How students can make conferencing work*. Retrieved September 5, 2010, from http://www.open.ac.uk/ pc4study/ documents/ how-students-can-make -conferencing-work-scr.pdf

Raleigh, D. (2000). Keys to facilitating successful online discussions. *Teaching with Technology Today.* Retrieved October 1, 2010, from http:// www.uwsa.edu/ ttt/ raleigh.htm

Rear, D. (2010). A systematic approach to teaching critical thinking through debate. Retrieved October 5, 2010, from http://blog.nus.edu.sg/ eltwo/2010/ 02/ 19/ a-systematic-approach-to-teaching-critical -thinking-through-debate

Rheingold, H. (1998). *The art of hosting good conversations online*. Retrieved October 16, 2010, from http://www.emoderators.com/ moderators/ artonlinehost.html

Richardson, J. C., & Swan, K. (2003). An examination of social presence in online courses in relation to student's perceived learning and satisfaction. *Journal of Asynchronous Learning, 7*(1). Retrieved October 7, 2010 from http://www.aln.org/ publications /jaln/ v7n1/ v7n1_richardson.asp

Rose, R., & Smith, A. (2007). Online discussions. In Cavanaugh, C., & Blomeyer, R. (Eds.), *What works in k-12 online learning* (pp. 143–160). Washington, DC: International Society for Technology in Education.

Rourke, L., & Anderson, T. (2002). Using peer teams to lead online discussions. *Journal of Interactive Media in Education, 1*(1), 1–21.

Rovai, A. (2007). Facilitating online discussions effectively. *The Internet and Higher Education, 10*, 77–88. doi:10.1016/j.iheduc.2006.10.001

Rovai, A. P. (2003). Strategies for grading online discussions: Effects on discussions and classroom community in Internet-based university courses. *Journal of Computing in Higher Education, 15*(1), 89–107. doi:10.1007/BF02940854

Sahbat, A. (2002). *The effect of religion and ethics teachers' attitudes on students' critical thinking skills*. Unpublished Master thesis. Selçuk Üniversitesi, Konya.

Sahinel, S. (2001). *Developing language skills integrated with critical thinking skills*. Unpublished dissertation. Hacettepe Üniversitesi, Ankara.

Salmon, G. (2002). *E-tivities: The key to active online learning*. Sterling, VA: Stylus Publishing Inc.

Schafersman, S. (1991). *An introduction to critical thinking*. Retrieved September 15, 2010, from http://www.freeinquiry.com/ critical-thinking.html

Scriven, M., & Paul, R. (1996). *Defining critical thinking: A draft statement for the National Council for Excellence in Critical Thinking.* [Online]. Retrieved http://www.criticalthinking.org/ University/ univlibrary/ library.nclk

Siribaddana, P. (2002). *How to improve student participation in online discussions*. Retrieved October 10, 2010, from http://www.helium.com/ items/ 1928716-how-to-improve-student-participation-in-online-discussions

Varaki, B. (2006). A reflection on three web-based teaching critical thinking: Toward a compromise approach. *Ankara University Journal of Faculty of Educational Sciences, 39*(2), 177–191.

Walker, S. A. (2004). Socratic strategies and devil's advocacy in synchronous CMC debate. *Journal of Computer Assisted Learning, 20*(3), 172–182. doi:10.1111/j.1365-2729.2004.00082.x

Wang, Q. Y. (2008). Student-facilitators' roles of moderating online discussions. *British Journal of Educational Technology*, *39*(5), 859–874. doi:10.1111/j.1467-8535.2007.00781.x

Wickstrom, C. D. (2003). A funny thing happened on the way to the forum. *Journal of Adolescent & Adult Literacy*, *46*(5), 414–423.

Yang, Y. T., Newby, T. J., & Bill, R. L. (2005). Using Socratic questioning to promote critical thinking skills through asynchronous discussion forums in distance learning environments. *American Journal of Distance Education*, *19*(3), 163–181. doi:10.1207/s15389286ajde1903_4

Zhang, J. (2010). *Clear expectations lead to less confusion in the online classroom.* Retrieved October 4, 2010, from http://deoracle.org/ online-pedagogy/ teaching-strategies/ clearer-expectation- and-less-confusion-in-online-classroom.html

Zhang, T., Koehler, J., & Spatariu, A. (2009). The development of the motivation for critical reasoning in online discussions inventory (MCRODI). *American Journal of Distance Education*, *23*(4), 194–211. doi:10.1080/08923640903294411

Zhu, E., & Kaplan, M. (2006). Technology and teaching. In McKeachie, W. J., & Svinicki, M. (Eds.), *McKeachie's teaching tips: Strategies, research and theory for college and university teachers* (pp. 229–251). New York, NY: Houghton Mifflin.

ADDITIONAL READING

Anderton, B. (2006). Using the online course to promote self-regulated learning strategies in preservice teachers. *Journal of Interactive Online Learning*, *5*(2), 156–177.

Astleitner, H. (2002). Teaching critical thinking online. *Journal of Instructional Psychology*, *29*(2), 53–77.

Atkinson, D. (1997). A critical approach to critical thinking in TESOL. *TESOL Quarterly*, *31*(1), 79–95. doi:10.2307/3587975

Black, A. (2005). The use of asynchronous discussion: Creating a text of talk. *Contemporary Issues in Technology & Teacher Education*, *5*, 5–24.

Brookfield, S. (1987). *Developing critical thinkers. Milton Keyes: Open University Press. Brookfield, S. D. & Preskill, S. (2005). Discussion as a Way of Teaching* (2nd ed.). San Francisco: Jossey-Bass.

Browne, M. N., & Freeman, K. (2000). Distinguishing features of critical thinking classrooms. *Teaching in Higher Education*, *5*(3), 301–309. doi:10.1080/713699143

Bruning, K. (2005). The role of critical thinking in the online learning environment. *International Journal of Instructional Technology and Distance Learning*, 2(5). Retrieved March 2010 from http:// www.itdl.org/ Journal/ May_05/ article03.htm.

Davidson, B. W. (1998). A case for critical thinking in the English language classroom. *TESOL Quarterly*, *32*(1), 119–123. doi:10.2307/3587906

Demiray Ugur. (1995). *Meta-communication.* Eskişehir: Turkuaz Publications.

DeVito Joseph, A. (2000). *Human communication.* New York City, NY, USA: Longman.

Dixson, M., Kuhlhorst, M., & Reiff, A. (2006). Creating effective online discussions: Optimal instructor and student roles. *Journal of Asynchronous Learning Networks, 10.* Retrieved April 6, 2010, from http://www.sloan-c.org/ publications/ jaln/ v10n4/ v10n4_dixson.asp

Gilbert, P. K., & Dabbagh, N. (2005). How to structure online discussion for meaningful discourse: a case study. *British Journal of Educational Technology*, *36*, 5–18. doi:10.1111/j.1467-8535.2005.00434.x

Greenlaw, S. A., & DeLoch, S. B. (2003). Teaching critical thinking with electronic discussion. *Journal of Economic Education*. Retrieved April 20, 2010 from http://www.indiana.edu/ ~econed/ pdffiles/ winter03/ greenlaw.pdf.

Hew, K. F., & Cheung, W. S. (2003). Models to evaluate online learning communities of asynchronous discussion forums. *Australian Journal of Educational Technology*, *19*(2), 241–259.

Hughes, W. (2000). *Critical thinking. An introduction to the basic skills* (3rd ed.). New York: Broadview Press.

Kuhn, D. (2005). *Education for thinking*. Cambridge: Harvard University Press.

Moore, B. N., & Parker, R. (2007). *Critical thinking* (8th ed.). New York: McGraw Hill.

Muirhead, B. (2002). Integrating critical thinking into online classes. *United States Distance Learning Association Journal*. Retrieved Jan. 25, 2010 from http://usdla.org.

Newman, H. M. (1981). Interpretation and explanation: influences on communicative exchanges within intimate relationships. *Communication Quarterly*, *29*, 123–131. doi:10.1080/01463378109369397

Paul, R., & Elder, L. (2004). *The Nature and Functions of Critical and Creating Thinking*. Dillon Beach, CA: The Foundation for Critical Thinking.

Paul, R. W., & Elder, L. (2002). *Critical thinking: Tools for taking charge of your professional and personal life*. Upper Saddle River, New Jersey: Pearson Education/FT Press.

Peirce, W. (2003). *Strategies for teaching thinking and promoting intellectual development in online classes. Electronic Communities: Current Issues and Best Practices*. U.S. Distance Learning Association: Information Age Publishing.

Pithers, R. T., & Soden, R. (2000). Critical thinking in education. *Review of Educational Research*, *42*, 237–249.

Smith, R. (2002). *Challenging your preconceptions: Thinking critically about psychology*. Belmont, California: Wadsworth/Thomson Learning.

Tsui, L. (2000). Effects of campus culture on students' critical thinking. *The Review of Higher Education*, *23*(4), 421–441.

Vaughn, L. (2008). *The power of critical thinking: Effective reasoning about ordinary and extraordinary claims* (2nd ed.). Oxford: Oxford University Press.

Walker, W. (2002). Critical thinking in asynchronous discussions. International *Journal of Instructional Technology & Distance Learning*. Retrieved June 09, 2010 from http://www.itdl.org/ journal/ Jun_05/ article02.htm

Wang, Q., & Woo, H. L. (2007). Comparing asynchronous online discussions and face-to-face discussions in a classroom setting. *British Journal of Educational Technology*, *38*(2), 272–286. doi:10.1111/j.1467-8535.2006.00621.x

KEY TERMS AND DEFINITIONS

Asynchronous Discussion: A discussion that students can join at any time.

Analyzing: Breaking a whole into its parts to unearth the nature, function and relationships.

Creativity: Generating, discovering, or restructuring ideas.

Critical Thinking: The use of thinking skills, such as analysis, synthesis, problem recognition and problem solving, inference, and evaluation.

Logical Reasoning: Drawing inferences or conclusions that are supported in or justified by evidence.

Meta-Communication: Communication about communication.

Online Discussion: A discussion that is made in a virtual environment.

Synchronous Discussion: A discussion that students can meet at the same time to talk about the issue at hand.

Synthesizing: Combining separate ideas, beliefs and styles.

Chapter 2
Building a Theoretical Background for Distance Education:
Towards Meta-Communicative Conversations

Gulsun Kurubacak
Anadolu University, Turkey

T. Volkan Yuzer
Anadolu University, Turkey

ABSTRACT

This chapter focuses on how to build a dynamic theoretical background of distance education, as a source of meta-communication, and how it affects the use of online learning for reflective meaning making to construct a knowledge society. Based on the main purpose of this study, the virtual world can provide online learners with an interactive milieu for problem solving, critical thinking, and personalized/group discussion, multimedia presentation of global resources, connectivity, and visualization of social aspects of discussion and communication. In this context, distance education can respond to concerns and issues to create digital self-representations through communication theories and learning theories together. Furthermore, discussing the main features of the cross-cultural implications of reflective conversations can construct a very powerful paradigm shift to establish public interests encompassing the reflections of every aspect of social networking with the enthusiasms, persuasions as well as judgments.

DOI: 10.4018/978-1-61350-071-2.ch002

INTRODUCTION

"I just became one with my browser software."
Bill Griffith

Meta-communicativeconversations in online learning affect the use of new media to build digital citizenships and focus on about how to utilize the theoretical background of distance education, which expresses the national and regional as well as global cultural dimensions. Reflective online communications can be built according to the analysis of the multicultural ideas across subordinates of a digital society. Furthermore, the authors hope that the underlying assumptions and theoretical constructs through the use of meta-communicative approach can help digital citizens understand management in an online community, and have knowledge and empathy with not only the whole the sight of communication sciences theories but also the prospect of learning theories. In spite of calls for enhanced reflective conversations among individuals, digital cultures and diverse backgrounds, there is still disagreement between online people and groups. Besides, they are hardly exposed to collective dilemmas, global troubles and local problems which demand mutual understanding for building a theoretical background of distance education. Based on this background, designing reflective communication activities in the online world through learning and communication theories helps digital citizens understand and appreciate diversities between different digital groups.

The use of meta-communicativeconversations empowers activist communications, which concentrate on authentic experiences in critical dialogues. On the other hand, basic socio-cultural assumptions and prejudices of reflective online communications can easily generate democratic-egalitarian inequalities. In distance education, therefore, online people should develop a transformative meta-communicativeapproach as well as social justice-oriented, critical and creative meta-communicative conversations. These conversations can go beyond power elites' mandates. As mentioned by Burge (2000), there is a need for investigating clearly how to design powerful collaborations among online people and build dynamic and democratic digital societies in distance education. Furthermore, dealing with how to negotiate the implications and usability of flexible online contents is very important for online people to realize and found on multicultural, common and interactive reflective online communications.

Meta-communicativeconversations provide online persons with diverse perspectives and individual cultural differences to give attentions to diversity and liberation. Therefore, these people can understand how to cope with their role tasks, give vigilant considerations to diverse online community, and recognize their important roles and responsibilities to integrate reflective online communications in their actions. The chapter, consequently, explores how to construct meta-communicativeconversations and reflective online communications through learning and communication theories as theoretical background of distance education.

Theoretical background of distance education can build, organize and implement not only the integration of new communication technologies but also leadership practices. Besides, theoretical background of distance education helps digital people characterize their responsibilities across the fields of communication sciences, lifelong learning and education.

Distance education should consider digital citizens as global online users come together to act and decide on issues of mutual interest using shared rules, norms, and structures. The working definition for this chapter is that meta-communicativeconversations and reflective online communications are interactive processes to engage two or more learning and communication theories together to achieve program outcomes online learners should accomplish independently in a digital group. Since learning and communication theories unexpectedly help distance education experts work in an executive framework as well as facilitate and utilize critical factors, which can exist in meta-communicativeconversations and reflective online communications. Those are investigated through the study of theoretical background of distance education, which is operationally, procedurally and culturally defined for this paper as an open and integrated process that fosters dialogical partnerships and encourages egalitarian leaderships, and also spread out digital connections beyond characteristic boundaries to achieve innovative outcomes.

Building Theoretical Background of Distance Education

To make stronger meta-communicativeconversations, there must be careful efforts to not only cultural reform but also support online people with ready interact to reflective online communications. These activities, therefore, provide digital persons with improving equal access opportunity to the system (Hodson, 1999; Powazek, 2002). Due to this diverse nature of the online world, theoretical background of distance education has different and effective dimensions. Diversity in distance education can cause difficulties to design knowledge networks and their cultures, and also complicates the integration of meta-communicative approach. It is reasonably understandable that learning theories learning and communication theories are inseparable from theoretical background of distance education. Distance education brings up new technologies and communication methods, the multicultural contexts, and diverse learning outcomes based on new media to support all types of meta-communicativeconversations.

The rapidly changing digital world often challenges digital people to communicate across several cultural boundaries and borders, and also diverse perspectives between the world's cultures. In this context, the main purpose of theoretical background of distance education should present responses to the following expressions:

To build theoretical background of distance education to integrate meta-communicativeconversations and reflective online communications, distance education should

- cover the challenges with fairness, expectations, respect, and communications inspired by the arts and critical dialogues
- share power and cultures
- help online people deeply engage in lifelong learning activities
- examine the dynamics of democratic changes in online community
- improve reflective practices for greater impact
- engage online people in critical civic responsibilities, dynamic academic curriculums and powerful social actions
- understand the possibilities and potentials of online people to make democratic decisions and dialogic leadership
- develop culturally responsive and integrated social justice communication plans
- include anarchist change models that promote inclusive online communications
- provide unique and diverse perspectives with their own methodological strengths and weaknesses
- obtain genuine equal opportunities and democratic participations in building online knowledge networks not characterized by power, dominance, hierarchy and competition
- discuss the philosophical foundations and backgrounds of concepts, insights and skills needed to accelerate democratic transformations
- challenge power elite mandates through points of tension
- promote critical communication activities for digital engagements in democratic decision-making

- promote authentic and high quality life-long learning experiences
- deal with the pressures for diversity and difference
- engage anti-racist, social activism and alternative communication practices through the arts and critical dialogues
- inform new models and approaches to diversity online communications.

The mission of the theoretical background of distance education is to integrate collective acts democratically to the fast developing philosophical, historical, political, and socio-culture backgrounds and contexts of new media that can bring together a community of people committed to liberal and transformative reflective online communications. Therefore, as mentioned by Preece, Rogers and Sharp (2002), online people, including theorists, theater workers, artists and others committed to transformative pedagogy and social equity, can represent a range of real-life experiences in their online societal works and critical praxis. Based on these concerns and also approaches, the theoretical background of distance education help distance education people develop frameworks related to the potentials and impacts of diverse online communications. Also, this background provides sound knowledge needed to understand the communication processes related to democratic and multicultural elicit issues, and the international dimensions of the challenges faced by education. As emphasized by Culwin, MacLeod and Lancaster (2001), online cultures can be egalitarian and liberating only when it prepares digital people for fully democratic participation in social life and equal claim o the fruits of economic activity. The theoretical background of distance education can develop strong the engagements for digital people to their shared responsibilities. The needs and expectations of these persons can bring about democratic decision-making for dialogic citizenships, and play an important role in affecting deep community change. These are crucial concerns to achieve their comprehensive responsibilities to build online socities.

Bringing theory to practice, the authors apply communication theories and learning theories. The approaches of analysis bring to attention the complex decisions required in the construction of meaningful contents designed to cross borders in distance education. Providing a dynamic and flexible framework to plan, deliver and evaluate online contents discusses the diverse dimensions and strategies of distance education, and design strategies to build online communities (Berg, 2000; Burniske and Monke, 2001; Huerta, Ryan, Igbaria, 2003; Kendall, 2003; Rosenberg, 2001; Salmon, 2000; Stephenson, 2001).

However, we need more specific concern, which focus on the theoretical and empirical issues about how to design and maintain online communications successfully. Distance education providers should help digital people to think critically about real-world problems, and collaborate with each other successfully, and respect others' ideas and values. Therefore, as suggested by Burniske and Monke (2001) and Howell, William and Lindsay (2003), distance education providers should be reform-minded individuals. In these contexts, meta-communicativeconversations should build multicultural learning contexts dealing with real-world problems, and have flexible contents for reflective communications. Therefore, online people can engage in their own learning to achieve course tasks effectively, improve their thinking skills critically, and share their feelings, concerns and ideas productively.

This critical approach encourages online providers and stakeholders to construct both meaningful and multicultural distance milieus for everyone. Therefore, they have to rethink about planning meta-communicativeconversations by gaining knowledge from global resources. On the other hand, over the past few years, lifelong learning has been explosively popular with the world, which is dealing with the enormous growth of the electronic communication environments. Therefore, interactions among online people should promote collaborative partnership environments for distance education. This foundation can enable them to understand problems and perspectives from the real world that these critical communicational activities can help these people focus on preparing real-life related problems in their online societies. In this case, building theoretical background of distance education should be not only a dynamic social and cultural activity as well as a goal-oriented process. Therefore, online persons can embrace this critical perspective to describe and analyze their lifelong learning projects. By examining real-life experiences of their partnerships in communicational situations, online people can know how to implement collective actions for moving beyond transmission model for social justice issues and implications for reflective communications.

Meta-Communicative Conversations and Theoretical Background of Distance Education

Not only do meta-communicativeconversations help online people facilitate multicultural ideals of inclusive, interactive, and collaborative activities, but also help these people perceive the world better, think critically and perform decisively. The milieus in distance education around the world manifest a new outlook and value the diverse qualities and capabilities of global online societies. Time and location independent learning opportunities are a consequence of the philosophy of dynamic and democratic distance education. Therefore, meta-communicativeconversations are powerful tools, which construct flexible learning contents and generate diverse online interaction possibilities related to multicultural contexts. In order to build the appropriate flexible online contents for online people, professionals and community should consider how they can expose the principles and strategies of sharing knowledge online. Meta-communicativeconversations can impact on delivering multicultural knowledge through online networks. These networks with interactive communication models and approaches have the enormous potential to promote the issues of justice, equity and human rights, and enhancing values and ethics for building reflective communication milieus. However, to make the philosophy of distance education significant, meta-communicativeconversations should cover these issues given below (Bolliger & Martindale, 2004; Huerta, Ryan, and Igbaria, 2003; Fisher, Wright, 2001; Kyrish, 2004; Nieto, 1996; Porter, 2004):

- enhance digital citizen academic achievements
- ink powerfully the theory, policy and practice of actual democratic and multicultural communications
- provide online people with an apprenticeships model
- make sense of their educational and personal experiences
- serve online people equitable and high-quality communication opportunities
- encourage interactive collaborations among online people from a wide perspective
- take account of the knowledge, experience, needs, interests and aspirations of each person, regardless of their social, cultural, economical and political backgrounds
- clarify the relationships among academic, technological and multicultural knowledge to benefit from personal experiences
- generate learning opportunities for online people
- help online people become critical thinkers and also productive members of a democratic online society
- encourage online people's attempts to rethink and reconstruct their ideas, views, needs, expectations, beliefs and attitudes toward cultural pluralism

- expose online people to different perspectives through several philosophical strategies

To better understand and construct online societies, it is vital to concentrate on the management strategies of global knowledge networks among societies. These strategies help digital citizens interact wisely with all knowledge sources from around the world and around the clock being aware of providing multicultural environments. To transfer gradually more overwhelming amount of knowledge among online people therefore, new media deal with the quandaries of digital diversity shaped by emerging communication technologies to build knowledge-based network societies. Meta-communicativeconversations, therefore, should have gradually involved in communication change process. Online people have to deal with the challenge to accomplish access and equity issues by integrating digital technologies with increasing knowledge qualities and quantities. Moreover, these people should appreciate the various learning needs and expectations of diverse groups around the globe. Also, as discussed by Huerta, Ryan, and Igbaria (2003), online people must progress generative enlightenments to build interactive online communications with multicultural e-content standards based on the philosophy of democratic education.

Communication Theories as Theoretical Background of Distance Education

Building global online culture via new communication technologies should focus on how radical changes are fostered by democratic rules and principles. As mentioned by Brosio (1994), a democratic online society can long survive if it does not allow elite powers and dominant groups to dictate the flow of information to generate the butterfly effect that was first described by Lorenz at the December 1972 meeting of the American Association for the Advancement of Science in Washington, D.C., brightly illustrates the essential idea of chaos theory. To be an online person as a digital citizen in the digital age means to make diverse choices. New communication technologies are only as successful as its empowerment of online people. In the complex times ahead, therefore, online person can share power and culture in various democratic as well as question what new communication technologies assume roles, what the pros and cons are effective these new media, and when new communication technologies make policy choices what norms and values are reaffirmed or threatened to online persons. The very survival of democracy may, in fact, depend upon this one thing. We now hear much about the speed of change and the way that new communication technologies should transform the political, economic and social landscape of online world.

To make the philosophy of global culture worthwhile, meta-communicativeconversations, therefore, should cover the organizational features of online knowledge networks that affect the process and outcomes of planned change cultural activities among online people and societies (Bates, 2000; Burke & Chidambaram, 1999; Chua & Ngee 2001; Fabos & Young, 1999; May, 1999; Neo, 2005; Resta, 2002; Schrum & Benson, 2002; Stevens-Long & Crowell, 2002):

- define required skills to build and support a milieu
- focus on working collaboratively with colleagues and global partners in global online culture through new communication technologies
- engage online learners in multicultural projects designed to be realistic, intriguing and relevant to real life experiences
- promote excellence through continuous process improvement and the creative pursuit of new ideas and systems in global on-

line culture through new communication technologies
- model how a communication theory transforms into practice on complex decision making process
- encourage online people independence in thinking critically in global context
- plan, communicate, motivate, manage, and lead successfully in professional development and lifelong learning actions in global online culture through new communication technologies
- propose situate communications in an authentic context by engaging digital citizens think deeply
- encourage online people to take ownership and responsibility for their decision making process when communicating online?

Building meta-communicativeconversations should be based on a philosophical, theoretical and political orientation that emphasizes the relationships between power and privilege. To develop positive attitudes toward others' diverse backgrounds, first of all, online people should accept that all people have equal rights. In addition, to accept people from the world, they must engage online participants in collaborative online activities with others. Meta-communicativeconversations can give carefully attentions on the self-esteem progress of the digital citizens. Without strong bases of self-confidence (Sheets-Hernandez, 2004), they cannot be successful online participants to value themselves, respect individual freedoms and take risk in making errors. In addition, as highlighted by Spring (1999) and Torres (1998), meta-communicativeconversations build various interaction milieus to match the social needs of online people who have the diverse race, gender, ethnicity, religious, language, size, cultural and social backgrounds with or without disabilities.

Not only is collective group actions the familiarities and awareness of facts, truths and information gained through experience, learning and self-contemplation, but also it means the confident understanding of a subject, potentially with the ability to utilize it for a specific purpose. Therefore, collective group actions are built up from collective interactions with the online world, and is organized and stored in each individual's mind (Scardamalia, 2003). The dynamic structure of collective group actions, however, requires more than collecting, acquiring and transmitting large amounts of information, data and experience. Knowledge emerges from the interactions of body, mind and soul by emerging from understanding the social word. Besides, as critically pointed out by Beaudoin (2003), meta-communicative-conversations help online persons have global memberships in digital society. Communication theories, therefore, have essential responsibilities to tie online individual self to collective actions due to significant improvements in both computing and communication areas.

The cutting-edge communication technologies can build powerful multicultural networks to share and exchange knowledge for the prosperity and well-being of its members. Meta-communicative approach help online people utilize an electronic network to send and receive information across any locations, devices and business services. Meta-communicativeconversations, therefore, can generate new forms and tools of gathering data, manipulating and storing knowledge, transforming information, and working together over distance and time. To establish online societies efficiently, meta-communicativeconversations encourage digital persons to effectively transfer their diverse knowledge to new multicultural contexts of distance education. As a result, digital people as lifelong learners can improve their complex critical thinking skills to construct, produce or demonstrate their knowledge.

Besides, online people can discover critical rubrics to assess lifelong criteria and promote egalitarian partnerships among diverse digital people. Building online knowledge societies should be the most important goals of building global culture in the online world. The existing milieus of meta-communicativeconversations focus on the integration of knowledge from diverse sources and domains across space and time. It is forced by uncertainty but also continuous radical changes, meta-communicativeconversations should provide radical infrastructure to send bits anywhere, anytime in mass quantities-radical connectivity. As strongly highlighted by Moore and Kearsley (2005), the exploration of collective group actions begin with a series of diverse concerns:

- introduce the philosophy for online communities
- underlie the concept of global culture
- provide digital citizens with successful activities and agreements
- work together without space and time obstacles,
- provide a general orientation and overview of global culture
- recognize the ethical, legal, and social implications of new developments in online communities
- reason about the analysis of global culture
- appropriate data processes and integration of knowledge from diverse sources from the world
- provide multicultural insights into cultural differences among people and communities
- accomplish innovative levels of interactivity by increasing in-depth concerns
- demonstrate the relationships and functional interactive communications across disciplines, languages and cultures.

Online people, therefore, can advance their extensive productivity, social opportunities and intellectual potentials through more focused advance strategies. More specifically, online global society can represent more well-planned and selective ways of looking for flexibility, value and beneficial arrangements within the global cultural, political and economic issues associated with the emerging communication technologies. As pointed out by McChesney (1999) and Kendall (2003), online global culture should generate collective commons committed to develop, legally build upon and share the variety of creative communication works available for their all members.

Alternative communication practices, therefore, can explore how a community of digital people committed to liberation negotiate and make sense of their social experiences in the online society. Alternative communication practices also represent a range of experience in online people as theorists, educators, theater workers, artists and others committed to transformative pedagogy and social equity in online community works for critical praxis. In this context, meta-communicativeconversations are not only activist processes but also complex decision making progressions in culturally diverse digital milieus (Porter, 2004).

Meta-communicativeconversations through online communication plans should expose on online critical dialogues that deepen our awareness of innate social and cultural biases, stereotypes and prejudices, and challenges the social construction of dominant elite and social inequalities in online collective activities. Therefore, digital persons are educational activists from Universities, Community Colleges, K-12 Schools and the wider community. Also, these people focus on critical communicational approaches for global culture. Moreover, these digital develop culturally responsive, social justice-oriented, critical and creative communication plans to go beyond elite power mandates. In this context, online communication plans ties digital citizens own well-examined experiences of race, racism, and whiteness to practical and essential concerns with social justice and the dismantling of racism and its supremacy within the online milieus. Meta-communicativeconversations, therefore, can present responses to the following concerns:

- Have developed practical cultural responses
- impact the race and diversity on digital people's consciousness and practices
- inform new models and approaches to diversity communication
- develop critical and creative pedagogical responses
- interrupt current one-size-fits-all educational mandates
- reproduce power and privilege
- promote inclusive communication
- recognize diverse perspectives, contradictory race, ethnic, class, gender, sexual, and ability experiences

By respecting individual differences, online communities with the ideas of multicultural strategies increase the quality of new media successfully. Since meta-communicativeconversations are social and cultural experiences, racial differences are irrelevant, intelligence is multidimensional and distributed. Besides, these networks must be equipped with not only high-tech systems but also new visions of global online societies for supporting their citizens to discover new plans for political resistance and power elites. In this context, meta-communicativeconversations through critical dialogues can make their points of agreement and disagreement explicit that order their citizens' perspective of the future by being aware of diverse cultural backgrounds determined by social movements.

Stating the existence of new and potential interesting subjects of interest for collective actions, on the other hand, does not tend to underestimate changes in the short run confounded by the vast, apparently endless obviousness of new unpredictable issues. To promote diversity in online societies including various interest groups to use multicultural resources for egalitarian transmissions makes fundamental changes in online citizens' main concerns according to the struggles between capitalist hegemony and its democratic challengers; and realizes the existence of new, potentially interesting subjects of interest for collective actions. Meta-communicativeconversations can be shared among diverse populations to shape the online public policy by involving efforts from a wide range of challenging social groups.

Distinguishing novel and emerging communicational relationships formulated by the large shared interests of new communication technologies that can structure according the power of whole communities. Alternative meta-communicativeconversations have great significance to emerge in sharing knowledge online, and having profound effects on critical thinking (Abbey, 2000). Unlike knowledge sharing in traditional milieus, online knowledge sharing to build powerful networks is relatively flexible, open and egalitarian that has instituted fundamentals changes in collective communication actions (Moore & Tait, 2002). These reform movements progressively support digital people and society partnerships based on the sound principles of communication theories. These improvements, therefore, must be concerned with the development of the whole collaborative interactions within digital multicultural knowledge-based societies.

Global online culture, therefore, has a radical potential to deliver global knowledge by promoting the democratic principles of liberation around the world. These location independent communication opportunities become a consequence of the philosophy of dynamic and democratic lifelong learning. Therefore, meta-communicativeconversations are powerful means to generate logical online possibilities and flexible contents. In order to build appropriate flexible lifelong contents for digital citizens, new media must focus on methods, techniques and principles as well as barriers to share and exchange knowledge in online communications. According to the philosophy of meta-communicativeconversations, alternative communication practices can be capable of designing and maintaining effective culture to provide these citizens with flexible collaboration contents. Besides, theoretical background of distance education helps distance education people become engaged citizens, informed individuals and dynamic members in their online society to improve their communication styles and abilities with each other. However, there are limited researches and theoretical articles about alternative meta-communicativeconversations to assist lifelong learning with real-life experiences.

Therefore, meta-communicativeconversations can bring a new ground by addressing key questions about the communication styles and abilities, and real-life experiences of digital people. Based on these concerns discussed above, the key inquiries in online communities must be:

- improve their communication styles and abilities via meta-communicativeconversations
- develop communication styles and abilities via meta-communicativeconversations
- describe communication styles and abilities via meta-communicativeconversations
- impacts the communication styles and abilities of digital people via meta-communicativeconversations

In this case, meta-communicativeconversations are active processes to obtain, evaluate and produce knowledge. Therefore, individuals can become active participants in their knowledge constructions rather than passive receptacles. In this constructivist milieu, digital people can work on complex global projects via meta-communicativeconversations.

Besides, these projects must be followed from communication theories to become meaningful and understandable. Lifelong learning environments with high levels of communication can be valuable tools to enhance interactive and collaborative communications through new media around the world. Therefore, culture provides invaluable information about the changing and evolving needs and benefits of lifelong learners. Furthermore, as underlined by Rosenberg, (2001), Sheets, (2005), and Scardamalia (2003), meta-communicativeconversations addresses the specific communication problems. Distance communication designers, policymakers, and scholars can concern a structured way to improve the communication styles and abilities of online people to look at practices and learn from evidences with reducing reliance on trial and error. Finally, online culture helps digital individuals rethink traditional communications and be aware of their communicational strengths and limitations in online societies.

Learning Theories as Theoretical Background of Distance Education

Individualism has great significance to emerge in sharing knowledge online, and having reflective effects on building global online culture (Picciano, 2002). Although individualism is widely recognized as a critical organizational resource irrespective of new communication technologies, powerful online networks can maximize the value of these resources without adequate understanding of how to leverage and share knowledge throughout the online society (Stephenson, 2004).

These reform movements progressively support digital people based on the sound principles of learning theories. These improvements, therefore, must be concerned with the development of the whole collaborative interactions within digital multicultural knowledge-based societies. These knowledge networks have radical potentials to deliver global knowledge by promoting the democratic principles of social justice around the world. The most essential elements of online culture are the social, political, economical, institutional, technological and educational backgrounds of online societies. Regardless of the developments and improvements in the online world over the decade, on the other hand, there are still many challenges and risks to establish, deliver and implement online contents in distance education.

Launching and maintaining new communication technologies need not only money and other funds, but also well-educated human resources for online support services. In this context, digital people can focus on the complex communication problems with their unique answers of their societies, and help their colleagues and stakeholders in community build not only progressive but also integrated global culture together. Moreover, these people can drive attentions on the principles, ethics and pitfalls of sharing and exchanging knowledge to work on critical communication policies based on the diverse opportunities of their society.

Flexible contents are an approach to new media which offer digital people choice in what to communicate, how it is interacted and collaborated, and when and where learning happens. Moreover, these contents provide a dialogical support for the design and development of effective new media designs for online community to share knowledge in their place and pace. To increase flexibility in online contents, digital people should seek how to increase the choice of professionals and community in one or more of these aspects of critical communication activities. These actions refer to both a multicultural philosophy and a set of techniques for flexible delivery, access and communication. To emphasize meta-communicativeconversations, the needs and interests of online people deal with diverse potentials the development of an enthusiasm for participation in distance education. In addition, the place of multicultural communication designs for a dynamic online learning milieu should concentrate on the communications models in distance education.

The processes involved in the design, development, delivery, evaluation, improvement and management of new media can be explored to take the multicultural chances to develop the higher-level thinking skills needed to share knowledge online. To provide real-life learning examples for digital people constructs flexible communication contents by enhancing the network-based technologies. Developing a critical understanding shows the needs, expectations and strengths of digital person as they interact with global online culture regarding their academic and social progress in distance education. In this context, also, meta-communicativeconversations can support how learning theories can fit into online societies. The availability of these cutting-edge communication technologies is crucial for not only digital people but also scholars, professionals and policymakers to make decisions for enhancing multicultural interactions about how they can provide flexible communication settings for diverse people.

Communication Theories and Learning Theories as Theoretical Background of Distance Education

Table 1 summarizes the dimensions and dynamics of the theoretical background of distance education. The table has two labels:

1. Communication Theories
    - Communication theories has five dimensions horizontally
        - collective group actions
        - alternative communication practices
        - online communication plans
        - arts and critical dialogues
        - diversity of meta-meaning
2. Learning Theories
    - Learning theories has five dynamics vertically
        - individualism
        - critical progress
        - diverse identity integrity
        - cultural values and perspectives
        - orientation for identity development

As focused on the table, the multifaceted responsibilities of distance education in support-

Table 1. Theoretical background of distance education

META-COMMUNICATIVE CONVERSATIONS						
Theoretical Background of Distance Education		Communication Theory				
		Collective Group Actions	Alternative Communication Practices	Online Communication Plans	Arts and Critical Dialogues	Diversity of Meta-Meaning
Learning Theory	Individualism	New Communication Skills	New Communication Skills	New Communication Skills	New Communication Skills	New Communication Skills
	Critical Progress	New Communication Strategies	New Communication Strategies	New Communication Strategies	New Communication Strategies	New Communication Strategies
	Diverse İdentity İntegrity	Common Vision for Liberation and Social Justice	Common Vision for Liberation and Social Justice	Common Vision for Liberation and Social Justice	Common Vision for Liberation and Social Justice	Common Vision for Liberation and Social Justice
	Cultural Values and Perspectives	Online People and New Roles	Online People and New Roles	Online People and New Roles	Online People and New Roles	Online People and New Roles
	Orientation for identity Development	Online People and Changing Responsibilites	Online People and Changing Responsibilites	Online People and Changing Responsibilites	Online People and Changing Responsibilites	Online People and Changing Responsibilites

ing digital society actively engaging in building their communities should investigate how digital people, theoretically and practically, recreate more dialogical and democratic forms of pedagogy and community engagements to focus on conscious and unconscious barriers and possibilities of building global online culture (Scardamalia, 2003). Communication theories, in this context, should explore the main characteristics of meta-communicativeconversations, and discuss how to reflective online communications promotes online collaboration to model how theory translate into practice, and integrate authentic partnerships by clearly stating the pedagogical guidelines to build online societies. As the 21st century begins, online societies are undergoing many profound changes associated with global social, societal, political and economic forces. Distance education, therefore, plays a leadership role in the global reflection on communication reform.

Although it provides a platform for meta-communicativeconversations on how best to adapt education systems to the emergence of knowledge societies in generating and delivering multicultural knowledge, it is often less responsive than its diverse challenges and obstacles of how to utilize new media in activist reactions to greater competency and assurance within its complex reality and comparative perspective. Investigating in various ways to both a prospered variety of inquiry and a deepen focus on the meaning of quality in culture empowers online communities. To fortify these organization performances, there must be careful efforts to reform communication system, and support knowledge management to provide stakeholders with improving equal access opportunity to the system (Moore & Kearsley, 2005). Quality in these online societies is a multidimensional concept. To accomplish in multifaceted efforts to improve the policy and practice of meta-communicativeconversations should support critical discussions of the criteria for evaluating the rigor and effectiveness of new media that reflect the broadened perspective on practice.

The critical issues of theoretical background of distance education, the identification of qualifications and develop international policies for globalization can merge the interests of international public goods, the higher education sectors, the needs of digital citizens and the worldwide public interest. Because today's world is complex and knowledge is developing fast, learning must go on throughout life.

Not only online adults but also digital youth in distance education should know how to deal with change that requires reformist actions in the quality of online organizations in all its aspects to accomplish excellence in communication. Identifying the issues, challenges, priorities and needs of online communities for knowledge management develops to prioritize the goals and major issues to enhance the relevance of communication by adjusting collaboration processes, multicultural contents and egalitarian knowledge management to embrace online organizations and their qualities (Kyrish, 2004). The major challenges of the theoretical background of distance education focus on global democratic citizenships, respect online human rights and social identities by measuring how to build dynamic knowledge management systems under a framework with suitable capacity-building to make critical decisions and construct powerful action plans.

On the other hand, the major priorities of theoretical background of distance education underline the necessary improvements, and promoting intellectual and scientific collaborations of online organizations that empower knowledge managements with regard to considering the global societal values. In addition, the major needs to utilize the advantages and potential of advanced communication technologies by guaranteeing quality and sustaining high standards for practices and outcomes ensure online facilities based on local, national and global networks, and increase online organizations efficiency as well as preserve their quality and significance. There should be efforts around the globe to reform the theoretical background of distance education, progressively considered as a critical action for being digital citizens to improve equity of access and opportunity, and strengthen communication milieus (Fisher & Wright, 2001). Knowledge obtained in setting can have suggestions for policy and practice in networked society, and researchers and policy-makers increasingly recognize the importance of comparative perspectives on distance education organization. There is an urgent need to plan and conduct learning and communication theories in a systematic approach that includes identifying needs, selecting the best strategies from among known options, monitoring changes as they occur, and measuring the influence of these changes.

Assessing the quality of online society culture, therefore, can provide digital people with an agenda as a communication process to answer various problems, dilemmas and obstacles about a wide variety of culture. Furthermore, this involves digital citizens in activist change actions to focus on authentic experiences in critical dialogues. There exists a common consensus on the authenticity of advancing meta-communicativeconversations that promote new critical approaches in organization culture. These online societies should give urgent priority to dealing with research measuring quality, increasing the relevance of online communication, quality for digital people, reforming the online communication system, and better collaboration systems. The credibility, viability and quality of either current or prospective theoretical background of distance education provide fundamental inquires for critical reflections. A better understanding and measurement of quality of the theoretical background of distance education in the diverse contexts of meta-communicative-conversations provides disadvantage individuals with quality opportunities to address these online people needs as well.

As mentioned by Picciano (2002), global online culture makes sure that new media presents ideas and values about building a sustainable future, give digital people the chance and learn about the global world. This can be build in-depth respect for diversity and differences. Rethinking global online culture by focusing on the more pressing social and societal problems of our time, and also understands the achievement challenges and assessment concerns of lifelong learning (Stevens-Long & Crowell, 2002; Worthen & Sanders, 1987). Finally, theoretical background of distance education provides digital people with pedagogical knowledge for the global online culture-oriented design in a multicultural view. These people gain a better understanding of how people of different cultures behave in the online world - their behavior, appearance and communication performances.

CONCLUSION

The main purpose of this study is to discuss how theoretical background of distance education empower online communications to build democratic digital societies. Like the use of traditional media, new media, therefore, are strongly related to the design models and strategies of constructing global online culture (Salmon, 2002; Torres, 1998; Williams, 2003). Therefore, digital people carefully redesign and revolutionize their new roles in online milieus together. These people should learn how to discover new communication technologies and their relationships to societal and educational change; focus on working collaboratively with each other regularly to promote excellence through continuous process improvement and the creative pursuit of new ideas and systems; plan, manage and lead effectively in professional development and life-long learning endeavors to construct knowledge networks, and investigate the relationship between meta-communicativeconversations and reflective online communications to build democratic and multicultural knowledge networks.

Building global culture through meta-communicativeconversations can help digital people actively engage in their communication progresses. This process, also, helps these people to effectively transfer their knowledge to new contexts. As a result, online participants can improve their complex critical thinking skills to create, produce or demonstrate their knowledge. Moreover, digital people can involve innovation in assessment to meet their changing needs and to realize new opportunities for sharing knowledge online. As discussed by Stephenson (2001), and Yang and Cornelious (2005), online societies, a type of micro-society where digital people work and live together on a daily basis, with certain rules and understandings about what is acceptable and what is not. The idea of an online community having a culture developed from the theoretical background of distance education must focus on meta-communicativeconversations and reflective online communications to respect diverse cultures in different contexts.

REFERENCES

Abbey, B. (2000). *Instructional and cognitive impacts of Web-based education*. Hershey, PA: IGI Global.

Bates, A. W. (2000). *Managing technological change*. San Francisco, CA: Jossey-Bass.

Beaudoin, M. F. (2003). Distance education leadership for the new century. *Online Journal of Distance Learning Administration, 6*(2). Retrieved November 11, 2004, from http://www.westga.edu/%7Edistance/ojdla/summer62/beaudoin62.html

Berg, G. A. (2000). Early patterns of faculty compensation for developing and teaching distance learning courses. *The Journal of Asynchronous Learning Networks* (*JALN*), *4*(1). Retrieved May 26, 2001, from http://www.aln.org/alnweb/journal/jaln-vol4

Bolliger, D. U., & Martindale, T. (2004). Key factors for determining student satisfaction in online courses. *International Journal on E-Learning, 3*(1), 61–67.

Brosio, R. A. (1994). *A radical democratic critique of capitalist education*. New York, NY: Peter Lang.

Burge, L. (2000). *The strategic use of learning technologies*. San Francisco, CA: Jossey-Bass.

Burke, K., & Chidambaram, L. (1999). How much bandwidth is enough? A longitudinal examination of media characteristics and group outcomes. *Management Information Systems Quarterly, 23*(4), 557–580. doi:10.2307/249489

Burniske, R. W., & Monke, L. (2001). *Breaking down the digital walls: Learning to teach in a post-modem world*. Albany, NY: State University of New York.

Chua, A., & Ngee, A. P. (2001). Relationship between the types of knowledge shared and types of communication channels used. *Journal of Knowledge Management Practice, 2*. Retrieved May 23, 2002, from http://www.tlainc.com/ articl26.htm

Culwin, F., MacLeod, A., & Lancaster, T. (2001). *Source code cyber-democracy in UK: The computing schools, issues, attitudes and tools*. (South Bank University Technical Report SBU-CISM-01-02).

Fabos, B., & Young, M. D. (1999). Telecommunication in the classroom: Rhetoric versus reality. *Review of Educational Research, 69*(3), 217–259.

Fisher, D. R., & Wright, L. M. (2001). On utopias and dystopias: Toward an understanding of the discourse surrounding the Internet. *Journal of Computer-Mediated Communication, 6*(2), 13. Retrieved July 2, 2002, from htpp://www.ascusc.org/ jcmc/ vol6/ issue2/ fisher.html

Hodson, D. (1999). Critical multiculturalism in science and technology education. In May, S. (Ed.), *Critical. ulticulturalism: Rethinking multicultural and antiracist education* (pp. 216–244). Philadelphia, PA: Falmer.

Hofstede, G. J., Pedersen, P. B., & Hofstede, G. (2002). *Exploring culture: Exercises, stories, and synthetic cultures*. Yarmouth, ME: Intercultural.

Howell, S. L., William, P. B., & Lindsay, N. K. (2003). Thirty-two trends affecting distance education: An informed foundation for strategic planning. *Online Journal of Distance Learning Administration, 6*(3). Retrieved June 25, 2006, from http://www.westga.edu/ ~distance/ ojdla/ fall63/ howell63.html

Huerta, E., Ryan, T., & Igbaria, M. (2003). A comprehensive Web-based learning framework: Toward theoretical diversity. In Aggarwarl, A. (Ed.), *Web-based education: Learning from experiences* (pp. 24–35). Hershey, PA: IGI Global. doi:10.4018/9781591401025.ch002

Kendall, L. (2003). Cyberculture. In Jones, S. (Ed.), *Encyclopedia of new media* (pp. 102–104). New York, NY: Sage.

Kyrish, S. (2004). Creating an online program. In Momolescu, D., Schifter, C. C., & Greenwood, L. (Eds.), *The distance education evaluation: Issues and case studies* (pp. 1–21). Hershey, PA: Information Science. doi:10.4018/9781591401209.ch001

Lorenz, E. N. (1972). Barotropic instability of Rossby wave motion. *Journal of the Atmospheric Sciences, 29*, 258–264. doi:10.1175/1520-0469(1972)029<0258:BIORWM>2.0.CO;2

Mamadouh, V. D. (1997). Political culture: A typology grounded on cultural theory. *GeoJournal, 43*(1), 17–25. doi:10.1023/A:1006892130880

May, S. (1999). Introduction: Towards critical multiculturlism. In May, S. (Ed.), *Critical multiculturalism: Rethinking multicultural and antiracist education* (pp. 1–10). Phladelphia, PA: Falmer.

McChesney, R. W. (1999). *Rich media, poor democracy: Communication politics in dubious times*. Urbana Champaign IL: University of Illinois.

Moore, M., & Kearsley, G. (2005). *Distance education: System view*. Belmont, CA: Thomson Wadsworth.

Moore, P. E., & Tait, A. (Eds.). (2002). *Open and distance learning: Trends, policy and strategy considerations*. Paris, France: UNESCO.

Neo, M. (2005). Web-enhanced learning: Engaging students in constructivist learning. *Campus-Wide Information Systems, 22*(1), 4–14. doi:10.1108/10650740510574375

Nieto, S. (1996). *Affirming diversity: The social context of multicultural education*. White Plains, NY: Longman

Picciano, A. G. (2002). *Educational leadership and planning for technology (3*[rd] (Columbus, O. H., Ed.). Upper Saddle River.

Porter, L. R. (2004). *Developing an online curriculum: Technologies and techniques*. Hershey, PA: IGI Global.

Powazek, D. (2002). Design for community: The art of connecting real people in virtual places. *Philosophical Perspectives on Constructivist Views of Learning, 29*(1), 37–48.

Preece, J., Rogers, Y., & Sharp, H. (2002). *Interaction design*. New York, NY: John Wiley & Sons.

Resta, P. (Ed.). (2002). *Information and communication technologies in teacher education: A planning guide*. Paris, France: UNESCO.

Rosenberg, M. J. (2001). *E-learning: Strategies for delivering knowledge in the digital age*. Washington, DC: McGraw-Hill.

Salmon, G. (2000). *E-moderation: The key teaching and learning online*. London, UK: Kogan Page.

Salmon, G. (2002). *E-tivities: The key to active online learning*. London, UK: Kogan Page.

Scardamalia, M. (2003). Crossing the digital divide: Literacy as by-product of knowledge building. *Journal of Distance Education, 17*, 78–81.

Schrum, L., & Benson, A. (2002). Establishing successful online distance learning environments: Distinguishing factors that contribute to online courses and programs. In Discenza, R., Howard, C., & Schenk, K. (Eds.), *The design & management effective distance learning programs* (pp. 190–204). Hershey, PA: Idea Group, Inc.

Sheets, R. H. (2005). *Diversity pedagogy: Examining role of culture in teaching-learning process*. New York, NY: Pearson.

Spring, J. (1999). *Wheels in the head: Educational philosophies of authority, freedom, and culture from Socrates to human rights*. Madison, WI: McGrawHill.

Stephenson, J. (Ed.). (2001). *Teaching and learning online: Pedagogies for new technologies*. London, UK: Kogan Page.

Stevens-Long, J., & Crowell, C. (2002). The design and delivery of interactive online graduate education. In Rudestam, K. E., & Schoenholtz-Read, J. (Eds.), *Handbook of online learning: Innovations higher education and corporate training* (pp. 151–169). Thousand Oaks, CA.

Torres, C. A. (1998). *Democracy, education, and multiculturalism: Dilemmas of citizenships in a global world*. Lanham, MD: Rowman & Littlefield.

Williams, P. E. (2003). Roles and competencies for distance education programs in higher education institutions. *American Journal of Distance Education*, *17*(1), 45–57. doi:10.1207/S15389286AJDE1701_4

Worthen, B. R., & Sanders, J. S. (1987). *Educational evaluation: Alternative approaches and practical guidelines*. White Plains, NY: Pitman.

Yang, Y., & Cornelious, L. F. (2005). Preparing instructors for quality online instruction. *Online Journal of Distance Learning Administration, 8*(1). Retrieved October 8, 2005, from http://www.westga.edu/ ~distance/ ojdla/ spring81/yang81.htm

Chapter 3
The Meta-Communicative, Yet Dancing 'Pink Elephants' in the Online Multicultural Teacher Education Classroom:
E-Racism, E-Classism, and E-Sexism

Christine Clark
University of Nevada Las Vegas, USA

Gwen Stowers
National University, USA

ABSTRACT

This chapter takes a contrary view of the "meta" aspect of meta-communication (where meta is defined as "behind" or "beneath") in the online multicultural teacher education classroom, arguing that such communication inhibits learning about (content) and through (pedagogy) sociopolitically-located multicultural teacher education by enabling e-racism, e-classism, and e-sexism to operate in largely covert manners in the distance education context. Accordingly, this chapter contends that digital meta-communication on issues of race/ethnicity, socioeconomic class, and sex/gender needs to be "de-meta-ed" or made explicit in order for the kind of liberatory reflective conversation on these topics to occur that is foundational to the adequate preparation of PK-12 teachers to effectively educate all students.

DOI: 10.4018/978-1-61350-071-2.ch003

INTRODUCTION

In this chapter, we will discuss how race/ethnicity, socioeconomic class, and sex/gender come up or come "through" in online communication. We examine the "appearances" of these dimensions of identity from the lens of how we, as online faculty, "see" them, and how they manifest in online course discussions in student-to-student communication. More specifically, we define the problem of e- or electronic racism, e-classism, and e-sexism as a meta-communicative (less than fully conscious), yet "dancing pink elephant" (blatant) in the online multicultural education classroom from the perspectives of how faculty perceive students' race/ethnicity, socioeconomic class, and sex/gender identities, as well how these identities become "transparent" in student e-conversation.

BACKGROUND

This chapter draws from/builds on three meta-communicative concepts. First, it engages Charles Lawrence's view that race and class are meta-communicative or covert conversational topics because they are "forbidden" (2005). Second, it connects to Mark Lawrence McPhail's notion that direct or non-meta-communicative dialogue about race is "(im)possible" or exceedingly difficult to meaningfully realize (2003). Third, it intertwines Paulo Freire's idea of "false generosity" in exploring the extent to which the meta-communicative aspects of e-racism, e-classism, and e-sexism can be surfaced in order to effectively and consistently develop PK-12 teacher disposition to teach from an ever-deepening critically conscious, sociopolitically-located multicultural educational point of entry across the curriculum (1970).

In "Forbidden Conversations: On Race, Privacy, and Community" (2005), Lawrence, an African American, describes a conversation he had with a white colleague about public schools. The conversation took place shortly after Lawrence's colleague moved to the Washington, D.C. area, where Lawrence already lived. The colleague asked Lawrence to recommend a "good" school for his children. Lawrence uses this conversation to illustrate the meta- or forbidden nature of conversation about race and class even between Blacks and Whites from the same socioeconomic class background, in this case the upper middle class. Lawrence argues that in asking for such a recommendation, his colleague was *really* asking him to tell him where the predominantly white, upper middle class schools in Washington, D.C. were, but without expressly stating so. Accordingly, Lawrence answers his colleague's question by referring him to areas of the District where all the public schools were predominantly white and upper middle class, instead of directly engaging him in a conversation about how he defines what a "good" school is and why. Lawrence analyzes this conversational exchange as a pre-choreographed conversational dance that he and his colleague had been conditioned to do with one another when issues of race and class emerged. Lawrence goes on to articulate that dancing this dance is the normative manner of communication between people from different racial groups in the United States when issues of race, and class as it pertains to race, emerge.

In essence, Lawrence is describing what Gloria Anzaldúa (1999) has characterized as a form of "border patrol"-like behavior that emerges when people approach situations (borders) in which honest engagement with each other might lead them to meaningfully bridge-the-gap between them (border cross). Avoiding these situations—staying on one's own side of the border—preserves the status quo social order that privileges Whites and, disproportionately, the rich, which is exactly why borders are policed and border crossing is "forbidden." But, Anzaldúa argues, because we have all been so thoroughly socially conditioned—pre-choreographed—to avoid the forbidden, we all operate as less-than-fully-conscious or meta border patrol agents in going about our own everyday lives. In this way, Michel Foucault (1995) suggests the "panopticon" becomes the people—we, all of us, learn to perform surveillance on others and, further, to even internalize this surveillance function in assessing ourselves. Applying Foucault's idea to the current political landscape in the United States, Michael Moore (2010) argues that as a consequence of this panopticonal self-assessment, working and middle-class Whites tend not to vote in their own economic self-interest (including not voting at all) because, at least at a meta-cognitive level, they have, once again, been socially conditioned—pre-choreographed—to avoid acting (forbidden to act) against the interest of the mostly White rich. They do this on one hand because racial borders (constructed around myths of biological superiority and inferiority based largely on skin color) have taught them to see these Whites as they see themselves (as sharing an identity), and on another hand because economic borders (constructed around the myth of class mobility) have taught them to believe that one day they will also be rich.

In "Race and the (Im)Possibility of Dialogue" (2003), McPhail expresses seeing the same meta or forbidden communicative dynamics that Lawrence describes. But for McPhail, at least initially, through a dialogic form of communication the meta- can be surfaced and meaningfully engaged such that the forbidden is not only eroded, it becomes the aspirational. Fortified by this belief, McPhail dedicates many years of his life to facilitating and/or co-facilitating (with a white co-facilitator) race-based intergroup dialogue (sustained, open and honest conversation about race and racism between people of color (especially black people) and white people). Over time, McPhail's belief begins to wane as a result of the prevailing nature of engagement—or rather, non-engagement—of Whites in these dialogues. Time and time again, no matter the care that McPhail (and/or his co-facilitator) takes to establish a unilaterally supportive framework for race-based intergroup dialogue for *all* the participants in it, the white participants repeatedly resist engaging as members of a racial group (as Whites versus as individuals) and, therefore, reject understanding the experiences of people of color as a function of racial group membership in relationship to structural inequalities in society, rather than simply as a function of individual capacity and/or effort. To add insult to injury, when this white resistance is met with expressions of pain, frustration, and anger from participants of color, white participants emotionally retreat in the dialogue (become hostilely silent) or physically run away from the dialogue (opt out), rather than directly engage with the counter-perspectives and related emotions offered to them by their co-participants of color. The cumulative effect of this repetitive cycle of withdrawal from race-based intergroup dialogue on the part of Whites leaves McPhail wondering if such dialogue is, in fact, possible. He does not extinguish all hope of its possibility, but he does lay the burden for its possibility at the feet of white people's willingness to not only join such a dialogue, but finish one.

In *Pedagogy of the Oppressed* (1970), Freire discusses the path to liberation from conditions of oppression (on the basis of race, class, sex, etc.) for both the oppressed and the oppressors. In the course of this discussion, Freire argues that the nature of oppression is such that seeking liberation from it for the oppressors is more contradictory than it is for the oppressed, precisely because while the oppressors are dehumanized by oppression, they also benefit from it. This is precisely why Whites initially join race-based intergroup dialogues, but ultimately retreat in and run from them. As a result of this contradiction, Freire argues that the oppressors are not "strong enough" to liberate themselves nor the oppressed from oppression, because attempts to do so will necessarily be compromised by "false generosity," or the desire to do justice (be generous) mitigated by the desire to maintain an unfair advantage in society (be false) through the systemic power and control that in race-based intergroup dialogue they deny exists. For this reason, Freire argues that only the oppressed are "strong enough" to liberate themselves and the oppressors from oppression, in part because their strength is not compromised by benefits derived from oppression, and in part because in being oppressed their strength is informed by consciousness of the utter inhumanity of oppression such that they will not seek to simply reverse the terms of oppression (i.e., to oppress the oppressor).

This chapter seeks to surface the meta-manner in which Lawrence's concept of the "forbidden," McPhail's concept of the "(im)possible," and Freire's concept of "false generosity" emerge in online multicultural education classroom dynamics. Only by surfacing or de-meta-ing these concepts, can the teacher education students in these classrooms learn to chart a path from liberatory reflective conversation to liberation from oppression for themselves and their future PK-12 students.

MAIN FOCUS OF THE CHAPTER

With this conceptual framework in mind, this chapter will explore student names, technical writing skills, and conversational content as race/ethnicity-, socioeconomic class-, and sex/gender-related online meta-communicative devices.

What's in a Name? Names as Meta-Communicative Devices Online

In this section, the discussion of student names will examine the manners in which sex/gender and gender identity/gender expression manifest in intra- and inter-cultural and androgynous names, as well as the ways in which primarily race, ethnicity, first language, geographic origin, and immigration status emerge in given and taken names in online conversation in the online multicultural educational classroom. Concomitantly it will examine the exacerbating/mitigating effects that cross-race (also often cross-class) marriages (and, domestic partnerships) have on the compounding advantages/challenges of students' PK-12 schooling.

In almost every online classroom, regardless of its content focus, various social identity group membership dimensions of faculty and students are revealed—both explicitly (known) and implicitly (assumed). For example, in the first week of an online course, the professor and students generally introduce themselves to one another by posting and responding to each other's introductory biographies. It is common in the biographies for marital status, parental responsibilities, and other sex/gender-related information to be disclosed. As a result, faculty and student sex/gender is often known early on in a course. However, this is not always the case, and, even when it is, it is not uncommon for faculty and students to forget personal details shared only at one point in (e.g., at the outset) and/or in one area of (e.g., in a specific discussion forum) the course. As a result, when the professor's or a student's name is cross-culturally gender ambiguous (e.g., "Chris") and/or the gendered nature of the name is not understood and, therefore, not recognized cross-culturally (e.g., "Sivagami"), course discussion can reveal default and/or erroneous gender-based assumptions that faculty and students make. For example, assuming—unintentionally or intentionally—that all names are male unless expressly informed to the contrary, and/or unconsciously or consciously interpreting the gender of a culturally unfamiliar name from the lens of one's own culturally influenced gender norms. But, professor and student sex/gender identity emerges in the online classroom in ways that have little to do with names. Research shows that how men and women communicate online mirrors their patterns of communication in the three-dimensional world (Clark & Gorski, 2002). Accordingly, women tend to engage in online communication with greater equivocation, qualification, and disclamation, use more descriptive language, and are more attentive to conversational exchanges (to being responsive to others, especially those who have engaged them directly) than men. Typically, in non-multiculturally conscious online courses, when these dimensions of identity and related reactions emerge in the classroom they are not attended to with deliberation—they are not considered important enough to either try to tie to the instructional focus of the course, or to engender taking time away from that focus. As result, student engagement with issues of difference remains largely at a "meta" level.

As alluded to in the preceding paragraph, cultural identity dimensions also emerge in the online classroom, perhaps intentionally through explicit disclosure in introducing oneself, and perhaps surreptitiously based on the assumptions made about one's name. In the online multicultural education classroom, it is not uncommon, precisely because of the explicit content focus of the course, for students to deliberately disclose things about themselves in their self-introductions that they might typically want to share in other contexts but are reluctant to for any number of reasons, not the least of which has to do with concern about whether the disclosure will have the effect of marginalizing them in the classroom community. One common unsolicited disclosure comes from white female students, from a variety of class locations, about their being married to, usually, working class Latino men, who often speak English as a second language. This disclosure serves many different purposes.

For some students this disclosure is a way of being racially authentic in the classroom, to interrupt assumptions classmates might make about their cultural identities based on their Spanish surnames, and to "claim" their whiteness/"own" their white privilege (as an unearned advantage), rather than simply "passing" for Latina. In these instances, these students are challenging the "forbidden," charging directly at it in order to deliberately "de-meta" it.

For some students this disclosure is predicated on the belief that if they are assumed to be Latina, the perception of their academic prowess could be negatively impacted by faculty racial/linguistic prejudice, and/or their immigration status could be called into question by the racial/linguistic prejudices of both the professor and/or their classmates. In these instances, the disclosure clearly reveals an awareness of the reality of prejudice (and the corresponding connections between this prejudice and their assumed and actual *or* erroneously assumed PK-12 schooling experiences), at the same time it reveals a willingness to invoke white privilege to avoid being the target of such prejudice. When this occurs, these students, perhaps unintentionally, contribute to the "(***im***)possible" nature of cross-race intergroup dialogue. Peter McLaren (2000) characterizes this behavior in Whites as follows: "To choose blackness or brownness merely as a way to escape the stigma of whiteness and to avoid responsibility for owning whiteness is still very much an act of whiteness. To choose blackness or brownness as a way of politically disidentifying with white privilege and instead identifying and participating in the struggles of non-white [sic] peoples is an act of transgression, a traitorous act that reveals a fidelity to the struggle for justice" (p. 43).

And, for some students this disclosure is an attempt to present oneself as "less White" or as "a good white person" or as "not prejudiced." In these instances, the disclosure reveals a desire to run away from recognition of one's unearned race privilege, as well as a lack of awareness of the reality that one's racial prejudices do not disappear simply because one marries someone from another racial group. Here students exhibit "false generosity" in seeking to appear committed to issues of equality but only to the extent these issues are unconnected to issues of equity—that is, only to the extent that such commitment does not cost them something personally.

It is important to acknowledge that the very same racial, ethnic, linguistic, geographic, immigration status-related, and/or class dynamics can and do manifest in white female-Latina or white male-Latino domestic partnerships, they just do so less often because these relationships are statistically less common, and because disclosure of this dimension of these relationships is also less common as a result of the added "forbidden" dimension associated with "coming out" as lesbian or gay given the larger heterosexist and homophobic societal context. While such added disclosure is, as discussed above, more likely in the multicultural education classroom, and even more likely in the online multicultural education classroom given the at least somewhat "anonymous" and "distant" nature of online learning (discussed further below) it is still quite rare (Clark, 2005b).

In the online multicultural education classroom, the revelation of cultural identity, especially dimensions of it based on race, ethnicity, first language, geographic origin, and immigration status, does not only emerge by chance (as it would in any online course), or merely as a function of student assumptions about what will be welcomed or expected (because of the multicultural content focus of the course), it is explicitly cultivated by—structured into—the course design. One of the most common ways that such revelation is scripted is through course discussion prompts that ask students to "tell a story" about one or more of their names—how they got it, what it means and/or means to them, what they feel or think of it, experiences they have had because of it, etc. While not expressly stated in the name story prompt, it is virtually impossible to tell a name story without referencing some aspect of one's race, ethnicity, religion, class background, caste, first language, geographic origin, or immigration status.

Facilitated with skill (expressed as faculty responses to and questions about students' stories), this activity has the potential to: 1) foster the development of interpersonal, cross-cultural relationships between students; 2) support the establishment of group norms in drawing out areas of common ground across student experiences based on their individual identities; 3) create the context for student engagement with issues of conflict in highlighting areas of difference across student experiences based on their group identities; and, 4) encourage students to come together to act against injustice, instead of acting oppositionally toward each another as a consequence/in unconscious or sub-conscious reaction to injustice (Clark & O'Donnell, 1999; Nagda, Gurin, & López, 2003; Nagda, Kim & Truelove, 2004; Nagda & Zúñiga, 2003; Zúñiga & Nagda, 1993; Zúñiga, Nagda & Sevig, 2002; Zúñiga & Sevig, 1997). As a result, this activity can, at once, walk through the forbidden, the (im)possible, and the falsely generous, enabling student engagement in liberatory reflective conversation.

It's Not What You E-Say, it's How You E-Say It: Technical Writing Skills and Online Meta-Communication

In this section, the discussion of technical writing skills will examine how the compounding advantages/challenges of students' PK-12 school experiences show up in their written communication online through their first and, where relevant, second language literacy and fluency, as well as through their command of grammar and American Psychological Association (APA) formatting.

The section will also examine the role of race and class issues in the development of student critical consciousness online. More specifically, this examination will explore how student critical consciousness is often facilitated by their membership in marginalized groups and impeded by their membership in dominant ones. Correlations between the presence and/or absence of this consciousness and the compounding advantages/challenges of students' PK-12 school experiences discussed in the preceding section will be drawn.

Because online education makes pursuing higher education more accessible to students who are working and/or parenting full-time, it is an option that, perhaps, disproportionately, working class students engage.

As a result, several trends in online communication based largely on race, first language, and class emerge.

The first trend is that working class, domestic (e.g., African American, Native American, Puerto Rican, Chicana/Chicano, among others) students of color tend to demonstrate high levels of critical consciousness related to multicultural content in the *content* of their online discussion posts, coupled with significant technical writing challenges in the *structure* of these posts. Both post characteristics here can be attributed to these students' experiences of marginalization in society based on race and class. Students live with the reality of their own experiences as working class people of color (including their sub-standard PK-12 schooling experiences) as in utter opposition to the master narrative that the United States is a race and class "neutral" society. For these students, knowledge of the "forbidden" is a part of their "everyday." To the extent these students hold this knowledge covertly, and/or in ways (through shame, defensiveness, or pride, or as a function of exhaustion (in coping with racism and classism)) that preclude them from seeking and/or accepting academic support to improve their writing, the "forbidden" will persist uninterrupted.

Skilled facilitation of these (and other) students' learning in the multicultural classroom (again, expressed as faculty responses to and questions about students' shared ideas and experiences) must expressly connect their consciousness and lived reality in the discussion area of the classroom. But skilled facilitation of *only* these students' learning must also be expressed in the form of direct, honest, supportive, timely, detailed, and comprehensively constructive feedback on their technical writing skills in the gradebook area of the course. Connection of this feedback to their consciousness and to their lived reality can engender a reduction in student shame, defensiveness, and pride. Further, connection of this feedback to the reduction of time spent on assignments as writing skills improve can help students muster the energy to take advantage of writing tutors and/or academic writing courses. Many faculty, especially white faculty, avoid giving this kind of private feedback to students, especially to working class students of color, in part because it is time-consuming to do so, and in part because it is simply easier to be "falsely generous" in the evaluation of student work. Giving and receiving compassionately truthful feedback is painful to both parties, especially when doing so crosses race and class lines—in its own way it is a form of cross-race, cross-class dialogue and, therefore, carries with it the burden of both the "forbidden" and the "(im)possible."

The second trend is that working class white students tend to embrace "English only" and "Standard English" educational policies and benchmarks in the *content* of their online discussion posts, coupled with the same significant technical writing challenges in the *structure* of these posts that their of color classmates do. For these students, the development of critical consciousness based on their own experiences as working class people (including their sub-standard PK-12 schooling experiences) is retarded and/or impeded by their race privilege. As a result, these students, again perhaps unintentionally, contribute to the "***(im)*** possible" nature of not only cross-race intergroup dialogue, but specifically cross-race, intra-class intergroup dialogue, as well as, simply, intra-class intergroup dialogue. While these students share more in common with their working class student of color classmates (and therefore stand to gain more from forging "forbidden" alliances with these classmates to act against class-based injustices in society), they, instead, aspirationally identify with middle and upper class white students who express reactionary ideals and, therefore, forge the type of alliances with these classmates that preclude social action of any kind.

Skilled facilitation of these (and other) students' learning in the multicultural classroom (again, expressed as faculty responses to and questions about students' shared ideas and experiences) must expressly connect their *lack of* consciousness and lived reality in the discussion area of the classroom. But, again, skilled facilitation of *only* these students' learning must likewise be expressed in the form of direct, honest, supportive, timely, detailed, and comprehensively constructive feedback on their technical writing skills in the gradebook area of the course. Connection of this feedback to their *lack of* consciousness and to their lived reality can *engender* shame, defensiveness, and pride, as well as pain and anger. For many of these students, being faced with the contradiction of their racist, meritocratic political philosophy in relationship to their own lack of meritocratic performance can be initially emotionally and intellectually overwhelming. Further, connection of this feedback to the need for them to spend the time to take advantage of writing tutors and/or academic writing courses in order to, in fact, merit good grades can be very off-putting to these students. Again, many faculty, especially white faculty, avoid giving this kind of private feedback to students, especially to working class white students, in part because it is time-consuming to do so, and in part because it is simply easier to be "falsely generous" in the evaluation of student work, especially when students perceive the quality of their work through similarly, though self-directed, "falsely generous" lenses—that is, when student self-evaluation is based on the myth of their merit that is, at once, predicated on race privilege and class oppression and a denial that such privilege and oppression exist. Once again, giving and receiving compassionately truthful feedback is painful to both parties, especially when doing so forces examination of race and class dynamics in relationship to a student's conflicting race and class locations and corresponding, now compromised, political philosophy. Again, developing and delivering this kind of feedback carries with it the burden of both the "forbidden" and the "(im)possible," making it an emotionally and intellectually "heavy lift" for faculty, especially white faculty, day in and day out. White, at least middle class faculty are typically unaccustomed to the exhaustion that direct engagement with racism and classism—even in only in academic contexts—can cause; accordingly, they also typically lack the coping skills for so doing and, for this reason as well, avoid constructing and conveying such feedback.

The third trend is a bifurcated one. This trend is that middle and upper class white students tend to either express progressive *or* reactionary ideals in the *content* of their online discussion posts, coupled with technical writing prowess in the *structural* expression of these ideals in their posts. For these students, the development *or* lack of development of critical consciousness cannot be linked with marginalization on the basis of race or class. Sometimes the development of such consciousness can be linked to experiences of marginalization on the basis of another dimension of social group membership (e.g., first language, geographic origin, immigration status, as well as sex/gender, gender identity or expression, sexual orientation, religion, and (dis)ability status, among others). Other times the development or lack of development of this consciousness is a function of how these students have come to see and understand oppression in society. Students who have been taught to think critically about social issues (taught to confront the "forbidden") in their privileged PK-12 schooling experiences, recognize and understand that oppression exists in society, largely as a function of the differential access to full participation in democracy afforded to people based on their race- and class-based social identity group memberships. Students who have not been taught to think critically about social issues (taught to avoid the "forbidden") in their privileged PK-12 schooling experiences, do not recognize that oppression exists in society, and, therefore attribute differential access to full participation in democracy that accrues to people based on their race- and class-based social identity group memberships to be a function of individual and/or group capacity (intelligence and/or ability), coupled with individual effort and discipline.

Finally, skilled facilitation of these (and other) students' learning in the multicultural classroom (again, expressed as faculty responses to and questions about students' shared ideas and experiences) must expressly connect their *consciousness or lack thereof* and lived reality in the discussion area of the classroom. But, once again, skilled facilitation of *only* these students' learning must likewise be expressed in the form of direct, honest, supportive, timely, detailed, and comprehensively constructive feedback *on their consciousness or lack thereof*. Too often, faculty spend less time engaging students through such feedback whose intellectual and/or technical skill sets are already strong, regardless of the ideals they express.

In the multicultural education classroom, all students must be supported and challenged in equitable ways, that is, in relationship to where their learning edges are—supported to stay engaged (to make the "(im)***possible***"), and challenged to grow in the ways their discussion posts and other assignments indicate are necessary based on the goals and objectives of the course (to confront and learn to move with diligence through the "forbidden") (Clark, 2005a; Nagda, Gurin, & López, 2003; Nagda, Kim & Truelove, 2004; Nagda & Zúñiga, 2003). This is, perhaps, the most difficult to accomplish in the multicultural education classroom with technically proficient students, regardless of race, who express progressive ideals. With these students, as well as all other students, it is paramount to search for points of contention in their consciousnesses (for example, an expressed belief in the fundamental oneness of all humanity juxtaposed with opposition to same sex marriage) and some area for improvement, however small, in their technical skill development.

It's Not How You E-Say it, it's What You E-Say if You E-Say It: Content and Online Meta-Communication

In this section, the discussion of student conversation content in the online multicultural education classroom will focus examination in two areas. The first area will examine how students express, if at all, what they feel, think, believe, experience, know, and understand in relationship to race/ethnicity, socioeconomic class, and sex/gender in online conversation. This examination will pay particular attention to how, if it all, students differentiate and/or learn to differentiate conjecture from actuality. The second area will examine the ways in which student internalized oppression can manifest as fidelity to racism, classism, and sexism, and how the "cover" provided by the relative anonymity of e-communication context can deepen this oppression and the manifestations of the e-versions of these isms.

Conjecture and Actuality

One of the unique benefits of online education is that students who might typically be less inclined to participate (based on personality (e.g., shyness) and/or internalized messages related social identity group membership (e.g., English language prowess, self-perceived validity of ideas based on sex, race, etc.)) in face-to-face education, are not only more inclined to participate in the online classroom; they *have* to because they simply cannot rely on the participation and/or overparticipation of their classmates to take up all the class discussion time. (While the asynchronous nature of online class discussion time means it technically never ends, it is usually internally structured to end at a certain point each week.) Similarly, students who might commonly have more difficulty in attempting to enter into class discussion (i.e., who are reluctant to "jump in," are used to raising their hands to get faculty or classmate attention before speaking, and/or who wait to be called on to speak) in face-to-face education, do not experience these challenges in the online classroom; there is less "air time" competition in online class discussion, and the "call" to discussion or discussion prompt greets all students in the same manner whenever they opt into the discussion (though some students do still compete to post their responses to discussion prompts first or most robustly). As a result, engendering equitable student participation online is somewhat less of a challenge than it is in the face-to-face setting.

But, while the question of *if* students participate may be a less challenging one in online education, precisely because students—all students—are participating (and often participating more) in such educational contexts, facilitating all of what they say (the sheer volume of it) is quite challenging. In the online multicultural education classroom, facilitating all of what students say (the sheer volume of it *as well as* the nature of it) is even more challenging because of the a priori-perceived politicized focus of the course content. What is most challenging in this regard is working with students to help them differentiate what they *feel*, from what they *believe*, from what they *think* (opinion), from what they *experience*, from what they *understand*, from what they *know* (fact), from what they can *prove* (based on rigorous academic research).

Because multicultural education focuses study on dimensions of differences based on all human social identity group memberships, it is, in fact, about everyone, and about us in very personal ways. Consequently, it is hard for students to suspend judgment for almost any length of time (hence the tendency toward immediate, knee-jerk response) or to defer judgment about the accurateness of the subject matter to the professor and/or course materials in the same way they might be customarily inclined to do, for example, in a physics classroom.

Hence, skilled facilitation of student learning in this area requires faculty deliberate and staid attention to the issue of "positionality," broadly conceptualized, in all that is said (written). Responding to student posts by asking positionality-focused problem-posing questions such as: Who benefits from this picture of reality and how? Whose interests does this idea serve and why? How did you come to believe this, by what process? Can you prove what you are saying here if you had to? How do you understand or make sense of this and why? What would it mean for you if what you think in this regard could be proven to be absolutely wrong and why? Why do you feel this way? How do you know this is true/false? Have you ever had this experience? Indeed these are "forbidden" questions, yet they are the only kind of questions, that when answers to them are crafted, have the potential to make cross-group dialogue (across all dimensions of difference) "(im)***possible***."

Further, the attention to the technical aspects of academic writing, again through individuated feedback in the gradebook area of the course, can be facilitative in building student learning in this area as well. While academic writing can be overly formulaic and dispassionate in ways that promote Eurocentric (and other) norms (and that should be acknowledged with students to do so), it can also be instructive in helping students learn how to construct and communicate their ideas in manners that require them and, therefore, reflect their ability, to situate these ideas: 1) relative to like ideas that have preceded and could follow theirs; 2) relative to ideas that both support and challenges theirs; 3) in a manner of organization that ensures that others can follow them; and, 4) in a tone of communication that encourages others to take them seriously. This dimension of skilled facilitation in the multicultural education classroom pushes past "false generosity" in seeking to prepare all students to succeed in the world as it currently exists (e.g., a world in which APA formatting is a measure of academic excellence), as well as to inspire them to change it for the better for all (e.g. a world in which multiple ways of knowing have equal value as indicators of learnedness).

Internalized Oppression

As previously alluded to, the relative anonymity of online education can have the effect of encouraging student participation in general, and online multicultural education can further this effect by engendering student disclosures relating to their social identity group memberships. But the online nature of education also has the effect of providing students "cover" in expressing their feelings, beliefs, and thoughts/opinions, as well as in describing their experiences, and demonstrating their understandings and knowledge in relationship to the course subject matter. In the online multicultural education classroom this can mean that students are not only more willing to share negative characterizations of people who are different from themselves, but also of people who are like them. While such characterizations can be and are also shared in face-to-face multicultural educational settings, in the online setting this sharing is often more cavalier and callous.

Discussed previously in relationship to working class white students' characterizations of people of color (different from themselves) and of poor people (like them), the latter aspect of this phenomenon also emanates from women about women, and people of color about people of the same color. This phenomenon is discussed in the social justice education literature (broadly conceived) as "internalized oppression" (Adams, Bell, & Griffin, 2007; Adams, et. al., 2010; Clark & O'Donnell, 1999). Such oppression manifests when people from non-dominant social identity groups internalize the negative messages about their own groups that are promoted by members of dominant groups both individually and systemically and then apply them to themselves, others in their group, and/or the group as a whole to explain their own, another person's, and/or the group's perceived lack of ability, value, and/or academic and/or economic progress. Alice Walker (2010) has commented on this phenomenon among African Americans arguing that it is not difficult to understand why black America might not want to identify with Africa (or Africans) when the vast majority of images of it portrayed in the U.S. media paints it as a poor and dirty place where people are suffering from starvation and disease. Henry Giroux (1996) has suggested that when what you are is made negative on a grand scale, the tendency is to run away from yourself, to disassociate yourself from your organic history and culture, to, in essence, develop a "fugitive identity." Adding insult to injury, Toni Morrison (2007) contends that in developing a fugitive identity, black Americans have also developed "images of whiteness" in their "black imagination." Said another way, the internalized oppression that many black Americans experience may be so profound that they no longer need to run from who they are, because their mind's eye has been permeated by white supremacy to such an extent that an authentic sense of who they were, are, and/or, could be apart from that supremacy may no longer exist, not even in their souls. Other people of color and women (as well as members of other non-dominant groups based on other dimensions of social identity group membership) experience and exhibit parallel identity conflicts, many of which show up in their discussion posts in the online multicultural education classroom.

Skilled facilitation of student learning in this area requires tremendous faculty empathy as differentiated from sympathy—that is, faculty must express "feeling *with*" the student whose posts demonstrate internalized oppression, not "feeling *for*" him or her. In "feeling *with*," faculty place themselves in the same position as the student, alongside her or him, instead of in a position apart from, outside, above, at a distance from, etc., that of the student. While there is the potential to fall into the trap of "false generosity" in expressing empathy as well as sympathy, not only is the potential greater with expressions of sympathy, the consequences of so doing are as well. As discussed previously in relationship to the "positionality" manifest in student posts, here the "positionality" of faculty responses to students' posts is likewise key.

When faculty express feeling *for* a student experiencing internalized oppression, it can have the effect of deepening that oppression by communicating to the student that what she or he is experiencing is emotionally and/or intellectually unfamiliar to the faculty member, making dialogue about the "forbidden" nature of the experience "***(im)***possible." If the faculty member is from the non-dominant group relative to the student's internalized oppression, the student can interpret the faculty member's sympathy as evidence that she or he is unaware of her or his own "inferiority." And, if the faculty member is from a dominant group relative to the student's internalized oppression, the expression of sympathy can signal to the student that their internalized oppression is warranted precisely because members of the dominant group do not experience it. Regardless of faculty identity relative to the student's internalized oppression, expressions of sympathy are ineffective in facilitating all students' learning in this area.

On the other hand, when faculty express feeling *with* a student experiencing internalized oppression, it can have the effect of mitigating that oppression by communicating to the student that what she or he is experiencing is emotionally and/or intellectually familiar to the faculty member, making dialogue about the "forbidden" nature of the experience "(im)***possible***." If the faculty member is from the non-dominant group relative to the student's internalized oppression, the student might be inclined to engage the faculty member's empathy further in an effort to discover overtly (by asking outright) or covertly (by asking tangentially related and/or indirect questions) how she or he copes with, responds to, manages, etc., her or his experience of this oppression. And, if the faculty member is from a dominant group relative to the student's internalized oppression, the expression of empathy can signal to the student that their internalized oppression is unjustified because members of the dominant group not only recognize it, recognize it as something warranting solidarity, allyship, and *leaning in toward*, **not** d-i-s-t-a-n-c-i-n-g a-w-a-y f-r-o-m. Regardless of faculty identity relative to the student's internalized oppression, expressions of empathy are effective in facilitating all students' learning in this area. These expressions of empathy should continue in individuated feedback to students in the gradebook area of the course.

It is important to note that, in contrast to sympathy, empathy does not necessarily imply kindness in the traditional sense of this word. Reverend James H. Cone describes the type of non-traditional kindness that often uniquely exemplifies empathy in this way: "G-d has a way of pointing you to the right thing if you remain open and listen to people who mean you well; *and, remember, the people who mean you well are not always those who say nice things…*" (2002). So, in empathizing with students experiencing internalized oppression, it may be necessary to "mean them well" by responding to their posts with commentary that may not always be nice. This is especially the case when the expression of internalized oppression is directed outward—at other members of the non-dominant group relative to the student's internalized oppression, as opposed to inward—at the student her or himself (that is self-directed) as a member of the non-dominant group relative to her or his internalized oppression. In these instances it is important not only for the student at focus, but for all students (from every identity group), to "e-see" and "e-hear" faculty interrogate, challenge, cite the erroneous origins of, provide counter perspectives to, identify weaknesses in, offer alternative understandings of, analyze from more comprehensive points of entry into, etc., manifestations of internalized oppression based on the research in multicultural education.

FUTURE RESEARCH DIRECTIONS

This chapter points to two key areas for future research. The first key area relates to developmental sequencing, and the second key area pertains to instructor readiness.

In thinking about how to predictably achieve the overarching multicultural educational instructional goal of preparing all teacher education students (but especially white middle class females) to effectively teach all students (but especially working class youth of color), it is clear that having a single multicultural education course in a teacher licensing program of study, while helpful, is not adequate. Further, where multiple such courses—either that contain multicultural educational components or are wholly multiculturally educationally focused—exist in a program, if attention is not paid to how the multicultural components and/or foci are sequenced, while student exposure may be robust, their cumulative knowledge, skills, abilities, and dispositions may be scant, spotty, and/or superficial. Accordingly, future research in multicultural teacher education needs to attend to the development of carefully reasoned scaffolds that are expressly designed to help students build progressively more comprehensive, insightful, and complex multicultural educational knowledge, skills, abilities, and dispositions from the beginning of a course to the end of it, and from one course to the next. With respect to the multicultural educational foci in this chapter, this would mean that students would, over time, develop reliably and demonstrably: 1) increased skill for and comfort with engagement with the "forbidden" and "(im)possible" aspects of especially cross-race intergroup dialogue; 2) greater critical awareness of the how the propensity for "false generosity" on the part of white participants in cross-race intergroup dialogue can threaten the dialogue's efficacy; and, 3) amplified strategic capacity for preventing "false generosity" from manifesting (in self and others) in cross-race intergroup dialogue, and for preserving the dialogue if it does. While there is emerging research in this area, it is not yet broadly, deeply, and differentially well developed enough to be meaningfully instructive in this regard (Clark & O'Donnell, 1999; Gurin, Dey, Hurtado, & Gurin, 2002; Hurtado, 2001).

Throughout this chapter there is an implicit assumption that the people who teach multicultural education courses possess the academic foundation and practical experience necessary to support students learning in the manners discussed. While this assumption is reasonable, it is also largely erroneous. While the literature on the nature of teacher and/or professor preparation required to accomplish these multicultural educational goals is growing, because it is an area of study typified by tremendous political economic conflict, much more research in this area is needed (Delpit, 2006; Mowry, 2005; Powers, 2006; Quinn & Meiners, 2007). Such research should seek to: 1) document the political and economic conflicts related to the development of multicultural educational prowess; 2) find areas of common ground between the parties engaged in the conflict, and articulate, to the extent possible, collaborative pathways forward for establishing constructivist "good practice" (*not* positivist "best practice") benchmarks for multicultural education; and ultimately, 3) explicate what multicultural educational knowledge bases and skill sets are needed and how they can be reliably developed and assessed.

CONCLUSION

This chapter undertook a critical examination of the myth of online communication/education as race-, class-, and sex-"blind" and, therefore, "bias free." In so doing, this examination uncovered meta-manners by which prejudice, discrimination, and oppression on the basis of social identity group membership—especially those related to race, class, and sex—emerge in and permeate conversation even in the multicultural education

Figure 1. People dancing with pink elephant

e-classroom. Once uncovered, this examination brought to light that the key to eroding and (hopefully) eradicating e-racism, e-classism, and e-sexism (among other forms of e-discrimination and e-oppression) lies in de-meta-ing the conversation on these topics—in short, in learning to dance ***with*** the pink elephants (Figure 1) in the e-classroom, instead of acting as though these elephants are not only not, pink and not dancing, but not even there.

REFERENCES

Adams, M., Bell, L. A., & Griffin, P. (Eds.). (2007). *Teaching for diversity and social justice* (2nd ed.). New York, NY: Routledge.

Adams, M., Blumenfeld, W., Casteñeda, C. R., Hackman, H., Peters, M., & Zúñiga, X. (2010). *Readings for diversity and social justice* (2nd ed.). New York, NY: Routledge.

Anzaldúa, G. (1999). *Borderlands/la frontera: The new Mestiza* (2nd ed.). San Francisco, CA: Aunt Lute Books.

Clark, C. (2005a, Spring). Intergroup dialogue as pedagogy across the curriculum. *Multicultural Education, 12*(3), 51–61.

Clark, C. (2005b, Fall). People of color coming "out" and being "out" on campus: A conversation with Mark Brimhall-Vargas, Sivagami Subbaraman, and Robert Waters. *Multicultural Education, 13*(1), 45–59.

Clark, C., & Gorski, P. (2002). Multicultural education and the digital divide: Focus on gender. *Multicultural Perspectives, 4*(1), 30–40. doi:10.1207/S15327892MCP0401_6

Clark, C., & O'Donnell, J. (Eds.). (1999). *Becoming and unbecoming white: Owning and disowning a racial identity*. Westport, CT: Greenwood Publishing Group, Inc., Bergin & Garvey.

Cone, J. H. (2002). *Liberation theology and multicultural community*. Border Crossing Speaker Series Keynote Address. University of Maryland, College Park, February 12, 2002.

Delpit, L. (2006). *Other people's children: Cultural conflict in the classroom*. New York, NY: The New Press.

Foucault, M. (1995). *Discipline and punish: The birth of the prison* (2nd ed.). New York, NY: Vintage.

Freire, P. (1970). *Pedagogy of the oppressed*. New York, NY: Continuum.

Giroux, H. A. (1996). *Fugitive cultures: Race, violence, and youth*. New York, NY: Routledge.

Gurin, P., Dey, E. L., Hurtado, S., & Gurin, G. (2002). Diversity and higher education: Theory and impact on educational outcomes. *Harvard Educational Review*, *72*(3), 330–366.

Hurtado, S. (2001). Linking diversity with educational purpose: How the diversity impacts the classroom environment and student development. In Orfield, G. (Ed.), *Diversity challenged: Legal crisis and new evidence* (pp. 143–174). Cambridge, MA: Harvard Publishing Group.

Lawrence, C. R. III. (2005). Forbidden conversations: On race, privacy, and community (A continuing conversation with John Ely on racism and democracy). *The Yale Law Journal*, *114*, 1353–1403.

McLaren, P. (2000). *Ché Guevara, Paulo Freire, and the pedagogy of revolution*. Lanham, MD: Rowman & Littlefield.

McPhail, M. L. (2003). Race and the (im)possibility of dialogue. In Anderson, R., Baxter, L., & Cisna, K. (Eds.), *Dialogue: Theorizing difference in communication studies* (pp. 209–224). Thousand Oaks, CA: Sage Publications.

Moore, M. (2010). *Capitalism: A love story*. Beverly Hills, CA: Anchor Bay Entertainment.

Morrison, T. (2007). *The bluest eye*. New York, NY: Vintage International.

Mowry, D. (2005, December 2). Cultural competence: Oregon style. *Oregon Catalyst.com*. Retrieved October 11, 2009, from http://www.oregoncatalyst.com/ index.php/ archives/ 20-Cultural-Competence; -Oregon-Style.html

Nagda, B. A., Gurin, P., & López, G. E. (2003). Transformative pedagogy for democracy and social justice. *Race, Ethnicity and Education*, *6*(2), 165–191. doi:10.1080/13613320308199

Nagda, B. A., Kim, C. W., & Truelove, Y. (2004). Learning about difference, learning with others, learning to transgress. *The Journal of Social Issues*, *60*(1), 195–214. doi:10.1111/j.0022-4537.2004.00106.x

Nagda, B. A., & Zúñiga, X. (2003). Fostering meaningful racial engagement through intergroup dialogues. *Group Processes & Intergroup Relations*, *6*(1), 111–128. doi:10.1177/1368430203006001015

Powers, E. (2006, June 6). A spirited disposition debate. *Inside Higher Ed*. Retrieved November 10, 2009, from http://www.insidehighered.com/ news/ 2006/ 06/ 06/ disposition

Quinn, T., & Meiners, E. (Summer 2007). Do ask, do tell: What's professional about taking social justice and sexual orientation out of classrooms? *Rethinking Schools Online*. Retrieved September 30, 2009, from http://www.rethinkingschools.org/ archive/ 21_04/ ask214.shtml

Walker, A., & Byrd, R. (2010). *The world has changed: Conversations with Alice Walker*. New York, NY: The New Press.

Zúñiga, X., & Nagda, B. A. (1993). Dialogue groups: An innovative approach to multicultural learning. In Schoem, D., Frankel, L., Zúñiga, X., & Lewis, E. (Eds.), *Multicultural teaching in the university* (pp. 233–248). Westport, CT: Praeger.

Zúñiga, X., Nagda, B. A., & Sevig, T. D. (2002). Intergroup dialogues: An educational model for cultivating engagement across differences. *Equity & Excellence in Education*, *35*(1), 7–17. doi:10.1080/713845248

Zuñiga, X., & Sevig, T. D. (1997). Bridging the "us/them" divide through intergroup dialogues and peer leadership. *Diversity Factor*, *6*(2), 23–28.

ADDITIONAL READING

Alimo, C., Kelly, R., & Clark, C. (2002, Fall). Intergroup dialogue program student outcomes and implications for campus racial climate: A case study. *Multicultural Education*, *10*(1), 49–53.

Banks, J. (Ed.). (2009). *The Routledge international companion to multicultural education*. New York: Routledge.

Banks, J., & Banks, C. (Eds.). (2004). *Handbook of research on multicultural education* (2nd ed.). San Francisco: Jossey-Bass.

Bigelow, B. (2006). *The line between us: Teaching about the border and Mexican immigration (paperback)*. Milwaukee, WI: Rethinking Schools.

Clark, C. (2002). Effective multicultural curriculum transformation across disciplines. *Multicultural Perspectives*, *4*(3), 37–46. doi:10.1207/S15327892MCP0403_7

Clark, C. (2002, Summer). Intergroup dialogue on campus. *Multicultural Education*, *9*(4), 30–31. doi:10.1207/S15327892MCP0401_6

Clark, C. (2004, Spring). Multicultural education as a tool for reclaiming schools organized as breeding grounds for prisons. *Multicultural Education*, *11*(3), 50–53.

Clark, C., & Gorski, P. (2001). Multicultural education and the digital divide: Focus on race, language, socioeconomic class, gender, and disability. *Multicultural Perspectives*, *3*(3), 39–44. doi:10.1207/S15327892MCP0303_7

Clark, C., & Gorski, P. (2002). Multicultural education and the digital divide: Focus on class. *Multicultural Perspectives*, *4*(3), 25–36. doi:10.1207/S15327892MCP0403_6

Clark, C., Jabonete-Bouis, G., Subbaraman, S., & Balón, D. (2004, Winter). Social justice from classroom to community. *Multicultural Education*, *12*(2), 55–59.

Freire, P. (2005). *Education for critical consciousness*. London, England: Continuum International Publishing Group.

Gorski, P., & Clark, C. (2001). Multicultural education and the digital divide: Focus on race. *Multicultural Perspectives*, *3*(4), 15–25. doi:10.1207/S15327892MCP0304_5

Gorski, P., & Clark, C. (2002). Multicultural education and the digital divide: Focus on disability. *Multicultural Perspectives*, *4*(4), 28–36. doi:10.1207/S15327892MCP0404_6

Gorski, P., & Clark, C. (2002). Multicultural education and the digital divide: Focus on language. *Multicultural Perspectives*, *4*(2), 30–34. doi:10.1207/S15327892MCP0402_7

Gorski, P., & Clark, C. (2003). Turning the tide of the digital divide: Multicultural education and the politics of surfing. *Multicultural Perspectives*, *5*(1), 29–32. doi:10.1207/S15327892MCP0501_6

Gurin, P., Gurin, G., Dey, E. L., & Hurtado, S. (2004a). The educational value of diversity. In Gurin, P., Lehman, J., & Lewis, E. (Eds.), *Defending diversity: Affirmative Action at the University of Michigan* (pp. 97–188). Ann Arbor, MI: University of Michigan Press.

Gurin, P., Nagda, R., & Lopez, G. (2004b). The benefits of diversity in education for democratic citizenship. *The Journal of Social Issues*, *60*(1), 17–34. doi:10.1111/j.0022-4537.2004.00097.x

hooks, b. (1994). *Teaching to transgress: Education as the practice of freedom*. New York: Routledge.

Horton, M., & Freire, P. (1990). Conversations on education and social change. In Bell, B., Gaventa, J., & Peters, J. (Eds.), *We make the road by walking* (pp. 1–296). Philadelphia, PA: Temple University Press.

Hurtado, S., Dey, E. L., Gurin, P., & Gurin, G. (2003). The college environment, diversity, and student learning. In Smart, J. S. (Ed.), *Higher education: Handbook of theory and research* (*Vol. 18*, pp. 145–189). Amsterdam: Luwer Academic Press. doi:10.1007/978-94-010-0137-3_3

Karno, D. (2008, April). *NCLB, Standardized curriculum, & privatization: Where does democratic education fit in?* Paper presented at the annual meeting of the Midwest Political Science Association (MPSA) Annual National Conference, Chicago, IL.

Ladson-Billings, G. (2006, October). From the achievement gap to the education debt: Understanding Achievement in U.S. schools. *Educational Researcher*, *35*(7), 3–12. doi:10.3102/0013189X035007003

Limburg, F., & Clark, C. (2006, Spring). Teaching multicultural education online. *Multicultural Education*, *13*(3), 49–55.

Lui, M., & Robles, B. Leondar-Wright, B., Brewer, R., Adamson, R., with United for a Fair Economy. (2006). *The color of wealth: The story behind the U.S. racial wealth divide* (paperback). New York: The New Press.

McLaren, P. (1997). *Revolutionary multiculturalism: Pedagogies of dissent for the new millennium*. Boulder, CO: Westview.

Milem, J., & Hakuta, K. (2000). The benefits of racial and ethnic diversity in higher education. In Wilds, D. (Ed.), *Minorities in higher education, 1999-2000: Seventeenth annual status report* (pp. 39–67). Washington, DC: American Council on Education.

Nieto, S. (1998). From claiming hegemony to sharing space: Creating community in multicultural courses. In Chávez Chávez, R., & O'Donnell, J. (Eds.), *Speaking the unpleasant: The politics of non-engagement in the multicultural education terrain* (pp. 16–31). Albany: State University of New York Press.

Nieto, S., & Bode, P. (2008). *Affirming diversity: The sociopolitical context of multicultural education (Fifth Edition)* (paperback). Upper Saddle River, NJ: Pearson Education/Allyn & Bacon.

Olson, C., Evans, R., & Shoenberg, R. (2007). *At home in the world: Bridging the gap between internationalization and multicultural education*. Washington, DC: American Council on Education (ACE).

Sleeter, C. E. (1996). *Multicultural education as social activism*. Albany, NY: State University of New York Press.

Tannen, D. (1999). Fighting for our lives. In D. Tannen, *The argument culture: Stopping America's war of words* (pp. 3-26). New York: Random House Publishing Group.

Thompson, M. C., Brett, T. G., & Behling, C. (2001). Educating for social justice: The program on intergroup relations, conflict, and community at the University of Michigan. In Schoem, D., & Hurtado, S. (Eds.), *Intergroup dialogue: Deliberative democracy in school, college, community and workplace* (pp. 99–114). Ann Arbor, MI: University of Michigan.

KEY TERMS AND DEFINITIONS

Critical Consciousness: Awareness developed through critical thought that enables one to see beyond the superficial to what is typically controversial because it threatens the hegemony or status quo.

e-Classism: The manifestations of prejudice and discrimination on the basis of socioeconomic class background (and/or employment status) in the electronic (or "e-"), online, and/or virtual realm.

e-Discrimination: The manifestations of unfair or unjust treatment, especially that which violates policy and law, on the basis of any dimension of social group identity (e.g., race, class, sex, etc.), especially toward members of "protected class," marginalized, and historically underrepresented groups in the electronic (or "e-"), online, and/or virtual realm.

e-Oppression: The manifestations of systemic discrimination—via overtly and covertly coercive mechanisms that operate in the political, economic, psychological, and physical spheres of society—from members of one or more dominant social identity groups (e.g., upper class, white, men, etc.), toward members of one or more non-dominant social identity groups (e.g., poor, of color, women, etc.) in the electronic (or "e-"), online, and/or virtual realm.

e-Racism: The manifestations of prejudice and discrimination on the basis of race (and/or ethnicity, tribe, religion, creed, color, and caste) in the electronic (or "e-"), online, and/or virtual realm.

e-Sexism: The manifestations of prejudice and discrimination on the basis of sex (and/or gender, gender identity, and gender expression) in the electronic (or "e-"), online, and/or virtual realm.

De-meta-ed: The process by which a covert phenomenon was made overt.

False Generosity: The inherently conflicted, and ultimately compromised, nature of commitment to equity expressed by members of dominant social identity groups who, on one hand seek social justice for all peoples, but on the other hand seek to maintain their unjust advantage over members of non-dominant social identity groups.

Internalized Oppression: The un- or subconsciously absorbed: 1) negative and/or inferior feelings, opinions, or beliefs about one's own non-dominant social identity group(s), and/or, 2) positive and/or superior feelings, opinions, or beliefs about dominant social identity groups of which one is *not* a member; both sets of ideas emerge in reaction to prolonged exposure to manifestations of systemic discrimination—via overtly and covertly coercive mechanisms that operate in the political, economic, psychological, and physical spheres of society—and that are actively promoted by members of dominant social identity groups.

Meta-: Behind or beneath.

Meta-Communication: Hidden and/or covertly underlying meaning; the deeper, alternative, and/or opposite meaning behind or beneath what is actually expressed.

Panopticon: A higher or strategic vantage point from which covert and/or overt surveillance can be conducted; the rifle tower in a prison; a prison or prison-like environment in which occupants are under constant scrutiny and, therefore, have no personal refuge and/or privacy.

Transparency: Openness, straightforwardness, directness; the absence of deception, coercion, duplicity; the skill, ability, and will to be honest even when honesty may compromise one's image, reputation, standing, etc., because it is the right thing to be.

Voice: Oral agency; the skill, ability, and will to express critically conscious—counterhegemonic or anti-status quo—feelings, opinion, beliefs, *and factual knowledge* about issues of oppression manifest in society at large and/or expressed by specific members of society.

Chapter 4
An Online Conversation among Southeast Asian Higher Education Institutions and its Observed Oppressions

Alexander G. Flor
University of the Philippine-Open University, The Philippines

Narong Sompong
Kasetsart University, Thailand

ABSTRACT

This study looked into the feasibility of a meta-communication approach, specifically the community of practice (CoP), in the design of a graduate degree program for natural resources and climate change management. The CoP is characterized as a modern day counterpart of the "invisible college" that developed curricula or learning programs during the birth of universities in the Middle Ages. Can a community of practice as a meta-communication approach, transcend institutional, geographical, disciplinal, and language oppressions for collaborative development of new curricula?

The study was implemented from Kasetsart University in Bangkok and the UP Open University in Los Baños, with the latter hosting the KM system and administering the online platform. However, it involved a community of practice that came from four countries: Thailand; Philippines; Lao PDR; and Indonesia. It found that the CoP model may indeed be used as capacity development approach for the design of a graduate degree program. Furthermore, Web-based learning management systems such as IVLE and Moodle can adequately serve as meta-communication platforms for such a CoP. However, it was observed that the language barrier, cultural sensitivities of Southeast Asian participants, intellectual intimidation, as well as access and connectivity clearly posed communicative oppressions.

DOI: 10.4018/978-1-61350-071-2.ch004

INTRODUCTION

"The problem of communication is a problem of consciousness."- Jurgen Habermas

One of the most discernable trends in this era of globalization and informatization is transnational education. Institutions of higher learning are no longer bound by national borders. Almost every major university in the world has programs that are addressed to learners based in countries other than its own. This trend has seen the rise not only of the global university but regional networks of higher educational institutions catering to a multinational student body. In the latter, several national universities established a regional consortium to jointly offer a program that may be availed upon by students of any nationality within the region. The institution that awards the graduate degree is based on the individual student's citizenship. In Southeast Asia, several university consortia or network initiatives are underway sponsored by the Southeast Asian Ministers of Education organization (SEAMEO), the Association of Southeast Asian Nations (ASEAN) and others.

This chapter is based on the online conversation that transpired among faculty members of higher educational institutions from four Southeast Asian countries who were in the process of designing a proposed regional graduate program on natural resources knowledge management. Knowledge management is synonymous to the sharing and reuse of intellectual capital. In other words knowledge management is likewise engaged in what Habermas (1984) calls the *communicative act*. This communicative act being the subject of the online conversation has transformed the online discussion for the proposed program into meta-communication, i.e., communication on communication or discourse (online discussion threads) on knowledge management (communication). The researchers documented the online conversation to test the efficacy of the platform used. In the process, however, they have uncovered certain oppressive factors peculiar to this setting that hindered the communicative act (i.e., knowledge management) and meta-communication (i.e., the online conversation) itself.

The Online Conversation

The online conversation was prompted by a pressing need: Southeast Asia is beset with natural resources management problems. Decades of unhampered resource exploitation in the watersheds of the Philippines and Indonesia by logging concerns are exacting their toll through landslides and flashfloods in the Visayas and Central Java. Land-locked areas in the Greater Mekong Subregion are now suffering the same fate. Coastal resources in the Sulu-Celebes Sea, home of the most biologically diverse marine ecosystems in the world, are being endangered by destructive fishing practices, mangrove destruction, and oil spills.

The initiative argued that the collective expertise of the region should be brought to bear on these problems through the establishment of a regional knowledge management (KM) system on natural resources, an online platform for the sharing and reuse of knowledge. Along this line, the capacities of both individuals and institutions for natural resources knowledge management should be built and strengthened. Thus, a program for developing these capacities was proposed and it was to be designed collaboratively through an online discussion forum among Southeast Asian universities.

Two alternative platforms for the online discussion forum were employed, the Integrated Virtual Learning Environment and the Modular Object Oriented Dynamic Learning Environment made available by the University of the Philippines (Open University).

Participants in the online conversation may be considered as part of the regional community of practice (CoP) on natural resources knowledge management. They came from Indonesia, Lao PDR, the Philippines and Thailand, mostly from national universities: Bogor Agricultural University; National University of Laos; University of the Philippines Los Banos; U.P. Open University; Kasetsart University; and Mahidol University.

Not all the participants were actively engaged in the online conversation. Some of them were *lurkers*, i.e., participants who monitored the online discussion forum but did not post nor reply to a discussion thread.

Objective

Technically, the researchers analyzed the feasibility of the community of practice or CoP concept as a model for natural resources knowledge management. Furthermore, they wanted to test the CoP as a capacity development venue specifically in the design of a learning program. The researchers revisited the curriculum development process with an added dimension, the Internet. The Internet has not only caused the death of distance. It has also destroyed exclusivity, undermined hierarchy, enabled nonlinear/ asynchronous interaction, and globalized education. The educational process now assumes a new label: *knowledge management*. Communities of practice may eventually become to knowledge management what invisible colleges were to the educational process. If, indeed, such is the case, can a community of practice engaged in an online discussion transcend institutional, geographical, disciplinal and language barriers to design new curricula? This paper attempts to answer this research question.

BACKGROUND

The conceptualization of this study was inspired by what educational historians refer to as the "invisible college."

Invisible College

Young (1998) describes the invisible college as a precursor to the Royal Society of the United Kingdom. It consisted of a group of scientists including Robert Boyle, John Wilkins, John Wallis, John Evelyn, Robert Hooke, Christopher Wren and William Petty. In letters written in 1646 and 1647, Boyle refers to "our invisible college" or "our philosophical college." The concept of an invisible college made up of a brotherhood of scholars exchanging ideas in restricted gatherings and correspondences spread throughout Europe and was exemplified by networks of astronomers, professors, mathematicians, and natural philosophers including Johannes Kepler, John Dee and Nicolas Copernicus. These societies adopted a common theme, to acquire knowledge through experimental investigation (Owen, 2004).

In earlier times, when knowledge was thought to be the purview of the privileged, the term was applied to secret societies and even to occult brotherhoods. Nowadays, invisible colleges often refer to the sharing and reuse of knowledge among academics, the free transfer of thought and technical expertise, outside of an institutional framework, spread within personal networks or informal apprenticeship (Owen, 2004).

The above description of the invisible college may very well be applied to the CoP concept.

CoP

The community of practice concept itself refers to both a process and a group of people. The most common definition of a CoP is "the process of social learning that occurs when people who have a common interest in some subject or problem collaborate over an extended period to share ideas, find solutions, and build innovations" (Cox, 2005). It refers as well to the stable group that is formed from such regular interactions.

The term was first employed by Jean Lave and Etienne Wenger (1991)who used it in relation to situated learning as part of an attempt to "rethink learning" at the Institute for Research on Learning. Later on Etienne Wenger (1998) extended the concept and applied it to other contexts, including organizational settings. More recently, Communities of Practice have become associated with knowledge management (Davenport and Prusak, 2000) as people have begun to see them as ways of developing social capital, nurturing new knowledge, stimulating innovation, or sharing existing tacit knowledge within an organization. It is now an accepted part of organizational development.

Others such as Wenger (1998) describe CoPs in terms of the interplay of four fundamental dualities: participation versus reification, designed versus emergent, identification versus negotiability and local versus global. Applying the CoP approach in graduate degree program development is theoretically biased towards participation, emergence, negotiability and globalism. The study intends to validate these theoretical biases.

Knowledge Management

Knowledge management or KM is traditionally defined as an evolving discipline that considers an organization's intellectual capital as a manageable and potentially profitable asset (Leibmann, 1999). It is based upon the assumption that today's global economy is knowledge-based and that knowledge is a primary commodity as well as a valuable resource. KM entails digitally capturing documented and tacit knowledge and storing these for sharing and reuse. Thus, knowledge is managed through an intranet system and guided by organizational policies that provide incentives to knowledge sharing.

The goal of knowledge management is the sharing and reuse of intellectual capital (Leibmann, 1999). Although, distinctions are made between undocumented or tacit knowledge and documented or explicit knowledge, both are captured digitally and stored in a knowledge base. These are also made available digitally in a variety of multimedia formats for sharing and reuse.

Many of today's grand academic traditions started out in invisible colleges, well-knit and tightly structured brotherhoods of hooded learned men governed by a culture of hierarchy, exclusivity, ritual and secrecy. In Paris, Oxford and Rome, these brotherhoods existed for the purpose of enlightenment. A progressive system of initiation, passing, and raising determined the degrees and the level of knowledge of a scholar. Under this system, disciplines began and areas of studies grew.

Today, the academe has discarded the secret handshake but still adheres to secret codes through the technical jargon inherent in any discipline. The hood and the robe have been retained in academic costumes. The system of seniority, the degrees and the rituals that accompany them have been maintained. Latin and Greek have been replaced with English as the academe's *lingua franca*. And invisible colleges are now being transformed into communities of practice.

CoPs have been used as the knowledge management model of choice among development sectors. In the book *eDevelopment and Knowledge Management* (Flor, 2001), a CoP is defined as a group of professionals informally bound to one another through exposure to a common class of problems, common pursuit of solutions, and thereby themselves embodying a store of knowledge.

Recently, CoPs have been gaining much attention because of the widespread influence that they have generated on several advocacies (Saint-Onge and Wallace, 2003). With little organizational or logistical support, CoPs are known to have: spearheaded knowledge sharing during the Asian SARS outbreak in 2003; influenced the policy process in 2004 leading to the World Summit for the Information Society; and decisively responded to the avian influenza threat in late 2005. The Asian Development Bank is currently applying KM protocols for an Asian CoP on Management for Development Results in support of the Millennium

Development Goals. This same approach may be adopted to address natural resources management constraints in Southeast Asia. However, the KM models employed by these CoPs have not been purposively constructed; and the KM systems have not been systematically documented (Flor and Sompong, 2007).

Operationalization

The constituent concepts enumerated in the aforementioned framework were operationalized as follows:

KM System

Knowledge management was operationalized through a KM system (essentially, an online communication system) that is co-located and administered at the UP Open University, operated as a module of the existing learning management system (LMS) powered by IVLE (Integrated Virtual Learning Environment) Version 4 and MOODLE (Modular Object Oriented Dynamic Learning Environment).

CoP

An NRM community of practice involving experts from the Philippines, Thailand, Lao PDR and Indonesia was activated to upload and share, download and reuse expert and local knowledge on NRM. Online discussions among the members were facilitated through consensus building.

Curriculum Design

Through online discussions of the CoP, a curriculum for a post-baccalaureate degree on natural resources knowledge management was designed. The program may be offered in both online and residential modes by Kasetsart University and the UP Open University. NRM professionals in all ten Southeast Asian countries may enroll in the program under sponsorship of development agencies or projects.

Institutional Involvement

The study was implemented from Kasetsart University in Bangkok and the UP Open University in Los Baños, with the latter hosting the KM system and administering the online platform. However, it involved a community of practice that came from four countries: Thailand; Philippines; Lao PDR; and Indonesia.

Thailand and Lao PDR were identified as participating countries because of their proximity, similarity in language, and the strong networking among their scientific communities. However, Lao PDR is landlocked and composed primarily of hilly land ecosystems. Thailand, on the other hand, has extensive marine, coastal and lowland ecosystems. NRM expertise is very much available in Thailand particularly in Kasetsart University, Mahidol University and Chang Mai University. Most NRM experts in Lao PDR have trained in Thailand.

The Philippines and Indonesia share parts of the Sulu Celebes (Sulawesi) Sea, a Vavilov center for marine biodiversity. Likewise, both have extensive lowland and upland areas, seventy percent of which have been deforested. Scientific and local knowledge on NRM management are also extensive in both countries. The documentation, however, is minimal primarily because of language and access issues.

DISCUSSION

Knowledge Management as a Communicative Act

The Dominant Discourse on KM

In the past decade, KM principles have been brought to bear upon pressing social and development concerns such as health, education, agriculture and the environment. The increasing recognition of KM by the international development assistance community is evidenced by the establishment of KM programs in most development agencies and the designation of a Chief Knowledge Officer or a Vice President for Knowledge, as in the case of the Asian Development Bank. In many instances, the levels of application have gone beyond the conventional organizational KM system and have entered sectoral domains cutting across institutions. Among the most critical in these sectoral domains is natural resources management or NRM.

An old adage states that, "Knowledge is power." Thus far, the dominant discourse on knowledge management has failed to look into the power relations surrounding KM, particularly as a communicative act. When knowledge is shared and reused within a given context, the dynamics of power sharing and using come into play.

Communicative Content

As applied to this study, the content of the communicative act is natural resources knowledge management. The inquiry adopted a "body of knowledge" perspective. It forwards that, like other bodies of knowledge, natural resources management is three-dimensional.

As a discipline, on one hand, natural resources management has three aspects: theory, policy, and practice. These three – theory, policy and practice – do not result from knowledge management per se but are products of knowledge generating activities, particularly, research. Theory refers to the product of basic research; policy, the product of policy research; and practice, the product of applied/action research or lessons learned in program implementation.

As an area of study, on the other hand, NRM has several themes, roughly classified as: land resource management (brown issues); water, coastal and marine resources management (blue issues); biodiversity conservation (green issues); air quality (grey issues); and energy resource management (red issues). Each thematic area would have its set of theories, policies and best practice (Table 1).

Communication Platform

As stated earlier, online discussion forums hosted and administered by the UP Open University Faculty of Information and Communication Studies were uploaded to the existing UPOU learning management system (LMS) running on two platforms: the IVLE (Integrated Virtual Learning Environment) Version 4 Platform, www.myportal.upou.org, and the Moodle (Modular Object Oriented Dynamic Learning Environment) Platform,

Table 1. Dimensions of NRM knowledge

Dimension	Theory	Policy	Practice
Land resource (Brown)	Theory $_1$... Theory $_n$	Policy $_1$... Policy $_n$	Best Practice $_1$... Best Practice $_n$
Water, coastal and marine resources (Blue)	Theory $_1$... Theory $_n$	Policy $_1$... Policy $_n$	Best Practice $_1$... Best Practice $_n$
Biodiversity (Green)	Theory $_1$... Theory $_n$	Policy $_1$... Policy $_n$	Best Practice $_1$... Best Practice $_n$
Air Quality (Grey)	Theory $_1$... Theory $_n$	Policy $_1$... Policy $_n$	Best Practice $_1$... Best Practice $_n$
Energy resource (Red)	Theory $_1$... Theory $_n$	Policy $_1$... Policy $_n$	Best Practice $_1$... Best Practice $_n$

www.myportal.upou.net. IVLE was designed and developed by the National University of Singapore. IVLE Version 4 used to be proprietary but its code has been opened when older versions were made available on the market. Moodle, on the other hand, was developed as an open source LMS application by Curtin University. Both sites are secure and password protected. User names and passwords for the COP members were provided. However, based on tests conducted during the country visits, it was decided to run the COP on the IVLE workspace and use the Moodle site as an alternate.

www.myportal.upou.org

The IVLE site (Figure 1) carries the following functionalities: online discussion board; messaging and collaboration; file transfer protocol; scheduling; document management; and others.

www.myportal.upou.net

The Moodle site (Figure 2) has the following functionalities: online discussion board; messaging and collaboration; file transfer protocol; scheduling; document management; and others.

Communication Participants/CoP

A total of eighteen (18) experts participated in the CoP. Four (22.00%) came from Indonesia. Another four (22.00%) came from Lao PDR. Six (28.00%) came from the Philippines. The remaining six (28.00%) came from Thailand.

Table 2 gives a breakdown of the CoP participants according to country of origin.

Figure 1. IVLE NRKM screenshot

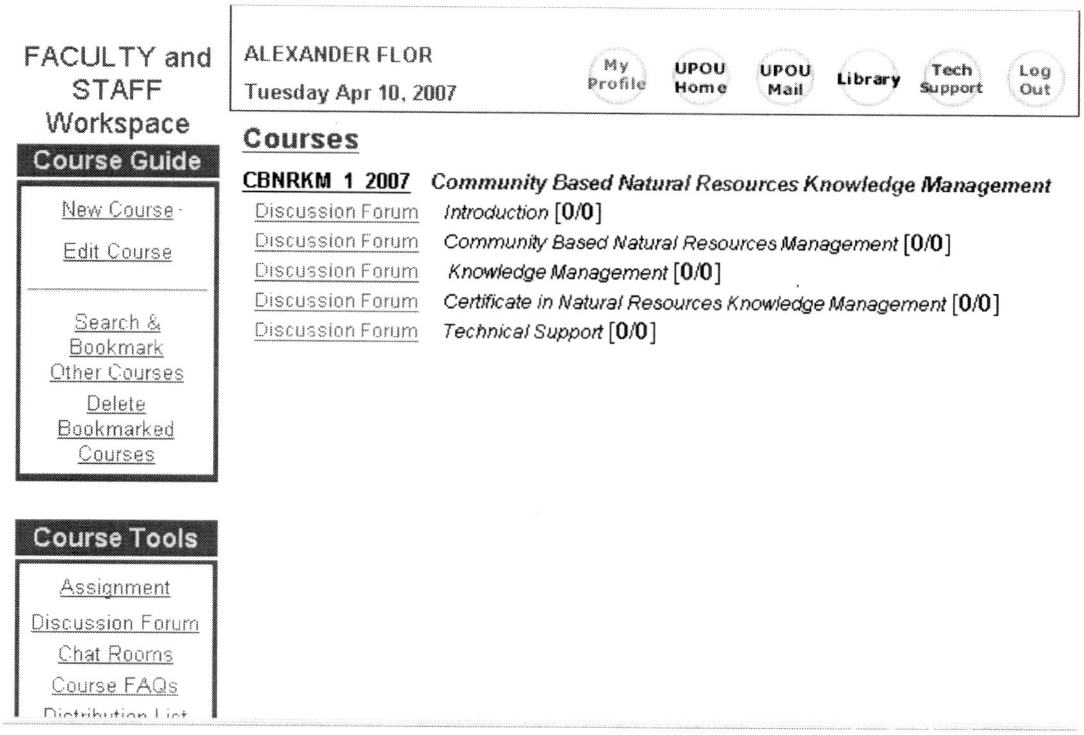

Figure 2. MOODLE NRKM screenshot

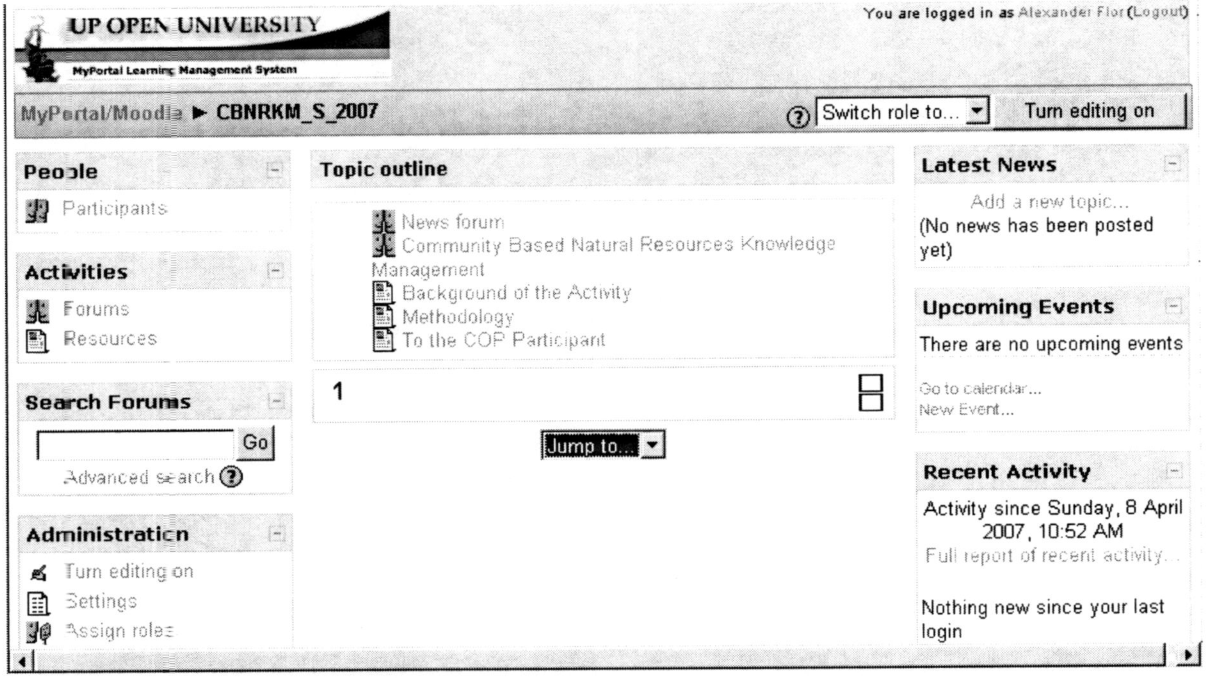

Communication Themes

The NRKM CoP site had a total of four discussion forums: Introductions; the CoP Process; the Post Baccalaureate Program; and General Comments. The following is a topic outline of the discussions:

1. Introduction (Forum 1)
   a. Meaning of Natural Resources: Leveling Off
   b. Natural Resources as Economically Viable Items or as Ecosystems?
2. Southeast Asian Community of Practice (CoP) on Natural Resources Knowledge Management (Discussion Forum 2)
   a. Definition of Knowledge Management
   b. The Goal of Knowledge Management
   c. Applications of Knowledge Management to Development
   d. Knowledge Management Model and System
   e. Good Practices
3. A Graduate Program on Natural Resources Knowledge Management (Forum 3)
   a. Rationale
   b. Program Description
   c. Institutions to Offer the Program
   d. Faculty
   e. Proposed Courses
4. Comments and Suggestions (Forum 4)
   a. On the Discussion Forum
   b. On the COP
   c. On the IVLE

The discussion threads initiated an online conversation on natural resources management, knowledge management and natural resources knowledge management. Forum 4 dealt with the online conversation itself.

The Outcome

The participants agreed on the need for a Graduate Program on NRKM with the following features:

Table 2. Participants breakdown by country

COUNTRY	NUMBER OF PARTICIPANTS	PERCENTAGE
Indonesia	4	22.00
Lao PDR	4	22.00
Philippines	5	28.00
Thailand	5	28.00
TOTAL	18	100.00

Description

The proposed Graduate Program on Natural Resources Knowledge Management will equip professionals to apply, share and reuse regionally appropriate information and knowledge to combat problems related to natural resources management. It is a post baccalaureate program with eighteen units of coursework. It will cover instruction on natural resources knowledge science, knowledge management, networking, and monitoring and evaluation. It is open to Southeast Asian professionals engaged in natural resources, research, instruction and management in the private, government of NGO sectors.

Institutions

It is proposed that the program be offered by Kasetsart University in the residential mode. The University of the Philippines Open University may offer the program in the distance mode. The program will initially use English as the medium of instruction. Thai and Bahasa Indonesian media of instruction may be considered in the future.

Faculty

Although Kasetsart and UPOU will offer the program, visiting faculty members from SEARCA's University Consortium will be encouraged to participate. However, the core faculty will come from the active members of the COP, who will contribute to the content. A team teaching approach will be employed, fielding several faculty members per course.

Tentative Courses

Results of key informant interviews and consultations have generated the following tentative listing of courses.

1. NRKM 201. Knowledge Management for Development (KM4D).
2. NRKM 210. Natural Resources Knowledge Science I.
3. NRKM 211. Natural Resources Knowledge Science II.
4. NRKM 205. Networking.
5. NRKM 220. Monitoring and Evaluation.
6. NRKM 250. Special Projects.

Online Conversation as Meta Communication

Transcripts

The exchange of ideas can be exemplified by the discussion threads and selected responses found below in Table 3.

Meta Communication

The discussions on the online conversation generated the following significant views:

- The CoP mode of exchanging (academic) views can be effective at the level where no consensus needs to be reached. I am not sure a web-based debate over a principle or theory or an empirical point that supports, reinforces or rebuts a theory can come up to any useful outcome.
- Maybe an appointment, say adjunct or affiliate faculty for UPOU and/or KU without additional compensation, may be pre-

sented to participants so that this document will be proof of having participated in this very relevant project. With an appointment as document, we can include NRKM participation in our respective Curriculum Vitae as addition official service to our University, country and the ASEAN region.

- The initiatives on wider applications of KM to cross sector domains make the knowledge base richer. With the complexity of environmental problems that we are facing, we need multi-disciplined approaches to address them. In order to have an effective natural resources knowledge management, experts from related disciplines who share common concerns and interests are needed.
- KM works under the principle of "unity in diversity" when various views over an issue or concern is ventilated by a heteroge-

Table 3. Transcripts of discussion threads

DISCUSSION THREAD	POSTED RESPONSE
ON KM: KM is traditionally defined as an evolving discipline that considers an organization's intellectual capital as a manageable and potentially profitable asset (Leibmann, 1999) It is based upon the assumption that today's global economy is knowledge-based and that knowledge is a primary commodity as well as a valuable resource. KM entails digitally capturing documented and tacit knowledge and storing these for sharing and reuse. Thus, knowledge is managed through an intranet system and guided by organizational policies that provide incentives to knowledge sharing. Do you think that we can apply knowledge management principles in our work as NRM researchers and educators? Can you cite examples?	I agree with this definition of KM. It is an evolving discipline because it is not a petrified discipline as in all dogmas. Its key idea is "knowledge" or "bits of information integrated together to reflect an improved understanding on the biological, physical and social environment within which man is a part. "Knowledge evolved from sheer memory of human perception of surroundings. Soon it became part of oral tradition of primitive human societies (some survives today as Indigenous Knowledge or IK) and, when writing was invented it first was recorded in scrolls, and then, with the advent of paper invention and printing, in published journals and books. Now, knowledge is stored in both modern libraries as well as electronically in CDs and computers.
ON THE GOAL OF KM: The goal of knowledge management is the sharing and reuse of intellectual capital (Leibmann, 1999) Although, distinctions are made between undocumented or tacit knowledge and documented or explicit knowledge, both are captured digitally and stored in a knowledge base. These are also made available digitally in a variety of multimedia formats for sharing and reuse. Do you agree that Southeast Asian researchers and educators should establish a knowledge base on NRM? Do you think this is feasible?	***Posting 1.*** The need for a knowledge base on NRM is probably beyond argument. It is the feasibility of doing so that requires serious thought. To this end, a COP could be useful in several ways: 1) it can clarify issues and establish boundaries and scope of the putative knowledge base; 2) start a knowledge pool by putting in their own tacit and explicit knowledge; 3) it can catalyze wider interest; 4) it might be able to present itself and what it has done so far to leverage resources to process materials in the knowledge base or important parts of it into such things as books (in hard copy and electronic form) ***Posting 2.*** Yes, it is feasible. There is a caution however that not all information constitutes what we call knowledge. Much information is generated within the spectacles of dogmatism and retards scientific problem solving, for example the nagging problem of reconciling development with environment. ***Posting 3.*** I think this is the way to go since many of our initiatives are common; hence, one common problem will unite us to come up with a common or collective solution although sometimes solutions have to be on a case-to-case basis as well. ***Posting 4.*** Establishing a knowledge base on natural resources is needed for Southeast Asian researchers and educators. The knowledge base should contribute to decision and policy making especially by the government. There are, however, many factors that need to be considered to make it feasible. Defining the scope, access, willingness to share that knowledge, facilities, usefulness or applications and many others. I agree with others that establishing a knowledge base requires careful thinking.

continued on following page

Table 3. Continued

DISCUSSION THREAD	POSTED RESPONSE
ON KM4D: In the past decade, KM principles have been brought to bear upon pressing social and development concerns such as health, education, agriculture and the environment. The increasing recognition of KM by the international development assistance community is evidenced by the establishment of KM programs in most development agencies and the designation of a Chief Knowledge Officer or a Vice President for Knowledge, as in the case of the Asian Development Bank. In many instances, the levels of application have gone beyond the conventional organizational KM system and have entered sectoral domains cutting across institutions. These ad hoc KM systems often operate on a Web-based workgroup platform run by an active community of practice or COP. What is your opinion on these initiatives?	***Posting 1.*** Probably easier to operate a KM activity in an organization or with a group which is homogeneous and have a common binding interest such as professional (engineers or, even more tightly, structural engineers. KM in a sector implies having participants with a common interest in a broader issue (than say, integrity of bridges) such as Natural Resources Management but also of more diffused areas of interests and specializations such as our own COP for this "course". But herein lies the greater challenge. If interests and specializations are widely varied, keeping the discussion points sharply focused might help. ***Posting 2.*** I think it's about time that all knowledge generated have to be captured, stored, and shared in practically all areas or disciplines. In this way, we could learn from one another but at the same time reflect on new ones resulting to new actions or adoption perhaps. The cycle of action-reflection-action prior to adoption of new knowledge is not only empowering but cost-effective and scientifically based as well. ***Posting 3.*** Since CoPs through forums have been recognized as the fastest and perhaps most practical way of information exchange lately, it is but logical to keep tab of those exchanges and unilaterally have a common practice if applicable. The difficulty perhaps would be on the willingness of some who have the knowledge but do not want to share. In many cases, even in research organizations, scientists do not want to share information because the other members could be a threat to them or the idea may be stolen from them. Yes, we have laws on IPR but due process does not always come in handy. It is important therefore to give credit to where credit is due especially in the light of NRKM. ***Posting 4.*** KM is an enabling tool to allow users (natural resources stakeholders or their representatives) retrieve vital information (e.g. spatial and temporal analysis of natural ecosystems as they change with stakeholders' management and/or feedback response from governance) in order that the right collective decisions meet challenges of sustainable resource use. It makes possible in community-base resource management the so-called informed decision-making. ***Posting 5.*** I agree we can be pragmatic while at the same time open to new ideas to properly address the yet elusive monster we call "sustainable natural resource management that is ken in satisfying ecological and social equity issues." This is where knowledge management comes in, vibrant and changing to remain relevant to issues and concerns to distinguish it from information management, which is just a simple systematic filing, storage and retrieval of voluminous information. Knowledge management also deals with information but it digests them and may make new synthesis out of them to become new learning experience that helps not to repeat past mistakes. Paradigms that have become stale should be replaced by new ones in a manner that we would not be accused as extremely liberal and/or extremely dogmatic. Last time "Green Revolution" was practical solution to food security at the local and international level (hence thought also to alleviate poverty) until environmentalists blame pesticides on the pollution of the environment while it also started to exact costs on the health of farmers and against biological resources (e.g. threat to wildlife, etc.). Now we are in the aftermath of the UNCED'S to be more careful hence we have multilateral agreements like the Convention on Biological Biodiversity (including ideas like the Precautionary Principle and measures like the Cartagena Protocol and Bioethics.)

continued on following page

Table 3. Continued

DISCUSSION THREAD	POSTED RESPONSE
ON THE NRKM DEGREE PROGRAM: The proposed Rationale of the program reads: The Southeast Asian Region is beset with natural resources management problems. Decades of unhampered resources exploitation I the watersheds of the Philippines and Indonesia by lumber companies are expecting their toll through landslides and flashfloods in the Visayas and Central Java. Land-locked countries in the Greater Mekong Subregion are now suffering the same fate. Coastal resources in the Sulu-Celebes Sea, home of the most biologically diverse marine ecosystems in the world, are being endangered by destructive fishing practices, mangrove destruction, and oil spills. The collective expertise of the region should be brought to bear on these problems through the establishment of a regional knowledge management system for natural resources management. Furthermore, the capacities of institutions for natural resources knowledge management should be built and strengthened. A Graduate Certificate in Natural Resources Knowledge Management is hereby proposed. Since the subject matter is focused on natural resources knowledge management, a certificate program is deemed most appropriate. Due to the highly specialized nature of the subject matter, the program should be offered at the post-baccalaureate level.	***Posting 1.*** Add the "coastal resources of the Gulf of Thailand and the Andaman Sea as among the resources that have been degraded and threatened with further degradation due to unplanned, unregulated and irresponsible practices." ***Posting 2.*** Add "pooling of experiences of practitioners that include managers, policy makers, civil society organizations, and fishers, farmers and foresters. ***Posting 3.*** The rationale is multipartite in nature. ***Posting 4.*** Knowledge sharing should be democratized so that participatory informed-decision making in establishing Marine Protected Areas result in empowerment instead of disenfranchisement. ***Posting 5.*** Add the following sentence after the word 'oil spills': In many areas of the region, natural habitats have been converted to other uses to respond to the needs of the growing population, urbanization and industrial development. These have resulted to the decline of the natural resources. ***Posting 6.*** Add the following before the sentence "The collective expertise..." While there are available expertise in the region and knowledge about the natural resources, access and use of these knowledge, for decision and policymaking has been a problem.
ON THE PROGRAM DESCRIPTION: The Program Description reads: The proposed Graduate Certificate Program on Natural Resources Knowledge Management will equip professional to apply, share and reuse regionally appropriate information and knowledge to combat problems related to natural resources management. It is a post baccalaureate program with eighteen units of coursework. It will cover instruction on natural resources knowledge science, knowledge management, networking, and monitoring and evaluation. It is open to Southeast Asian professional engaged in natural resources, research, instruction and management in the private, government of NGO sectors.	***Posting 1.*** Suggestion to re-structure as follows: "... to apply, share and reuse for research, education and management, information and knowledge that are applicable to problems in the region." Another suggestion: "to apply, share and reuse regionally appropriate information and knowledge to plan and execute solutions to cross-cutting problems related to natural resources management in various modes (such as corporate, community-based or agency-based decision-making) in the region."

continued on following page

neous group who has down-to-earth experiences on the same issue or concern. Our goal is to see that humanity's "Common Good" is always target. The group should be homogeneous (e.g. all professionals capable of communicating with patience to each other's diverging views) to facilitate putting together our product after one month of on-line forum. While we are homogeneous because we are all professionals, we may at the same time heterogeneous because each of us come to the forum as representatives to different interests under the common goal of designing a viable sustainable natural resources knowledge management graduate program. Some of us may represent aquatic environment, others terrestrial, others come to represent respective institutional interests, while some purely academic. A long time ago, I have learned to be patient with diverging views and have experienced collective resolution

Table 3. Continued

DISCUSSION THREAD	POSTED RESPONSE
ON INSTITUTIONAL COMMITMENTS: Although the program will be offered by KU and UPOU, visiting faculty members from SEARCA's University Consortium will be encourage top participate. The core faculty will come from the active members of the COP, who will contribute to the content. A team teaching approach will be employed, fielding several faculty members per course	For an in-residence course such as envisioned for KU, it would obviously cost more if a team consists of "teachers" from different countries. Couldn't a hybrid approach be developed in which KU and Thailand-based faculty could administer modules/lessons contributed by faculty from other countries, but with a provision for internet-based support from the "core" faculty?
ON PROPOSED COURSES: Results of key informant interviews and consultations have generated the following tentative listing of courses: **NRKM 201**. Knowledge Management for Development (KM4D), 3 units. A survey of KM4D concepts, operationalization. **NRKM 205**. Networking, 3 units. Principles and strategies of institutional, electronic, formal and informal networking. **NRKM 210**. Natural Resources Knowledge Science I, 3 units. An Introductory course on how natural resources Knowledge is currently structured and systematized by the research and development sector. **NRKM 211**. Natural Resources Knowledge Science II, 3 units. An advanced course on how natural resources knowledge is applied by decision makers and policy makers. **NRKM 220**. Monitoring and Evaluation, 3 units. KM4D success indicators and M&E methodologies to gather and analyze data on these indicators. **NRKM 250**. Special Projects, 3 units. Design, development and testing of NRKM systems.	***Posting 1.*** Our students should have background courses on "Biography: Focus in Southeast Asia," "Geography with emphasis on Asian Cultures and Man-Nature Relationships," "East-West Cultural Exchanges that Bridge Development with Environment," and probably a course called by Dr. Malayang as "Political Ecology" and from Jonathan Porritt's "Seeing Green-The Politics of Ecology." ***Posting 2*** Courses look balanced but I am not sure a whole 3-unit course on KM is needed. Give a thought to a merger of 201 and 205. This would then allow a course that might sequel nicely with 211 (Applications of NRM knowledge in policies and programs), which could be "NRM Policy Tools and Practices." This course could discuss such concepts as environmental or ecological services and their valuation; the worldviews of natural resources management from deep ecology to cornucopian; conservation vs development; trade offs and their impacts on welfare; giving voices to the poor aquatic users on policies and programs; and enabling their participation in conservation and development programs. I agree with the merging of 201 and 205 as networking is essential in KM. ***Posting 3.*** Can we have something on participatory communication?

reconciling diverging views. In UP we promote sharing of ideas but at the same time we are on-guard that the promotion of critical thinking is sustained.

- The COP model is like a smorgasbord that you do not gulp all dishes on the table. You take only the relevant ones (information or experience from COP) that cater to applications that have heuristic value on case-to-case basis. In COP model, there should be room for tolerance because it is always possible that participants come from different interests, sectors and philosophies (e.g. anti-globalization versus pro-globalization, pro-GMO versus anti-GMO, pro-centralized governance versus pro-decentralization or devolution, pro-industrialization versus pro-sustainable development). There is a saying that a crowd of mixed experiences can extract the right solutions to a problem better than a monolithic crowd would have done. The latter tends to make solutions that are only variations of the same theme (moving in circles), the former tends to experiment radical solutions that may work (moving in many directions, greater chance of hitting the target!). Solutions that failed are not all bad, because they are recorded in KM as learning experiences so that mistakes will not be repeated and better solutions crafted.

CONCLUSION

At the beginning of this chapter, we stated that the Internet has not only caused the death of distance, but has also destroyed exclusivity, undermined

Table 4. Participation in the CoP

DISCUSSION FORUMS	MAJOR THREADS	REPLIES
Introductions	13	21
CoP Process	5	14
Grad Program	5	19
Comments	3	4
TOTAL	26	58

hierarchy and enabled nonlinear/ asynchronous interaction. If, indeed, such is the case, can a community of practice engaged in an online conversation transcend institutional, geographical, disciplinal and language barriers to design new curricula?

Based on the outcomes enumerated and the discussions provided above it would appear that online metacommunication may indeed neutralize many of the oppressive elements inherent in the communicative act. The researchers would have accepted this as a result of their observations if it were not for the online discussion participation data that were auto-captured by IVLE and MOODLE. According to these statistics, the rates of participation were quite disappointing. They were in fact very low. For the entire duration of the online discussion boards, the total number of posted responses to the twenty-eight discussion threads was fifty-eight (58) replies only.

Table 4 provides a breakdown of the posted replies per discussion board.

What accounted for this hindrance in the discourse?

Perhaps the biggest reason for the lack of participation is the language barrier. English was the medium used by the CoP and a mastery of the language was required. An inability to contribute substantively to the discussion due to language problems prevented active participation. The online conversation may have transcended institutional and geographical barriers but it did not transcend the language barrier. Language remained an oppressive element in the communicative act.

Furthermore, an unwillingness to make ideas public among some of the experts was observed. Posting an idea for others to assess may have been considered risky. Volunteering one's personal insights among colleagues may have been thought of as presumptuous even when encouraged to do so. This is more of a function of Southeast Asian culture and it can be said that the online conversation failed to transcend cultural barriers. Culture remains part of the communicative act's most influential elements or oppressions.

Then there is also an element of intellectual intimidation considering the novelty of the subject matter. After all, academic debate has always been encouraged or tempered by academic rank. Thus, it may be said that the online conversation failed to transcend disciplinal as well as hierarchical barriers also. The structure of the academic enterprise remained an oppressive element.

However, perhaps the most critical factor that affected participation was the connectivity of the participants at the institutional level and individual level. Online discourse requires a telecommunications infrastructure and bandwidth that unfortunately cannot be made available among resource poor institutions and faculty members. Connectivity was an indeed an issue, particularly in Lao PDR. Thus, the biggest oppression for this communicative act was inherent in the medium of the online conversation itself.

REFERENCES

Cox, A. (2005). What are communities of practice? A comparative review of four seminal works. *Journal of Information Science*, *31*(6), 527–540. doi:10.1177/0165551505057016

Davenport, T. H., & Prusak, L. (2000). *Working knowledge. How organizations manage what they know* (2nd ed.). Cambridge, MA: Harvard Business School Press.

Flor, A. G. (2001). *E-development and knowledge management: ICT applications for sustainable development*. Los Baños, Philippines: Southeast Asian Regional Center for Graduate Study and Research in Agriculture.

Flor, A. G., & Sompong, N. (2007). *The design, development and testing of a knowledge management model for natural resources management in Southeast Asia*. Los Baños, Philippines: Southeast Asian Regional Center for Graduate Study and Research in Agriculture.

Gingrich, O. (2004). *The invisible college*. London, UK: Penguin Books.

Habermas, J. (1984). The theory of communicative action: *Vol. 1. Reason and the rationalization of society (trans. T. McCarthy)*. Boston, MA: Beacon Press.

Lave, J., & Wenger, E. (1991). *Situated learning: Legitimate peripheral participation*. Cambridge, UK: Cambridge University Press.

Leibmann, M. (1999). *A way to KM solutions: Things to consider when building knowledge management solutions with Microsoft technologies*. Seattle, WA: World Wide Technical Services, Microsoft Corporation.

Saint-Onge, H., & Wallace, D. (2003). *Leveraging communities of practice*. London, UK: Butterworth Heinemann.

ADDITIONAL READING

Ardichvilli, A., Page, V. and Wentling, T. (2003). Motivation and barriers to participation in virtual knowledge sharing in communities of practice. *Journal of Knowledge Management, 7*, 64–77.

Barton, T., & Tursting, K. (2005). *Beyond Communities of Practice: Language Power and Social Context*. Cambridge: Cambridge University Press. doi:10.1017/CBO9780511610554

Duguid, P. (2005). *The Art of Knowing: Social and Tacit Dimensions of Knowledge and the Limits of the Community of Practice. The Information Society*. London: Taylor & Francis Inc.

Flor, A. G. *Towards a Global KNET: Setting-Up the Sub-Regional Infrastructure for a World Brain*. Virtual Global Super Projects Conference, World Development Federation, November to December 2001

Flor, Alexander G. *ICT and Poverty: The Indisputable Link. Asia Development Forum III*. World Bank, Asian Development Bank, ADB Institute, and UNESCAP, June 14, 2001, Bangkok

Nonaka, Ikujiro (1991). The knowledge creating company. *Harvard Business Review* 69 (6 Nov-Dec): 96–104

On the Invisible College. Crane Diana (1972) *Invisible colleges. Diffusion of knowledge in scientific communities*. Chicago and London: The University of Chicago Press

Sveiby, K.-E., & Simon, R. (2002). Collaborative climate and effectiveness of knowledge work - an empirical study. *Journal of Knowledge Management*, *6*(5), 420–433. doi:10.1108/13673270210450388

Tu, C.-H. (2002). The management of social presence in an online learning environment. *International Journal on E-Learning*, (April–June): 34–45.

Wagner, C. S. (2008). *The New Invisible College: Science for Development*. Washington DC: Brooking Press.

Lomas, Robert (2002). *The Invisible College: The Royal Society, Freemasonary and the birth of modern science*, London: Headline Book Publishing On Communities of Practice.

Wasko, M., & Faraj, S. (2000). "It is what one does": why people participate and help others in electronic communities of practice. *The Journal of Strategic Information Systems*, *9*, 155–173. doi:10.1016/S0963-8687(00)00045-7

Wenger, E. (1998). *Communities of Practice: Learning, Meaning, and Identity*. Cambridge: Cambridge University Press.

Wenger, E., McDermott, R., & Snyder, W. M. (2002). *Cultivating Communities of Practice*. Boston: Harvard Business Press.

Section 2

Dynamic Models of Meta-Communication and Reflective Conversations

Chapter 5
Avatar Manager and Student Reflective Conversations as the Base for Describing Meta-Communication Model

Vardan Mkrttchian
HHH Technology Incorporation, Australia

ABSTRACT

This chapter describes the meta-communication model and illustrates its applicability. The model integrates previous discursive approaches to reflective practice and extends them with additional relevant concepts. The meta-communication model concepts are mainly based on Avatar Manager and Student Reflective Conversations pedagogical theory. By means of the case examples, this chapter also illustrates how the model can be used for making meaning in experiential and theoretical based online educational courses and collective sense-making, i.e. the articulation and contesting the meaning and relevance of ideas. This chapter argues that the model provides a way for systematically and meaningfully structuring and organizing meta-level conversations in virtual classroom. The use of reflective pedagogies has long been considered as critical to facilitating meaningful learning through experientially based curricula; however, the use of such methods has not been extensively explored as implemented in virtual environments. The study reviewed utilizes a combination of survey research and individual interviews to examine the student perceptions of the meaningful learning which occurred as a result of their participation in two Web-based courses which are utilized reflective pedagogies. One course focuses on topics related to the service-learning and the second on the placement-based internships. All of them were instructed using online coursework based in reflective pedagogies to the compliment on-site placements within

DOI: 10.4018/978-1-61350-071-2.ch005

local communities. Thus, created software of Meta-Communication Model applicable for using in virtual education process and in virtual research collaboration works at the Astrakhan State University (Russian Federation) and at All Armenian Internet University (Australian Federation and the Republic of Armenia) for the development of avatars has significant potential to enhance realism, automation capability, and effectiveness across the training environments variety.

INTRODUCTION

Teaching is a process of conveying ideas to the students. Good teaching means, mostly, more effective communication between learners. The prerequisite has been due to the fact that because teachers "maybe" have studied ideas longer, they understand them better and are therefore better able to communicate them. Other requirements, which are important to control, are that the strategies and methods used by us are empirically based and validated. Whatever, the level of the distance education or teaching organization, many factors make teaching a distance education course different from the teaching in traditional classroom. When using the technology tools the material should be developed from the good point of learning theories. Our work experience in virtual classroom explains what intelligent avatars or computer characters could be used to support or even to replace teachers in the classroom. The devotee is the human that makes sure the avatar and the student are properly matched. Virtual classroom is a social network service environment focuses on building and reflecting of social networks or social relations among people, e.g., who shares interest and/or activities. A social network service essentially consists of the representation of every user (often a profile), his/her social connections, and a variety of additional services. Most social network services are web based and provide means for users to interact over the internet, such as e-mail and instant messaging. Although online community services are sometimes considered as a social network service in a broader sense, social network service usually means an individual-centered service whereas online community services are group-centered. Social networking sites allow users to share ideas, activities, events, and interests within their individual networks. Information- and communication technology (ICT) provides us with a better prerequisite for open distance learning. Now although the region has yet to fully tap the immense learning potential of a 3D virtual environment, educators believe it's the only matter of time. HHH University's latest release Avatar has made online virtual worlds such as the Second Life (SL) more popular than ever as audiences sit up and take notice of the possibilities of these sites. Users are currently using these sites to socialize and to connect using free voice and the text chat through personalized avatars or computerized self-representations. However, these sites also hold out the possibility to become places where educators are discovering academic possibilities. SL, for example, provides virtual homes for some of the world's most prestigious universities such as Harvard and Stanford who have bought virtual land with Linden Dollars. Although this seems to be somewhat of a trend in the West it has yet to catch on in the South Caucasus. Campus Notes spoke to educators in the Armenia to gauge how long it will take before students take their seats in the virtual classroom. There is a widely accepted view that information systems entail a multitude of assumptions and claims, and that they serve some interest at the others expense. Therefore, discussions among all stakeholders for reaching mutual understanding about the desired features of systems are viewed as essential. For example, by regarding an information system in principle as a complex communication tool, several authors in the Language-Action Perspective used the notion of meta-communication to refer to communications about system's communication concepts. They emphasized that many areas of information systems from specification to design, implementation and use involve meta-communications. Others, without using the notion of meta-communication, emphasized the importance of discourses and reflections conceptual framework theoretically provides wider discursive concepts for reflective practice. Still others suggested further extensions of discursive approaches in order to deal with global challenges. The purpose of this chapter is to take the conceptual development of the research on reflective practice in information systems one step further. Previous discursive approaches have made valuable contributions by the application of "hhh" technology ideas. This chapter describes a meta-communication model which integrates the previous approaches and extends them with additional relevant concepts from discourse ethics and information systems literature. Thus, it provides a wider spectrum for reflective practice. The model can be used for collective sense-making, i.e. the articulation and possible contesting the ideas meaning and significance. It allows systematic and meaningful structuring and organizing of meta-level conversations, in order to enable effective meta-communication processes. Instructional approaches which facilitate reflective, critical dialogue provide students with opportunities to make the meaning from experiential based learning. When facilitated via Internet, curricula emphasizing such pedagogies hold the potential to guide and encourage a diverse range of students as they make meaning from learning situated in experiences. The increased technological tools integration (such as synchronous conferencing platforms, asynchronous discussion structures, social networking environments, video sharing websites, and so forth) in educational programming provides the means to implement instructional approaches that are current, relevant and efficient. As a result of their academic leaders survey at 1200 Russian Federation institutions, double-digit growth rates in online post-secondary enrollments for the sixth consecutive year, clearly indicating a preference among this student population for studying using educational media. As technologies are increasingly integrated into curricula, there is a growing need for the strategies development which mobilizes ways to create collaborative, interactive and relevant applications specifically within the experiential learning framework. Moreover, the introduction of technology into practice-based learning allows the broad access which enables the diverse learning communities' development that may not be possible among geographically bound college populations. Collaborative learning which is constructed in such communities has the potential to reach beyond a single classroom to impact local communities on uniquely personal levels. The potential for reflective pedagogies to facilitate significant learning for distant students engaged in applied studies is specifically explored in this study.

"VIRTUAL BIOLOGY TEACHER" PROJECT OBJECTIVE

Virtual Biology Teacher (VBT) Project is a two-year Russian National Science Foundation (RNSF) effort whose objective is to develop and to evaluate realistic avatar interfaces as portals to intelligent programs capable of relaying knowledge and training skills for virtual biology school teachers. This interface aims towards support of spoken dialog within a limited domain and capabilities for learning to maintain its knowledge as current and accurate. Research objectives focus on the integration of speaker-independent continuous speech recognition technology with a context-based dialog system and real-time graphics rendering capability derived from live subject motion capture traces. The motion capture traces are used by the avatar to provide spoken interaction with gestural expressions. Next, an example subset of its RNSF protocols knowledge was encoded in a grammar-based speech interpretation system and context-based reasoning system. These systems were integrated with the VBT Responsive Avatar Framework to enable the avatar to receive spoken input and generate appropriate verbal and non-verbal responses. The system demonstrates conveyance of knowledge within a limited domain such as RNSF project reporting requirements. Working toward improving the realism of the avatar, long-term efforts toward creating a toolbox for generalization to other training applications, and results of evaluation of how users respond to different characteristics that contribute to realism in an avatar are discussed. The VBT project is investigating intelligent avatar interfaces suitable for a range of question answering and training applications. The project objective is to enable the domain-specific conversation with a realistic avatar supported by an intelligent engine capable for online learning. We address three specific characteristics of this interface that increase naturalness in interaction for various narrative and tutorial-style training applications:

1. A life-like embodiment of a particular person which a trainee can orally address,
2. The use of non-verbal cues including expressions by the avatar, as well as a real-time trainee location tracking and means for the user to designate a focal point within the virtual world,
3. A knowledge-driven backend that can respond intelligently to questions and can be learnt through its interactions.

Many existing Decision Support Systems (DSS) for tactical and training purposes rely heavily on the traditional keyboard-style input devices and display their output in the form of a written text or schematic/graphic representations such as maps and charts. On the other hand, an avatar-based interface in some certain applications can reduce the trainee's machine interface workload and allow the trainee focus more completely on the task being trained rather than on the user interface to the DSS. Initially, research in this project developed a traditional keyboard/text interface for a DSS called VarDSS *by* Vardan Mkrttchian (2010). With VarDSS as a starting point, the first phase objective of the VBT project was to create an avatar-based interface for user interaction. We have developed an avatar for this purpose, one that supports a limited dialogue, and have evaluated several operational effectiveness aspects of the current implementation with numerous users. We refer to this avatar as Vard Avatar. The following sections describe the design of the current Vard Avatar, production generalization approaches using a graphical asset pipeline, observed system performance, and progress toward the eventual goal of a completely realistic avatar.

AVATAR MANAGER: STUDENT SYSTEM DESIGN

The avatars for the virtual teacher and the virtual student are supported by integrated components consisting of a Speech Recognizer (SR), Dialog Manager, and Speech Generation module. They roughly correspond to the avatar's tasks of hearing, understanding, and responding, respectively. Each module is executed as a separate thread and communicates with the others using a handshaking protocol created to enforce synchronization constraints between links. Voice input from the microphone headset is provided to the VBT and the student Recognizer module that performs speaker independent continuous speech recognition on the input waveform to produce two forms of recognized speech data. The first result is a list of the most likely domain-specific concepts detected using a domain specific grammar-driven recognizer. The second form of recognized speech data produced is an ASCII text of the Russian words in the phrase as recognized using a generic non-customized grammar-free lexicon. The Dialog Manager uses both sets of data to more fully disambiguate the speech input. The Dialog Manager also maintains the current context which indicates the focus of the conversation using domain specific knowledge. It provides the current context back to the Recognizer to help focusing the recognition task. The Dialog Manager also selects or generates a text response string to be spoken by the avatar which is passed to the Speech Output system to perform text-to speech and gesture generation. Each system is described in detail below.

The VBT Recognizer module was designed using a layered model for modularity that can support a range of Commercial-Off-The-Shelf (COTS) speech recognition engines. Figure 1 shows the Speech Recognizer Control (SRC), Speech Recognizer Engine (SRE), and Smart layers in the SR.

The SRC is at the lowest layer and allows using of compatible COTS recognition engines. The prototype is currently implemented using Microsoft Speech API (SAPI) version 5.1 from Microsoft Development Network. The SRC translates the audio waveform into both textual formats with the help of Chant Speech Kit middleware from Chant Software. Chant middleware components simplify the process using the Software Development Kits (SDKs) from multiple speech technology vendors to increase portability and to reduce development time. The SR is activated by the Dialog Manager to initiate processing of microphone input only at appropriate times in the dialog to prevent miss-recognition due to spurious noise. Activation invokes the primary recognition strategy which is grammar-based. The grammars are used by the SR to provide a stream of domain-specific concepts with a certain degree of confidence as its primary output similar to research by G. Ryabichkina (2009). Simultaneously with the custom grammar-based resolution links, the second instantiation of a SAPI process performs recognition in standard dictation mode using a non-domain-specific SAPI lexicon to attempt an audio-to-text conversion on the same waveform.

Figure 1. The layered speech recognition architecture

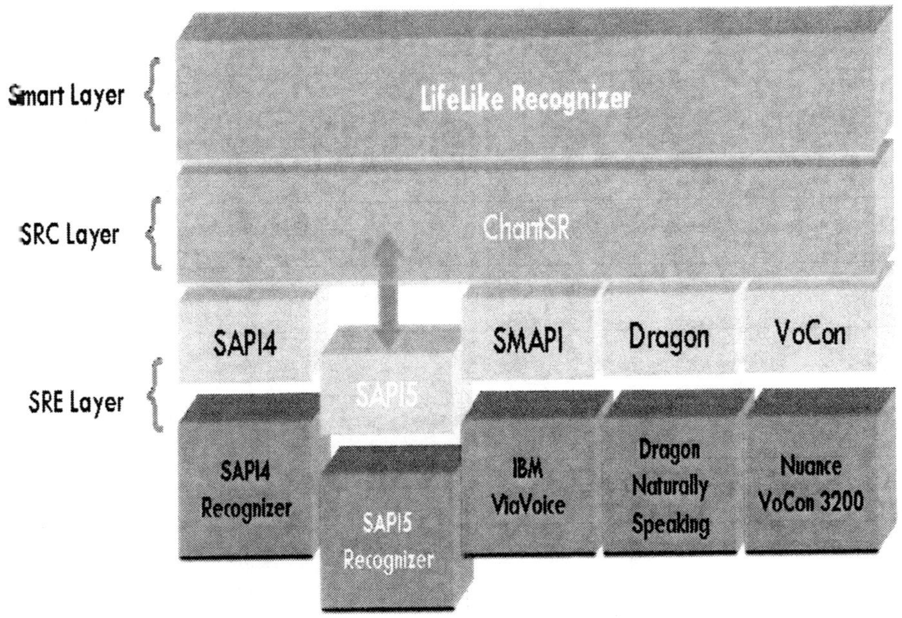

Therefore, two independent recognition pathways use multiple sets of COTS programming APIs, all of which are controlled by the SR module implemented in the C# language. Although the current version of the SR uses the Microsoft SAPI 5.1, the layered design using Chant allows compatibility with other recognizer engines such as Nuance's Dragon Naturally Speaking and IBM's Via Voice. SAPI 5.1-compatible grammars provide a recognition framework for domain-specific entries in the lexicon. These are partitioned and organized by context to reduce the size of the search space and to improve recognition accuracy.

An additional innovation in SR processing is that grammars are generated semi-automatically from a relational database that facilitates dialog development, maintenance, and portability. The SQL database contains the structural knowledge of the concept instances, and the relationships between them, which are then extracted for dialog management. New speech information regarding the project can be added automatically next time when the SR module starts by invoking transfer of database content into grammars automatically by using a set of rewriting rules. A small embedded script reads the database and rewrites the grammars with a new data set. The long-term objective which has been partially met in the current prototype is to generate new grammars for speech recognition as necessary without needing to compose all grammars and their variations manually. An extension to this technique could be used to refine grammars each time the system is used. The role of the Dialog Manager (DM) is to interpret the text streams provided by the Speech Recognizer to determine the context, decide how to react to contextual shifts, and coordinate the communication between the subsystems accordingly. The DM system also attempts to disambiguate likely candidate phrases using the information already in its database concerning the users and I/UCRC program.

Conversational goal management is achieved using a context-based approach. A *context* refers to a particular situation that is dictated by the configuration of internal and external circumstances such as the internal state of the conversation agent and the perceived state of the human trainee. For every context, there is an associated goal condition and a group of relevant actions that can be executed to achieve this condition.

A *goal condition* is defined as an end state that an agent desires to reach to impart specific knowledge to the trainee.

It is imperative that a dialog system is able to properly manage conversational goals, as the user can have multiple goals and may introduce new goals at any time. Henceforth, the system must be able to service many goals at the same time, as well as to be prepared to take on more goals, unannounced. This need to be able to jump between different goals in real-time lends itself to the Context-Based Reasoning (CxBR) technique used by G. Ryabichkina (2009). CxBR agents provide responses that are directly related to its active context. The fact that contexts correspond to accomplishing particular goals combined with the idea that conversational goals take on a very fluid nature yields the assertion that goal management can be facilitated using CxBR methods.

Figure 2 shows the architecture of the DM, which consists of three components: Speech Disambiguation, Knowledge Manager, and CxBR-based Dialog Manager. The Semantic disambiguation serves as a listening comprehension filter, where heard noises (the SR output) are converted to conversationally-relevant content to be processed by the person, known as the Disambiguated Input. The Knowledge Manager acts as a person's rote memory. The Speech disambiguation and the Dialog Manager send keyword-based requests to it as inputs, and the Knowledge Manager outputs relevant information in the form of a contextualized data base. The Dialog Manager serves to provide the proper responses output to the user. It takes in input from the Speech disambiguation, as

Figure 2. Lifelike responsive avatar framework

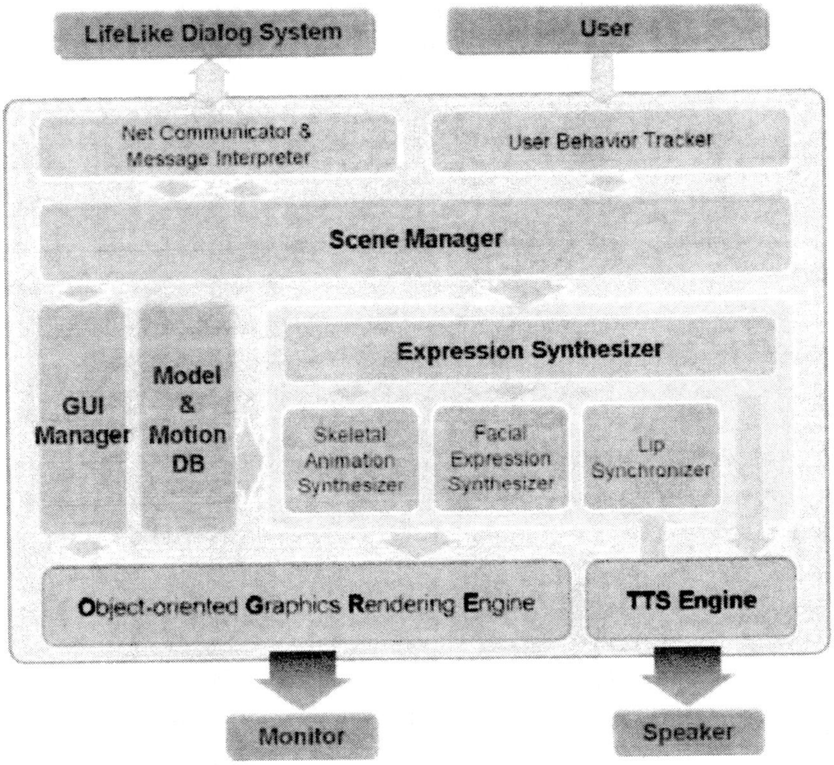

well as its own internal context-based mechanisms to determine this output response.

Goal management in the Lifelike Dialog Manager involves three parts: 1) goal recognition, 2) goal bookkeeping and 3) context topology. Goal recognition refers to the process of analyzing user input utterances to determine the proper conversational goal that is to be addressed. This is analogous to the context activation process in CxBR methods, goal bookkeeping deals with keeping track of the identified goals in an ordered manner. Bookkeeping simply services the recognized goals in the order they are received, using a stack.

Context topology refers to the entire set of speech acts of the conversation agent. This structure also includes the transitional actions of moving between contexts when a goal shift is detected. The context topology carries out the responses needed to clear out the goal bookkeeping stack. Goal recognition is accomplished using linguistic analysis of each user utterance. This is similar to the inference engine found in CxBR systems, where conditioned predicate logic rules determine the active context according to the environmental state.

The difference with the goal recognizer, however, is that the context is resolved using keywords and phrases which are extracted from a parts-of-speech parsing of input responses. With the aid of a contextually organized knowledge base, the user utterance is interpreted, and the context associated with this understanding is activated.

Creating a realistic active digital representation of a particular human being is a challenging and multifaceted task. Initially, investigations were conducted to identify and to evaluate the interoperability of COTS packages for facial modeling, rendering of real-time graphics, motion-capture, and text-to-speech synthesis. The result was a customized Graphical Asset Production Pipeline which encapsulates the tasks needed to create a visual representation of a human character. Furthermore, the options and best practices for recording vocal mannerisms and non-verbal mannerisms were evaluated and identified. FaceGen, a tool used by researchers Mkrttchian (2010) for face recognition was used. FaceGen generates three-dimensional (3D) head and face models using front and side photographic images. The technique was used to develop the highly acclaimed video game. We anticipate altering the motion-captured data in real-time while the avatar is moving so that dynamic, naturalistic behaviors can be synthesized. Real-time graphics required selecting a capable engine with the right blend of features and within any budget. After evaluation of several possible open source graphics engines, we decided to use Object-oriented Graphics Rendering Engine (OGRE) as our underlying graphics library for the avatar framework. OGRE provides both a high-level interface for interacting with graphical objects as well as a low-level shaded control to create specialized visual effects that will be used in the future for more realistic avatars creation. Its plug-in based architecture also provides greater ability to interoperate with other software tools. For the text to speech synthesis, Microsoft SAPI 5.1 was chosen as the Application Programming Interface (API). MS-SAPI provides an event generation mechanism to report the status of phoneme or word changes during the synthesis of voice in the real time. These events can be used to create realistic phoneme based lip animations. Furthermore, a number of commercial speech systems provide an interface to SAPI so that an application can transparently leverage a multitude of speech systems.

Figure 2 shows the Lifelike Responsive Avatar Framework (LRAF) that controls the avatar and provides connectivity to the SR and DM. The LRAF drives the avatar's operation to create a realistic representation capable for speech input, emotive response, and vocal response. The LRAF has two separate input sources. One is the Life-like Dialog Manager which provides sentences that are intended to be spoken by the avatar. The other is the user's behavioral information such as eye-gaze. Currently, as an approximation for eye-gaze tracking, we are using an infrared camera to track retro-reflective markers on a head-band. A current objective is also to track the user location while speaking with the avatar.

The most significant component of the LRAF is the Expression Mkrttchian which is responsible for taking the 3D models and applying the motion-capture data to produce a sequence of facial and body animations that fit the discussed context. Three major components of the Expression Synthesizer are: 1. The Skeletal Animation Synthesizer, 2. the Facial Expression Synthesizer, and 3.the Lip Synchronizer.

The initial version of LRAF uses only static animation playback.

However, the research is in progress toward more complicated algorithmic animations control. For example, the motion-captured skeletal animations could be varied (through exaggeration or attenuation) to correspond to the avatar's subtle emotional changes.

This will enable a more complex and believable personality avatar behavior model.

THE APPLICATION OF AVATAR MANAGER AND STUDENT REFLECTIVE CONVERSATION IN VIRTUAL CLASSROOM

To frame a discussion related to the development and implementation of the reflective pedagogies in applied settings, literature focusing on the importance of providing opportunities for guided reflection in experientially based learning was explored. Moreover, because the courses examined in this study were conducted in virtual classrooms, literature related to online instructional delivery as it relates to experiential learning was also investigated. Previous research indicates that the experiential learning definition is widely interpreted, analyzed and debated, however, for this study purposes it is defined as a structured learning activities set that promotes critical inquiry and reflective discourse through a deliberate combination of technologies and instructional methods such as structured discussions, directed writing assignments, and on-site placements in local communities.

The methods by which reflection is taught to students within the life-long and experiential learning contexts have been of specific focus over the last several decades. Many educators have identified critical inquiry, engaged dialogue and reflective practice as essential to furthering substantive learning in experiential settings. Sedrak Sedrakyan (2006) suggested structured reflection to be the key to learning from experiences; Sedrakyan elaborated, identifying structured reflection as critical to meaningful academic learning. Sedrakyan specifically defined reflection as central to "... the process of stepping back from an experience to ponder, carefully and persistently, its meaning to the self through the inferences development" noting that engaging such processes forms the foundation for future decision making and behaviors. Sedrakyan found that experientially based learning enabled students to both "...sharpen the focus of their own instruction and learning [as well as] deepen their level of inquiry through questioning, making connections, and honoring multiple perspectives". Opportunities for reflective learning facilitate cognitive, affective and moral development; without such reflection learning is not sustainable. The development of critical thinking and meta-cognitive skills are particularly important outcomes of students' participation in applied learning experiences. Sedrakyan found that for the meaningful reflection it must be continuous, connected, challenging and contextualized. Connected reflection facilitated through engagement in asynchronous discussions that utilize guided questions emphasizes the importance of integrating experiences with academic learning. Both continuous self-dialogue and collaborative inquiry is made possible by participation in activities constructed within synchronous conferencing platforms require individual reflection and group processing to occur before, during and after structured learning experiences. The process of challenging students' self reflective methods as demonstrated through the use of web-based journals and e-portfolios encourages them to critically think in new ways, producing unique and individualized approaches to problem solving. Knowledge, then, results from the culmination of navigating, internalizing and transforming learning experiences.

Mkrttchian (2010) identified reflection as an important component to facilitating the development of civic, social, cultural and language literacies in experiential learning. Web-based courses that feature reflective practice as the foundation for pedagogy have emerged as a structured means for students to not only engage with their local communities, but also to participate in collaborative inquiry and discourse with geographically dispersed peers. In the same way as learning occurring in physical settings is dependent upon effectively engaging all members of the service triad (that is, members of the virtual learning community, the instructor and colleagues/peers at on-site placements), so it is in learning environments that enable engaged reflection utilizing emerging technologies found the combination of active discussions and structured assignments to form a foundation for both individualized reflection as well as collaborative learning when utilized within technology rich classrooms. Similarly, Mkrttchian found technologies to profoundly impact learning as a result of their capacities to facilitate interaction and communication. Mkrttchian's research (2010) indicated that distant students report a strong sense of learning in those online classes that provide open environments for discussion, mediation and resolution of difficult dialogues that ultimately reinforce complex understanding. Learning technologies provide a particularly important link between on-site learning experiences and classroom activities; such media become even more significant when the primary mode of instructional delivery occurs via the Internet (Mkrttchian 2010). Discussions structured to facilitate reflective inquiry are particularly effective when facilitated in a virtual environment: instructional methods promoting explorations of, for example, issues related to social equity, are easily migrated for examination in Web-based classrooms Mkrttchian (2010) found virtual classrooms indeed provide environments in which reflective discourse can be fostered and critical inquiry nurtured to extend positive, collaborative educational transactions. They propose a three-tiered approach for the delivery of meaningful learning experiences via the Internet; their "Community of Inquiry" approach provides a comprehensive framework that reinforces the development of critical thinking skills within a context of reflective pedagogies which utilize a media range. This model indicates that experiential learning is initiated as a cognitive presence result (e.g., the ability to construct meaning through ongoing reflection and discourse), sustained through evolving social presence (a support to the cognitive process that enables the relevant relationships development that encourage ongoing engagement), and results in learning as an teaching presence outcome (the instructional methods design that intentionally reinforce critical reflection and inquiry). The "Inquiry Community" model not only establishes a framework for realizing the potential for the reflective pedagogies usage in virtual environments, but also identifies important components to high quality and accessible learning. Mkrttchian (2010) observed that such pedagogy "... recognizes that how we learn should reflect how we live and learning should be an active process that is resource-centered and inquiry-based and that develops the student's skill in collaborative problem solving". The role assumed by technology in web-based courses is so significant that it has the potential to become an "intellectual partner" with students as they pursue learning goals. When used in conjunction with instructional methods that promote inquiry and collaboration, technological solutions become important components to facilitating experiential learning. A Web-based learning management system provided the technical infrastructure for the online classes, featuring a mechanisms variety to enable ongoing communication and interaction among peers, instructors, on-site colleagues and the learning environment itself. Additional technological applications were integrated as relevant to curricular goals and manageable by participants in such ways as to move beyond simple information sharing to the development of substantive dialogue related to meaningful learning rooted in applied experiences Both instructional methods and educational technologies were selected based on their capacities to support the following goals: 1.facilitate collaboration, promoting work with peers to generate shared learning goals and solve common problems; such activities are made possible through the virtual conferencing platforms integration that enable text, audio and video interactions; 2. ensure continuous one-to-one and one-to-many communications in order to facilitate reflection upon readings and discussion of placement experiences, by using email, chat and blogs; 3. enable information management to distribute course content using file sharing, text-based lectures, podcasts and eBooks; 4. exploit and/or minimize geographic differences through the strategically combined use of synchronous and asynchronous activities and events; 5. promote consistent and universal access by implementing standard minimum requirements for software, hardware and bandwidth; 6. advance functionality to promote skill development related to general use, navigation, and a range of applications and plug-ins; 7. archive relevant artifacts from the courses, such as learning objects and transcripts collectively created by the membership; and, 8.

coordinate a range of administrative functions that typically accompany instruction, such as identifying participation patterns or generating and recording assessment data (Sedrakyan, 2006).

The exploratory nature of the study led to a qualitative approach to the research design. The purpose of this study was to explore students' perceptions of reflective pedagogy in experiential based courses offered online. Exploring possible learning and potential impact was gained through a qualitative design aimed at constructing this information through a brief survey and accompanying interview. This study's approach examined the phenomenon of experiential learning and reflection on the learning through narrative writing and other media. The qualitative research field is constantly challenging the distinction between that what is "real" and constructed, that all events are made real through interaction, discourse, conversation and narratives (Mkrttchian 2010). This study attempted to understand the phenomenon of learning through the combination of qualitative surveys and interviews. The qualitative nature of the survey provides student narratives and perceptions of reflection. The brief seven-question survey was created to collect demographic information and initial reactions to reflective pedagogy. General demographic information collected included age, gender, major, academic level, ethnicity, and frequency of online courses taken. Open ended questions such as, "How do you define reflection?" "How do you best make meaning for the experiences you have?" "What reflection forms are required for the course you are currently enrolled in? And "What other types of reflection would be useful for you to make meaning of your experiences?" were asked. The final survey question asked participants for their willingness to participate in a follow up interview. The primary task in interviewing was to understand interview statements and the meaning assigned to them (Mkrttchian 2008). The interview design allowed for both main and probing questions (Mkrttchian 2010). Main questions were prepared for the interview ahead of time and were consistently delivered to all participants. Additionally, probing questions were used to clarify participants' responses as appropriate or needed. Fifteen students participated in an interview either via telephone or Web-based audio conferencing, which lasted 20 to 40 minutes. The interview gathered direct quotations, a basic source of raw data essential to the qualitative study. Such direct quotations revealed the respondents' emotional presence in the learning experiences, the ways in which they organized their worlds with respect to individualized learning and reflection, their thoughts about what were happening, their experiences, and their basic perceptions. Direct quotations provided meaningful information with regard to the participants' perceptions of their learning and the meaning and the reflection impact as a participation result in an online course. Potential participants were contacted by gaining access through the institution's academic department in which the courses were offered. Participants in four experiential based courses that focused on internships and service-learning were contacted. During the interview, 53 students were enrolled in one of the four experiential based courses. Once a list of possible participants was verified, individuals were contacted via e-mail with a link directing them to the online survey. Among the 53 students contacted, 37 completed the survey for a return rate of 70%. Among the 37 that completed the survey, 21 consented to be interviewed and 15 were actually interviewed.

Mkrttchian (2010) suggested researchers to explore a study's themes before collecting initial data; by researching the topic area before collecting data. Research was initially accomplished through the literature review and reflection on personal experiences as both students and faculty members instructing in online learning environments. Three ways of organizing and reporting the data gathered, description, analysis, and interpretation, were used. In the final analysis, transcripts from the interviews were read and re-read; data that aligned with the refined codes were highlighted. Phrases and words were used to determine codes for each participant. Emerging themes were identified in those instances in which similar ideas surfaced in three or more student transcriptions. Once all of the emerging themes were studied, relationships among those themes were examined.

As previously noted, a total of 37 undergraduate students (Astrakhan State University-Russian Federation) responded to an invitation to participate in this study. Among the 37 students who responded to the brief survey, 21 were between 20-24 years old, 9 were between 25-29 years old, 5 were between 30-40 years old and 2 were between the ages of 41-55. Thirty students identified themselves as Caucasian and 7 identified themselves as a minority; 3 were Asian, 1 was multiracial and 3 were Europeans. The students responding majority were female, and only 11 respondents were male. Ten students stated that they only took classes online and 27 students took both classes in both online and face-to-face formats. The majority of students were in their fourth year of full time coursework where five students were in their third year, one was in his second year and two were in their fifth year. Among the 37 students who responded, 21 stated that they typically take 0-1 online course in a semester, 14 typically take 2-3 online courses in a semester and 2 take 4-5 online courses in a semester.

Students participating in this study identified themselves as majoring in a wide disciplines range. Business, including management and accounting majors, were the most represented with 13 students; 6 students studied computer science; 6 students studied criminal justice and legal studies; 4 students majored in communications; political science was presented by 2 students; and, global studies, history, psychology, mathematics, biology and chemistry were presented by one student correspondingly. Twenty two students in this study were motivated to take one of the experientially based online courses because it is fulfilled as a general education requirement, 9 students responded that it is fulfilled as a requirement for their major and 5 reported motivation to enroll out of their personal interest. Among the students who responded to the survey, 26 were enrolled in an online service-learning course and 11 were enrolled in an online internship-based course.

In order to better understand students' perception of reflection as a whole, both on the survey and during the interview, study participants were asked to define reflection. Among the 37 survey responses, 32 students defined reflection in terms of analyzing and learning from past experiences, 3 students mentioned learning from present experiences, one student mentioned future learning and one student defined reflection as involving past, present and future experiences. On the survey, one student responded that reflection was, "The process of examining the actions and reactions of situations and scenarios in order to understand the deeper meanings and process it took to come full circle." A second student described reflection as, "Looking back at your experiences and examining what you learned from those experiences." Yet another student defined reflection "...as the process of thinking back upon what you have experienced over a certain time period and assessing what you learned from that experience." A fourth student wrote that reflection meant, "Pondering experience and assessing what can be learned from it." When we followed up with this same student during the interview, she defined reflection as "Thinking about experiences and then figuring out what can be learned from it. In every experience there is a lesson to be learned." This student explained how one could reflect and learn from everything he/she does. She continued by noting, "...reflection becomes a habit rather then something you have to do for any class." Each of these students defined reflection as examining past experiences and making meaning from lessons learned.

Four students during the interview specifically defined reflection as being an active process in which a person is engaged in his/her own learning, an often-challenging process. One student stated,

"...reflection requires the ability to engage in a higher level of personal honesty, a willingness to engage in self-directed positive criticism and a rejection of „easy answers." Another student defined reflection in terms of "...actively analyzing previous perceptions and emotions and reevaluate the circumstances that influenced them. It is not an easy stuff." One student defined reflection in terms of looking at past, present and future experiences. On the survey he reported reflection to be "... the process of analyzing an event for relationships pertaining to the past, present, and future." In the interview, the same student was asked for his reflection definition and he responded, "Critically thinking about what has happened, what is happening and what will happen. There are so many connections to our experiences; reflection helps us to see all of the relationships between them." Better understanding of the participants' reflection definitions and the reflective process provides a strong context for exploring their perceptions related to reflective pedagogy in an online environment.

Students participating in the survey were asked to identify those forms of reflection used in their online experientially based courses, selecting as many answers as applicable from the following four methods: reflection journals, essays and papers, online discussions, and Web-based interactive presentations. Among 37 participants: 36 students identified using reflection journals, 28 described using essays and papers, 20 noted using the online discussion feature as a reflection form, and 3 responded that they presented through the courses' Web-based conferencing platform as a form of reflection.

All 15 students interviewed agreed that any of these methods facilitated reflection and, as such, extended their learning in the online experientially based course(s). During the interview, a follow up question from the survey relating to the reflection types used in the course was asked. Students were asked, "On the survey you stated that the course you are enrolled in uses different reflection types. Are these reflection types helpful?" Fourteen of 15 students responded that all reflection types used in the course were helpful. One student specifically said, "Yes, these reflection types were helpful. When I think about it, all types had some benefit to my learning. The second student, who self-reported that she took all of her classes online, stated the structured reflection opportunities provided had a particularly positive impact on her learning, responding;

All of the reflection types were useful in this class. The journals made me continually reflect on the experience I was having at my site. The essays pushed me to think critically about the new material and relate it to my experience and the online discussions got me to think about my opinion in relation to others. This was a way different experience than any of the other online classes I have taken. I really learned in a whole new way. I wish more online courses were like this. When he was asked whether structured reflection provided with the best environment to the critical think and learn about his experience, the third student stated, "I never thought about making meaning from an experience until it was discussed in class. I never even thought about online discussions as a reflection, but this course helped me to understand that." The same student went on to explain how he had "never been in a class that was so powerful. I rolled my eyes when I saw structured reflection in the description, but it turns out that this has been so applicable to life." This student further explained that the opportunities for structured reflection provided in the online courses had a positive impact on his learning.

During interviews, students shared their structured reflection opportunities perceptions in the experientially based online courses in which they were enrolled. While all students reported that the reflective nature of the course resulted in a positive impact on their learning, several students specifically noted that this perception changed over the semester. For example, as a semester began several students reported negative attitudes toward the reflection required in the course. However, they continued with noting that this perception changed over the course of the term due to the range of methods offered for structured reflection.

Reflection Journals

Both of the online experientially based courses examined in this study implement journals to facilitate structured reflection. The internship course requires students to write each time they are at their placements; the service-learning course requires that an entry is made per every four hours of the community service. Overall, students indicate that maintaining written journals is a means of reflecting especially beneficial to their learning. One student enrolled in an online service-learning course noted, "The reflection journals were so helpful in forcing me to think about my service experience. I have never journeyed before, but I really think that it helped me to get the most experience output." The second student reported, "After this class I think I will register it more often. I had the negative thoughts about it at first, but once I felt more comfortable with it, it made sense. It turned out to be a good thing". While this student explained initial negative feelings about recording structured reflections in a written journal, he came to understand the benefits by the end of the class. The student enrolled in the internship focused course said, "I register personally and did not want to do it for this class since it was required. However, I totally get why it is important and when the class ended I was glad I did it." While this student wrote in her personal journal, she was not excited to do it for class because it was a requirement. While initially reluctant, she eventually reported the benefits from such a course requirement.

Reflective Essays

The second method, the use of formal written assignments in the form of essays and papers, is used in the online service-learning class. During the interview process students explained reflective essays were especially beneficial to their learning. One student noted, "We did two reflective essays in the course I attended. It was such a different way of analyzing material and then relating it to my community service experience." This student reported that such assignments forced her to relate the course material to the service experience in the class. Another student stated, "I struggled with the reflective essays we had in class. It was a good struggle. I mean, when I got done relating two historical leaders and figuring out how that informed my service, I got it. What a clever assignment." This particular student explained how relating two historical leaders to the service she performed was a challenge, but ultimately rewarding. In responding to reflective essays as a form of structure reflection, a student said, "The essays pushed me to apply what I read to what was going on with me at my site. What a cool way to think about the [course] material in a new way." Each of these students stated that these structured written assignments had a positive impact on their learning online discussion. Structured questions guided online discussions in both experientially based courses. Guided questions focused around course materials reinforced learning outcomes, requiring students to integrate applied experiences at internship or community service sites with theoretical concepts. One student explained that she typically disliked required discussions assigned in online courses, but enjoyed this feature of this specific course because it enabled her to consider her own experiences. She reported "I normally hate it when we are required to post thoughts for our class, but I really loved it in this class. It was not as formal because we were bringing in our own experiences. It allowed us to build relationships which I don't have with other classmates in my online courses".

Another student stated, "I loved the questions our instructor posed. They were thought provoking and got me thinking about how the material is applied in our real life." The third student responded, "The discussions posted on our class site were very cool. That was the best way for me to reflect. I normally have to discuss things and this was the same thing. This was better than the journals." This specific student identified that reflecting through discussion rather than writing in a journal provided her the more productive option for meeting course goals, noting that asynchronous online discussions were a better fit to her learning style. Building relationships through online discussion was another benefit that made a positive impact on students learning. A student who self-reported only taking online courses said, "My self and another student always seemed to be on the discussion board at the same time. We were talking in almost real time. It was a great way to reflect on the material."

The reflection process as cognitive and affective development mean, particularly as facilitated in web-based courses, was a new concept for many students. One student explained that while she had heard the word "reflection" before the class, she had not considered its meaning; the class in which she participated enabled her to "test it out." The second student remarked that she "... actually looked forward to this class because it took what I was doing and allowed me to learn from that instead of the new information regurgitating." In order to provide opportunities for students to reflect on individual aspects of learning and self-report identified impacts, each of 15 students interviewed were asked the following question: "Has the reflective nature of this course made an impact on your learning any way?" All students interviewed unanimously reported that the reflective nature of the online experientially based courses had a positive impact on their learning. From these responses, three emerged themes were found: building relationships with classmates, increased learning through theories application, and identifying reflection as a new learning way. Twenty-seven percent of students responded that activities promoting reflection assisted them in building relationships with others in the course. This achievement was particularly important in as much as participants were geographically dispersed throughout the United States. One student specifically noted, "Having reflection be a part of online courses made me more connected to others in the course. When you share personal thoughts it builds relationships." The second student reported, I would not have said this in the beginning of the semester, but after this class I am a believer. I believe that reflection is a powerful thing, especially in online classes where often you are an island doing your own work not really interacting with other classmates. This was a positive way to interact with folks across the country, heck, and world doing cool things. Using real world experiences around which to frame various theories related to applied studies was also a common perception of students; in fact, thirty percent of students specifically stated they felt their learning was positively impacted through reflection on connections made between theoretical concepts and practice. One student stated, "I know I learned more because I would always be thinking about how to make connections for my journals and reflective essays. I was in the grocery store shopping once when I realized I was thinking about the class." Another student said that he brought various "ah-ha" moments he had during online discussions into his professional conversation, noting, "I just feel that I learned more in a well-rounded perspective."

Eighty percent of students interviewed for this study reported the greatest impact of the reflective nature of the online experientially based courses which offered a new approach to critical thinking that enabled meaningful and deep learning that extended throughout multiple areas of their lives.

One student explained, "I would say I learned more in this class because of the reflective nature…I like people and like searching deeply. Making it a requirement made me to find time to reflect." Another student said, "We heard several times in our class how reflection was making meaning from experiences. Once I really got that, I started looking at this class and I guess learning in a totally new way. It does not sound cheesy, but I can be a learner of life and learn from anything and everything. I just need to reflect – make meaning from whatever it is. Several students noted that learning about the concept of reflection actually enabled them to change their learning styles and processes. One student reported "I am so thankful I learned about this reflection concept. It took me about half of the semester to really get why reflecting on what you do is so important. As our instructor constantly said, to make meaning from what you learn. The results of this study indicate that reflective pedagogies have the potential to dramatically facilitate and extend significant learning when implemented in online learning environments. In such classrooms meaningful learning consists of cultivating a capacity for self-awareness through opportunities for structured reflection, developing collaborations to explore individualized awareness and perceptions, understanding complex theoretical concepts within a cognitive processing framework, and applying reflective material resulting from both individual impressions and collaborative relationships in both academic and "real world" contexts. These pedagogies become even more significant when delivered as a means to connect geographically dispersed students in the development and achievement of shared learning outcomes. Mkrttchian (2010) substantiated the link between the integration of new media in curricula and meaningful opportunities for learning, noting that such connections are made stronger in virtual environments in their potential to extend beyond individual classrooms, impacting the organizations and larger communities in which students serve. Most notably, students' perceptions of the potential for structured reflection to positively impact their learning related to individual as well as collaborative learning, and both active (for example, participation in discussions) and passive (such as recording impressions in journals) means of reflection were perceived to be beneficial.

In Astrakhan State University G. Ryabichkina (2009) identified that for reflection to be meaningful it must be continuous, connected, challenging and contextualized. To ensure such relevancy it is critical that curricula impose structures that enable a scaffolding of students' insights, interpretations and analyses. Because meaning making results from both individual and collective processes, reflective pedagogy most appropriately seeks to balance instructional direction with learning autonomy. Such strategies can be negotiated through using open-ended questions that guide discussions, constructing parameters in the development of journal entries, and framing reflection within the context of targeted readings and assignments, as well as by encouraging honest and respectful interactions and communications with peers at placements as well as in virtual classrooms. It is noteworthy that these approaches are similarly well suited for both virtual and on ground learning environments; however, they appear most appropriately used in asynchronous virtual settings in which students have opportunities for considered, thoughtful and well-researched responses. Posing opened-ended questions (e.g., as used to direct the discussions, essays and journals content) is key to guiding the reflection process; students particularly value an emphasis on interpretation as opposed to predetermined conclusions and generalizations. Questions that specifically relate their learning experiences and evolving outcomes, thoughts, and feelings allow students to focus on very unique and individualized ideas and impressions. Open-ended questions such as, "What were your initial reactions to the site at which you are working?", "What has been the biggest lesson you have learned while engaged at your site?", or "What are some of the challenges you face in your experience?" enable students to capitalize on opportunities to create language around sometimes challenging, elusive and contradictory thoughts, feelings and conclusions.

The use of narrative journals promotes critical reflection insofar as its focus is structured to facilitate insights and analyses formed in response to assignment requirements. For example, the instructors for the courses of focus for this study require that reflection journals include a minimum of 20 unique entries, each consisting of 500 to 750 words; such parameters reinforce the importance of reflective processes to overall learning and development as well as provide often-needed guidance related to expectations and learning outcomes. Additionally, students are instructed to limit descriptions of factual content of journal entries to 25 to 40 words per entry so that their narratives specifically convey subjective insights, reactions, thoughts, feelings and lessons learned. Moreover, questions strategically introduced enable sequenced learning; for example, the non-imposing questions exclusion, such as, "What do you think about the resources (monetary, human, etc.) available to service recipients at your site?" as a course commences provides groundwork for students as they form responses to more difficult questions, such as, "How would you distribute limited, but much-needed resources to those who receive services at your site?" Implementing guidelines related to interaction and communication, for example, requiring honest and respectful responses between peers in online discussions, and framing reflection in the context of readings are two additional strategies that promote inquiry and self-discovery. Creating a community of learners who values honesty, respectfulness, and support as well as challenge and confrontation is important in promoting the development of reflections that are productive and meaningful; modeling this level and style of communication is critical to creating a constructive classroom environment. Framing reflection on experiences within the context of specific readings similarly reinforces student learning related to both curricular content as well as individualized experiences. For example, focusing reflective discourse and self-inquiry around reading current events or biographies enables opportunities for comparison, contrast and analyses that reinforce learning outcomes. While reflective pedagogies provide a rich context in which to examine experiential learning in a virtual environment, it is important to acknowledge challenges inherent in providing highly interactive experiences to a distributed group of students placed in diverse service placements and settings. For example, assisting students with a range of learning styles and preferences to develop skills in reflection and critical inquiry requires a substantial commitment by educators; such a commitment of time and focus competes within current contexts of maintaining growing enrollments. For example, students may be reluctant to make themselves vulnerable by recording personal impressions within large classrooms; such concerns must be dealt with directly and immediately so that students are able to continue to reap the benefits of developing reflective skills and abilities. Certainly the participation of students from around the globe enables access to a wide variety of experiences that promotes interdisciplinary thinking and collaboration. However, assisting students to integrate such diverse experiences as they struggle to form individual identities requires a consistent level of engagement and motivation by both students and teachers. Sustaining an awareness of highly personalized meaning is especially challenging in asynchronous classrooms where interaction is not instantaneous. Finally, the continuous integration of evolving technologies into instruction while meeting curricular goals, monitoring student capabilities, and managing provider needs requires ongoing attention, often necessitating curricular modification as applications are developed and updated.

CREATING MODEL SOFTWARE FOR DISCOURCE-BASED META-COMMUNICATION

HHH University and Astrakhan State University research team (2010) crated special software of model for discourse based meta-communication and use in distinguishes between communication action and discourse. Team argues that, when communicating, actors raise validity claims and that communication breaks down when any validity claim becomes problematic. This leads to a reflective mode of communication, i.e. to a discourse about the controversial validity claim. Depending on the validity claims challenged, the validity basis of communication can be made thematic at the discourse level in different types of discourses, in which participants reflects on contested validity claims and attempt to vindicate or criticize them through arguments.

Actions can be communicative or non-communicative. Accordingly, reflections can refer to communicative as well as non-communicative actions. Reflections can take place in an individual's mind, but also be dialogical. The term 'meta-communication' used here implies dialogical reflections among actors about communications.

In Sedsrakyan' discourse theory; the discourse level is entered to reflect on the communication action level. In our case, the meta-communication level (i.e. the second level) is entered to communicate about the communication action level (i.e. the first level). Communications at the meta-level themselves can raise validity claims, which can then become controversial and lead to discourses. Accordingly, in the general architecture of the meta-communication layer, two levels are distinguished: the *conversation for clarification level* for communicating about the communication action level, and the *discourse level* for argumentative examination of controversial claims. Thus, in the model, discourses are viewed as part of the meta-communication layer.

This differentiation allows us to place various types of discourses proposed by Sedrakyan into the discourse level. Discourses provide a structure and orientation for disputing controversial validity claims raised at the lower level(s). However, they do not structure the conversation for clarification level. Hence, the questions arise: Can the conversation for clarification level also be structured – like the discourse level - to ensure that conversations take place systematically? In the case that conversations deal with the communication and action aspects of information systems, then what are the basic issues that need clarification and explicit attention at the meta-level?

THE META-COMMUNICATION MODEL PROGRAMMING CONCEPTS

Figure 3 presents the programing concepts that we place in the conversation for clarification level as well as at the discourse level. In the following, we will briefly explain them and their relationships. At the conversation for clarification level, we use the extended version of the *philosophical staircase* for reflective practice suggested by Sedrakyan. Using the staircase metaphor, Sedrakyan provided an arrangement of several basic issues and validity claims involved in information systems definition, design, and development. They are originally called semiotic steps (syntactic, semantic, and pragmatic clarity), epistemological steps (expressive, empirical, and normative validity) and practical-philosophical steps (instrumental, strategic and communicative rationality). In Mkrttchian and Lazovskaya final report (2011), the staircase has been reviewed and two additional steps added, i.e. the physical clarity and aesthetic rationality. These steps are relevant especially in designing international user interfaces Mkrttchian(2011). A detailed description of the steps of the staircase will be provided later on. The idea is that the staircase organizes basic issues and can thus support researchers and practitioners in the

Figure 3. The generic connection framework classes

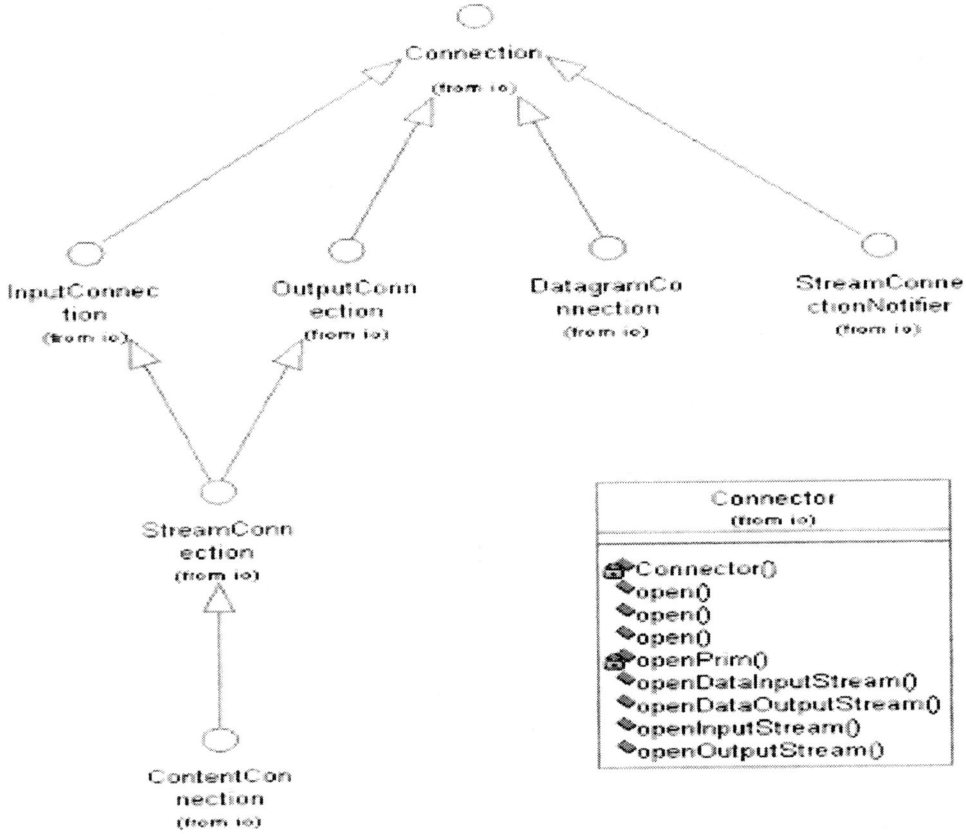

process of identifying and scrutinizing diverse issues they face in any information systems development project. It provides a way of sorting and structuring conversations at the conversation for clarification level. At each step of the staircase conversations for clarification can take place and the discourse level is entered when controversies arise, which require argumentative examination.

The discourse level contains several types of discourses and reflective media proposed by Mkrttchian. The types of discourses are: *Explicative discourse* where the comprehensibility (or well-formalness) of symbolic expressions is schematized as a controversial claim; *theoretical discourse* for disputing truth claims of expressions and the efficacy of actions; and *practical discourse*, which is further differentiated in Sedrakyan later works: Pragmatic, ethical, and moral discourses as well as legal discourse. *Pragmatic discourse* is concerned with the justification of technical and strategic recommendations, i.e. with the purposiveness of choices. *Ethical discourse* refers to individuals or communities with differing value systems, and is concerned with the justification of regulations from a cultural perspective, i.e. from the perspective of what is 'good' for them. However, duties of justice, i.e. whether the corresponding practice is *equally* good *for all*, can be rationally justified in *moral discourse*. *Legal discourse* deals with grounding of legitimacy of legal norms of a community. In addition to these discourses, Sedrakyan introduced two further reflective media for problematic expressive and evaluative expressions. These are *therapeutic critique*, which is related to the validity claim of truthfulness or sincerity of expressions, and *aesthetic criticism*, which is related to the adequacy of value standards as a controversial claim. Let us briefly describe the steps of the staircase and their relations to the discourses in more detail. The steps of the staircase themselves are concepts borrowed from semiotics, e.g., Sedrakyan concepts of validity and rationality.

1. *Physical clarity* is strongly related to the media. It deals with the clarification of the perceptibility or visibility of signs (e.g., "Can you see the new pictures on my homepage?").
2. *Syntactic clarity* refers to structures and rules for composing complex signs. Different rules and syntactic conventions may cause breakdowns or misinterpretations, which require the clarification of syntactically correct formulations of signs (e.g., "Should we use the 'day/month/year' or the 'month/day/year' format?").
3. *Semantic clarity* deals with the clarification of the meanings of signs, i.e. of a word or a complex sign (e.g., "What do you mean by 'meeting time: 8 o'clock'? 8 am or 8 pm?"). When controversies arise at any of these three steps, actors can enter *explicative discourse*, to argumentatively examine the comprehensibility, well-formalness or rule-correctness of symbolic expressions.
4. *Relevance* (an aspect of pragmatics) deals with the clarification of whether a sign (or the content) of a design is relevant (e.g., "What fields do we need in a résumé template?"). Controversies in the relevance of the content have to take place in *pragmatic discourses*, in which the relevance of choices with respect to their purposiveness is justified.
5. *Expressive validity*, i.e., whether it reflects sincere pragmatic intentions (e.g., "Do we really mean that?"). If the expressive validity of an expression becomes controversial, the reflective medium *therapeutic critique* can be entered for challenging and argumentatively defending.
6. *Empirical validity*, i.e., whether it refers to the true (commonly believed) state of affairs (e.g., "Does this message agree with the fact?"). The *theoretical discourse* serves as the related forum for disputing and grounding contested truth claims.
7. *Normative validity* (or appropriateness), i.e., whether it is communicated in accordance with accepted social norms (e.g., "Is it appropriate to say that?"). In his earlier work, Sedrakyan regarded practical discourses as the place for testing "both the rightness of a given action in relation to a given norm, and, at the next level, the rightness of such a norm itself. Following his later differentiation, we regard the legal discourse as the place where the rightness of an action/expression in relation to a given norm or rule is examined, whereas the rightness of a norm itself remains a matter of moral discourses.
8. *Instrumental rationality* refers to means-end rationality. That is, it deals with the efficient use of means, the choice of the most effective means or the effective planning of the application of means for a given purpose (e.g., "Do we need to design so many pages to communicate this content?"). Social aspects are not considered here.
9. *Strategic rationality* is a purposive but also a social concept of rationality. That is, the behavior of other rational actors is taken into account. It involves egocentric calculation of success, deception, and power. Its validity is determined by the effectiveness in influencing others for achieving a given purpose. A design can be assessed according to its efficacy in influencing social actors to do what is desired (e.g., "Should we disable the page numbers in order not to put readers off?"). When the empirical basis or effectiveness of an instrumental or strategic

rationality becomes controversial, actors can enter the *theoretical discourse*.

10. *Aesthetic rationality* of a design can be judged according to its aesthetic beauty, i.e., whether a design is in accord with or deviates from culturally established standards of aesthetic value (e.g., "isn't it too white?"). This type of rationality is added to three ideal types of rationality proposed by Sedrakyan. The place for reflection on aesthetic experiences is *aesthetic critique*.
11. *Communicative rationality* refers to the communicative achievement of mutual understanding among actors. This step allows actors to reflect retrospectively on what they have achieved so far and to seek mutual agreement with respect to the content and normative basis of an information system (e.g., "Does everyone agree with what we have achieved so far? Finally, when a communicatively achieved consensus with respect to one or several aspects of a communication action is challenged, actors can enter corresponding discourses.

Note that the discourses are interrelated and that there are not only the explicit paths from the staircase to discourses as shown in Figure 4, but also multiple (implicit) paths among discourses themselves.

Actors can go back to earlier steps in the staircase in need of further clarifications or switch between discourses when in a discourse issues arise that require argumentative examinations in other discourses (e.g., a moral issue in pragmatic discourse requires entering moral discourses). Finally, discourse is not just talking, but rather argumentatively examining validity claims. In the network of different types of discourses, different types of reasons can be brought to justify the corresponding claims.

FUTHER REFLECTIONS ON THE PROGRAMING USAGE OF THE MODEL

Software Situations for Entering Meta-Communication

So far, we have introduced and illustrated the concepts of the meta-communication model. In fact, the model can be used in different action situations for reflective practice. Reflections can take place before, during, and after an action. Accordingly, taking action as a basis, we can distinguish between three types of meta-communication:

1. *Ex ante meta-communication*, taking place before an action;
2. *Meta-communication-in-action*, taking place during an action; and
3. *Ex post meta-communication*, taking place after an action

Mkrttchian (2011) distinguished between *ex post* meta-communication (taking place when breakdown occurs) and *ex ante* meta-communications (referring to proactive discussions about future communication). However, breakdowns can occur during and after an action. Thus, the action-oriented characterization of meta-communication types can do more justice to describe the situations for reflections. We therefore introduce the *Meta communication- in-action*, in the sense of "reflection-in-action". The continuous reflections taken place in three different action situations can support the continuous co-evolution of the communication action concepts (figure 5).

Using the Programing Staircase for Conversations and the Discourses

The staircase used at the conversation for clarification level suggests that the basic issues represented as steps of the staircase need to be clarified step by step, from the lowest step up to the highest

Figure 4. The create meta-communication model using sequence diagram

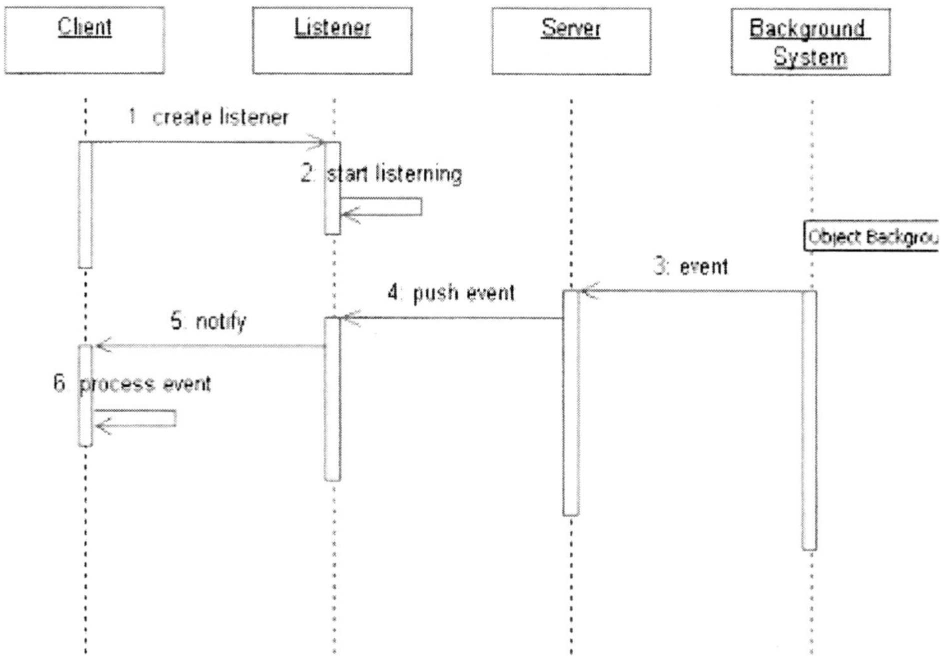

Figure 5. The diagram of situations for entering meta-communication

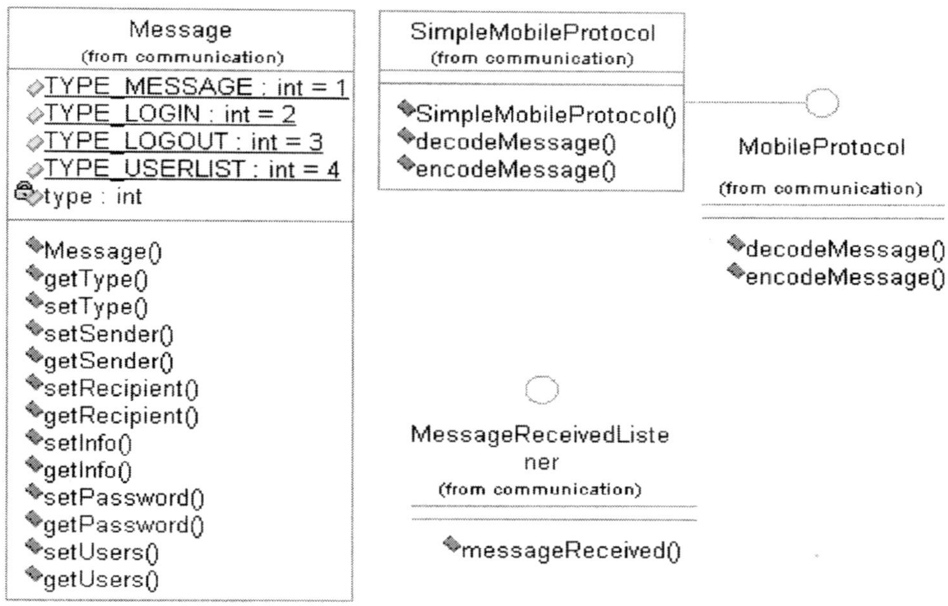

step. Mkrttchian (2008) justifies the arrangement of the steps of the staircase, among others, also with the argument that the clarification of one step may require the clarification of previous steps, for example, the issue of relevance may require semantic clarity (figure 6).

On the other hand, in many cases, the relevance or normative validity of the signs needs first to be established before the clarification of its physical, syntactic, and semantic aspects. Thus, it may not always be efficient to use discourses along the staircase and to carry longer controversial disputes on the comprehensibility of a sign in explicative discourses before examining its relevance or normative validity in practical discourses. Since previous discursive approaches considered only one or two discourse types, the sequence of discourses has not been discussed. For the meta-communication model with several discourses, this issue gains significance. Depending on the purpose and objects of meta-level discussions, the priority of discourses may change. But, from the perspective of discourse-ethics, the practical discourses have the highest priority.

Thus, participants may communicate along the steps of the staircase, and at the same time, put controversial issues in related discourses, but leave them undecided until they have stepped to the highest step 'communicative rationality'. They can then retrospectively clarify open issues, starting from practical discourses (e.g., pragmatic or legal discourses as illustrated using examples 2 and 3 in section 4).

Software Implementation Options

The model can be implemented in an online environment to support computer-mediated discourses. In its realization, two versions are possible:

Figure 6. The diagram of staircase for conversations and the discourses

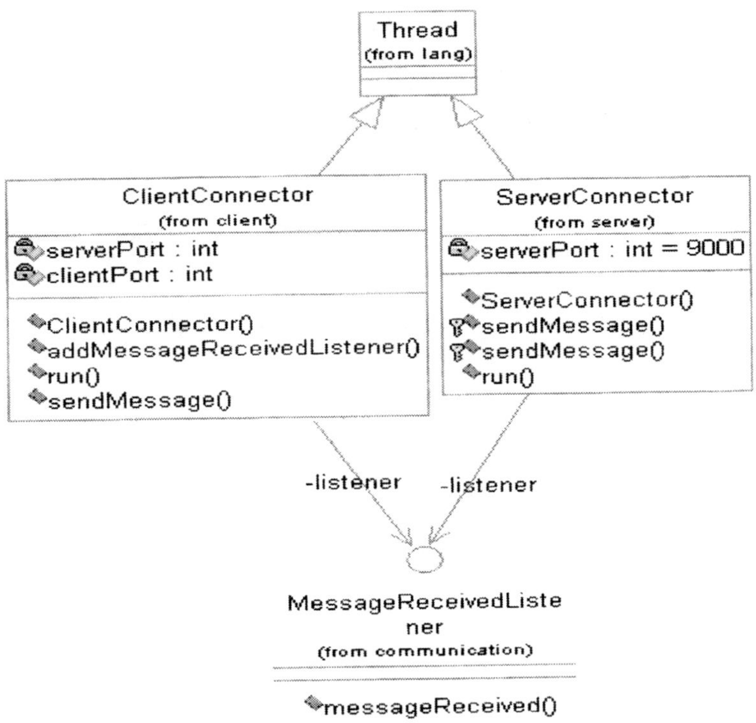

1. The implementation of only the discourses as discussion spaces and the integration of the steps of the staircase into related discourses; or
2. The implementation of both levels of the meta-communication layer so that the discourses and the steps of the staircase can be used as separate 'discussion spaces'. In the first case, actors can reflect within each discourse on related aspects of an issue (e.g., in explicative discourse on the comprehensibility of signs with respect to their physical, syntactic, and semantic aspects). In contrast, the second option allows actors the separation of "just talking" from argumentative disputes and thus can reduce the information overload for those who are only interested in controversial positions on specific issues rather than in conversations for clarifications or vice versa. In addition, the separation of the clarification level allows actors and moderators (if any) to use this level for facilitating discourses (Figure 7). For example, when the abstract concepts and their interrelationship may become confusing for the actors, supportive conversations for orientations can take place at this level. In addition, actors who prefer expressing views in their culturally preferred forms, e.g., using narratives, rather than providing confrontational arguments, can use this level. The narratives can be 'translated' by others (or mediators) into 'confrontational arguments'.

The model can also be realized as a functionality of user interfaces, e.g., in form of pop-up menus, which can open spaces for discourses on selected user interface objects. This option would provide users with means to articulate the breakdowns and problems experienced during the interaction with the system, and thus to initiate

Figure 7. The create implementation options for model

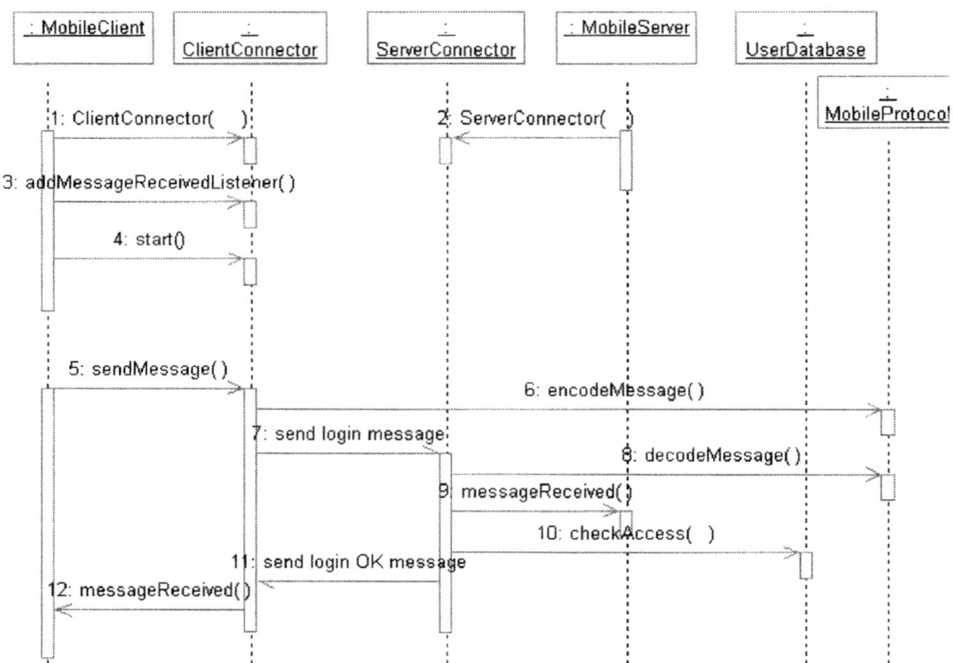

further discussions for the improvement of the system functionalities.

FUTURE RESEARCH DIRECTIONS

More testing of the system is being undertaken to improve its performance. In our particular test scenario, Vard Avatar used direct query to identify a user whose identity could be found in a database containing 200 first and last names of people related to the I/UCRC program. The test Vard Avatar system was 100% effective after it asked the user for his identity not more than three times. By controlling the context of the conversation in real-time, the appropriate group of grammars to be used is selected for that context. This minimizes the speech recognition search space, improves performance and minimizes duplication of grammar items.

A follow-up demonstration system is currently being developed to expand the feature set of the first Vard Avatar prototype. In essence, it expands upon the original design by adding two key features: temporal awareness and multi-user capability. Temporal awareness refers to the idea that the avatar can retain and recall chronologically relevant user specific data. For example, the avatar is being enhanced to reference episodic memories concerning previous conversations in the current conversation. The multi-user feature currently under development will allow the avatar to conduct a group meeting, where two or more human users wearing headsets can interact with the avatar, which will turn to face each person being addressed.

Research results in the virtual biology teacher project permit the creation of an entirely new teaching program and software in the following fields – mathematics, physics and informatics virtual teacher and virtual law.

CONCLUSION

As evidenced by this study, reflective pedagogies provide a framework in which to facilitate the achievement of a wide range of competencies and literacies. This approach appears particularly powerful in web-based learning environments in which critical inquiry and engaged discourse are complimented by participation in "real world" on-site experiences. The synergies possible when geographically dispersed students join to explore issues related to experiential learning, civic engagement, and "making a difference" in local communities provide an exciting context for additional study; these synergies are boundless when reflective pedagogy and experiential learning combine with technology-based systems that enable broad access to educational opportunities.

In this chapter, we have described a meta-communication model, which extends the spectrum of earlier discursive approaches to reflective practice by integrating discourse-ethical concepts as well as additional relevant insights from information systems literature. As illustrated, the model deals with issues of ambiguity and conflict in general, and therefore it can support collective sense-making both in local and global contexts. The network of different types of discourses allows actors to bring different types of reasons and to argumentatively examine and to justify controversial claims.

It should be noted that the model cannot overcome some difficulties that the realization of discourse theoretical concepts face, especially in global contexts. Its application requires a minimum of value congruence or openness to discursive resolution of conflicts.

Communication in global context remains a challenge and the value-consensus formation nearly impossible in the short run.

Yet, we argue that the model provides a way for systematically and meaningfully structuring and organizing meta-level conversations. Thus, it can be used in several application domains, in order to enable effective meta-communication processes. It also provides structures for capturing human knowledge.

Once implemented in an online environment, empirical work needs to be carried out for testing the usability of the model abstract concepts. It can include, for example, investigating how naive users translate the breakdowns occurring in their use context into the abstract concepts of the meta-communication model and exploring whether a human facilitator is needed for enabling the use of the model, in the sense of technology use mediation as well as for enabling discourses through communication processes structuring.

REFERENCES

Mkrttchian, V. (2008). Development of educational Web-based simulator and its evaluation. Preprint of the 17th IFAC World Congress. Seoul, 2008, (pp. 9802-9806).

Mkrttchian, V. (2008). *E-learning and social perspective in all Armenian Internet University*. Preprint of the 17th IFAC World Congress. Seoul, 2008, (pp. 8109-8112).

Mkrttchian, V. (2010). E-learning in Armenia: Has established the pioneering usage of "HHH" technology. In Demiray, U. (Ed.), *E-learning practices* (*Vol. 1*, pp. 55–75). Eskisehir.

Mkrttchian, V. (2010). Modeling and simulation of the framework for the effective implementation of "HHH" technology in Armenia. *Proceeding of 22nd International Conference on Systems Research, Informatics and Cybernetics*, (pp. 78-90). Baden-Baden, 2010.

Mkrttchian, V. (2010). Use "HHH" technology in the transformative models of online education. In Kurubacak, G., & Yuzer, T. V. (Eds.), *Handbook of research on transformative online education and liberation: Models for social equality* (pp. 340–351). Hershey, PA: IGI Global.

Mkrttchian, V., & Lozovskaya, M. (2009). Possibilities of virtual campus for distance learners of diploma biologist in Russia. *Proceeding of V International Conference on Multimedia and ICT in Education (m-ICTE2009),* Lisbon, 2009, (pp. 169-171).

Ryabichkina, G. (2009). *Some problems of substandard socio lexicography: Theoretical and applied aspects*. Dissertation, Pyatigorsk.

Sedrakyan, S. (2006). *The suggesting structured reflection to be key to learning from experiences.* Urartu. HHH University & Astrakhan State University. (2011). *Database, electronics handbooks, testing systems and avatars for virtual university.* Patents of Russian Federation N°2011613106, from 19.04.2011

Chapter 6
Science for All through Reflective Interactions:
Analyzing Online Instructional Models, Learning Activities and Virtual Resources

Jennifer J. Neakrase
New Mexico State University, USA

H. Prentice Baptiste
New Mexico State University, USA

Ashley N. Ryan
New Mexico State University, USA

Elsa Q. Villa
New Mexico State University, USA

ABSTRACT

One of the goals of science education is to ensure that the discipline of science is accessible to all individuals. By many organizations this has been termed "Science for All," and those who promote this idea also advocate the connection to science literacy. Teaching science in the online environment has been one way to offer science content to many different individuals, who do not necessarily need to be in the same location. Discourse in the science classroom is framed under situated cognition theory, whereby interactions between individuals are part of the normal culture of the classroom. For science knowledge to be adequately constructed by a student these interactions must be meaningful ones. This is especially important in an online science course where typically learning occurs through interactions between the students and the instructor, the students with one another, and within the individual themselves. As part of these online interactions, good reflective practice includes the different forms of feedback and the quality of this feedback. However, even with quality reflective interactions, there are barriers to science concept construction in an online environment. These barriers are discussed, and future research directions are suggested based on this review.

DOI: 10.4018/978-1-61350-071-2.ch006

INTRODUCTION

Science education reform efforts in the U.S. emerged following the launch of Sputnik in the late 1950s to enable American competitiveness in the space race. In the aftermath of this event and with funding from government agencies, scientists and educators collaborated in developing hands-on science programs to equip young Americans with the necessary knowledge and skills to address this challenge. While many school districts adopted these materials soon after their release, these materials soon faded in all but a few districts across the nation (National Science Resources Center (NSRC), 1997). In the 1980s and 1990s science education reform efforts re-emerged in response to the Reagan administration's publication of *A Nation at Risk,* which underscored the challenges of public schools in adequately preparing students in mathematics and science to meet the technological workforce needs of the nation. National efforts in reforming mathematics and science education re-emerged to address this mandate. One such effort was the establishment of the NSRC by The National Academies and the Smithsonian Institute.

In 1997 the NSRC published *Science for All Children: A Guide to Improving Elementary Science Education in Your School District* to facilitate the establishment of science education programs grounded in research-based pedagogy and materials. Another effort, titled Project 2061, founded by the American Association for the Advancement of Science (AAAS) produced a publication called *Science for All Americans*, which outlined benchmarks of scientific concepts and processes that students should master at strategic grade levels and upon exit from high school (AAAS, 2008). This publication provided the impetus for creating national science education standards, which have been integrated into most states' science education standards (NSTA, 2009). "Science for All" then is a vision for all Americans to acquire scientific literacy by the 21st century. Scientific literacy embodies the ability of individuals to use scientific reasoning in making decisions for personal and societal benefit. "Science for All" also promotes the discipline of science as being accessible to all individuals, regardless of culture, socioeconomic status, gender, or other barriers to the learning of science.

To achieve this vision of all Americans attaining science literacy, these aforementioned organizations and others support a pedagogical strategy informed by sociocultural and constructivist theories of learning; that is, learning is a process whereby learners derive meaning from, and make sense of, science phenomena through observation, research, questioning, and dialogic encounters with peers and experts (Brooks & Brooks, 1993; Fosnot & Perry, 2005; Vygotsky, 1978). In this pedagogical approach, teachers are guides and facilitators of learning who understand that learners use prior knowledge, social interaction, and critical reflection in their construction of deep understanding of science concepts.

With the recent technological advancements in online education, a plethora of instructional models are available to enhance the classroom experience in exploring science phenomena. This fact notwithstanding, face-to-face classrooms in progressive educational communities have been able to utilize state-of-the-art materials and effective pedagogy to increase student learning in science. While many such communities are in affluent areas such as Silicon Valley and Montgomery County in Maryland (NSRC, 1997), one notable community where progressive science teaching and learning happens is Imperial County, California located on the U.S. and Mexico border. This school district successfully implemented a reform effort with financial support from the National Science Foundation. Five recommended elements for successful reform were infused into the curriculum, instruction, and district policy: 1) high quality curriculum; 2) sustained professional development; 3) materials support; 4) community and administrator support; and 5) program assessment and evaluation (NSRC, 1997). This particular school district dramatically improved their science achievement and increased literacy scores (Klentschy & Molina-De La Torre, 2004). While these communities thrive under these reform efforts, too many American communities continue to struggle, particularly with the demands of standardized testing with its emphasis on low-level skill development (Sleeter, 2005).

While this example of successful science instructional reform in a face-to-face format is one of many, in order to truly provide science accessibility to a greater number of individuals science has been ported to the online environment. Online education offers an alternative to face-to-face classroom interaction with its inherent access to more resources and structured activities informed by research-based practices, such as data-driven investigation, modeling, collaboration, scaffolding and critical reflection (Hoadley, 2002; Simons & Clark, 2005; Williams, Linn, Ammon, & Gearhart, 2004). In particular, science web-based programs like WISE (Web-based Inquiry Science Environment), Kids as Global Scientists: Weather, and The Reconstructors were developed using the precepts of learning theories grounded in cognitive science and sociocultural theories (Linn, Clark, & Slotta, 2003; Miller, Moreno, Willcockson, Smith & Mayes, 2006; Songer, Lee, & Kam, 2002)). Furthermore, online instructional models have

potential... (to) support problem solving and precise instructional guidance through highly structured tasks and timely feedback. Instruction is said to fit the student's needs and to provide scaffolding and support at unprecedented levels of resolution. (Larreamendy-Joerns & Leinhardt, 2006, p. 584)

Furthermore, online education has promise for dismantling discriminatory practice through its discursive interaction in communication (Goldstein & Puntamekar, 2004; Tallent-Runnels, Thomas, Lan, Cooper, Ahern, Shaw, & Liu, 2006) where an asynchronous mode allows students "more time to think about their responses... (which) improved the depth and quality of responses" (Tallent-Runnels et al., 2006, p. 96).

BACKGROUND

The learning of science has been described as occurring through two metaphors: acquisition and participation (Scott, Asoko, & Leach, 2007; Sfard, 1998). The acquisition metaphor refers to knowledge as something that is gained over time. In this metaphor knowledge is seen as "stored or held somewhere" (Scott, Asoko, & Leach, 2007). The basic units of knowledge are concepts, which can be combined to form more complex cognitive structures. The focus is on the individual learner as constructing knowledge. Theories of science concept learning that utilize the acquisition metaphor include those within cognitive (conceptual change), sociocultural, and social constructivist perspectives.

Within the theory of conceptual change (Posner, Strike, Hewson, & Gerzog, 1982) an individual constructs their beliefs about the natural world, rather than being received. When examining how individuals learn science concepts through this lens, strong commonalities have been found in relation to how these individuals think about the natural world (Scott, Asoko, & Leach, 2007). However, it is also recognized that within conceptual change theory prior experiences and a person's existing ideas regarding a subject has a large influence on future learning in that subject (Ausubel, 1968).

In the move towards a more community oriented process of learning, Vygotsky (1978) provided a theoretical framework for learning concepts that includes a social aspect. Individuals are introduced to new ideas within a social situation first, and are then able to reflect on and make sense of these new ideas on an individual basis. Therefore there is a transition between the social and individual processes of learning new information. In terms of learning science concepts specifically, an individual needs to learn the "social language of the scientific community" (Scott, Asoko, & Leach, 2007). This language is introduced to the learner through an instructor or other individual who is knowledgeable about the scientific community. Thus, while the social context is not ignored in the acquisition of science concepts, the individual still plays a significant role in how the knowledge is constructed.

The participation metaphor provides a fundamentally different approach to knowledge where the learner is viewed as an active participant in the learning process, rather than individually accumulating knowledge. The learner is a member of a community, which includes the learner, instructor, and other learners. It is within this community that knowledge is constructed. Theories of science concept learning through this metaphor have largely followed that of situated cognition (e.g. Lave & Wenger, 1991). Within this perspective learning is seen as a process of enculturation. Individuals participate in socially organized practices, and it is within this participation that specialized skills are developed, either through apprenticeship in thinking (Rogoff, 1990) or through legitimate peripheral participation (Lave & Wenger, 1991). It is within the situated perspective that inquiry-based approaches to science teaching and learning developed (Roth, 1995). Roth (1995) has suggested that this can be accomplished through "authentic activities", whereby students can learn in context, experience uncertainties, engage in learning based on their prior knowledge, experience and participate in being part of a community of knowledge, practices, resources, discourse, and expertise.

The learning of science also requires individuals to "talk science" which was described by Lemke (1990). Often this is referred to as "scientific discourse". Through this approach students learn science as participants who communicate in the language of science and as members of the community who speak this language. Therefore, through this perspective the learning of science is a process whereby there is a development, through participation, of the practices of the scientific community. The learner becomes an apprentice under the expert participant, the teacher. The science concepts learned through this perspective involve aspect of actual practice and/or discourse.

Scientific Inquiry

Through these different frameworks for the learning of science concepts, science curricula have been developed around the idea of scientific inquiry. As mentioned in the introduction these reformed curricula have been in existence since the post-Sputnik era when the NSF funded science education endeavors for this reformation. However, since this time the term "inquiry" had become a phrase that encompasses many different aspects of science education (Anderson, 2007). When an attempt is made to define this term, there are many resources that can be drawn on, all with slightly different views of what "inquiry" in science instruction is.

Given that scientific inquiry is grounded in the previously discussed models for the learning of science concepts – situated cognition and constructivism – there are four elements about inquiry in the science classroom that are generally accepted (Anderson, 2007; NRC, 1996). These four elements as described by Anderson (2007) are:

1. Learning is an active process of individuals constructing meaning for themselves; significant understandings are not just received.
2. The meanings each individual constructs are dependent upon the prior conceptions this individual already has. In the process, these prior conceptions may be modified.
3. The understandings each individual develops are dependent upon the contexts in which these meanings are engaged. The more abundant and varied these contexts are, the richer are the understandings acquired.

4. Meanings are socially constructed; understanding is enriched by engagement of ideas in concert with other people. (Anderson, 2007, p. 809)

Given these four elements as necessary for inquiry in the science classroom it is clear that the environment for learning science is not limited to the face-to-face classroom, but can be other environments such as online or informal education environments.

In the teaching of science inquiry it is also generally accepted that students need to participate in activities that promote the active role of the student. Activities need to provide opportunities for students to: ask their own questions, design their own activities, interpret, explain, hypothesize, and share authority for answers. The work that students do need to emphasize reasoning, reading and writing for meaning, solving problems, build from existing cognitive structures, and explain complex problems (Anderson, 2007). How these characteristics of science inquiry look in practice in both the face-to-face and online classrooms has been discussed elsewhere by the authors (Baptiste, Neakrase, & Ryan, 2011).

Scientific Discourse

With the situated learning perspective as the basis for science inquiry, the learning of science has been successfully described as through a process of discourse. In order to fit into the "Science For All" emphasis, student access to science is best accomplished through "engagement in the social and symbolic words comprising the knowledge and practices of specialized communities" (Kelly, 2007). Science instruction therefore does not have to be done within a traditional classroom, and for it to really be a global discourse, may best be delivered in an online format.

Discourse can be defined to be the language in use within a discipline. Thus, in the science classroom the language in use would be that of the discipline of science. This can be in the form of text, signs, symbols, and physical objects (Gee, 2001). Discourse in science needs to include how language is used in social contexts, connected to social practices (Anderson, 2007; Gee, 1999). Gee (2001) also argued that science discourse needed to include "ways of being in the world…forms of life which integrate words, acts, values, beliefs, attitudes, and social identities as well as gestures, glances, body positions, and clothes" (p. 526).

Given the pedagogical necessity to include scientific discourse in the science classroom, it is important to include this in the online science classroom. However, given the interactive nature of this discourse between the students and the instructor there are areas that are easily approached in a traditional, face-to-face classroom that are not as easily approached in the online classroom. One of these areas involves feedback between students and instructors, as well as students with other students. Thus it is necessary to define feedback and its role within online science instruction.

FEEDBACK IN ONLINE SCIENCE INSTRUCTION

Online education has become a major point of discussion within recent years. Not only has there been a rise in discussion, but also a huge want and need for online courses at all grade levels. As a society we have become accustomed to the world being only a keystroke away. Online science education is not a new topic, however there are various outlets within online science education that have not been explored or discussed. For instance, reflective communication, or feedback within general online courses has often been researched, discussed, and implemented. However, there are various facets to reflective communication and/or feedback that should be explored and implemented in online classrooms. When science discourse is considered in the online science classroom this reflective communication is extremely important to define and consider. Feedback is a term that is widely used within many curricular, pedagogical, and academic circles. More importantly, there are various definitions of feedbacks, as well as various forms of implementation. Due to the fact that online courses, including science courses, require students, and instructors to focus on written feedback it is important to understand the various forms of feedback. Within the current section feedback will be looked at from various realms, including teacher to student feedback, student to teacher feedback, cooperative or collaborative feedback, as well as the role of the teacher in student group feedback.

Pedagogy and Theory

Online education possesses two notable pedagogical features that were inefficient in earlier generations of distance education. One is communication; the other one is cooperation. In terms of communication, teachers are able to now work together with the student or the whole class more efficiently comparatively when distance learning was mainly print, radio, and television. The communication between teacher and student has changed from one-way communication to two-way communication. The Internet makes communication between physically separated course participants more effective. In terms of cooperation, students have the opportunities to learn with the other students, to share ideas, and to create knowledge. At the earlier ages of distance education, there was only one source of learning materials. Now in online learning, students can easily extend their learning experience by linking to other resources. Learning then becomes more authentic and cooperative.

Despite the new teaching and learning experiences derived from these two pedagogical features, there are some challenges associated with them deserving the online instructors' attention. The ultimate challenge for all types of distance education including e-learning is the problem of "transactional distance." Moore defined transactional distance as "...a psychological space of potential misunderstandings between the behaviors of instructors and those of the learners..." (Moore & Kearsley, 1996, p. 200).

Another distance education theory that is related to interaction and collaboration is Holmberg's (1960) "Guided Didactic Conversation" theory. Since most of the online courses use text-based asynchronous communication methods, Holmberg's theory can be used as a guide to the design of online course content as well as text-based communication between teacher and learner online. He argued that if the students feel typical traits of conversation, learning will occur. According to his theory, there are two types of conversations: the real conversation and the simulated conversation. The real conversation is the communication reflected by correspondence, telephone, personal contact, and so forth. Simulated conversation is achieved by internalized conversation in a text and the conversational style of course authors. More precise details of this theory are presented in his later publications (Holmberg, 1986, 1995). Holmberg (1986) believed that the feeling of a personal relationship between teacher and learner is the most influential factor in distance education. The atmosphere, language, and friendly conversation favor feelings of a personal relationship that is important for learning motivation. Holmberg (1986) stated his theory relates "teaching effectiveness to the impact of feelings of belonging and cooperation as well as to the actual exchange of questions, answers and arguments in mediated communication" (p. 123).

In web-based courses, if students are only allowed to passively learn from the materials posted on the web site, didactic conversation between teacher and learner is impossible. As a result, "real learning," as Holmberg called it, will not occur. The central idea in his teaching theory is that learning pleasure will be promoted if personal relations, study pleasure, and empathy exist between students and teachers. Because of the personal learning atmosphere, language, and conversation, students will be able to learn to make decisions, construct meaning, and solve problems. Since currently most communication in online courses is text-based, Holmberg's (1986) guided didactic conversation fits well with such an online learning environment.

Teacher Verbal Immediacy

Teacher verbal immediacy refers to teachers' verbal communication behaviors that reduce psychological distance in the interaction between teacher and student. Immediacy is defined as "communication behaviors that reduce social and psychological distance between people" in the field of interpersonal communication (Mehrabian, 1971). Andersen (1979) was the first scholar to connect the construct of immediacy with instructional communication. Immediacy behaviors are often divided into two categories: verbal (e.g., using humor, personal example, "our" instead of "my") and nonverbal immediacy (e.g., eye contact, smiling, positive head nods). Both teacher nonverbal and verbal immediacy have shown to have a positive influence on students' affective (Baker, 2004; Gorham & Christophel, 1990; Pogue & Ahyun, 2006; Sanders & Wiseman, 1990) and cognitive learning (Allen, Witt, & Wheeless, 2006; Baker, 2004; Christophel, 1990; Sanders & Wiseman, 1990). However, the relationship between teacher immediacy and cognitive learning is less clear than with affective learning, especially in the online learning environment. In the online learning environment, verbal immediacy may be more relevant as most of the online communication is through text, such as, email and threaded discussion. However, it is only in recent years that the construct of immediacy has been studied in the field of online learning. When considering teacher verbal immediacy within a science classroom, especially and online science classroom, another layer is added. When students are being asked to conduct hands-on activities and/or experiments in an environment at a distance from the instructor how quickly the instructor can respond and provide feedback is very important. In some cases it is an issue of safety, depending on the experiment the student is being asked to perform. At other times it can be due to the student being a novice in the area and not having the proper skills to complete the activity, such as with a simulation program on the computer.

The Nature of Online Feedback and Communication

According to Ober (2005), "tone in writing refers to the writer's attitude toward the reader and the subject of the message. The overall tone of a written message affects the reader just as one's tone of voice affects the listener in everyday exchanges" (p. 88). In "Setting the Tone" (n.d.), Stone states, "just as the pitch and volume of one's voice carries attitude and tone at parties and meetings, the choice of words and the way we put our sentences together convey a sense of attitude and tone in our writing" (paragraph, 2). Stone (n.d.) further states "tone is attitude, whether you want to be subtle or bold, tone is conveyed through word choice, sentence structure and even font" (paragraph, 4). Writing that is complex, ambiguous, and/or indirect may lead to misinterpretation of the intended message. Selecting all caps or bold may be interpreted as shouting, screaming, or aggression. Changes in font size, style, or color may create confusion or misinterpretation since the receiver may not understand the meaning or intention behind the changes.

In online science education, written communication is a primary form of communication between the institution and students, as well as faculty and the students. Consequently, it is important for administrators and faculty to be aware of "tone" in writing so the message being sent is not misinterpreted or lost in translation. This is especially pertinent in the online science classroom where many times students have a fear of learning science or performing the mathematics necessary to complete the science activity. If the tone of the feedback and communication is not "just right" it may cause the student undue stress, thus impeding and sometimes regressing the learning of the science concepts.

Feedback as Part of Reflective Communication and Cooperative Feedback

Feedback therefore is a key element in all forms of online learning. Because students have a desire to know, understand, and grow from coursework, it is ultimately the teacher's responsibility to acknowledge the student's work. Through feedback, students have the ability to better their sense of understanding, and gauge their progress in the course. Without adequate feedback from the instructor, students are not capable of understanding what they are doing incorrectly, or correctly. The idea of merely giving a student their grade, and not commenting on their assignment is unheard of in an online forum. Reflective communication is the basis, or tool to success in an online course. A reflective mind is one that takes a reasoned thinking process seriously, and is the trademark of critical thinking (Schroyens, 2005). Studies regarding student teachers have suggested that self-awareness and mindfulness contribute to nurturing reflective practices (Collier, 1999; Tillema, 2000; Titone et al., 1998) and that "providing feedback" is an effective method of increasing self-awareness and mindful learning (Titone et al., 1998). Similarly, Steele (2001) noted that by interacting with others, learners can reflect and exchange ideas, which contributes to mindful learning. Cooperative instructional designs, within online education, increases "peer feedback" and "teacher feedback" simultaneously. While peer feedback is mainly provided through online discussions, group work, and lab work teacher feedback is provided through grades, exams, and other online interactions.

When student have a sense of self-awareness, as well as a sense of belonging to a group they are more likely to become involved in cooperative feedback. Due to the fact that within online course students remain, for the most part, anonymous, they are "allowed" to speak their mind, offer opinions, and begin to explore their identity. This aspect of online education can be extremely valuable to an individual. More importantly, by working with a group, sharing information, giving and receiving feedback, students are able to express who they are without prejudice. Granted it is important to note that there are some boundaries in an online forum, students cannot make outrageous claims and not receive backlash, but students can begin to understand the difference between opinion based information and fact based information. With feedback from group members, the instructor, and students are more likely to achieve higher scores on coursework, begin to explore various sources of research, and appreciate the true value of feedback (Etzioni, & Etzioni, 1998). An example of this comes from a current course one of the authors is teaching. The students in this course must complete an online science module, where the students first complete individual work and post their findings/discussion on a discussion board. When this process is complete the group members critique the individual's work, as well as begin to answer questions that were posed by the individual. The group members then receive feedback from all of their colleagues, and the process continues until the entire module is complete. When students were asked to discuss their feelings on feedback from their group members, many stated that they felt more at ease with the assignment, and the process of the science module. This in turn shows that by including cooperative feedback in an online course may allow students to feel more at ease with the course work, as well as their colleagues.

Within cooperative feedback group members must establish rules or norms around what is and is not appropriate. For instance, "yelling, screaming, or fighting for the sake of fighting should not be tolerated" because, within online learning students are anonymous, they may feel that there may be no consequences for bad behavior (Etzioni, & Etzioni, 1998, p. 242). Once rules are in place students have will feel more capable, willing, and invested in sharing ideas, thoughts, and opinions with one another. Wen and Tsai (2008) state that feedback from student to student can often be more valuable than instructor feedback for many reasons. Because students are invested in learning, sharing ideas, and working towards a common goal, students may form feedback in a more valuable format. Also, because students share a common sense of being (i.e. going to school, working on course work, and are focused on achieving a high grade in the class), students frame their feedback in a way that is of most value (Wen, & Tsai, 2008). Feedback, at times, can become daunting, and impersonal, however when students become invested in a shared goal the feedback presented is often framed around the task at hand. More importantly, students share a common language, and use current phases that have meaning for their group.

The role of the instructor, when looking at cooperative feedback, is important. However, the instructor must be careful to not intrude on the current communication by becoming too involved in the feedback loop. Cooperative feedback entails many different aspects of group dynamics, and outsiders, in this case an instructor, may hinder the process (Edge, 2006). When an outsiders attempts to breakdown or understand the group dynamics, and intrudes in the feedback loop of the group, group communication may come to an end. Within online learning these dynamics become more difficult to breakdown. Due to the fact that much of the feedback may be done within emails, or personal online communication, the outsider may become lost when attempting to understand the groups' work. Therefore, the instructor must remain as an outsider, however the instructor must also be a director and gatekeeper for the course. Working with the group, observing various rounds of feedback, and acknowledge the group dynamics will ultimately allow the students, and group, to become comfortable (Edge, 2006). On the other hand the instructor must be aware of any issues with feedback, or problems groups may experience. The instructor should make it known that all group must report back at various times in the course, have requirements for group feedback, and encourage groups or individuals to discuss any issues that may arise (Paulus, & Phipps, 2008).

ISSUES IN ONLINE SCIENCE DELIVERY

While state-of-the-art online science instructional models have and are being developed using research-based inquiry principles, impediments impacted by human forces prevent these models from full implementation as intended by the developers. When one thinks about how "science for all" can be enacted in the online science classroom the realization is made that there are barriers that might affect the learning experience. Moreover, these barriers will affect the reflective practice that instructors might be promoting within the course, or students might be enacting within themselves through the learning process.

Influences Obstructing Online Science

It is generally accepted that face-to-face or online classroom environments, as sites of social interaction, are susceptible to discriminatory and racial bias in materials and pedagogical strategies. Along with that are the concerns related to other cultural artifacts as related to the teaching of science. For example, some students, because of economics, do not have access to computers and other digital resources that would give them fair access to the online materials that are being delivered by the instructor. To further compound that, institutional resources are not provided at some of the schools and community sites (e.g., libraries, churches, etc.); these sites are not fully equipped as one will find in more economically advantaged communities. Not only is limited access an issue, up-to-date infrastructure necessary for wideband communication may be lacking in such communities, such as adequate capacity in modems and routers (Norris, 2001). Furthermore, too often the structural infrastructure does not support the budget for continuous maintenance of hardware updates for the instructional models currently in place. For example, some communities will receive grants to install hardware, which at that time are up-to-date and sufficient, but the community does not also receive monies to support the software maintenance that is necessary for best utilization of the hardware that has been made available. Newly developed software may demand compatible hardware to run such software. Consequently, full advantage of the digital age is not available to these groups. This lack of institutional support leads to certain cultural groups at an extreme disadvantage for online education in the teaching of science (Baptiste, 1999).

Similarly, the Internet, much like any other medium of public media, may function in a socially, culturally, or politically biased manner (Agre, 1998). Not only can biased digitized material sustain for an indeterminate length of time, other issues arise as noted in Larreamendy-Joerns and Leinhardt's (2006) overview of online education research:

Issues of audience location, instructional autonomy, audience specificity, and formality are important because they shape the assumptions that designers make about the students' prior knowledge and learning goals, and they determine the depth and breadth of instructional explanations as well as the types of scaffolding provided. (p. 583)

With the rapid advancement of technology, online instructional models are proliferating at the same pace, which has potential for generating varying degrees of quality and exacerbating the issues. Furthermore, the issue of physical access is further complicated by the extent to which learners are proficient in the dominant language of science and is intensified by the dearth of research in this particular domain. This poses many questions for educators: To what extent do online instructional designers consider learners' cultural and linguistic backgrounds? If and how is knowledge privileged? What prior knowledge is assumed for engagement in scaffolding? To what extent are learners from underprivileged and diverse backgrounds at a disadvantage?

Teachers and Online Instruction

Where adequate technology and digital tools are available, pedagogical issues further complicate their use. Becker (2000) found that technology use in low-income schools tended to be drill and repetitive activities. This finding is congruent to what multicultural scholars claim occurs with traditional classroom approaches in low-income and impoverished communities (Sleeter, 2005). This is further exacerbated by the tendency for teachers to be authoritative and controlling where the teacher is a knowledge giver and the student is the consumer of such knowledge (Apple, 1979; Freire, 1998). To corroborate this notion, Hamilton, Dahlgren, Hult, Roos, and Söderström (2004) touch on a potential use of technology as a tool for knowledge delivery rather than a communication system for generating learners' knowledge in a sociocultural context, a valued tenet of education in their home country of Sweden where education is "attention to learning 'in the making,' through 'engagement in social practice' (p. 850).

While online instructional models have potential for increasing learning and self-management, Webb (2005) noted that teachers are critical to the process and need to develop their pedagogical skill in facilitating technology use in the classroom. Likewise Wallace, Kupperman, Krajcik, and

Soloway (2000) found that students in an online science environment tended toward focusing on delivering a product rather than engaging in a process of investigation. This notion was corroborated by Rogers (2010) who claimed that the teacher's role in technology environments was to facilitate student autonomy and more investigative thinking, discussion, and interpretation of results, rather than focusing on a product. These studies recommend teachers learning pedagogies of engagement in online environments to facilitate and guide students in order to maximize the effect of technology use on students' conceptual understanding and communication skills. Yet in their overview of computer technologies in the classroom, Sutherland et al. (2004) remind us of the issues in teachers' understanding of teaching and learning:

There is an extensive research base on teaching and learning 'without technology' which could inform teaching and learning 'with technology' (Donovan & Bransford, 2005; Greeno, Collins, & Resnick, 1996). Such research has not systematically been drawn upon by policy makers when developing curriculum and guidelines for teachers on how to use technology in the classroom. There is a tendency to think that technology is so 'new' that its use will be accompanied by 'new' pedagogies that will somehow transform teaching and learning. This utopian vision often leads policy makers and practitioners to ignore theoretical perspectives about teaching and learning, which in our view are central to all learning with or without technological tools. (p. 413)

As such, teachers are a critical element for online instructional models to be effective; they should and must examine their belief systems and dispositions regarding teaching and learning in every social stratum and context. Only then can we authentically realize "Science for All" in a future world with technology in every classroom.

FUTURE RESEARCH DIRECTIONS

Science for All is a vision of numerous stakeholders throughout the world in creating a scientifically literate populace. As cited in this chapter, too often underprivileged communities do not have adequate access to online instructional models and exemplary and pedagogically skilled teachers who understand how to effectively structure communication among and between students and teachers. The authors of this chapter recommend that researchers further investigate those societal obstacles that continue to lead to these inequities among various cultural groups.

It is also clear that more research needs to focus in the context of science online instruction in terms of the amount and quality of reflective communication that is presented and offered to students. Given the different types of pedagogical models used by online science instructors it is imperative that researchers explore the level of communicative practice and feedback present in these courses. Since research in this area is still in the beginning stages, much of the research is found in varying disciplines outside of science education, such as education technologies and distance education. A comprehensive study of what kind of communication is present in online science courses would be beneficial to the community at large.

CONCLUSION

If students are not given the opportunity to reflect on their own learning and how the communication is progressing in the online environment it is clear that the discourse and constructivism models for learning science concepts are compromised. With science inquiry being taught within a community of learners, learning becomes a situated social endeavor. Communication in general, and feedback in particular, are essential components to good reflective practice in an online environment. Without these components it is difficult to know whether students have adequately learned the material.

It is also clear that this communication component is an important aspect of science literacy. If students do not learn the science material and are not given the opportunity to build a foundation for communication and feedback, then students will have a difficult time demonstrating the scientific literacy necessary for participation in today's society. A lack of quantity or quality of communication also contributes to the barriers that prevent all individuals from accessing science in a meaningful way. One then needs to ask whether "Science for All" is really being promoted and in what way.

REFERENCES

AAAS, American Association for the Advancement of Science. (2008). *Project 2061* (Electronic Version). Retrieved from http://www.project2061.org/

Agre, P. (1998). The Internet and public discourse. *First Monday, 3*(3). Retrieved September 17, 2010, from http://firstmonday.org/ htbin/ cgiwrap/ bin/ ojs/ index.php/ fm/ article/ view/ 581/ 502

Allen, M., Witt, P. L., & Wheeless, L. P. (2006). The role of teacher immediacy as a motivational factor in student learning: Using meta-analysis to test a causal model. *Communication Education, 55*(1), 21–31. doi:10.1080/03634520500343368

Andersen, J. F. (1979). Teacher immediacy as a predictor of teaching effectiveness. In Himmo, D. (Ed.), *Communication yearbook 3* (pp. 543–559). New Brunswick, NJ: Transaction Books.

Anderson, R. D. (2007). Inquiry as an organizing theme. In Abell, S. K., & Lederman, N. G. (Eds.), *Handbook of research on science education* (pp. 807–830). Mahwah, NJ: Lawrence Earlbaum Associates, Inc.

Apple, M. (1979). *Ideology and curriculum*. London, UK & Boston, MA: Routledge & K. Paul. doi:10.4324/9780203241219

Ausubel, D. P. (1986). *Educational psychology: A cognitive view*. New York, NY: Holt, Rinehart, & Winston.

Baker, J. D. (2004). An investigation of relationships among instructor immediacy and affective and cognitive learning in the online classroom. *The Internet and Higher Education, 7*(1), 1–13. doi:10.1016/j.iheduc.2003.11.006

Baptiste, H. P. (1999). Science educators in the next millennium: Needed a new paradigm for the Y2K of science, mathematics, and technology. *Proceedings of the 40th Annual Conference of Science Teachers Association of Nigeria: Evaluating Science, Technology, & Mathematics Education*. Nigeria: Heinemann Educational Books.

Baptiste, H. P., Neakrase, J. J., & Ryan, A. N. (2011). Relevant issues that challenge the designing of transformative, liberating online science courses. In Kurubacak, G., & Volkan Yuzer, T. (Eds.), *Handbook of research on transformative online education and liberation: Models for social equality*. Hershey, PA: IGI Global Publishing.

Becker, H. J. (2000). Who's wired and who's not: Children's access to technology and use of computer technology. *Children and Computer Technology, 10*(2), 44–75.

Brooks, J. G., & Brooks, M. G. (1993). *In search of understanding: The case for constructivist classrooms*. Alexandria, VA: Association for Supervision and Curriculum Development.

Christophel, D. M. (1990). The relationship among teacher immediacy, student motivation, and learning. *Communication Education, 39*, 323–340. doi:10.1080/03634529009378813

Collier, S. T. (1999). Characteristics of reflective thought during student teaching experience. *Journal of Teacher Education*, *50*(3), 173–181. doi:10.1177/002248719905000303

Donovan, S., & Bransford, J. D. (2005). *How students learn: History, mathematics, and science in the classroom*. Washington, DC: National Academies Press.

Edge, J. (2006). Computer-mediated cooperative development: Non-judgmental discourse in online environments. *Language Teaching Research*, *10*, 205–227. doi:10.1191/1362168806lr192oa

Etzioni, A., & Etzioni, O. (1998). Face-to-face and computer-mediated communities: A comparative analysis. *The Information Society*, *15*, 241–248. doi:10.1080/019722499128402

Fosnot, C. T., & Perry, R. S. (2005). Constructivism: A psychological theory of learning. In Fosnot, C. T. (Ed.), *Constructivism: Theory, perspectives, and practice* (pp. 8–38). New York, NY: Teachers College Press.

Freire, P. (1998). *Pedagogy of freedom: Ethics, democracy, and civic courage*. Lanham, MD: Rowman & Littlefield Publishers, Inc.

Gee, J. P. (1999). *An introduction to discourse analysis: Theory and method*. New York, NY: Routledge.

Gee, J. P. (2001). Literacy, discourse, and linguistics: Introduction and what is literacy? In Cushman, E., Kintgen, E. R., Kroll, B. M., & Rose, M. (Eds.), *Literacy: A critical sourcebook* (pp. 525–544). Boston, MA: Bedford/St. Martins.

Goldstein, J., & Puntambekar, S. (2004). The brink of change: Gender in technology-rich collaborative learning environments. *Journal of Science Education and Technology*, *13*(4), 505–552. doi:10.1007/s10956-004-1471-1

Gorham, J., & Christophel, D. M. (1990). The relationship of teachers' use of humor in the classroom to immediacy and student learning. *Communication Education*, *39*, 46–62. doi:10.1080/03634529009378786

Greeno, J. G., Collins, A. M., & Resnick, L. B. (1996). *Cognition and learning*. New York, NY: Macmillan.

Hamilton, D., Dahlgren, E., Hult, A., Roos, B., & Söderström, T. (2004). When performance is the product: Problems in the analysis of online distance education. *British Educational Research Journal*, *30*(6), 841-8754. DOI: 1080119204200027953O

Hoadley, C. M. (2002). Teaching science through online, peer discussions: SpeakEasy in the knowledge integration environment. *International Journal of Science Education*, *22*(8), 839–857. doi:10.1080/095006900412301

Holmberg, B. (1960). *On the methods of teaching by correspondence*. Lund, Sweden: Gleerup.

Holmberg, B. (1986). *Growth and structure of distance education*. London, UK: Croom Helm.

Holmberg, B. (1995). *Theory and practice of distance education* (2nd ed.). New York, NY: Routledge.

Huffman, J. L., Wu, H.-K., Krajcik, J. S., & Soloway, E. (2003). The nature of middle school learners' science content understandings in the use of on-line resources. *Journal of Research in Science Teaching*, *40*(3), 323–346. doi:10.1002/tea.10079

Kelly, G. J. (2007). Discourse in science classrooms. In Abell, S. K., & Lederman, N. G. (Eds.), *Handbook of research on science education* (pp. 443–469). Mahwah, NJ: Lawrence Earlbaum Associates, Inc.

Klentschy, M., & Molina-De La Torre, E. (2004). Students' science notebooks and the inquiry process. In Saul, E. W. (Ed.), *Crossing borders in literacy and science instruction: Perspectives on theory and practice*. Arlington, VA: NSTA Press.

Larreamendy-Joerns, J., & Leinhardt, G. (2006). Going the distance with online education. *Review of Educational Research, 76*(4), 567–605. doi:10.3102/00346543076004567

Lave, J., & Wegner, E. (1991). *Situated learning: Legitimate peripheral participation*. New York, NY: Cambridge University Press.

Linn, M. C., Clark, D., & Slotta, J. D. (2003). WISE design for knowledge generation. *Science Education, 87*, 517–538. doi:10.1002/sce.10086

Mehrabian, A. (1971). *Silent messages*. Belmont, CA: Wadsworth Publishing.

Miller, L., Moreno, J., Willcockson, I., Smith, D., & Mayes, J. (2006). An online, interactive approach to teaching neuroscience to adolescents. *Life Sciences Education, 5*, 137–143.

Moore, M. G. (1973). Toward a theory of independent learning and teaching. *The Journal of Higher Education, 44*, 661–679. doi:10.2307/1980599

Moore, M. G. (1989). Three types of interaction. *American Journal of Distance Education, 3*(2), 1–6. doi:10.1080/08923648909526659

Moore, M. G., & Kearsley, G. (1996). *Distance education: A system view*. Belmont, CA: Wadsworth Publishing.

National Academies Press. (2010). *National science education standards*. Accessed September 16, 2010, from http://www.nap.edu/ openbook.php? record_id=4962

National Science Resources Center. (1997). *Science for all children: A guide to improving elementary science education in your school district*. Washington, DC: National Sciences Resource Center, Smithsonian Institution.

National Science Teachers Association. (2009). *National science education standards*. Retrieved from http://www.nsta.org/ publications/ nses.aspx

Paulua, T. M., & Phipps, G. (2008). Approaches to case analyses in synchronous and asynchronous environments. *Journal of Computer-Mediated Communication, 13*, 459–484. doi:10.1111/j.1083-6101.2008.00405.x

Pogue, L., & Ahyun, K. (2006). The effect of teacher nonverbal immediacy and credibility on student motivation and affective learning. *Communication Education, 55*(3), 331–344. doi:10.1080/03634520600748623

Posner, G. J., Strike, K. A., Hewson, P. W., & Gerzog, W. A. (1982). Accommodation of a scientific conception: Toward a theory of conceptual change. *Science Education, 66*, 211–227. doi:10.1002/sce.3730660207

Rogers, L. (2010). *Does ICT in science really work in the classroom?* GIREP Seminar-Udine 2003. Retrieved from http://10.1.1.111.4688.pdf

Rogoff, B. (1990). *Apprenticeship in thinking: Cognitive development in social context*. Oxford, England: Oxford University Press.

Roth, W.-M. (1995). Teacher questioning in an open-inquiry learning environment: Interactions of context, content and student responses. *Journal of Research in Science Teaching, 33*, 709–736. doi:10.1002/(SICI)1098-2736(199609)33:7<709::AID-TEA2>3.0.CO;2-R

Sanders, J. A., & Wiseman, R. L. (1990). The effects of verbal and nonverbal teacher immediacy on perceived cognitive, affective and behavioral learning in the multicultural classroom. *Communication Education, 39*, 341–353. doi:10.1080/03634529009378814

Schroyens, W. (2005). Knowledge and thought: An introduction to critical thinking. *Experimental Psychology, 52*(2), 163–164. doi:10.1027/1618-3169.52.2.163

Scott, P., Asoko, H., & Leach, J. (2007). Student conceptions and conceptual learning. In Abell, S. K., & Lederman, N. G. (Eds.), *Handbook of research on science education* (pp. 31–56). Mahwah, NJ: Lawrence Earlbaum Associates, Inc.

Sfard, A. (1998). On two metaphors for learning and the dangers of choosing just one. *Educational Researcher, 27*, 4–13. doi:10.3102/0013189X027002004

Simons, K., & Clark, D. (2005). Supporting inquiry in science classrooms with the Web. *Computers in the Schools, 21*(3-4), 23–36. doi:10.1300/J025v21n03_04

Sleeter, C. E. (2005). *Un-standardizing curriculum: Multicultural teaching in the standards-based classroom*. New York, NY: Teachers College Press.

Songer, N. B., Lee, H.-S., & Kam, R. (2002). Technology-rich inquiry science in urban classrooms: What are the barriers to inquiry pedagogy? *Journal of Research in Science Teaching, 39*(2), 128–150. doi:10.1002/tea.10013

Steele, D. F. (2001). Using sociocultural theory to teach mathematics: A Vygotskian perspective. *School Science and Mathematics, 101*(8), 404–415. doi:10.1111/j.1949-8594.2001.tb17876.x

Stone, T. (n.d.). *Top Ten Reviews^{TM}*. Retrieved from http://writing-enhancement- software-review.toptenreviews.com/ setting-the-tone.html

Sutherland, R., Armstrong, V., Barnes, S., Brawn, R., Breeze, N., & Gall, M. (2004). Transforming teaching and learning: Embedding ICT into everyday classroom practices. *Journal of Computer Assisted Learning, 20*, 413–425. doi:10.1111/j.1365-2729.2004.00104.x

Tallent-Runnels, M. K., Thomas, J. A., Lan, W. Y., Cooper, S., Ahern, T. C., Shaw, S. M., & Liu, X. (2006). Teaching courses online: A review of the research. *Review of Educational Research, 76*(1), 93–135. doi:10.3102/00346543076001093

Tillema, H. H. (2000). Belief change towards self-directed learning in student teachers: Immersion in practice or reflection on action. *Teaching and Teacher Education, 16*(5–6), 575–591. doi:10.1016/S0742-051X(00)00016-0

Titone, C., Sherman, S., & Palmer, R. (1998). Cultivating student teachers' dispositions and ability to construct knowledge. *Action in Teacher Education, 19*(4), 76–87.

Vygotsky, L. S. (Ed.). (1978). *Mind in society: The development of higher psychological processes*. Cambridge, MA: Harvard University Press.

Wallace, R., Kupperman, J., Krajcik, J., & Soloway, E. (2000). Science on the Web: Students online in a sixth-grade classroom. *Journal of the Learning Sciences, 9*(1), 75–104. doi:10.1207/s15327809jls0901_5

Webb, M. (2005). Affordances of ICT in science learning: Implications for an integrated pedagogy. *International Journal of Science Education, 27*(6), 705–735..doi:10.1080/09500690500038520

Wen, M. L., & Tsai, C. C. (2008). Online peer assessment in an inservice science and mathematics teacher education course. *Teaching in Higher Education, 13*, 55–67. doi:10.1080/13562510701794050

Williams, M., Linn, M. C., Ammon, P., & Gearhart, M. (2004). Learning to teach inquiry science in a technology-based environment: A case study. *Journal of Science Education and Technology, 13*(2), 189–206. doi:10.1023/B:JOST.0000031258.17257.48

ADDITIONAL READING

Aborisade, P. (2009). Investigating a Nigerian xxl-cohort wiki-learning experience: Observation, feedback, and reflection. *Electronic Journal of e-Learning, 7,* 191-202.

Aikenhead, G. S. (1996). Science education: Border crossing into the subculture of science. *Studies in Science Education*, *27*, 1–52. doi:10.1080/03057269608560077

Annetta, L. A., & Shymansky, J. A. (2006). Investigating science learning for rural elementary school teachers in a professional-development project through three distance-education strategies. *Journal of Research in Science Teaching*, *43*, 1019–1039. doi:10.1002/tea.20106

Bell, P. (2000). Scientific arguments as learning artifacts: designing for learning from the web with KIE. *International Journal of Science Education*, *22*, 797–817. doi:10.1080/095006900412284

Brem, S. K., & Rips, L. J. (2000). Explanation and evidence in informal argument. *Cognitive Science*, *24*, 573–604. doi:10.1207/s15516709cog2404_2

Brown, B. A. (2004). Discursive identity: Assimilation into the culture of science and its implications for minority students. *Journal of Research in Science Teaching*, *41*, 810–834. doi:10.1002/tea.20228

Brown, J. S., Collins, A., & Duguid, P. (1989). Situated cognition and the culture of learning. *Educational Researcher*, *18*(1), 32–42.

Bruner, J. S. (1960). *The process of education*. Cambridge, MA: Harvard University Press.

Campbell, K., & Ellingson, D. A. (2010). Cooperative learning at a distance: An experiment with wikis. *American Journal of Business Education*, *3*, 83–89.

Celani, M. A. A., & Collins, H. (2005). Critical thinking in reflective sessions and in online interactions. *AILA Review*, *18*, 41–57. doi:10.1075/aila.18.05cel

Chittleborough, G. D., Mocerino, M., & Treagust, D. F. (2007). Achieving greater feedback and flexibility using online pre-laboratory exercises with non-major chemistry students. *Journal of Chemical Education*, *84*, 884–888. doi:10.1021/ed084p884

Fosnot, C. T., & Perry, R. S. (2005). Constructivism: A psychological theory of learning. In Fosnot, C. T. (Ed.), *Constructivism: Theory, perspectives, and practice* (2nd ed., pp. 8–38). New York: Teachers College Press.

Frederiksen, J. R., White, B. Y., & Gutwill, J. (1999). Dynamic mental models in learning science: The importance of constructing derivational linkages among models. *Journal of Research in Science Teaching*, *36*, 806–836. doi:10.1002/(SICI)1098-2736(199909)36:7<806::AID-TEA5>3.0.CO;2-2

Gaytan, J., & McEwen, B. C. (2007). Effective online instructional and assessment strategies. *American Journal of Distance Education*, *21*, 117–132. doi:10.1080/08923640701341653

Hand, B., Hohenshell, L., & Prain, V. (2004). Exploring students' responses to conceptual questions when engaged with planned writing experiences: A study with Year 10 science students. *Journal of Research in Science Teaching*, *41*, 186–210. doi:10.1002/tea.10128

Kittleson, J. M., & Southerland, S. A. (2004). The role of discourse in group knowledge construction. *Journal of Research in Science Teaching*, *41*, 267–293. doi:10.1002/tea.20003

Lopez, R. E., & Tuomi, J. (1995). Student-centered inquiry. *Educational Leadership*, *52*(8), 78–79.

Marcus, S. (2005). Does online participation matter? A case study of a hybrid theatre arts course. *Campus-Wide Information Systems*, *22*, 77–87. doi:10.1108/10650740510587092

Moscovici, H., & Nelson, T. H. (1998). Shifting from activitymania to inquiry. *Science and Children*, *35*(4), 14–17.

Post, G. V. (2005). An expert system helps students learn database design. *Decision Sciences Journal of Innovative Education*, *3*, 273–293. doi:10.1111/j.1540-4609.2005.00070.x

Schön, D. A. (1983). *The reflective practitioner: How professionals think in action*. New York: Basic Books, Inc.

Sherman, G., Byer, A., & Rapp, S. (2009). Evaluation of online, on-demand science professional development material involving two different implementation models. *Journal of Science Education and Technology*, *17*, 19–31. doi:10.1007/s10956-007-9075-1

Vess, D. L. (2005). Asynchronous discussion and communication patterns in online and hybrid history courses. *Communication Education*, *54*, 355–364. doi:10.1080/03634520500442210

KEY TERMS AND DEFINITIONS

Cooperative Feedback: A process in which a group discusses/communicates their opinions, feelings, or arguments about a piece of work. Following this process an individual within the group uses the information communicated to improve upon their work. The process is infinite.

Face-to-Face: Traditional classrooms where teachers and students occupy the same physical space.

Feedback: the process in which an individual, or group, communicates feelings, opinions, or information about a piece or work. A discussion between an author, and another individual, critiquing a piece of work, resulting in various outcomes. The process can take a few moments or may be done over the course of a few years this process is infinite.

Inquiry Instruction: Instruction where the teacher guides and facilitates students in investigating science phenomena to make sense of, and derive meaning from, such phenomena.

Online Instructional Unit: Integrated and comprehensive online unit providing students with guidance and direction for successful completion.

Science for All: Publications by the National Science Resources Center (NSRC) and Project 2061 of the American Association for the Advancement of Science (AAAS) advocating science literacy for all students in the 21st century. Generally refers to science as being accessible to all individuals regardless of culture, gender, age, socioeconomic status, or other factors.

Science Literacy: The ability of individuals to use scientific reasoning in making decisions for personal and societal benefit.

Traditional/Authentic Approach: Traditional approach is teacher-centered with the teacher delivering knowledge for students to consume; authentic approach is one informed by inquiry instruction where children are self-regulated and autonomous learners rather than consumers of knowledge.

Chapter 7
Multimodal Communication:
A Case Study of Organizational Discourse and One-to-One Mentoring at an Online University

Melanie Shaw
Northcentral University, USA

Susan Stillman
Northcentral University, USA

Gayle Cicero
Northcentral University, USA

David Cross
Embry-Riddle Aeronautical University, USA

Dennis Lessard
Northcentral University, USA

ABSTRACT

This chapter includes information about communication patterns and organizational discourse at an online university, which utilizes a mentoring model to educate students. The mentoring approach involves the assignment of individual students to work one-to-one with a faculty mentor for each course of the degree or certificate program in which the student is enrolled. To address the types of communication inherent in this virtual education model, a mentor, a doctoral dissertation committee member, and a student shed light on their experiences of communication at the university. These diverse prospectives serve as a meta-communication model that can be implemented to enhance the effectivness of discourse at other institutions—particularly those seeking to implement a one-to-one mentoring approach.

DOI: 10.4018/978-1-61350-071-2.ch007

INTRODUCTION

Communication is a process that involves encoding, message transmittal, decoding based on knowledge, experience, values, and prior observations to decipher meaning, and feedback (Green, 2005, p. 87). In order to effectively communicate, educators must develop an understanding of communication within organizations. Communication is often represented symbolically because of the complexity involved in adequately addressing all components of message decoding (Razik & Swanson, 2001).

Within any single organization, there are many forms of communication that occur on a daily basis from e-mail correspondence, to face to face meetings, to nonverbal nuances. For this study, the authors collected personal examples of communication in an entirely online university to build a broader understanding of the meta-communicative patterns existing within the organization. The collective experiences of contributing authors acted as a meta-communicative framework from which to understanding organizational discourse. Each contributor wrote from his or her own perspective to share experiences of communicating in the online environment. In this institution, one-to-one mentoring is the method of instruction. Instead of enrolling in a cohort, each student is assigned a faculty mentor who facilitates learning with the course. If the student is enrolled in the doctoral program, in addition to course mentors, he or she will be assigned a dissertation committee with a chair and two committee members. All communication is through the Internet or through the telephone.

Communication in the Literature

A literature review on the topic of communication helped identify a broad spectrum of research. From the information obtained, five common themes were identified pertinent to communication in educational organizations:

1. Communication is enhanced when educators demonstrate an active interest in the students. When educators display behaviors such as demonstrating interest and responding to questions, students held positive perceptions of teacher power (Turman & Schrodt, 2006).
2. Non-verbal communication is an important tool for student motivation and learning - Effective educators demonstrate strong verbal and nonverbal communication skills (Pogue & Ahyun, 2006).
3. Communication is enhanced through collaboration- Trusting and respectful relationships develop between students, parents, and teachers when educators capitalize on communication through collaboration. Collaborative learning experiences strengthen the learning process (Gonsoulin, Ward, & Figg, 2006). Collaboration is essential to school success as it encourages communication among stakeholders (Zygmunt-Fillwalk, 2006).
4. Technology is an effective communication tool - Computer based communication increases interaction (Hirvela, 2006).
5. Communication is enhanced through peer review – Reiber (2006) noted that communication improves with the use of peer review in the school setting (p. 322). Peer review promotes discussion and evaluation within groups.
6. Meta-communication is a complex process whereby communication is multi-leveled and highly interactive. Messages are sent, received, controlled, and interpreted in hierarchical ways (Bateson, 1951).

Models of Communication

Hersey, Blanchard, and Johnson (2006) examined three communication models to highlight effective communication methods:

- The Linear Model – communication can be shown as a one-sided activity traced from the leader to the follower. First, messages are encoded, then thoughts are interpreted as symbols, and finally the message is transmitted via verbal, nonverbal, and paralanguage cues to the recipient.
- The Interactional Model – Unlike the linear model which does not analyze the role of the follower, but represents a one-way communication method in which back and forth communication is largely overlooked, this model considers the follower's point of reference. After a message is received, the message is decoded to form meaning. The follower can give feedback and a message in return.
- The Transactional Model – This is the only model that accounts for the continual process of communication that involves messages, symbols, encoding, decoding, feedback, the leader, follower, and the channels of communication. This model also accounts for external and internal noise, semantic noise, pacing, and listening – which all complicate or strengthen communication.

Essentials for Promoting Interactivity

Interactivity was also noted as a critical aspect of educational communication. Both student and mentor must have access to common technological resources to facilitate interactivity. In order to maximize such interactivity, it is necessary to:

- Establish an effective online community through the promotion of user and administrative tools, course forums, discussion forums, course resources, and technology (Downes, 2001).
- Develop a commitment from all individuals involved - Administration must be committed to providing the needed technology, acting as a liaison between student and mentor, and ensuring continued growth of the organization to conform to emerging best practices. The learner must be committed to pursuing knowledge, completing coursework, and communicating needs. The mentor must commit to assisting the learner, communicating with the school and individuals enrolled in classes, and continuing to evolve with the profession.
- Create an environment where collaboration is encouraged - Collaboration must occur among all stakeholders for full success.

In order to promote interactivity, it is necessary to:

- Focus on learning goals (Downes, 2001) - All members of the online community must have a similar vision for the educational endeavor. By clearly defining the goals of the administration, instructors, and learners, overlapping objectives and ambitions can be the foundation for educational success.
- Integrate content and communication (Downes, 2001) - This is a critical component of interactivity as it allows for a blending of instructional content and higher-ordered activities.
- Allow for free access to needed resources - All members of the online community must have access to informational texts, library resources, and assistance, when needed.
- Build a community that bridges the learning experience from enrollment to beyond graduation.

The Value of Synchronous Communication

In an asynchronous education setting, students have the ability to log onto the university website any time, day or night and complete coursework. Even in discussion forums, where learners have a chance to 'meet' fellow learners, online interface occurs without the need for a designated time and place for such interaction. Yet, without the immediacy of synchronous activities, the online academic journey can be a lonely one. Synchronous interaction brings some of the positive elements of the face-to-face classroom into the online learning arena. Such activities afford students the chance to immediately interact with instructors and other students (Hines & Pearl, 2004). This interaction can enhance the instructional experience for all involved. Questions and issues can be addressed in the moment, and snychronous learning activities add a collaborative dimension that is not possible in an asynchronous environment.

By building in synchronous opportunities, mentors help students who need more frequent interaction to stay on-task. In addition, such interaction allows for mentors to tailor the learning experience to the specific learning style preferences of the students, thus attending the learners' unique needs. Because many online educational formats do not require synchronous interaction, the educator should develop ways to bring this element to the courses taught. Some ideas for such interaction include virtual office hours, where the mentor is available for students via messaging, phone, or e-mail; "chat room" discussions (Hines & Pearl, 2004), where cohorts of students can come together to discuss topics of interest; and through the inclusion of an instant messaging program so that communication can occur instantaneously.

MULTIMODAL COMMUNICATION: SHARED AUTOBIOGRAPHICAL EXPERIENCES

The Online Mentor

A learner who just successfully completed her program recently sent me a thank you card noting my "passion for developing others." I was pleased and intrigued by her comment and decided to review emails from other former learners to look for common themes. In these, I found consistent appreciation for honest, constructive, detailed instructions and feedback. Learners enjoyed being allowed flexibility and choices and appreciated the challenge to become better scholars and educators. They consistently valued being seen as more than faceless learners; they felt good being consulted for their opinion, being sent an article of interest, and being heard when expressing ongoing concerns in their personal or professional lives. One learner viewed mentoring as a "morale booster… [and] theory [put] into action." These comments inspired me to delve deeper into the underlying communication between mentor and learner. What are the important messages mentors send to learners, outside of the course content? What is the impact of this meta-communication on learner achievement and outcomes? What skills must online mentors possess? I realized as I was writing this chapter and talking about it with others, that being a mentor is a weightier responsibility than sometimes assumed when the word is used synonymously with online instructor. Through their meta-communication, mentors not only teach, but listen, support, engage, inspire, challenge, cheerlead, coach, and commit to "bringing out the best" (Freedman, 2007, p. 14) in learners.

While learner outcomes are critical, meta-communication is also a two-way street that impacts mentor and learner alike. Meta-communication comprises not only the underlying messages sent by mentors, but also the response of learners, and the subsequent reply of mentors. It is not only the words typed on a page, but also the underlying messages and the feelings they provoke. Emotions are powerful partners in mentoring learners. I feel valued when learners attach a note to an assignment thanking me for some assistance. I feel ecstatic when dissertation learners successfully complete their final oral reviews. These emotions are energy sources for future actions. So, too, meta-communication, the underlying messages and the emotions that drive them, may energize the learner/mentor relationship in profound ways.

Meta-communication is used to describe not only what is said between mentor and learner but also the relationship context or enveloping system for all communication that occurs. This relationship wrapper may be influenced by mentor and learner life circumstances and history, vision and goals, and the knowledge, competencies, and attitudes that both bring to the table. While the mentor/learner relationship may also be affected by demographic differences, such as ethnicity, age, gender, religion, and socio-economic status, through attention to meta-communication, powerful, authentic, and effective relationships based on equality, respect, and mutual trust can be sustained.

One theoretical proposition that underpins each section of this chapter is that personal reflections may lend important voice to a study of educational practices (Pinar & Pautz, 1998). I will therefore extrapolate from of my own experience to bring to light some themes relating to my own mentoring practice. A second framework, intertwined with the first, is my overriding belief in the importance of emotional intelligence and its role in enhancing meta-communication. I believe that the more mentors reflect on emotional intelligence competencies, the more enriched our meta-communication will become, and therefore the more rewarding our own experience and that of our learners.

An Autobiographical Pipeline

The pipeline (Holden, 2010) leading to my present work in online mentoring began in New York City, where I grew up and attended a public high school for gifted girls. While my mother pinned her hopes for my future on marriage, my school conveyed a meta-communication of a different sort. Teachers taught us that, with a healthy dose of self-efficacy, it was possible to do just about anything. It was not until forty years later that I earned my doctorate, but, in part, my motivation came from the internalization of this message. As a mentor, I try to support the empowerment and achievement potential of all my learners and help them surmount obstacles.

Undergraduate years at a prestigious university were both exciting and challenging due to the tremendous social and political upheavals in the 1960s. While studying psychology and sociology, the events of the war in Vietnam, the draft, the assassination of Martin Luther King, and the wave of protests occurring in colleges and communities across the world had a dramatic impact on me and in many ways overshadowed my studies. Here, I first realized that learning is contextual and continually intertwined with social forces. Swayed by the events of the decade, I chose to complete my undergraduate education at a small progressive college with a dedication to a social justice mission. With no mentor to guide me, I was never sure I made the right decision. Knowing that, I believe my responsibility to learners goes beyond the course content. I believe mentors need be open to learners' uncertainties about their journey, available to help learners reflect on their choices, and refer them to advisors and counselors for further assistance.

I began my graduate studies with a Masters program in Teaching, but soon realized, given my interest in psychology and social contexts, that counseling was a more appropriate major. Through theory and practice, I learned to hold clients in high positive regard, find solutions rather than import blame, focus on restructuring thoughts to enable effective action, and seek to understand the context within which all behavior and learning occurs. I learned to actively listen, give constructive feedback, and help clients develop the self-awareness and the social emotional skills to be successful. As first a mental health and then later a school counselor, I worked with many groups, families, school personnel, and students. These experiences reinforced the importance of meta-communication on relationships, motivation to learn, and academic achievement.

In the mid-90s, I learned about emotional intelligence, or the ability to be self and socially aware and use both thoughts and feelings to meet life's challenges, develop meaningful relationships, and achieve one's goals (Goleman, 1995)Mayer & Salovey, 1997; Salovey & Mayer, 1990). While introducing social emotional learning (Elias et al., 1997), a set of critical skills derived from emotional intelligence, into my school community, I began to see its immense value, and, when researchers confirmed its impact, my lasting espousal of this important framework began. Subsequently, I had my first opportunity to work with adult learners in a state university counseling and school psychology program where emotional intelligence was valued and imbued in educator practice. I came to understand the importance of engagement, motivation enhancement, inclusion, relationship building, and the value of effective feedback when working with adult learners. During this transformational year, I decided to pursue a doctorate in educational leadership and change.

I chose a distributed doctoral program with a commitment to diversity and social justice. My most effective mentors were outstanding communicators, enthusiastic and engaging, and supportive and encouraging while giving constructive feedback. My dissertation chair assiduously contacted me every two weeks, without fail, and provided extensive writing feedback. Most importantly, she radiated a belief in my abilities and conviction that I would be successful. For my dissertation, I chose grounded theory methodology, which required me to carefully ground analysis in data, avoiding all preconceptions about the nature of a problem or its solution. I came to appreciate the fundamental importance of critical thinking, of not making assumptions, of integrating diverse voices, and of scholarly writing. In a final course on online learning, I explored distance education from a social justice perspective and the importance of developing social presence in the online environment.

These experiences were the pathways for my becoming an online mentor. When appropriate, I share some of my history with learners, and in my welcome letter, let them know that it was not long ago that I stood in their shoes.

Mentors Matter

Meta-communication, as discussed earlier, is the enveloping framework for all communication that occurs between the mentor and learner. As described by Watzlawick, Bavelas, and Jackson (1967), "Every communication has a content and a relationship aspect such that the latter classified the former and is therefore a meta-communication" (Watzlawick et al., 1967). Meta-communication involves both the beliefs that shape the nature of the relationship between mentor and learner and also how these beliefs are operationalized and communicated in the mentor/learner relationship.

(Tubbs & Carter, 1978) categorized all communications as destructive, neutral, or therapeutic:

Destructive when they leave participants more vulnerable than before to the strains of future interactions; they are neutral when they add information but do not affect underlying values or attitudes; they are regarded as therapeutic when they provoke insight or reorientation--and when they enable persons to participate in more satisfying ways in future social encounters (p.6).

Unexamined, the relationship between mentor and learner may suffer from, at best, neutral and, at worst, possibly destructive communication. It is only by purposefully examining one's practice and reflecting on the meta-communication that exists that one can begin to open the door for more consistently empathic and transformative relationships to occur. What must be conveyed to learners goes beyond the written word. "Failing to create and sustain the proper atmosphere can undermine even the best, most informed teaching content" (Simmons, 2010, p. 35).

One preliminary task for mentors is to get to know their learners and to communicate, in a welcome letter and in subsequent encounters, in such a way as to encourage motivation, allay fears, provide needed structure, prompt reflection and insight, and develop trust. How to accomplish that? From my perspective, a mentor's ability to create an effective and meaningful learning relationship, via meta-communication, is related to their level of emotional intelligence.

Emotional Intelligence is the Energy Source for Meta-Communication

Emotional intelligence is often described as the ability to recognize one's own and others' emotions, and utilize them effectively in the service of a goal, thereby promoting emotional and intellectual growth (Mayer & Salovey, 1997). The competencies are typically categorized as self-awareness, self-management, social awareness and relationship skills, conflict resolution, and decision making (Goleman, 1998). Researchers have found that emotional intelligence comprises a set of essential skills for leading organizations and developing strengths in an organization's constituents (http://www.casel.org; http://www.6seconds.org). Similarly, emotionally intelligent educators and administrators have been found to develop more supportive student/teacher relationships, better manage their own stress, reduce the risk of a "burnout cascade," (Jennings & Greenberg, 2009, p. 493) and promote optimal student outcomes ((Patti & Tobin, 2006). When educators are emotionally literate, they are able to exhibit more empathic behavior, engage in more effective communication, and create a safer environment for learning (Brackett et al., 2009).

Emotional intelligence may be understood as the energy source for meta-communication, as it can help mentors deepen their own self-awareness, establish meaningful relationships with others, make effective choices, resolve conflicts, and maintain a focus on their ultimate goals.

An iceberg analogy conveys the importance of understanding "the drivers of behavior that live beneath the surface" (Freedman, 2007, p. 82). The underlying and hidden meanings and influences on our actions and performance are a graphic and powerful way to think about meta-communication. As mentors understand how their communication with learners is impacted by their emotions and those of others, by their habitual patterns, and by their choices and long range goals, they may be able use this awareness to transform their work and, indeed, their own lives for optimal results and greater fulfillment.

According to one emotional intelligence model, people develop competencies in three main pursuits: Know yourself (increasing self-awareness), Choose yourself (using self management and becoming more intentional), and Give yourself (aligning with a purpose, increasing self-direction) (http://www.6seconds.org). The development of competencies in these three emotional intelligence areas facilitates meta-communication in support of a caring, authentic, compassionate, and effective mentoring relationship.

In Know yourself, mentors might use emotional literacy to become aware of their own feelings as they work with learners and recognize their own habitual patterns of behavior. Along with increased self-awareness, I try to read between the proverbial lines to ascertain learner feelings and respond to these as well as I can. When I recognize my own emotional patterns such as annoyance or frustration with learner issues, I try to not respond automatically but instead to examine my reactions and choose the most effective way to deal with them. I attempt to address learner patterns, such as chronic lateness or disregard for feedback, forthrightly and with attention to caring communication, which might be a direct request for phone call, or might be a sensitive response to a message. All meta-communication is enhanced by the emotional literacy and pattern recognition of Know Yourself.

In Choose yourself, mentors apply consequential thinking, evaluating the costs and benefits of choices, in order to put positive change into effect. I ask myself—what will happen if I respond to a learner issue this way? How will the learner feel? How will I feel? What will be the result? For example, when confronted with a high plagiarism score in the online Turn It In program, I try to consider the most effective way to respond, emphasizing the seriousness of the issue and asking myself what would help the learner to grow? In constructing feedback on any assignment, I consider carefully the message that I want to convey, so that learners' defensiveness will not be activated. Rather than reacting with impulsivity, I try to explore options. In Choose yourself, one reflects on how well one navigates emotions. Sometimes, during my work with learners, I notice that I am feeling angry, bored, or stressed. Unexamined, these feelings can become noxious, but with reflection, I can accept my own feelings and use them for insight, decision making, and better direction. Within the Choose yourself pursuit, mentors also may consider their intrinsic motivation, reminding themselves of the values behind their decision to be a mentor. Just thinking about my attitude towards my mentoring, in preparation for writing this chapter, has refreshed my intention and allowed me to reconnect with my passion for the work. Tapping into intrinsic motivation allows mentors to be champions for their learners and support them enthusiastically. At the same time, meta-communication around intrinsic motivation is essential in helping learners persevere through challenges, such as when faced with lack of progress in doctoral milestones. Meta-communication is evident in conflict situations where mentors must also not only resolve issues but also acknowledge learner emotions such as anger and fear. Finally, in the Choose yourself category, mentors must engage optimism and help learners to do the same. This competency is not about seeing the world through "rose colored glasses" but instead being proactive, unlocking energy and potential by recognizing options and helping learners negotiate their present challenges. Mentors adept at engaging optimism remind learners that setbacks are temporary, should be viewed as isolated events and not indicators of irradicable failure, and with effort may be overcome (Seligman, 2006). Meta-communication around intrinsic motivation allows mentors to set up a climate of support whereby learners find the strength to do the "impossible"(Freedman, 2007, p. 11).

In the final category of Give Yourself, mentors may increase empathy for their learners, remembering the real person behind the computer screen and the impact a negative comment may have on that life. By increasing empathy, mentors develop a non-judgmental stance towards learners' feelings and genuinely care about their welfare, balancing their own concerns with those of their learners. Mentors use empathy to establish deep connections with learners and form sustaining relationships, which may last only for the length of one course or may endure for the entire dissertation process and beyond. I find that flexibility, immediacy of response, acknowledgement of diversity, attention to learners' special needs, and personal sharing aids in increasing empathy. Freedman (2007) stated, "empathy is the key to finding lasting solutions" (p. 190). It is equally necessary for mentors to have empathy for themselves, take breaks as needed, and replenish their energy source. Mentors sometimes believe that online facilitating requires a 24/7 availability, but mentors who increase empathy for themselves find ways to disconnect in order to "sharpen the saw" (Covey, 2004, p. 287) and self-renew.

One important aspect of developing one's emotional intelligence rests on the identification and pursuit of noble goals (http://www.6seconds.org). When we, as mentors, reflect on our own noble goals, we connect with our long-term vision, re-engage with our motives for the work, and align our thoughts and feelings with our actions. Mentors who acknowledge and reflect upon their noble goals retain a sense of direction and integrity in their work. Pursuing a noble goal enables mentors to navigate difficult situations with courage and conviction (http://www.6seconds.org). Pursuing noble goals also allow us, as mentors, to engage, inspire, and help learners connect with their purpose and vision (Freedman, 2007).

Summary

The use of emotional intelligence to understand and direct our meta-communication allows for powerful, insightful, compassionate, and trusting relationships, which create the context for optimal learning and performance. As I reflect on my autobiographical narrative and pathways to my mentoring role, I uncover my evolving noble goal: to help others live their lives with passion, integrity, health, peace, and authenticity. Through mentoring, emotional intelligence and meta-communication are fused to create ripe conditions for this vision to occur.

THE ONLINE DISSERTATION COMMITTEE MEMBER

I have had the opportunity to serve on a number of master and doctoral committees. Going through a masters or doctoral program is tough, and completing a program in an online environment adds both opportunity and challenges. Mentoring in an online environment is very different from mentoring in a traditional classroom/office setting. When working on a thesis/dissertation, a new element is introduced: working with a second (or third) committee person. This complicates the normally direct communication when working one-on-one with a student, since now up to four people may be involved.

First, the process. No matter how clear the communication may be, without a good process (tracking mechanism), problems will plague us. Here is what I have found to be successful:

For the Committee Members

1. Determine, within the committee, how you want to communication to flow. Do you want the student to send each revision to everyone simultaneously for feedback, or do you want the committee to *flow* the revisions (student sends to committee person A, committee person A reviews it, sends it to committee person B, who then sends it back to the student for changes)?
2. Set up a process whereby questions/disagreements within the committee are resolved WITHIN the committee, before the student is involved. Few things are more frustrating for a student than getting conflicting direction from different committee members.
3. In today's environment, a large percentage of faculty are part time. Some work for multiple schools, while other have more traditional jobs in addition to teaching. Sometimes, it is necessary to remind people of the difference between procedure and technique. Schools normally issue guides/templates to use. Make sure all committee members have the most recent version of the school's requirements. I have occasionally worked with another committee member who was extremely knowledgeable in an area. Knowledge is good, but an extreme opinion can be a very bad thing. In this case, a committee member wanted the student to change direction toward where the member wanted the student to go (not because of a problem with the student's direction, but because of the passion a committee member had for a particular area within the student's topic). Sometimes, we need to remind (and be reminded) that we are here to guide students to learn about the research process, not advocate our particular point of view.

4. We deal with a bell curve of instructors; some are phenomenal, returning quality feedback amazing quickly, and yet some always promise something in a more few days... a few more days... rarely to return anything meaningful. Unfortunately, I have worked with committee people who were absent 90% of the time. As instructors, this puts us in an unfortunate position of delaying the students while holding the other committee member(s) accountable, or doing the work of two committee members so as not to delay student progress.
5. Referencing #2 above, get phone numbers of all committee people! This alleviates problems on two fronts. First, e-mails do occasionally get eaten in cyberspace, or get pushed down the list in the Inbox, so it is a great tool to follow up (people tend to respond better after a phone call). Secondly, I have a full-time job which requires a lot of travel, sometimes to places without reliable Internet. A quick telephone call of "I am gone the next four days, so can you respond to Mary's latest version" keep student progress going. This also lets the other instructors know they can do the same, rather than just not responding when their time does not allow.
6. Work from the same version. Have your student rename each version sequentially (e.g., Cross1, Cross2, Cross 3) so there is NO question as to which version is being discussed.
7. Have the student verify he/she has the style guide with them. Often times I will have my student *refer to page XXX of the XXX guide for examples* (see below).

Obviously quality, specific feedback is the main goal. There are a number of techniques to accomplish this. Here are some of the techniques that have worked well for me:

For the Students

1. Know your schools requirements/template/style guide. Know it cold. Have the guide physically available (electronic or paper) to reference throughout your thesis/dissertation.
2. Actually comply with the school requirements! If the template states *Introduction - 2 pages maximum*, make sure the Introduction is physically limited to no more than 2 pages. I have seen a number of instances where the Introduction exceeded this. I immediately sent the draft back with a comment stating "Per the template, the Introduction is 2 pages max. Make sure you read all the requirements before sending me a copy to review. Fix this, send me a new version, and then I will read everything." This message has been very successful, in that the students learn very quickly that THEY are responsible for knowing what is required of them. They also realize that I will not do a complete scrub and point out/fix it for them.
3. Give them specific feedback. Feedback such as "give me more" rarely helps a student. I will not write it for him/her, but a comment such as "great start, take your three major themes and develop them (perhaps some history, challenges, legal implications)" give specific guidance without getting too detailed. Another technique I have found successful is to include comments/questions. Examples include
   - Why did this happen?
   - How did this happen?
   - What were the results of this?

Asking these types of questions can help prompt a student with ideas of how to expand a topic.

4. For format issues, I refer a student to the style guide. For example, if a citation is incorrect,

I will often give feedback such as "refer to APA page 177 for examples of how these citations should be formatted. Check all your citations throughout your paper against page 177." Also, be aware that many schools have exceptions to the respective style guides, so, as faculty, be familiar with these exceptions.

5. Encourage feedback from your students. As a faculty member, the most frustrating thing I deal with is when a student sends a new version and has not made my last set of corrections. (That is why I always have a student update the same document and rename it--I can check my previous comments and corrections.) I always encourage my students to ask about any comment he/she does not understand BEFORE sending a new version.
6. Stay positive! So often critique is seen as negative. Make sure to throw in comments such as "perfect explanation" or "nice job on condensing this to 250 words." We are there to help and guide students through a very tough process; receiving only negative feedback can make that journey even tougher. Always find something positive to say.
7. Sometime a telephone call is worth a thousand comments. When the back-and-forth goes well, great! Sometimes though, without face-to-face communication a possibility, misinterpretation and frustration can occur. At that point, a telephone call can be a great help. When a student is having problems, sometimes I e-mail and arrange a time to talk. This system has a lot of benefits, including
   - I, as an instructor, become more than an e-mail
   - Students can now *hear* that you are genuinely interested in their success
   - I can listen to their thought process
   - On more than one occasion, after listening to a student, I realized that I had mis-read what he/she wrote, and the original writing was correct
   - This gives the student a chance to ask a myriad of questions, write down the answers, and clear up a number of issues all at once
8. Update at least once per week. Have the student keep regular contact with you, even if no progress has been made. This helps to keep the work at the forefront of the learner.

The online environment presents some unique challenges for communicating within the thesis/dissertation environment. The key to minimizing problems is to have solid processes in place. Not every process works for every instructor/student combination, but I have found these to be a great system for me to use.

THE ONLINE LEARNER

As I attempt to convey pieces of my journey that led to becoming an Ed. D. through an online university I am reminded of the many challenges and highlights that were part of the learning process. No doubt, I learned more about myself than anticipated and left with newly found confidence as a learner, scholar, and a writer. The journey has inspired me to consider how I will participate in the virtual learning community to support others as they pursue their own learning goals. I sincerely hope that my honest reflections regarding the thought process that brought me to an online learning environment with a mentor model accompanied by a recollection of communication norms and challenges will be useful to future online students learning in a virtual world. As a trained counselor I know that who I am and what I brought to the learning experience were critical factors, although difficult to measure, and were important to the learning experience.

It is challenging to articulate the discord experienced as a new online Generation X, female, doctoral learner. Perhaps this is difficult to convey because the journey was a process of continuous surprises and a level of growth that was unanticipated. In particular, having an extroverted disposition and counseling background combined with multiple years of graduate school experiences in a traditional learning format seemed contrary to even seeking a doctoral degree online. Age and generation are significant aspects, as I was not raised in a digital environment. In fact, home and office computers were not commonplace until I was several years into my career in public education. While I am technologically literate, I am by no means a well established geek; and I grossly underestimated the impact of technology on the learning process in the twenty-first century. Interestingly, colleagues suggested that an online program of study would be far easier than traditional programs; however, the rigor I experienced during my doctoral journey far surpassed prior graduate studies.

An important reason for choosing an online university was the perceived ability to complete a rigorous course of study while maintaining a demanding full-time professional career. Flexibility and alignment with professional aspirations were critical factors. Finally, developing relationships with mentors was important, and I felt that selecting a program with an individual mentor model would support my need for strong relationships. On a personal level, taking risks and learning new content in any learning environment comes much easier when I have a strong relationship with the teacher. Experience supports that relationships are equally important in a virtual learning platform. Online learning was a surprisingly different experience than interacting with other students and a professor in a traditional classroom setting.

The time commitment and the intensity of learning that resulted from the introverted and introspective nature of learning in an online environment in a mentor-student model was surprising. The writing expectations far exceeded prior experiences in a traditional graduate classroom because all communication with mentors was written. For the first time I knew that my level of understanding, ideas, and contributions would be judged solely on the ability to express myself by writing succinctly. As I became more confident and experienced with the process, I learned that my writing took on a unique voice much like the individualized quality of my own speaking voice. This discovery was perhaps my greatest asset in navigating the dissertation process. Over time and throughout the process I had developed an understanding and confidence in my written voice.

The unforeseen benefit to my online learning experience was that I truly owned the outcome and quality of learning, and the mentors existed in the backdrop to provide feedback, encouragement, or redirection throughout the process. This meant that for the first time I was the person most responsible for the quality and scope of learning, not the teacher. This did not minimize the importance of the mentor, as the written feedback provided by the mentor was critical in moving forward and thinking differently. Every word a mentor wrote on an assignment took on added value because this was the only feedback available. It seemed that mentors, much like learners, were forced to rely on the quality of their written voice to facilitate the learning process. Other student work was not seen in courses so the only way to gauge progress was through comments provided by the mentor.

One strategy I employed early in the learning process was to engage with a peer to discuss, debate, and share writing samples. In part I began this process as a way to talk about new learning, gain additional feedback regarding writing, and to meet my needs as an extroverted temperament. This strategy allowed multiple opportunities to process new material and writing conventions with a trusted colleague and ultimately supported the most growth in my own learning and writing. Participating with a peer fills in the gap when a mentor fails to provide adequate feedback or when content is particularly difficult to grasp. The value of feedback in learning cannot be overstated, and online learners must find a way to get continuous feedback because the personalized nature of learning in a one to one mentor model does not always meet that need.

Working with individual mentors can be a benefit and a challenge. The benefit is that in each course a learner has an opportunity to build a relationship with an individual mentor and can use this as a platform to discuss areas of interest for research linked to the dissertation. Additionally, learners can work with their advisors to experience mentors with a variety of backgrounds to broaden their learning circle and perspectives. Ideally, individual mentors provide considerable feedback on the writing assignments in order to help learners prepare for the dissertation. One shortcoming of the mentor student model is that some mentors do not provide adequate feedback throughout a course. Additionally, if there is a problem with a mentor, it can be challenging to handle because there is no peer group in which to discuss the problem. This underscores the importance of the learner taking personal responsibility to address problems successfully. Perhaps this is not really a negative because, in my view, doctoral learners must own the outcome of all that they do. While I have not experienced a traditional classroom environment for doctoral studies, I think it is safe to say that there can be problems in all learning platforms, and students will have to negotiate those challenges in order to succeed.

One particular challenge that is paramount in an online learning model is the amplified importance of written communication. While effective writing is critical in all graduate and doctoral programs, it is important to realize that in an online model, writing is often the only way to communicate with mentors. Relationships are built through online communication, and all learning is assessed through written assignments. This means that if writing skills are not excellent, both the learning process and the relationships can be less than satisfying. Not only are writing conventions important, but word choice and tone take on additional significance, and I believe that when learners fail to pay attention to these aspects of writing they can jeopardize their ability to build strong relationships online.

The emphasis on writing is timely because ultimately learners are expected to successfully complete a dissertation or capstone project that is comprehensive and requires outstanding writing skills. The practice obtained through the coursework is a huge advantage if learners take the time to focus on the quality of writing and seek feedback about their writing from mentors and online resources. Learners then must be self-regulated and at a sophisticated level in their own metacognitive development. Completing a dissertation requires a great deal of self-regulation, dedication, and self-awareness.

Two additional factors that are important to the dissertation process are the ability to write succinctly and the ability to build relationships with mentors. The writing is the most obvious skill to learners, but the relationship aspect is equally important because of the necessary reliance on mentors to give candid feedback that can be heard and accepted. It is hard enough to accept writing criticism, but I believe it is nearly impossible to accept and process that criticism without a relationship. The candid feedback is not meaningful if the learner is not able to really absorb, process, and use the information for improvement.

Once the dissertation was completed, preparation for the oral presentation began. Interestingly, in my online program, the oral presentation, referred to in some other schools as an oral defense, was completed as a one hour conference call. The experience was unusual because it included a PowerPoint presentation and phone communication but no visual contact with participants. While the participants were respectful, interested, and engaged, I felt like the sales people I have seen on TV selling products and talking enthusiastically about their product for hours. In essence, I felt like an energized salesperson for my dissertation. I have often wondered if other students felt the same way or if my response was unusual. Regardless of the analogy to a television salesperson, it was affirming to interact with researchers, professors, and other interested participants to discuss various aspects of my study. The audience appeared genuinely interested and treated the occasion as if it were a celebration. Indeed the oral presentation was an opportunity to celebrate my commitment and journey to becoming an Ed. D.

Graduation was the final experience to celebrate my learning success. This was the first opportunity I would have to meet key mentors who had supported and encouraged me long distance throughout the process. My dissertation chair and one member of my committee attended, and I was able to thank both of them in person for their commitment, kindness, and time. I could finally hug the people that invested so much in my growth and stood by my side relentlessly throughout a very important part of my life. Graduation was also a chance to meet students that I had built relationships with online. It is difficult to describe the overwhelming joy and gratitude I experienced at the graduation ceremony. This part of the experience was a reminder that celebrating experiences and successes are an essential part of the journey.

Recommendations for online learners seeking a doctoral degree include: (a) strengthen writing skills by using a writing center or taking formal courses, (b) build a relationship with a peer to share and critique writing throughout the process, (c) build a relationship with your advisor and work together to select mentors throughout the program who will enable you to experience multiple perspectives, and (d) take the time and make the effort to build relationships with mentors in each course. Ultimately, it is the learner's efforts and willingness to reach out to mentors that will result in strong relationships that allow candid feedback to emerge. Online learning within a mentor student model is powerful, but largely dependent on the learner's writing capacity and online interpersonal skills.

CONCLUSION

Students enroll in online courses and degree programs for many reasons. Often, students are adults who have full time careers, families, and commitments that prevent a more traditional face-to-face learning experience. Such learners are drawn to the online community as a place to pursue professional goals and personal interests. O'Lawrence (2006) noted that the online learning format has "increased opportunities for adult learners to accomplish educational goals" (p. 47). Distance learning research suggests that online learning offers significant benefits if regular interaction occurs among learners and faculty members (O'Lawrence, date). Such interaction contributes to the sense of community, despite the fact that learning often occurs asynchronously and in distant locales. Chen (2003) noted the factors that contribute to an effective online community include "interactivity, opportunities for collaboration, a meaningful and motivational context, and a continuously available learning environment" (p. 35).

As Liao (2006) suggested, meeting the needs of adult learners requires mentors to engage learners with real-world issues. Ally (2004) emphasized that students have access to learning resources at any time. This allows learners to work on instructional tasks at convenient times. However, because online courses provide an asynchronous format, assistance may not be readily available. Therefore, faculty must interact with students regularly and provide frequent guidance to ensure successful course completion. Berge (2006) wrote that the online instructor serves several functions - pedagogical, social, managerial, and technical. These diverse functions must be accomplished to ensure the success of online facilitation and effective communication within the organization. By developing an understanding of the implications of online learning and the needs to establish a sense of community among learners, faculty members can enhance the educational experience for each student through best communication practices.

Every day, educators engage in many types of communication. Faculty send and read e-mail, make calls to colleagues, verbally and nonverbally communicate with students, and convey content knowledge. Effective communication strengthens organizations, improves relationships, and increases learning. From the extensive research on communication, it is clear that in order to effectively communicate; educators must develop an understanding of communication within organizations. By establishing a strong communication framework, stakeholders can ensure and effective learning environment.

This study provided a meta-communicative framework through shared autobiographical experiences of a mentor, a doctoral committee member, and a student. The 'voice' of each contributor emphasizes the personal nature of communication and highlights the value of attending to the nuances of message transmittal in the online educational environment. In order to effectively convey knowledge and understanding, educational stakeholders must develop a systematic understanding of diverse modes of communication. This study serves as a qualitative testament to communication patterns existent in online mentoring. The mentoring approach provides a unique opportunity to maximize one-on-one communication for both the educator and the learner. When mentoring is blended with online learning, it is possible to produce a new meta-communicative paradigm, which can be employed at educational institutions utilizing distance education practices.

REFERENCES

Ally, M. (2004). *Foundations of educational theory for online learning*. Retrieved from http://cde.athabascau.ca/ online_book/ ch1.html

Bateson, G. (1951). *Communication: The social matrix of psychiatry*. New York, NY: Norton.

Berge, Z. L. (2006). *The role of the online instructor/facilitator*. Retrieved from http://www.emoderators.com/ moderators/ teach_online.html

Brackett, M. A., Kremenitzer, J. P., Maurer, M., Carpenter, M., Rivers, S. E., & Katulak, N. A. (2009). *Emotional literacy in the classroom: Upper elementary*. Portchester, NY: Emotionally Intelligent Schools.

Chen, T. (2003). Recommendations for creating and maintaining effective networked learning communities: A review of the literature. *International Journal of Instructional Media, 30*(1), 35–45.

Covey, S. (1989). *The 7 habits of highly effective people*. New York, NY: Fireside.

Downes, S. (2001). *Building a learning community*. Retrieved from http://alumni.ncu.edu/ course/ default.asp?TB=TABResources&course _code=FMD5012& learner_course _ id=44019&assignment _number=2

Elias, M., Zins, J., Weissberg, R., Frey, K., Greenberg, M., & Haynes, N. (1997). *Promoting social and emotional learning: Guidelines for educators*. Alexandria, VA: ASCD.

Freedman, J. (2007). *At the heart of leadership: How to get results with emotional intelligence*. San Mateo, CA: Six Seconds.

Goleman, D. (1995). *Emotional intelligence: Why it can matter more than IQ*. New York, NY: Bantam.

Goleman, D. (1998). *Working with emotional intellligence*. New York, NY: Bantam.

Gonsoulin, W. B., Ward, R. E., & Figg, C. (2006). Learning by leading: Using best practices to develop leadership skills in at-risk and gifted populations. *Education, 126*(4), 690–702.

Green, R. L. (2005). *Practicing the art of leadership. A problem based approach to implementing the ISLLC standards* (2nd ed.). Upper Saddle River, NJ: Pearson Merrill Prentice Hall.

Hersey, P., Blanchard, K. H., & Johnson, D. E. (2005). *Management of organizational behavior: Leading human resources* (8th ed.). New Delhi, India: Prentice-Hall.

Hines, R. A., & Pearl, C. E. (2004). Increasing interaction in Web-based instruction: Using synchronous chats and asynchronous discussions. *Rural Special Education Quarterly, 23*(2), 33–36.

Hirvela, A. (2006). Computer-mediated communication in ESL teacher education. *ELT Journal, 60*(3), 233–250. doi:10.1093/elt/ccl003

Holden, J. (2010). *Pipelining: A grounded theory of officer training* [draft title]. Manuscript in preparation. School of Educational Leadership and Change, Fielding Graduate University, Santa Barbara, CA.

Jennings, P. A., & Greenberg, M. T. (2009). The prosocial classroom: Teacher social and emotional competence in relation to student and classroom outcomes. *Review of Educational Research, 79*(1), 491–525..doi:10.3102/0034654308325693

Liao, S. C. (2006). Creating learning scenarios: A planning guide for adult learners. *Convergence, 39*(1), 101–103.

Mayer, J. D., & Salovey, P. (1997). What is emotional intelligence? In Salovey, P., & Sluyter, D. (Eds.), *Emotional development and emotional intelligence: Educational implications* (pp. 3–31). New York, NY: Basic.

O'Lawrence, H. (2006). The influences of distance learning on adult learners. *Techniques, 81*(5), 47–50.

Patti, J., & Tobin, J. (2006). *Smart school leaders: Leading with emotional intelligence* (2nd ed.). Dubuque, IA: Kendall/Hunt.

Pogue, L. L., & Ahyun, K. (2006). The effect of teacher nonverbal immediacy and credibility on student motivation and affective learning. *Communication Education, 55*(3), 331–335. doi:10.1080/03634520600748623

Razik, T. A., & Swanson, A. D. (2001). *Fundamental concepts of educational leadership* (2nd ed.). Upper Saddle River, NJ: Merrill Prentice Hall.

Seligman, M. E. P. (2006). *Learned optimism: How to change your mind and your life*. New York, NY: Vintage.

Simmons, O. (2010). Is that a real theory or did you just make it up? Teaching classic grounded theory. *The Grounded Theory Review, 9*(2), 15–35.

Tubbs, S. L., & Carter, R. M. (1978). *Shared experiences in human communication*. New York, NY: Transaction Publishers.

Watzlawick, P., Bavelas, J. B., & Jackson, D. D. A. (1967). *Pragmatics of human communication: A study of interactional patterns, pathologies, and paradoxes*. New York, NY: Norton.

Chapter 8
Building Knowledge through Dynamic Meta-Communication

Mary Beth Klinger
College of Southern Maryland, USA

Teresa L. Coffman
University of Mary Washington, USA

ABSTRACT

Sharing knowledge through collaboration and community using distance learning tools is an important component of today's 21st century education. Distance learning is growing in educational institutions worldwide, and instructors are developing enhanced teaching strategies focused on incorporating meta-communication that engages and empowers students in their quest for understanding. This chapter focuses on knowledge building through interactivity, social engagement, and communication technologies in a distance learning environment. Emphasis is placed on online collaboration and community building to encourage collaborative learning and ultimately knowledge acquisition. Theoretical constructs surrounding social constructivism and practical application to instruction are provided to the reader to enhance a distance learning course using meta-communication strategies.

INTRODUCTION

The focus of this chapter is on building knowledge through dynamic meta-communication in an online classroom. The ability to apply knowledge principles can improve student learning and new knowledge creation as well as knowledge sharing and application within the course environment.

DOI: 10.4018/978-1-61350-071-2.ch008

Knowledge management is a strategy that helps to identify and distribute knowledge so that a transfer of knowledge and learning takes place. It is a systematic coordination of instructional technologies within the classroom – either online or face-to-face - to enhance knowledge sharing and intellectual growth. Within this chapter, emphasis is placed on creating an optimal learning environment within the context of distance learning and how best to bring students together so that they can exchange information and focus on knowledge creation, transmission, transformation, and eventual assimilation of course content to add and create value.

The growth in distance learning is staggering. Since early 2000, online enrollments have been growing substantially faster than overall higher education enrollments with over 4.6 million students taking at least one online course during fall 2008. This is a 17 percent increase over the previous year during which the overall higher education student population saw only a 1.2 percent increase in growth ("Learning on Demand", 2009).

The growth in distance education courses shows no signs of slowing down anytime soon. As more longitudinal research becomes available, the results appear to confirm that online courses are working for students. They provide dynamic and diverse ways to interact with course content from different locations around the world, given that an Internet connection is available. According to research completed by Sloan-C: A Consortium of Institutions and Organizations Committed to Quality Online Education, more than one in four higher education students reported taking at least one class online ("Learning on Demand", 2009).

As distance learning evolves, so too does the value and excellence within online education. Within the online environment, more and more instructors are incorporating meta-communication models into their courses to create collaborative and supportive learning opportunities. This chapter explores three meta-communication constructs that influence high-quality teaching and effective student learning in a distance learning environment:

1. interactivity,
2. social context, and
3. communication technologies

As distance educators look to incorporate various strategies, methods, and technology tools to provide online learners with quality teaching and equitable access to content, instructors must also be aware of and integrate effectively interactivity, social context, and appropriate communication technologies into the course environment to engage learners in the process of learning the course objectives (Tu & Corry, 2002). A constructivist model of collaboration, communication, and interactivity comes to the forefront of the course planning process.

The constructivist theory has the potential to provide a rich didactic communication model that can provide diverse opportunities for learners to test their mental models with other learners through active participation and manipulation of content. This begins the process of knowledge construction through a social and blended context. This chapter explores the meta-communication model of collaboration and community through the practice of active learning modalities and communication technologies, all within a knowledge oriented context.

BACKGROUND

The Meta-Communication Model

The meta-communication model of interactivity, social context, and appropriate communication technologies requires students to participate in reflective thought and applied analysis, which in turn must be communicated to peers and the instructor through dynamic participation. This active engagement in an online social learning context embeds collaborative communication technologies into the process of learning. Students are therefore afforded the potential for higher level thinking due to opportunities presented by other learners as well as the instructor to challenge their understanding through a meta-communication method.

Interactivity

Interactivity is an important component to build into a distance learning course. Instructors create learning environments that encourage students to work in small and/or large groups through discussion and debate with the goal of sharing new knowledge and at the same time challenging existing knowledge schema or previous understanding.

Instructors design opportunities for learners to think critically about topics and content by challenging peers and their own previous knowledge. This can be done through research projects and presentations, the creation of concept maps or mental models, or creating videos to share with the group, all with the purpose of eliciting questions and critical analysis from other learners.

Within this participatory environment, learners form a community where they actively share personal knowledge and understanding with the members of their learning group, especially as a sense of trust develops between the group members and the instructor. The cultural environment developed within the course is a key component to ensuring that critical knowledge and information flow within the class. It consists of norms, routines, and spoken as well as unspoken rules about how things are done in the course.

A culture committed to knowledge is one that embraces and welcomes change and is committed to innovation and new ideas. The instructor serves as a role model and reward systems (e.g. assessments) should promote, support, and value student interactions that facilitate cultural acceptance of knowledge practices and processes.

Within this online collaborative environment, instructors serve as facilitators of knowledge instead of knowledge dispensers. In addition to foundational knowledge, opportunities are provided for learners to discover and interact with new information through a process of active learning and social interactions. These include activities such as:

- online debates,
- problem statements,
- writing blog posts to summarize readings and ask critical questions, or
- creating a timeline of an event or process

All of these activities encourage active participation with the content through the manipulation and reworking of content into a new format. Within this interactive distance learning environment, learning is not a competitive process but instead is seen as collaborative and inclusive.

Planned interactivity is aligned with learning goals within the course, thereby allowing learners to deepen their overall understanding of the content and build connections by using real world situations with the planned activity (Tu & Corry, 2003). Studies conducted on small group instruction with the incorporation of interactive elements have shown a positive influence on student achievement in a distance learning environment. The cognitive disequilibrium that is induced by the interactive real world activity helps the learner to develop an understanding of course content and to elicit questions that build on their overall knowledge of the learning objectives (Ocker & Yaverbaum, 1999; Slavin, 1991).

Within a constructivist learning environment and through the incorporation of meta-communication methods, active learning is promoted through the participation with other learners and contributing to the dialog of the learning process itself with the intent of deep inquiry. As learners work within the online course environment, exploring course problems and questions, they begin to construct knowledge around the course topics and themes.

This construction ultimately leads to knowledge retention as learners ask questions of themselves and their classmates and begin presenting new information to their community of learners. When using a constructivist learner-centered model with the central focus being knowledge construction, the communication tools used to support a learner's construction of knowledge become important (Kimball & Sibley, 1996).

These technology tools must strengthen the meta-communication model implemented within the course in order to promote reflection and thought around the content being explored. This construction of knowledge is developed through doing, by actively participating in the process of discovery and learning through experience by using the scientific method of questioning in a systematic process (Dewey, 1966). In an online environment, instructors develop learning experiences for students tied into social interactions and questioning.

By providing social interactivity, learners have an opportunity to communicate and interact with classmates and in turn observe and identify inferences of other learners constructing meaning around similar problems. This proactive interactivity constantly and consistently tests the learner's beliefs and understandings so new knowledge can occur.

Social Context

The social context of the meta-communication model is important as well. Interactivity is increased when learners are engaged in an activity which encourages them to be social, such as small and large group activities. Within this social environment, learners again have the opportunity to test their understanding and to compare it with others through the process of social negotiation. This allows learners to determine if they are accurate in their knowledge acquisition. The role of the instructor is that of a facilitator who guides the learner through direct and indirect questions (Perkins, 1991; Vygotsky 1978; Piaget, 1973; Bruner, 1966).

In order for the social context of a distance learning course to be successful, all learners must actively participate by sharing new knowledge. The instructor ensures that all learners are challenged appropriately, the learning activities are structured to achieve relevant learning goals as well as are meaningful and applicable, and learners utilize appropriate communication technologies.

If each of these elements are in place, learners identify with the content instead of just absorbing information offered by the instructor. Through this active participation with the content and other learners in a social context, meaning is created with the new information which allows learners to think critically about the content and to make connections in a real world context. The meta-communication model of collaboration and interactivity has the potential to provide constructive conversations between learners and the instructor, thus creating a dynamic learning experience where knowledge easily flows in multiple ways within the community of learners (Sorensen, Takle, & Moser, 2006).

Vygotsky (1978) stated that through language, which he identified as a cognitive tool, learners have the potential to develop ways of creating meaning that help develop a sense of the world around them. This sense of understanding can be created and implemented in a distance learning environment where instructors implement active learning and communication tools to help learners negotiate and manipulate the content, discuss and debate their manipulations, and present their ideas in new and diverse ways. Throughout this process, learners are consistently reflecting on their new understanding and aligning it with real world application.

Communication Technologies

In using the meta-communication model of interactivity, collaboration, and communication in a distance learning environment, technology is the tool that both delivers content and allows the learner to interact and communicate with others in the learning environment. Modes of communication can be either asynchronous or synchronous.

Appropriate technologies can help encourage peer-to-peer interactions and learner-instructor interaction with content (Cooper & Robinson, 1998). Each method of communication in a distance learning course should provide opportunities for the technology to aid in fostering learner engagement with the content.

In order for the communication to be effective within a distance learning environment, it must be consistent, relevant, and help enhance the cognitive development of each student. Technology tools allow learners to create and exchange information about course content and then reflect on possible connections. This critical reflection and thought benefits the learner by providing cognitive dissonance which allows learners to question understanding and ultimately create a shared and coherent knowledge structure developed through collaborative interactions within the learning community (Sorensen et al., 2006).

Using a written method of communication within an online learning environment has the potential for learners to think about the content and provide clear and consistent ways of explaining and applying the content to others within the community. This constant meta-reflection, meta-awareness, and meta-learning can be focused on a learner's practice. Methods of written reflective thought within the online learning environment include journal writing, reflective narratives, presentations, and discussions (Sorensen et al., 2006).

MAIN FOCUS OF THE CHAPTER

Online Collaboration and Community

In order for online collaboration and a knowledge community to be effective in a distance learning environment, it is important that the instructor be present within the community from the very beginning of the course. Without this engagement from the instructor, the learners will feel disconnected from the content, the instructor, and other learners. The instructor must actively participate within the learning environment, showing a presence in each activity. In addition, the design of the course should be clear, consistent, and focused on the intended learning goals.

Management of each element from feedback, assignments, and learner interactions must also be identified early in the course. Understandable, regular, personal, and timely feedback to all students should be provided in the assessment process (Yelland, Cope, & Kalantzis, 2008). Rubrics are often developed for this purpose.

The instructor takes on the important role of helping to provide learners with a sense of social presence within the course. Technology tools provide applications for announcements, discussion forums, and e-mail communication between the instructor and learner and between learners. Through this technology, learners can be encouraged to think about the learning objectives and form understandings and then test these understandings within the newly formed community of learners.

The community developed within the online course environment has the potential to become a support system where theories can be tested and debated. The presence provided by technology tools also has the potential to give learners feedback on their progress throughout the course activities so they do not feel isolated and ultimately lost in their individual process of learning (Tu & Corry, 2003). A true knowledge-oriented culture of learning is formed.

Group Work

Assignments within an online course environment can be done individually or in small groups. Each method of instruction provides benefits for the learner. The instructor must provide opportunities for learners to work together by giving thoughtful comments and feedback to student work. This would be the same as in a face-to-face class where the instructor encourages learners to discuss, debate, and think about content using a discussion, questioning session, or debate forum.

Within an online course this interactivity with the content itself, combined with the perspectives of other learners, is important because it encourages engagement and helps to develop stronger connections with the content (Tu & Corry, 2003; Yelland et al., 2008).

Although group work can be difficult for learners in an online environment due to time constraints and availability, this remains an effective method for learners to become active and engaged with the content and to begin thinking about specific learning objectives. This method also allows learners to meta-cognitively think about their own learning, by testing their ideas with the thoughts and understandings of their classmates.

During group work, learners test their theories and hypotheses and begin the process of constructing their knowledge by working on the task of an assignment, questioning their understanding and the understanding of their peers using technology tools such as email, chat, or conferencing technologies to help answer questions and ask for input. Within this interactive learning process, the instructor does not have to assign specific technology tools for learners to use but instead can make a variety of communication tools available for students to use that help them communicate and work in collaborative supportive groups (Yelland et al., 2008).

The main purpose for collaborative learning in a distance learning course is to provide rich interactive experiences for students to challenge one another's thinking. Once this is accomplished, students are thinking critically about the content, exchanging information, and applying this newly constructed knowledge directly to their own experiences (Sorensen et al., 2006).

The Application of Knowledge to the Meta-Communication Process

A knowledge strategy encompasses knowledge management principles with operational goals and objectives so that knowledge resources can be leveraged and a sense of direction obtained. An effective knowledge strategy provides a road map that can be used by the instructor to identify and prioritize course objectives, tools, and processes so that long-term educational objectives and strategies are met.

Successful implementation of knowledge focuses on analysis and planning of course content, knowledge sharing and acquisition of information, the class culture, and instructional processes. The overall use of a knowledge strategy can be seen as a dynamic chain of events to create, identify, collect, review, validate, share, adapt, and use knowledge. When these events are managed well, individual knowledge becomes community knowledge, which then becomes class knowledge. As a result of this collaboration and validation, the course now has dynamic knowledge.

Capturing, sharing, and applying knowledge requires the instructor and learners to share knowledge freely throughout the course. The best classes are those that encourage collaboration and networking.

- Capturing knowledge in a collaborative environment includes identifying, collecting, adapting, organizing, and storing knowledge.
- Knowledge sharing of best practices allows students to share ideas to obtain specific information and advance their own learning.
- Knowledge application permits new information to be applied, preferably through real-world application, or secondarily through discussion and discourse with other learners.

The traditional transmission model of instruction where the instructor posts a discussion and the student provides a response has not been found to be effective. Instead, having learners engaged in the process of discovery by asking questions of other learners and questioning the understanding of their peers, ultimately allows the learner to question their own understanding and discover new knowledge and perceptions of self-efficacy (Gabriel, 2004).

The theory of constructivism provides a process of situated learning where learners are provided, through the design of the online course, transformative elements that support learners in the construction of knowledge. This shared learning space must be developed by the instructor in a learning community.

The instructor creates a learning environment that provides multiple and diverse opportunities for student understanding of the intended learning objectives through the multimodal expression of linguistic, visual, audio, and spatial elements to help learners grasp the message of the content and have discourse freely with other learners so meaning can be made. The idea that knowledge is shared among the group must be the central pillar of the course and its construction (Yelland et al., 2008; Gabriel, 2004).

For example, when preservice teachers take an online course, such as a Foundations of Education course, the instructor must allow for and incorporate multimodal expressions into the design of the course in order to encourage debate and discourse over important topics such as the law and educational practice in the classroom and throughout the school. By allowing for and providing opportunities for learners to debate and question their understanding using multiple methods, a collaborative community can be formed and knowledge construction gained (Gabriel, 2004).

Continuing with the preservice teacher example, the instructor can provide a landmark court case through primary documents that include both written proceedings and oral arguments. Students can be asked direct questions about the case and then be asked to analyze the case and provide arguments on the case's impact and how the case could be questioned today. This co-construction of knowledge helps learners to understand how school policies and procedures are formed and how they can be questioned in the future.

Through these multimodal expressions, learners have opportunities to communicate their understanding of the legal system and begin identifying how this system would impact their professional lives as teachers within a public school environment (Yelland et al., 2008). This is a true application of knowledge using the meta-communication process.

Collaborative Learning

Collaborative learning experiences must be cultivated for each member of the community. Learners must learn how to work in this virtual space, developing collaboration skills, and develop new strategies to work online and at a distance. Learners new to distance learning must learn new tools to work within this environment and communicate effectively with peers at distant locations.

For the instructor teaching the distance learning course, there may be a need for increased contact with learners due to the heightened interactivity and social collaboration. This may be accomplished by providing thoughtful feedback and/or redirection, personal emails or posts on a discussion forum frequently. This increased contact can be time consuming. Because of this, the instructor must be well organized and design an effective interactive course that is specifically aligned with learning objectives and learning goals. Otherwise, both the instructor and the learners will be overwhelmed and lost, resulting in frustration of both parties (Gabriel, 2004).

The idea of collaboration using the meta-communication model of verbal communication through discussion forums and group projects where learners are working on real world problems using collaborative technology tools such as GoogleDocuments (http://docs.google.com) to design a lesson plan with other classmates or creating a collaborative picture book about synonyms using MixBook (http://www.mixbook.

com) is not new. This collective responsibility that each learner must feel a part of the community of learners is important for students to experience or there is a disconnect with the course and ultimately the content. In order to become connected and engaged in the co-collaboration of knowledge creation, students must feel a part of the social responsibility of creating new knowledge for the group and ultimately for themselves.

Community Knowledge Building

As learners form a collective community, there is a growing sense of responsibility to encourage community knowledge construction and development. This building of knowledge and its ideas helps to advance the learning of the collective group.

This is different from the idea of individual instruction with the premise that the student will learn solely by the teacher's instruction. In this meta-communication model, using a collaborative learning theory as a guide, the goal is for learners to build on the ideas and contributions of the group and to think critically about these ideas, helping each member of the group to build deeper understanding. There is a collective responsibility established within this community of learners (Zhang, Scardamalia, Reeve, & Messina, 2009).

The instructor must identify big idea questions and important problems that focus the learner on the key ideas of the learning objectives, tying together concept understanding by engaging and stimulating the learner through the process of asking important questions with the purpose of facilitating meta-discourse (Coffman, 2009). The student feels a sense of collective responsibility and is encouraged to focus on the evolution of knowledge construction of the group through classroom discussions and debate (Zhang et al., 2009).

This collective responsibility helps to develop meaningful discussion among learners that has the potential to facilitate reflective thinking. This reflective thinking requires learners to ask thoughtful and effective questions that are built upon their higher levels of domain knowledge and metacognitive skills developed through the course and collaborative design (Choi., Land, & Turgeon, 2005).

When instructors develop the course, it is important to build in a peer-questioning scaffolding framework that will help facilitate the necessary meta-cognition and learning that will allow for the knowledge transfer in an online discussion, for example. This framework helps to create the meta-cognitive knowledge necessary for learners to begin generating meaningful interactions and develop higher order knowledge construction to work on complex problems surrounding the intended learning objectives.

The ideal knowledge sharing culture is one where communication and coordination between groups is emphasized, where experts (e.g. teachers) share rather than guard their knowledge, and where knowledge construction is actively and visibly encouraged at all levels of the classroom through recognizing and rewarding knowledge sharing.

Knowledge re-construction can help trigger a cognitive dissonance, or a gap, between a learner's beliefs and their experiences. This conflict is necessary for construction of knowledge at a higher level. The instructor builds on this conflict by asking probing questions and encouraging students to ask good questions of their classmates. This ultimately allows all students to build on their knowledge creation and overall understanding (Choi et al., 2005; Piaget, 1985).

When learners receive different perspectives or questions from their peers about their explanations revolving around course topics within a meta-communication device, such as a discussion forum, students begin to justify their own responses and revisit their prior understanding in defense of the statement. Eventually, through peer questioning and the multiple responses and perspectives to this same discussion by their peers, the learner recognizes differences within understanding and with guidance from the instructor recognizes the strength and weaknesses in their own response. This articulation of gaps of understanding through verbal discourse is the beginning of a learner's knowledge construction (Choi et al., 2005).

Social Constructivism

Social constructivism is a theory that is readily integrated within a distance education course. Its core foundation is built from the need for learners to reflect on their own learning experiences and to actively participate in a social-dialogical process. The central premise of constructivism provides opportunities for instructors to create an active environment where learners are able to construct their own knowledge, with a mixture of social interactions among other learners, with the purpose of sharing knowledge and testing new knowledge construction (Woolfolk, 2010). Thus, this theory fits nicely into the Chapter discussion and serves as the underlying premise.

The social constructivist theory suggests that learning should be both holistic and authentic with less emphasis placed on isolated skills and rote memorization. This hands-on experience can be built into distance courses providing varied opportunities for students to actively engage with the content by debating and analyzing important topics with their peers in a learning community environment.

The primary focus in constructivism is that each learner must have learning opportunities built into the environment that are authentic, meaningful, and interesting. Building authenticity into a lesson requires that students are provided with opportunities to work in collaborative and supportive groups allowing them to share ideas and new knowledge freely, thus building on their own knowledge creation and testing this new knowledge with the understanding of their peers.

Through this collaborative supportive learning structure, learners share their new understanding through varied communication methods in the online course. Communication methods can include chat, email, discussion forums, or web conferencing. In order for learning to occur, students must adjust their existing mental models to accommodate new experiences. Communicating with group members and learning peers within the distance learning environment using various communication technologies is an important step for each learner to question content, one another, and to begin thinking critically about the material being presented and reviewed.

Solutions and Recommendations

The solution to building knowledge through meta-communication strategies in a distance learning course is to focus on collaboration and community in an interactive context. It also requires the use of appropriate technologies so that students can feel connected to each other and the instructor. The role of technology is not to flood students with information or take it from them, but instead to provide a valuable link in transferring knowledge (Gilmour, 2003).

In developing effective online courses, instructors should understand the value students will take from the class. Teachers should focus on understanding why some students are more adept than others at gathering knowledge and customizing it for their own use. Seek out students who consistently do a good job applying newly gained knowledge and understanding, watch how these learners interact with others, and look for common techniques (Jacobson & Prusak, 2006). Try to model these techniques to other students to enhance their own understanding and knowledge creation.

FUTURE RESEARCH DIRECTIONS

We want students to develop a cognitive understanding of major course concepts, not just rote memorization of facts and figures and a superficial basic knowledge. Education in the 21st century means interactivity, social collaboration, and integration of appropriate technologies – all with the end goal of developing knowledge learners.

In order to do this, instructors must develop learning environments and meta-communication strategies that are student-centered and guide the student throughout the learning process. This requires developing activities that incorporate multiple opportunities for sustained inquiry.

Meta-communication models of direct interaction through discussion and debate are an important and necessary opportunity for teachers within a distance learning environment. Students need opportunities to defend and discuss their understanding with classmates and the instructor until they develop deeper knowledge.

More research is needed to help provide distance learning instructors with helpful guidelines and best practices to aid them in both the design and management of student-centered, collaborative learning environments. Applied research is also needed in bridging the gap between knowledge management practices and meta-communication strategies in education.

CONCLUSION

The future for building knowledge through meta-communication is dynamic and exciting. Inherent in knowledge are the concepts of creativity, innovation, and ultimately change so that students learn how to expand their understanding and function more efficiently and effectively in all levels of their lives - educationally, personally, and if applicable, professionally.

The past is no longer representative of the future. What worked well for education in the 1980s and 1990s no longer applies. Today the best classrooms are obtained by having an orientation towards open communication, along with integration of multiple technologies working together to enhance student knowledge of various content areas. This transparency allows ideas to be leveraged more quickly and successfully throughout the online course environment so that they can be examined, manipulated, and then effectively implemented.

Effectual knowledge educators are needed for leadership in 21st century schools. Collaboration and sharing of information using technology allows for more effective communications within the online course. Today the Internet can be used as a powerful tool to capture creativity and encourage innovation so that classroom dialogue and exchange can flourish. The second half of that equation is our students who are knowledge ready, open and accepting of this change paradigm.

The future of the online classroom in terms of building knowledge through dynamic meta-communication is bright. It relies on the abilities of the educational system, the instructor, and ultimately the student to encourage and support the transformation of knowledge into a valuable and successful competency. Knowledge now serves as a basis for almost every task performed in an organization, whether in an educational institution or a for-profit business. What an engaging opportunity to integrate it into student coursework so that it can be applied and used outside of the classroom 'walls'. Now that's progress!

REFERENCES

Bruner, J. S. (1966). *Toward a theory of instruction*. Cambridge, MA: Belknap Press of Harvard University.

Choi, I., Land, S., & Turgeon, J. (2005). Scaffolding peer-questioning strategies to facilitate metacognition during online small group discussion. *Instructional Science*, *33*(5-6), 483–511. doi:10.1007/s11251-005-1277-4

Coffman, T. (2009). *Engaging students through inquiry-oriented learning and technology*. Lanham, MD: Rowman & Littlefield Education.

Cooper, J., & Robinson, P. (1998). Small-group instruction in science, mathematics, engineering and technology (SMET) disciplines: A status report and an agenda for the future. *Journal of College Science Teaching, 27*(6), 383-388. Retrieved October 6, 2010, from http://www.wcer.wisc.edu/ archive/ cl1/ CL/ resource/ smallgrp.pdf

Dewey, J. (1966). *Democracy and education: An introduction to the philosophy of education*. New York, NY: The Free Press.

Gabriel, M. A. (2004). Learning together: Exploring group interactions online. *Journal of Distance Education, 10*(1), 54–72.

Gilmour, D. (2003, October). How to fix knowledge management. *Harvard Business Review.*

Jacobson, A., & Prusak, L. (2006, November). The cost of knowledge. *Harvard Business Review.*

Kimball, C., & Sibley, P. (1996). *The technology use plan primer*. San Diego, CA: Edmin Open Systems.

Ocker, R. J., & Yaverbaum, G. (1999). Asynchronous computer-mediated communication versus face-to-face collaboration: Results on student learning, quality and satisfaction. *Group Decision and Negotiation, 8*, 427–440. doi:10.1023/A:1008621827601

Perkins, D. N. (1991). What constructivism demands of the learner. *Educational Technology, 39*(9), 9–21.

Piaget, J. (1973). *Memory and intelligence*. New York, NY: BasicBooks.

Piaget, J. (1985). *The equilibration of cognitive structures: The central problem of intellectual development* (Brown, T., & Thampy, K. L., Trans.). Chicago, IL: University of Chicago Press.

Slavin, R. E. (1991). Synthesis of research of cooperative learning. *Educational Leadership, 48*(5), 71–82.

Sloan Consortium. (2009). *Learning on demand: Online education in the United States*. Sloan-C: A Consortium of Institutions and Organizations Committed to Quality Online Education. Retrieved December 1, 2010 from http://sloanconsortium.org/ publications/ survey/ learning_on_demand_sr2010

Sorensen, K. E., Takle, S. E., & Moser, M. H. (2006). Knowledge-building quality in online communities of practice: Focusing on learning dialogue. *Studies in Continuing Education, 28*(3), 241–257. doi:10.1080/01580370600947470

Tu, C. H., & Corry, M. (2002). E-learning community. *The Quarterly Review of Distance Education, 3*(2), 207–218.

Tu, C. H., & Corry, M. (2003). Building active online interaction via a collaborative learning community. *Computers in the Schools, 20*(3), 51–59. doi:10.1300/J025v20n03_07

Vygotsky, L. (1978). *Mind in society*. Cambridge, MA: Harvard University Press.

Woolfolk, A. E. (2010). *Educational psychology* (11th ed.). Upper Saddle River, NJ: Allyn & Bacon.

Yelland, N., Cope, B., & Kalantzis, M. (2008, August). Learning by design: Creating pedagogical frameworks for knowledge building in the twenty-first century. *Asia-Pacific Journal of Teacher Education, 36*(30), 197–213. doi:10.1080/13598660802232597

Zhang, J., Scardamalia, M., Reeve, R., & Messina, R. (2009). Designs for collective cognitive responsibility in knowledge building communities. *Journal of the Learning Sciences, 18*(1), 7–44. doi:10.1080/10508400802581676

ADDITIONAL READING

Bates, A. W. (1999). *Managing technological change: Strategies for academic leaders*. San Francisco, CA: Jossey Bass.

Buzzeo, T. (2002, September). Disciples of collaboration. *School Library Journal, 48*(9).

Cecez-Kecmanovic, D., & Webb, C. (2000). A critical inquiry into web-mediated collaborative learning. In Aggarwal, A. (Ed.), *Web-based learning and teaching technologies: Opportunities and challenges*. London: Ideal Group Publishing.

Coffman, T., & Klinger, M. B. (2010). Emphasizing diversity through 3D multi-user virtual worlds. In Kurubacak, G., & Yuzer, T. V. (Eds.), *Handbook of Research on Transformative Online Education and Liberation: Models for Social Equality*. Hershey, PA: IGI Global.

Danielson, J., Lockee, B., & Burton, J. (2000). ID and HCI: A marriage of necessity. In Abbey, B. (Ed.), *Instructional and cognitive impacts of web-based education*. London: Ideal Group Publishing. doi:10.4018/9781878289599.ch007

Davis, R., & Schlais, D. (2000). Learning and technology: Distributed collaborative learning using real-world cases. *Journal of Educational Technology Systems, 29*(2), 143–156. doi:10.2190/RXU0-B22T-PB14-0H9A

Dede, C. (1996). Distance learning, distributed learning: Making the transformation. *Learning and Leading with Technology, 23*(7), 25–30.

Duck, J.D. (1993, December). Managing change: The art of balancing. *Harvard Business Review.*

Jerald, C.D. (2009, July). *Defining a 21st century education*. Alexandria, VA: Center for Public Education.

Johnson, D. (2004). *Proactivity and reflection: Tools to improve collaborative experiences*. Minneapolis, MN: Minnesota Media.

Jonassen, D., Davidson, M., Collins, M., Campbell, J., & Haag, B. B. (1995). Constructivism and computer-mediated communication in distance education. *American Journal of Distance Education, 9*(2), 7–26. doi:10.1080/08923649509526885

Langer, E. J. (1988). *The power of mindful learning*. Cambridge, MA: Perseus Publishing.

Lemke, J. L. (1990). *Talking science: Language, learning, and values*. Norwood, NJ: Ablex.

Levy, F., & Murnane, R. J. (2007). How computerized work and globalization shape human skill demands. In Suarez-Orozco, M. M. (Ed.), *Learning in the global era: International perspectives on globalization and education* (pp. 158–176). Berkeley, CA: University of California Press.

Manouchehri, A. (2001). Collegial interaction and reflective practice. *Action in Teacher Education, 22*(4), 86–97.

Milbury, P. (2005, May/June). Collaboration: Ten important reasons to take it seriously. *Knowledge Quest, 33*(5).

Montiel-Overall, P. (2005). *Toward a theory of collaboration for teachers and librarians*. School Library Media Research.

Oblinger, D. G., & Maruyama, M. K. (1996). *Distributed learning*. Boulder, CO: CAUSE.

Persichette, K. A. (2000). A case study of lessons learned for the web-based educator. In Abbey, B. (Ed.), *Instructional and cognitive impacts of web-based education*. London: Ideal Group Publishing.

Roberts, T. S. (2004). *Online collaborative learning: Theory and practice*. Hershey, PA: IGI Global.

Rovay, A. P. (2004). A constructivist approach to online college learning. *The Internet and Higher Education, 7*(2), 79–93. doi:10.1016/j.iheduc.2003.10.002

Scott, T., Cole, M., & Engel, M. (1992). Computers and education: A cultural constructivist perspective. *Review of Educational Research, 18*, 191–251.

Sorensen, E. K. (2002). *Part of the online teachers curriculum: Designing for collaborative knowledge building online*. Society for Information Technology and Teacher Education International Conference, 995-999.

Walsh, J. P., & Maloney, N. G. (2007). Collaboration structure, communication media, and problems in scientific work teams. *Journal of Computer-Mediated Communication, 12*(2). doi:10.1111/j.1083-6101.2007.00346.x

Warschauer, M. (1997). Computer-mediated collaborative learning: Theory and practice. *Modern Language Journal, 81*(4), 470–481. doi:10.2307/328890

Wenger, E. (1998). *Communities of practice: learning, meaning, and identity*. Cambridge, UK: Cambridge University Press.

Willingham, D. T. (2007, Summer). Critical thinking: Why is it so hard to teach? *American Educator, 31*(2), 8–19.

Zhu, E. (1998). Learning and mentoring: Electronic discussion in a distance-learning course. In Bonk, C. J., & King, K. S. (Eds.), *Electronic collaborators: Learner-centered technologies for literacy, apprenticeship, and discourse* (pp. 233–259). Mahwah, NJ: Erlbaum.

Zumbach, J., & Reimann, P. (2003). Influence of feedback on distributed problem based learning. In B. Wasson, S. Ludvigsen & U. Hoppe (Eds.), *Designing for change in networked learning environments*, 219-228. Dordrecht, The Netherlands: Kluwer Academic Publishers.

KEY TERMS AND DEFINITIONS

Active Participation: Learner-centered instruction where students are engaged in the process of learning and take an active role by asking questions, making informed decisions, and questioning classmates ideas as well as their own.

Collaborative Supportive Learning Structure: A flexible learning environment created by the instructor that allows each member of the community to learn from both formal and informal interactions.

Constructivism: A learning environment that emphasizes social interactions and communication and where the instructor serves as a facilitator to support student learning.

Distance Learning: Courses provided at a distance and online.

Knowledge Construction: Students create their own personal understanding of the world through their experiences.

Multimodal Expressions: Distance learning courses have multiple ways for students and the instructor to communicate with one another, providing opportunities for discussion, demonstration and debate.

Preservice Teacher: Training provided to student teachers before they have undertaken any full-time teaching.

Section 3

Designing Online Messages for Reflections

Chapter 9
Designing Asynchronous Message Board Assignments for Deep Learning Discourse:
A Longitudinal Heuristic Case

Shalin Hai-Jew
Kansas State University, USA

ABSTRACT

Asynchronous message boards provide a critical space for university students to learn collaboration, support each other, and develop critical thinking skills in freshman and sophomore composition and research writing classes. How asynchronous message board assignments—icebreakers, discussion questions, summaries, reading analyses, lead-up assignments (research topic proposals, source evaluations, outlines, and drafts), and cumulative projects—all work towards building reflective online conversations and deep learning. This chapter addresses the evolving strategies that have been used in the deployment of publicly viewable assignments used on asynchronous message boards for freshman and sophomore writing classes since 1997 through the consortium WashingtonOnline (WAOL), which consists of 32 community colleges in Washington State.

INTRODUCTION

The information-based economy assumes a level of information sophistication and literacy to function in a complex global space. This literacy often requires many years of work to acquire and apply. At the university level, freshman and sophomore students begin to explore information in more depth in foundational composition and research writing courses; they look at where information comes from, how it is captured and packaged (in genres, in writing, and in print and electronic

DOI: 10.4018/978-1-61350-071-2.ch009

forms), how to vet information for credibility, and how to participate in that informational universe by honing their own self-expression, voices, and writing skills. Deep learning in this context involves multiple dimensions.

Deep Learning about Information

Deep learning differs based on the particular disciplinary field. Traditionally, deep learning involves plenty of analyses, sustained and critical discussions, and hands-on applied experiences (including simulations). Deep learning implies transferability of the skillset and knowledge to different learning contexts; it also suggests longitudinal (life-changing) learning.

The Self in Relation to the Information Universe

It is said that while writing is very personal on one level, it has to have social value to make it into publication. It has to offer something of benefit to others, whether that is knowledge or insight or even a sense of aesthetic appreciation. One important deep learning aspect involves knowledge of the information that one has and how one has come by this information and the standards that one applies in vetting what they believe. A critical and difficult lesson for younger students is differentiating between experienced versus inherited information. Many young learners confuse what they have heard from others or seen on the Internet or television (mediated experiences) with their own experiences; they will fall into easy parroting of others' ideas without a sense of their own lack of expertise in a particular area. Mastering the sense of one's relationship in the information universe to the larger world involves metacognition (awareness of one's thinking and learning) and an honest assessment of one's own skill sets and potential for contributing to the larger world of applicable information. They need to understand discourse as part of a broad range of information exchange and an ongoing social activity; they need to explore the various informational artifacts in the real world—in terms of articles on digital repositories or libraries; scripts; short stories; essays; poems; plays; movies, and multimedia files. They need to synthesize information across various streams and create semi-coherent understandings of a range of topics.

Reading Accurately

Deep informational knowledge involves the ability to read a variety of university-level works openmindedly and to be able to extract the main idea, the evidentiary supports, the writing genre, the writing tone, the writing strategies, the sources of information, the apparent purpose of the writing, and the target audience. They have to articulate and represent an original work comprehensively and accurately. They have to cite a work correctly so as to avoid plagiarism. They also have to avoid being manipulated by false information or emotional language.

Ideally, they would be able to apply particular frameworks of analysis—socio-cultural (historical, Marxist, feminist, psychoanalytical, and other schools of critique), textual (formalist or "new" criticism, structuralist, and deconstructionist), and personal schools of critique: author biographical and reader-response criticism. Ideally, learners may be able to identify satire, irony, symbolism, and other more complex forms of analysis.

The socio-cultural schools of literary critique include the following approaches. Historical criticism draws upon the historical circumstances of a piece of literature—to capture a sense of the larger setting and environment, particularly in terms of social and political concerns. Marxist critique focuses on the class structure of the society and the tensions between those with power and those who do not (or the bourgeois vs. the proletariat). Feminist critique involves the analysis of power dynamics between males and females. Psychoanalytic critique involves drawing on various psychological theories in analyzing the actions and thoughts of various characters in a work—including Freudian concepts of the self (as an id, ego, and superego), Jungian ideas of archetypes and the collective unconscious, and others.

Textual schools of critique focus on the textual aspects of a work independent from its social or historical context; rather, what's more important involves the uses of various literary devices and techniques. Textual critiques involve analyses of names, themes, characters, dialogue, binary oppositions, symbolism, various stylistic turns, the uses of point-of-view, voice, and tone, and word choices. Structuralist critique examines the component element's of a work's structure and what that says about the coded meanings in a text. Deconstructionism involves the breaking down of various elements: the verbiage, the symbols, the action, the plot, the characters, and other aspects in the work.

Personal schools of criticism involve two general approaches. One focuses on the author's biographical details and how they have been shown to have a direct effect on the writing. (**Note:** One critical error to avoid here is to not reverse-engineer a factual biography from fictional writing, which is a work of the imagination. Novice learners tend to over-assert beyond the evidence.) Reader-response critique involves the role of the reader in making meaning—based on his or her prior experiences and mental models. The situatedness of the various readers will shed different light on a work.

The evidence used to support an interpretation has to be found in the text, and learners have to be able to make a sound case for a particular interpretation. They have to be able to draw out the assumptions of the respective writers, if those are indicated, and they have to understand their own assumptions. They have to differentiate between objective and factual information as compared to subjective and analytical information. This learning then has to be transferable beyond the current academic terms and have to apply to future learning—in a discipline and self-regulated way.

When reading works from different time periods, learners need to see how those different contexts may have affected the extant ideas, and they need to develop a deep sense of empathy (and yet critical analysis) with the various writers.

Readers need to be able to engage the ideas raised by a particular work by cross-referencing other readings and bringing in from-life observations (which assumes wider reading beyond the classroom); they need to articulate these concepts originally. They need to vet the author's sources and decide how credible the line of argument is. They have to consider the logical end conclusions of the ideas (What would happen in the real world if such ideas were applied?) and analyze whether the work has practical merit. After all, ideas do not exist in a vacuum; ideas, like actions, often have consequences.

Writing Effectively and Analytically

The practical aspects of reading and writing may culminate, in a sense, in the writing—whether it is analytical (derivative from other writing) or more wholly original and innovative. In their writings, learners need to be aware of how the relevant disciplines and professions have set standards for information validity. They need to be aware of the different genres of writing and the demands of those genres for informational validity. (For example: A short story does not have to have any informational validity as compared to a non-fiction essay.) Learners should be able to engage complexity and ambiguity in their work and not fall into logical fallacies of over-simplification. Their work should show a nuanced understanding of the expectations of various writing structures and forms. They also need to be able to write effectively to a particular audience to achieve a particular purpose—whether it's to describe an experience, compare two different objects, categorize the types of a thing, or persuade others to a particular action or point-of-view.

Learners need to consider how specific disciplines and professions set standards for informational validity. They have to consider whether a work fits into a particular prose genre and then how well the author has executed the writing in that context. The informational source has to be cited accurately, with clear citations and provenanced information. Learners have to use informational graphics and visuals accurately to explain their ideas.

Research

Deep learning in university-level reading, writing, and research also involves being able to sift through information, to vet it for relevance, and to use information tactically to achieve particular research and writing aims. This ability assumes the ability to use electronic research tools effectively. Sophisticated learners should also be able to triangulate and cross-reference data to test for validity. They need to be able to maintain ambiguous understandings but also to identify contradictions in order to learn to explore further for possible resolutions of logical conflicts. Learners need to be able to extract how research was done. Learners also must be able to cite sources accurately to avoid plagiarism and to give credit where it's due.

Figure 1, "Sifting Secondary Information for Research Papers," lays the groundwork for evaluating information for possible relevance and use in a student paper. This ability to vet information will enhance the learner's ability to read more critically for sourcing.

Learners need to apply a clear sense of ethics and values in their selection of information and in their methods of collecting information and then in their uses of the data. Learners have to see the implications of information and develop a sensitivity as to how others might use that information:

> *In such a globally connected world – where published words and images give rise to bombing and burnings – teachers need to know how to instruct students in intercultural rhetoric, that is, how to persuade people to understand the way in which others located in different global contexts perceive, analyze, and produce situated knowledge (O'Brien, Alfano, & Magnusson, 2007, p. 126).*

Some applied principles in the uses of information include the rigor needed to capture facts and truths; the importance of not misrepresenting information or misleading readers (through incomplete, biased, unverified, archaic, emotionally manipulative, stereotypical, defamatory, or other types of information); the clear explanation of how information was attained; the protection of the identities of research sources, and the application of the idea that concepts have effects and do not exist in social vacuums. Ideas do get disseminated and have effects in the world. Figure 2, "Source Credibility," emphasizes the importance of using information that is close to the target source and that is verifiably valid.

Originality

One of the central values in non-fiction writing is to offer original information to a wider readership in a way that is beneficial. This requires knowledge of the extant writing in the world and an understanding of what would make the writing unique and original. Learners must be able to analyze what they know and select the data that would be relevant for a piece of writing created for public consumption. They must be able to analytically sift through their own experiences and empathetically understand what may have benefit for others. Learners also must train themselves to convey their own ideas with a unique sense of style. In the Western traditions, writing must be concise, accurate, and engaging to readers—but without using manipulative information or emotions.

Figure 1. Sifting secondary information for research papers

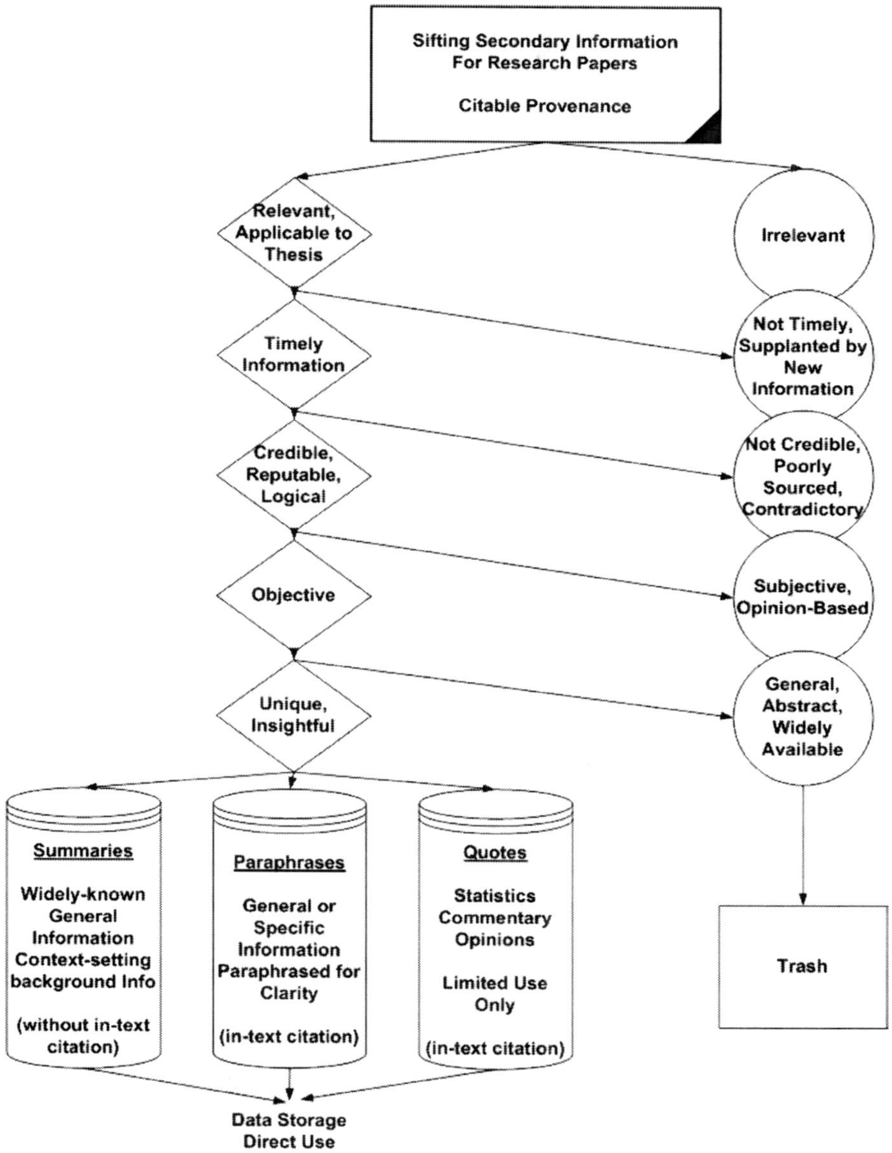

Self-Regulation and Follow-Through

All this is nontrivial learning. The human mind will be deeply taxed. After all, modern American learners are known to make it through high school without ever having once read an entire book. More than 40 percent, in standardized university entrance exams, do not fulfill the minimum requirements for college-level courses and have to take developmental ones. The non-complete rate in US high schools is more than 30 percent. Widely cited research suggests that 80 percent of modern college students have engaged in academic misconduct in the form of plagiarism. From 15 years of teaching online, this author has only encountered two papers (out of thousands) that had no mechanical, grammatical, syntactical or word choice mistakes.

Figure 2. Source credibility

Source Credibility

Insider (Direct) Sourcing

- Reach: Access to critical information, closeness to the topic, collection of primary data
- Background: Experience with the topic
- Probing and Reflective Approach: Credible questions, reasoning and ideas
- No Spin: No ulterior motives (spin or bias), no "sell," no desire for particular actions from information release, high stakes or low stakes, high or low pressure
- Logical: Clear use of logic, clarity
- How: Knowledge of how something works (causation)
- Why: Knowledge of why something works (underlying deep understanding)
- Authenticity of Authority: Clear lines of authority, training, documented support
- Timely Info: Timely information, not superseded by other data
- Cross-Referencing: Verification through several streams of information
- Proof: Authentication of ideas through physical "inviolable" (or at least credible) proof, use of "warrants" for assertions
- Knowing: Knowledge of others' motives and self-awareness of own motives
- Perspective: In-depth understanding in full complexity or in-depth understanding of a portion of topic
- Non-bias in Info Collection: Clean non-biased techniques
- Fair Interpretation: Critical analysis of facts

Outsider (Indirect) Sourcing

- Lack of access to primary information, no direct relation to the topic
- Strong opinions without facts, over-reaching in terms of conclusions
- Lack of consideration for full information, insufficient data
- No or little expertise in the field, no recent experience in the field
- Surface understanding
- High emotional involvement with the issue or topic, desire for particular end results from information release
- Unclear motives (spin or bias)
- Unclear logic
- Unclear "trail" or provenance of knowledge (primary or secondary)
- Unclear authority re: the issue, unproven track record
- Potential "sell" or promotion of particular ideas or agendas
- Potential corruption or contamination of data
- Defensiveness and anti-learning approaches, biased information gathering, inaccuracies, focus on the wrong information (e.g. personality vs. data),
- Political motivation to interpret information a particular way
- Logical fallacies in analysis and conclusions (false premises, hasty generalization, over generalization, red herring, straw man, ad hominem attacks, bandwagon effect, reference to authority)
- High stakes, controversial issues, or high pressure on sources

One artifact used to provoke learner thinking is the "Ladder of Inference," broadly adapted from Peter Senge's concepts that show how people's assumptions will affect what information they pursue and lead to erroneous conclusions. While Senge's "systems theory" ideas suggest a deeper level of rigor, there is a value to this concept of a learner as a tool in the environment to collect information and to make the best and most accurate use of it. If people do not know how to broaden their own informational horizons and to test assumptions, they may well short-circuit the process and bypass real experience and valid data. In the real world, this may have serious, negative implications.

Figure 3, "An Adaptation of Peter Senge's 'Ladder of Inference,'" shows how learners need to hone themselves as tools of research. They need to maintain an open mind but also a logically critical spirit about the information they engage. They need to keep that channel of research open until they have sufficient information to engage. They need to avoid traps such as defensiveness, blindness, wishful thinking, and so on. This is a tool to enhance learner metacognition.

The Challenges of Contemporary American Students

More than 50 percent of American students work in addition to going to school. Others also have many family responsibilities. These draws on time, energy, attention, and will—mean that it's harder to meet deadlines. Many will read quickly (skimming and scanning) and so miss critical information. Many will do the work in a non-thinking way. They will not go to the actual folders with the directions for the particular assignments and follow the directions. They will not conduct due diligence and research extra information in order

Figure 3. An adaptation of Peter Senge's "Ladder of Inference" for research writing. Adapted from Senge, 1994.

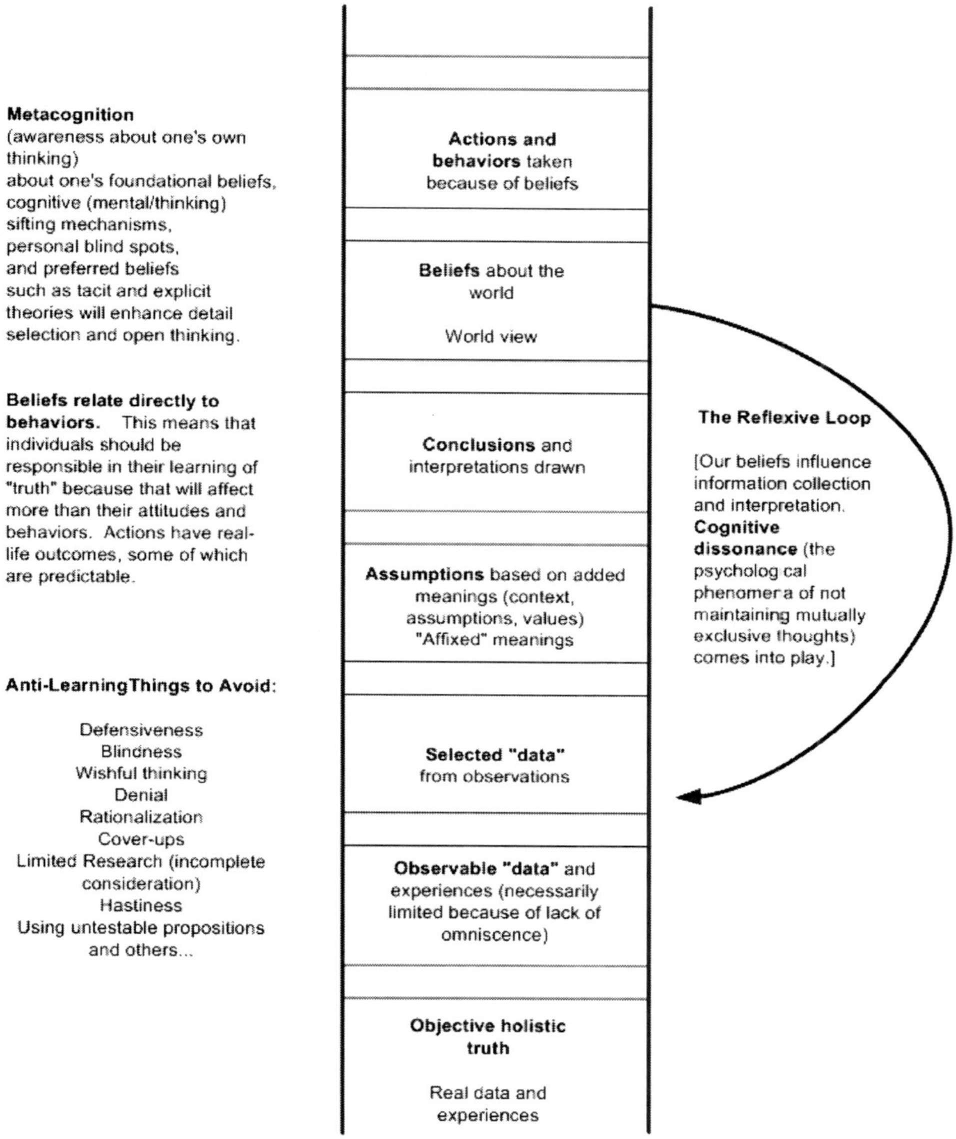

to add value to their responses. They will read a work and take it at face value, and they will more often than not have a context or system for vetting what is real or not (an observation made by Neil Postman in a prior generation in *Amusing Ourselves to Death*, from 1985).

They need to stretch contemporary attention spans that have often been trained to be short-term and flickering—with the fast cutaways of Hollywood movies and online games—in what has been termed cultural attention deficit hyperactivity disorder (ADHD). They must discipline themselves to read so they may actually understand the original writing in sufficient depth. They must brainstorm relevant questions and have the skills to track down the relevant information. They must be able to handle ambiguity and multiple ways of understanding a particular work, which is polysemic or many-meaninged. This is asking a lot of novice learners.

A Literature Review

Conventional face-to-face courses involve limited student-to-student and student-to-teacher interactions in comparison to online "high-tech high-touch" courses, which focus on online human-facilitated interactivity. The asynchronous message board offers ways for learners to share insights and digital files, provide support to each other, debate ideas, and bring more of themselves into the learning. Asynchronicity removes some of the pressures of synchronous learning (which is much more fast-paced), and it replaces it with time for learners to reflect and to maintain longer trains of continuous discussion. Researchers contend that such interactions enhance knowledge creation: "Discourse is central to knowledge creation because it is the means through which knowledge is formed, criticized, and amended" (Scardamalia, Bereiter, & Lamon, 1994, as cited in Lamon, 2005, p. 358). Dialogic arguments may be honed online with supporting evidence and the addressing of counterclaims (Kuhn & Goh, 2005, p. 346).

Online learning also may use peer review to create effective quality assurance (Bauer, Figl, Derntl, Beran, & Kabicher, 2009). While online courses emphasize the importance of individual telepresence and group social presence, researchers have found that pseudonymous interactivity has value for learning and "is compatible with responsible online behavior" (Kilner & Hoadley, 2005, p. 278).

The learners in online courses may be seen to be part of a knowledge building community which engages "real ideas and authentic problems"—by sharing diverse ideas (which are all treated as "improvable"), holding discourses to build on shared knowledge, supporting the original contributions of each participant, and "democratizing knowledge" (as having shared ownership of group progress and knowledge building) (Lamon, 2005, p. 360). Meaning-making requires "the inter-animation of more than one perspective," observes one researcher (Wegerif, 2005, p. 707).

The processes in virtual workshops may be understood as a permutation of Kolb's experiential learning cycle (1984). This theorist's model moves from concrete experience to reflective observation to abstract conceptualization to active experimentation (Kolb & Boyatzis, as cited in Sternberg & Zhang, 2001, p. 229). In the online workshop, learners observe, perform, acquire feedback, reflect, and then reapply their work, with cumulative learning and synergistic supports from their peers. Group members support and encourage individuals' efforts: "Moreover, working with peers tends to reduce anxiety as learners share solutions to complex tasks, increasing satisfaction with the process and results" (Gerosa, Pimentel, Fuks, & Lucena, 2005, p. 160).

Online courses may be considered a type of asynchronous learning network which promotes "student-instructor interaction, emphasize(s) student-to-student collaboration, and generate(s) active participation with appropriate software" (Hiltz & Turoff, 2002, p. 56). Tactical uses of questions achieve a variety of aims. Short answers may be elicited for information verification, decision-making, clarifying concepts, defining features, determining quantities; long answers may be elicited for defining concepts, eliciting examples, comparing objects, interpreting data, clarifying causal relationships, enabling a particular action, clarifying expectations, and eliciting judgments; and task oriented endeavors may be organized for promoting effective group dynamics, monitoring group activities, encouraging self-directed learning, clarifying prior statements or information, and requesting specific actions (Hmelo-Silver, 2002, p. 201).

The asynchronicity in online courses (which are semi-public spaces) occurs within the framework of the semester or quarter term, often with week-based deadlines, during which the interactivity and shared work has to be uploaded, along with critiques or other feedback loops. Also, instructors will facilitate the interactivity oftentimes by stimulating conversations, reflecting on the variety of opinions, leveraging cognitive conflicts, highlighting critical ideas, sharing resources, and coordinating the learning efforts. Instructor presence also may mean more sophisticated scaffolding of learning for ill-structured problems and projects. The instructor encourages interdependence among the learners and awareness about each other's works (Sorensen, 1999).

Human Facilitation

Early on in an online course, the instructor has created an electronic environment for the situated cognition of the learners. In this case, the space is set up as a reading and writing workshop where learners will engage with various texts in the "communications triangle." This concept suggests an interaction between the individual learners, the instructor, and the various texts, and their own created texts. The reciprocity and tensions between each of these elements promotes a space in which different perspectives may be shared. Learners must apply an "activity awareness" to the work of others in the online spaces for the most effective interactivity.

An Environment of Safety

The instructor's role involves setting up social icebreakers (activities which allow people to socialize without discomfort) early on to help learners get to know each other and to form a level of comfort in providing feedback and commentary to each other. Individuals are asked to post textual biographical profiles of themselves as a self-introduction. The sharing of identities among all participants provides a sense of equal voices and rights of presence; the acknowledgments of these identities affirm the dignity of learners. A continuing sense of identity involves the definition of roles in a class and the responsibilities of those roles. For example, students will sometimes ask the instructor to choose a topic for their writing—and the instructor must decline because that is within the role and responsibility of the individual learner.

Why is an atmosphere of safety so critical? For people to learn and to take risks in their learning, they need to have an environment in which they are not penalized for their explorations and creativity. An atmosphere of safety is also critical for professional support of learners. Learners often begin classes with a sense of fast trust, and it's the instructor's to lose by mismanagement or lack of care (Hai-Jew, 2007). An environment of safety is created in multiple ways.

First, learners are informed of the regulatory environment. They are notified of the instructor's responsibilities to them and their rights and responsibilities. They learn of learner privacy. These involve the privacy protections of the Family Education Rights and Privacy Act (FERPA), which protects learners' private information like grades, contact information, and other non-catalog details.

The instructor's provision of a private channel (usually email and telephone) for interactivity is also critical in order to address learner concerns. For some students, they will request to write on personal topics as a form of both learning and catharsis, and they would rather not share their work online for others' perusal, and accommodating that is also important for both the academic learning and the student's personal development. This means that the instructor works with the student by email or other off-public-channel modes and then maintains learner secrets into perpetuity.

Another aspect of learner privacy is the creation of an online "learner lounge" in an asynchronous message board to allow for informal chat and relaxation of learners among themselves. This is an instructor-free space, which means the instructor never goes in to see what students have posted and never posts messages there—except in the rare situation of a break-down in student relationships requiring some sort of mediation. (Note: The author has never yet had occasion to go into an online student lounge.)

There's the anti-plagiarism policy and academic honesty provisions that apply to the learning. This assumes full revelation of the policies and then follow-through in enforcing the policies. This means using lead-up assignments that students evolve in order to submit a work to the course—from brainstormed topic to source evaluations to outlining to developing the various sections of a paper. This also suggests the calling out of students who have submitted plagiarized works and not rewarding dishonest academic behaviors.

An instructor's respect for learners' intellectual property rights means that he or she must attain rights to use a particular student work. This also means that he or she must surface all known rules of IP for students who may be interested in publishing their works. This alignment of laws, values, and practices is critical for an environment of professional safety.

Civility clauses at the course level establish a modicum of respect for others' dignity and differences of opinion—particularly in courses where controversial issues may be addressed. The instructor, too, must abide by all civility policies, and he or she should never use an online class as a bully pulpit to spread pet ideas, politics, or values. The classroom should be a safe space from any sort of ideological taint.

This information is addressed in a transparent way. With full knowledge, learners have a stronger sense of self-efficacy and an understanding of the rules of engagement that all must abide by.

Second, the instructor creates an environment of accountability—in which all learners are accountable to themselves, the instructor, their respective educational institutions, the ethics of the field, and the larger publics. This is achieved through modeling, through statements, and through the design of the learner works.

The uses of learner peer review for quality assurance and learner training in critique and diplomacy have high value in online writing and research workshops. Such interactions help build learner tolerance for others' critiques of their works without the usual defensiveness. This experience also mimics the professional role of peer review which is widely used in academia. Peer review helps learners be accountable to the values of the field and to each other's well-being in the course.

Third, the long-term persistence and archival of the online course protects the official work record and puts all interactions into a recorded situation in case any review is necessary. Having all asynchronous message threads and all digital contents available from the beginning and available all term (even though closed threads are moved to the bottom of each message board) enables learners to review past work and to peruse others' work as time allows. It is a rare occurrence to delete learner messages (usually only at their request or only if works were posted multiple times accidentally—for the course housekeeping's sake).

Fourth, fair treatment of all students and clear abiding by the course policies is critical in terms of a safe environment. This involves clear and regular feedback—in this case, responses to all student postings and line-by-line formative critiques of all assignments and essay drafts. Such tailored attention (with comments interspersed in the text) makes the online course experience much more personalized and customized to the individual. One researcher notes: "Annotating digital documents is believed to offer many advantages for asynchronous discussions because the context of the annotation is clear to other readers" (Brush, 2002, p. 542). This instructor attention to detail involves a high cost in instructor time, but it's critical for actual learning to occur. Any questions that are asked have to be addressed in full measure—whether the question is posted in the public forum in the online classroom or is emailed from the learner's private email account. There cannot be a discrepancy between a public and private face.

Fifth, instructor flexibility and care are also important for creating safety. This flexibility applies to pacing the course—sometimes requiring a de-escalation in the pace over segments that students find difficult, for example. In other times, students may need personal accommodations because of personal emergencies. This also suggests acceptance of a wide range of learner proposed topics for exploration and research, so the assignments have personal relevance to learners.

The power of instructor-led courses is in the capability to accommodate for ill-structured, divergent, and open-ended learning vs. convergent and close-ended learning. The thinking is that learners need to learn the rules, but they also need to learn the confidence to break the rules when necessary for a particular effect or purpose. This flexibility taps into learner motivations. Because such foundational classes attract learners from a range of academic disciplines, instructors must accommodate a range of interests—from the arts and humanities, social sciences, empirical sciences, and other fields. Also, if an instructor has made a mistake, he or she needs to correct that mistake promptly and transparently. That openness is another important aspect of safety.

A sense of instructor care also may be conveyed through the offering of some extra credit opportunities, which provide paths for extra learning. Having grade floors for a particular assignment may also provide a sense of protection for learners who may have met the basic requirements of an assignment even if some other aspects were deficient. (Note: This not does suggest a buy-in to the common student idea that they begin with perfect points and have points "taken away" from them by the instructor. This assumption is apparent when students ask why they "lost" points on a particular assignment. It's important that students do not have the assumption of grade entitlement—the common idea that they start out with all points possible.) A "floor" could assume a student's right of re-submittal of an assignment that he or she misunderstood at the first go-around.

Sixth, learners need a sense of where they are. This is achieved through rich and regular feedback loops—such as prompt (1-2 days) responses on all student assignments with in-depth feedback; full responses to all posted queries and emailed messages; accessible grades throughout the term (beginning from the Pre-week or so-called Week Zero when the course is opened a week before the course actually begins), and constant and regular notifications of course issues, pacing, and performance on the assignments. The methods for grading need to be transparent and expressed in tools like grade sheets and rubrics—to set a baseline understanding and then with unique comments on the work to support learners where they're at. Learners who prefer consistent structure may prefer the continual uses of grade rubrics, but many will use rubrics to set expectations and then offer more free-form feedback on the learner works.

The responsibility for full disclosure falls on the instructor because he or she has access to the critical information to promote the learning. There is no reason to withhold. Full transparency early on and throughout enables learners to pace their own work within the larger weekly deadlines, and it enables them to be more successful by working ahead and doubling-back as needed.

A Longitudinal Heuristic Case

In this particular case, two foundational undergraduate courses, English Composition and Research Writing, are addressed. Both of the courses were created by curricular development teams led by faculty hired by WashingtonOnline (WAOL), a consortium of 34 colleges in Washington State. These courses were built on different learning / course management systems (L/CMSes) and ported over to different structures as the consortium's work evolved. Compared to other courses, these tend to be very highly text-based and also "high-tech high-touch," with a strong emphasis on instructor engagement with learners. (**Note:** This high human-facilitated interactivity is one reason why classes are capped at 31 students per term With the usual percentage who are non-participants—for all the invitation to engage in the class—this makes for a workable instructor workload.)

The Technologies: Learning/ Course Management Systems (L/CMSes) and Asynchronous Message Board Assignments

Online courses are often taught through learning / course management systems (L/CMSes), or Web-based socio-technical systems that enable digital delivery of contents, online interactivity, and class coordination with grading, and other features. Students may create profiles to introduce themselves to each other. Asynchronous message boards, which consist of topic-based threaded discussions, are a critical part of these systems because they allow for both semi-public student submittal of work and text-based intercommunications.

Basic features of asynchronous message boards are the following: the ability to start a message thread and to reply to any number of messages; the archival of all messages; the ability to attach digital files (up to a certain file size limit); the ability to change the subject line in response to others' messages; the ability to search for particular key words in the message board; the ability to sequence the original threads in a message board into a certain order, and the ability to name message boards based on a certain topic or learning sequence (or any other way that information may be sequenced or ordered using words). Add-on features based on different L/CMSes involve ways for learners to rate the popularity of a particular posting with stars or other measures.

As many have noted, tools are transformed during the activity itself. The mental models built around a conversation, for example, may imbue the intercommunications with a higher sense of purpose and conceptualization beyond the interchanged messages themselves. The ideas may evoke readings and trigger new ideas that exist well beyond the text of the concepts.

Asynchronous message boards may house a theoretically infinite level of discussions, depending on how far participants want to pursue a particular thread. In practice, one particular thread can go approximately 15 – 20 messages deep depending on the directions of ideas and the levels of student and instructor interest. Some conversations continue across multiple threads and multiple forums, particularly in online courses that use a theme-based textbook that supports the deepening conversations around a particular topic.

Hoadley and Enyedy point out how information and communication media enhance social activities and enable the movement between dialogue (with others) and monologue (with the self) as a way to promote learning—and they show the importance of the "middle spaces" between dialogue and monologue as critical for computer supported collaborative learning technologies (Hoadley & Enyedy, 1999, n.p.). Dialogue is interactive; monologue is reflective. In a sense, the faculty member as a facilitator also enhances the fluidity of such middle spaces.

Asynchronous message boards then are used in the context of multi-threaded discourses with multiple methods of formal and informal communications. The collaborative online learning environment exists on public, semi-public, and fully private channels. Figure 4, "Conversation Flows around Nodes of Contents, Tasks, and Personalities and Communities," offers a depiction of how the intercommunications occur in an online classroom—around contents, tasks, people's ideas, and the larger world.

Figure 4. Conversation flows around nodes of contents, tasks, and personalities and communities

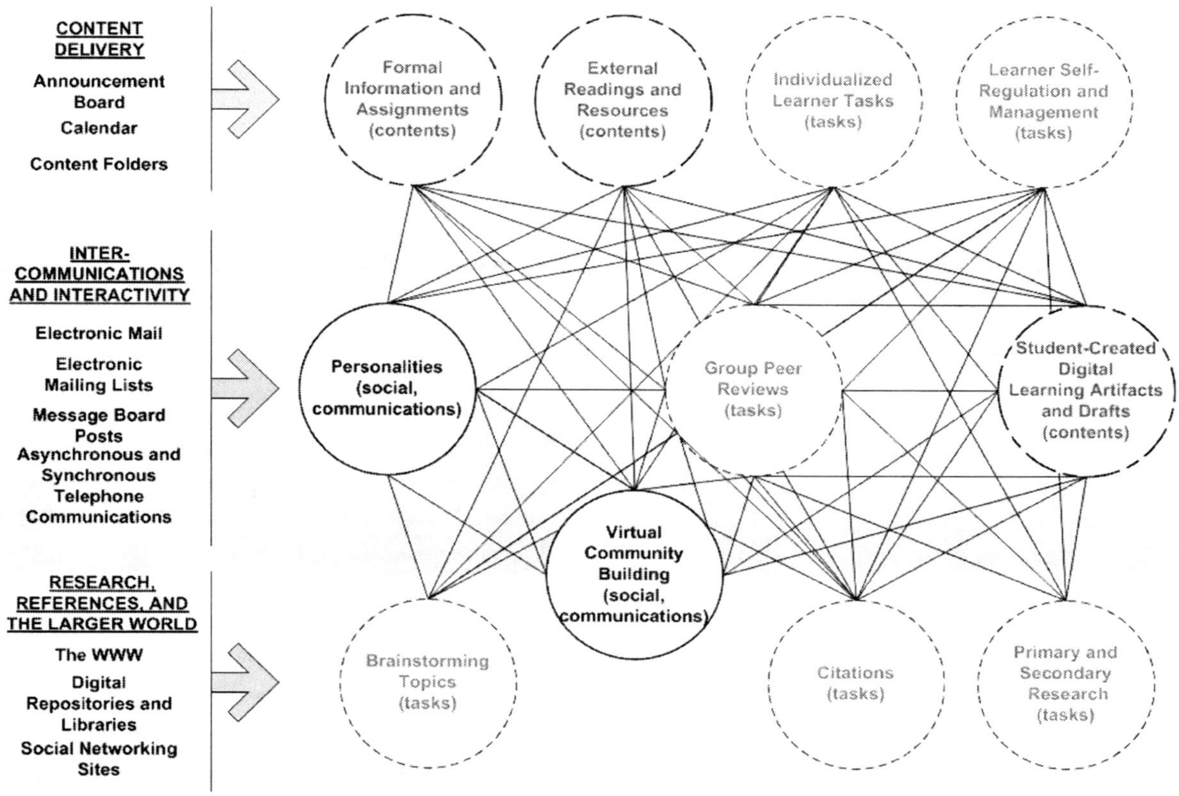

The Setup of Message Boards

Most asynchronous message boards are listed by the week that the work is due and the topic of the assignments due. The overall e-learning path and trajectory are obvious by perusing the topic names alone. When the assignments and interactivity for the particular message boards have reached the deadline, the forums are closed by a mark in the heading, but they're kept open and accessible all term.

The self-introductory threads and other low-value early assignments provide opportunities for learners to post works and experiment with the L/CMS technologies without too much embarrassment or social costs. There may be orphaned messages that are not part of the "reply-to" structure or mis-posted files that may need retraction or covering over. Learners begin to create that discursive coherence based on the lines of argument and information that came before. They also introduce new concepts into the discussions and engage others with messages that have a more personalized touch.

The goal of assignments (set up on asynchronous message boards) then is to build to a high standard of learning given many limits. The limits involve the amount of work that students can expect for a five credit course balanced against the requirements of learning experiences for course transferability. There is the need to train students to be able to succeed in successive courses and also to prepare them to compete well in future college courses. The L/CMSes involve affordances and constraints—and those provide hedges and limits to what may be done. The instructor's depth of experience and approaches to the teaching and learning also offer limits.

Deep Learning about Information in Intertextual Exchanges

The following then is a rubric for measuring deep learning in intertextual exchanges on an asynchronous message board in freshman and sophomore composition and research writing classes (see Table 1).

Porous Boundaries: The Classroom and the World

While online classes maintain a place of safety for risk-taking and new and deep learning, these classes are also very closely tied to the real world. Each student is only a few clicks away from sharing a wide range of contents with the world. In this particular learning context, learners may be encouraged to publish—if they're emotionally and professionally ready to. Being "ready" also involves knowing the rules of publishing (in terms of intellectual property, avoidance of libel, privacy protections, and other elements). Learners also need to realize the diversity of peoples who will be recipients of the information being shared.

To that end, it's important to address clean writing from the beginning to make sure that all works are legitimately created and ready to be shared in commercial spaces. Figure 5, "Five After: The Application of Commercial Standards to Intellectual Property Issues in Class," suggests the importance of student awareness of their risks and benefits in going into the world with their works. This also shows the importance of building with clean intellectual property (IP) and other habits, so the porous wall between the online classroom and the world may be more easily and beneficially traversed.

Indeed, all successful students have to eventually go out into the world with their skill sets, so early senses of sampling the world and engaging it would be beneficial for some learners.

Future Discourse

The building of asynchronous message board assignments for deep learning will differ depending on the particular disciplinary field. This chapter opened with a definition of deep learning in terms of interacting with information—as readers and writers. This then highlighted how asynchronous message boards were built for reading and writing courses at the freshman and sophomore levels in instructor-team created courses taught in the WashingtonOnline (WAOL) consortium. This suggests the importance of the design of the environment, the design of assignments, and the facilitation work of the instructor and learner peers in order to successfully achieve deep learning discourse, which involves all text interchanges on the asynchronous message board and some digital contents in the content areas and other parts of an online learning environment. Figure 6, "A Heuristic Model for Designing Asynchronous Message Board Assignments for Deep Learning Discourse," shows the interactivity among the various elements of this model—originating strategies from the definition of deep learning in the discipline, and going through a trial-and-error model of building asynchronous message board assignments, and then measuring results—and making proper changes in the assignments from there.

Future writing may address the design of asynchronous message board assignments for deep learning discourse in other domain fields. This assumes a definition of the desired deep learning for the field, long-term observations of student behaviors in online courses, and extracted methods of assignment building based on what works.

Figure 5. Five after: The application of commercial standards to intellectual property issues in class

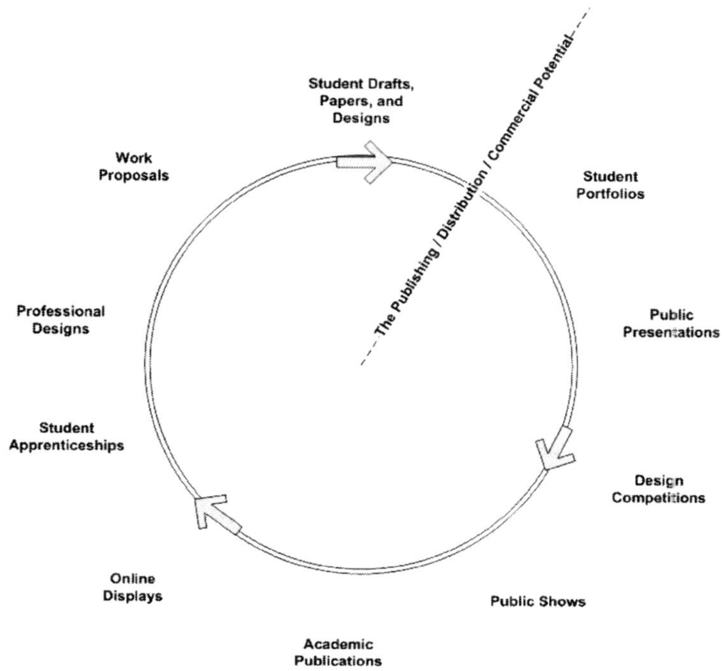

Table 1. A rubric for measuring deep learning about information in intertextual exchanges

Deep Learning Goals	Strategic Asynchronous Message Board Assignments
The Self in Relation to the Information Universe • Does the learner show awareness of personal vs. public writing? Does the learner understand what the "social value" of a piece of writing is? • What is directly experienced information vs. inherited information? Why is original information more valuable than repeated information from others? • Does the learner demonstrate clarity about his / her own writing skills and knowledge base? Does he / she know how to broaden his / her reading experiences and access to relevant information? • Do the learners show an understanding of the importance of discourse as part of the larger context of information exchange? • Do the learners show an awareness of the various ways that information may be packaged and delivered to various audiences? • Are the learners able to synthesize information from various sources in a coherent way?	**Topic Selection:** Learners are asked to propose topics for essays based on their own lived experiences. This will allow them a basis from which to select relevant information, and it will also give them a framework from which to evaluate researched information. Learners are encouraged to choose topics about which they have something to learn and benefit from knowing. (Novice writers will often gravitate towards pre-existing topics with plenty of essay samples available online instead of proposing anything about which they have direct experiences. They also often will not align their topic selection with anything in their lives, which would be more efficient.) The proposal of topics also shows how well learners can gauge their ability to conduct relevant research, read a particular amount of writing, form a coherent thesis, and write a term research paper. This is where scaffolding for the lead-up assignments is particularly useful. Topic proposals can show how well learners understand and conceptualize the assignment. Conceptualizing the requirements and then ensuring one's proposal's fit to the assignment is beneficial—particularly in understanding writing organization, purpose, effective use of information, and the values of the profession (originality, style, proper crediting, and others). It also sometimes shows whether the learners take the initiative to read the student sample essays of the students who came before, in order to help them in the conceptualization of the wide possible range of work. **Sourcing:** Students can use the occasional video, primary email-based interview, and other sourcing in a research paper. (Using cross-format types of sources may enhance their senses of where information resides and how it may be harnessed for practical purposes.)

continued on following page

Table 1. Continued

Deep Learning Goals	Strategic Asynchronous Message Board Assignments
Reading Accurately • Do the learners read open-mindedly? • Are the learners able to extract the main ideas relevantly? • Are the learners able to extract the evidentiary supports used by the respective authors? • Do the authors show an understanding of the various demands of the various writing genres, based on culture and prior practice and certain functional demands? • Are the learners able to identify the writing tone? • Are the learners able to identify the writing strategies? • Are the learners able to identify the various sources of information in a particular work? Can they tell how valid these possible sources of information are from the work? • Are the learners able to identify the apparent purpose of the writing? • Are the learners able to identify the target audience? • Are the learners able to summarize a work comprehensively and accurately? • Are the learners able to cite works correctly (using the assigned citation method) to avoid plagiarism? • Are learners able to engage the ideas of a work by cross-referencing other readings and applying from-life observations? • Are they able to vet the author's sources and decide how credible the particular line of argument is? • Do the learners consider the logical end conclusions of the ideas? Are they able to analyze whether the work has practical merit? • Are the learners aware of how different time periods may have affected the writing? • Are the learners able to apply the apt frameworks of analysis to the particular reading in order to extract valuable information and insights? • Are the learners able to make a coherent and supportable argument based on evidence from the text?	**Formulating Questions for Peers:** Students are asked to create analytical questions for peers to consider based on particular literary works. They are to avoid creating "generic" questions that do not show an understanding of the literature or the schools of literary critique. Formulating effective questions and seeing where these questions lead is a powerful way to text student mental models and knowledge. **Cross-Cultural Understandings:** Offer works that are outside of the students' comfort zones. Put them in a situation of analyzing a work which is from an unfamiliar time or background. Analyze how fairly they engage the works. What efforts do they take to understand the writing? Do they open up to the works, or do they shut down and just apply their own worldview? **Engaging Complexity:** See how learners engage with satirical works. Do they catch the tone and purpose, or do they read a satire as straight argumentation? Debrief their interactions, and bring a clearer sense of understanding of the works. Help learners achieve a comfort with ambiguity but still maintain a critical sense of analytical logic in understanding a situation. **Beyond Self:** Offer ways for learners to engage a work beyond the reader-response school of literary critique. Too often, readers will merely give their own response, without understanding that that alone is limited and not of any particular value. There is importance in being able to apply a framework to analytically and informatively engaging a work. **The Power of Ideas in the World:** Engage how ideas affect learner decision-making. Then, bring in some historical understandings. Show how ideas move people and societies…and have effects in the world. Engage systems complexity. If one action is taken, what are the intended or unintended effects? How can particular actions be construed or misconstrued? **Articulating Standards:** Help learners articulate what standards they apply to information to understand something to be true. Offer other models for vetting information. Help learners understand the life cycle of information…and how it is evolved over time. **Identifying Writing Strategies:** Work with learners to identify tone, metaphors, symbols, binary oppositions, similes, monologues, dialogues, and other aspects of writing that affect the reading experience. Analyze the theories and thinking behind the melding of fictional features and non-fiction prose in "New Journalism," for example. **Avoiding Manipulation:** Help learners develop a mental toolkit to perceive when they are being manipulated by writers with propaganda, emotionalism, unsubstantiated assertions, incomplete information, inapplicable analogies, or other writing strategies. **Encourage Cross-Referencing:** Help learners cross-reference information from various sources.

continued on following page

Table 1. Continued

Deep Learning Goals	Strategic Asynchronous Message Board Assignments
Writing Effectively and Analytically • Are the learners aware of how the relevant disciplines and professions set standards for informational validity? Are the learners aware of the genre of writing and the information validity of that genre? • Are learners able to engage complexity and ambiguity in their work? • Are learners aware of the writing conventions and features of various writing structures and forms? • Are the learners able to write in various writing structures and forms? • Are learners able to strategically write to a particular audience to achieve a particular purpose? • Are learners able to cite the sources professionally and ethically?	**Disaggregating Pieces to a Longer Writing Project:** To focus learner attention on particular requirements for particular aspects of a piece of writing, disaggregate the pieces in order to analyze each of the pieces alone. In other words, require separate postings of the thesis, lead-in or introduction paragraphs, and the conclusion of an essay. Define what each piece has to achieve. For example, a lead-in needs to attract reader attention, properly reflect the contents of the essay, introduce the narrative voice, and introduce the thesis or main idea. **Genres and Organizational Conventions:** Expose learners to various rhetorical modes and genres of writing. Highlight the aspects of these texts to show why they fit into a particular form. Then, assign work so that the learners may practice these various forms. Assign the writing of outlines to explicitly address the issues of structure and writing strategy. **Audience Awareness:** Help your learners write strategically to a designated audience to achieve a particular aim. Help them apply structure, tone, information, logic and reasoning, evidentiary support, and other ethical methods to communicate with an audience. (**Note:** The typical assumed audience for a college writing class is their peers or other college students.) **Citation:** Learners often struggle to understand why they need to cite and why they need to cite in a particular way—both in-text and in the References that follow. It is important to help learners understand the information life cycle and the ethics behind citing sources. It is also important to show why the different citation methods take particular approaches to cite particular information.
Research • Are learners able to discern between relevant and irrelevant information for a particular purpose? • Are learners able to effectively conduct research using contemporary electronic research tools? • Are learners able to extract how cited research was done? Are they able to articulate research methods in their own writing? • Are the learners able to triangulate and cross-reference data for validity? • Are the learners able to cite sources accurately (so as to avoid plagiarism but also to give credit where it's due)? Are learners able to maintain accurate records of their research sources? • Do the learners use research and researched information ethically?	**Sifting Information:** One common assignment used is to assign learners to conduct research using multiple methods: digital repositories, physical libraries, and so on. In higher level courses, students would be sent out to do primary firsthand research, but that is not advisable without full student preparation and training (to avoid potential harms and to align with legal requirements). **Source Evaluations:** Ask students to cite their sources using bibliographical citations, and then have them to comprehensively summarize the contents of the sources. Make sure that they closely summarize how the original authors conducted their research; after all, novice learners think their work is done once they've cited a "reputable" source; they need to train to look beyond the name to the methodology of information collection. Then have them add an evaluation of the validity of that source and how that source might or might not support their thesis. Encourage students to include sources that support and that refute the student author's stance. Work with students to see the tie between their ideas and relevant supporting information. **Assertion-Support:** Emphasize the importance of having evidence for all main assertions. Highlight any observed disjunctures between assertions and the evidence backing up that assertion. **Logical End Conclusions:** Help learners explore some of the potential repercussions of the research and writing. Show how ideas have implications.

continued on following page

Table 1. Continued

Deep Learning Goals	Strategic Asynchronous Message Board Assignments
Originality • Are learners able to personalize their ideas and show how the data they hold relates to them? • Are the learners about to offer fresh information that has not been published before? Are they able to offer original thoughts? • Are learners able to convey their own ideas with a sense of unique style? • Do learners write in a way that is tailored to a particular audience? • Do the learners write with proper concision? • Are the learners accurate in their writing? • Do the learners avoid the use of manipulative information or emotions? • Do the learners apply professional and personal ethical guidelines to their works?	**Self-Knowledge:** Help learners ruminate a little about what experiences they have that they would like to explore in a writing class. In classes that do not yet include research, students only have themselves to draw from, so they need to select aspects of themselves that would be beneficial to explore. **Self and the Future:** Have students write a paragraph about some of their ambitions, goals, and interests. These provide powerful fodder for research topics—because most students will find ways to benefit from what they learn in the course of writing a research paper. **Understanding Originality:** Students often struggle with knowing what it is about themselves that may have value for other readers. They struggle with the idea that they may have anything of value for others. It is important to show them that if they can write based purely on their own lives and experiences and personalities, they will have an original piece of writing…because no one else has the same lives or perspectives as they have had. It is more impossible to write a plagiarized piece similar to someone else's writing than it is to write a fully original piece of writing.
Self Regulation and Follow-through • Are the learners able to discipline themselves for the learning? • Do the learners meet the deadlines? • Do the learners read the directions in sufficient depth to do the work? • Do the learners hone themselves as learning tools based on accurate meta-cognition? • Are the learners able to do the required work while upholding high standards of academic integrity? • Are the learners able to apply the proper mechanics, grammar, syntax, and word choice to their writing?	**Scaffolding:** Asynchronous message boards can be scaffolded to help students self-regulate with the proper pacing of the work, and the posting of deadlines. **Instructor Support:** Instructor feedback about the appropriateness of the submitted work (in terms of fit to the assignment) and his or her flexibility in supporting revisions will be important for learner success.

CONCLUSION

This longitudinal heuristic case culminates many years of online teaching and learning. It captures the subject matter expert (SME) level of insight in a particular field—research writing—and how asynchronous discussion board assignments may be set up and presented for deeper learning. This chapter presents a simplified model for approaching how to create asynchronous message board assignments for deeper learning by offering an example and then a general conceptualization that may support work in the online teaching and learning field and practice.

ACKNOWLEDGMENT

Thanks to Dr. Sandra Madsen and Hildy Helgeson at Walla Walla Community College, for such effective direction and support. I am also grateful to Connie Broughton, Mark Carbon, Brook Bane, and Monique Kovalenko, of the State Board for Community and Technical Colleges and WashingtonOnline for all of their collaborative support over the years. It truly always takes a team. Their encouragement of deep learning has enhanced the learner experience and my work as an instructor. Thanks to R. Max.

Figure 6. A heuristic model for designing asynchronous message board assignments for deep learning discourse

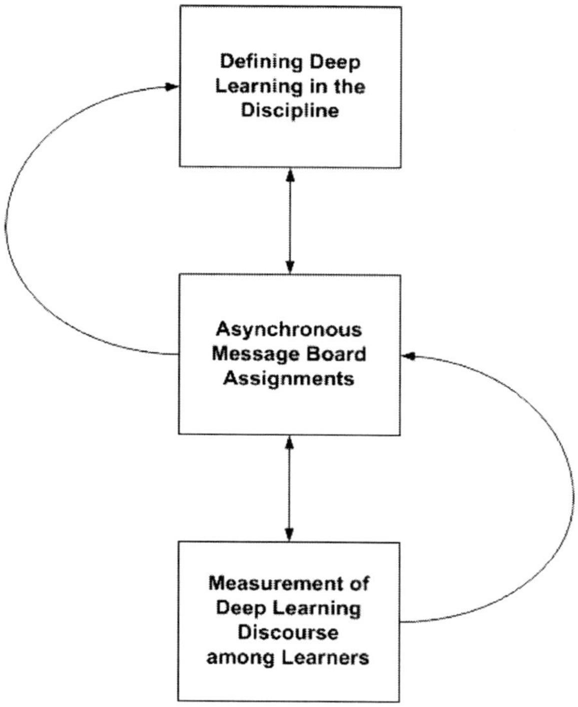

REFERENCES

Bauer, C., Figl, K., Dernti, M., Beran, P. P., & Kabicher, S. (2009). The student view on online peer reviews. In the *Proceedings of the 14th ACM –SIGCSE Annual Conference on Innovation and Technology in Computer Science Education* (ITiCSE '09), Paris, France. (pp. 26–30).

Brush, A. J. B. (2002). *Annotating digital documents: Anchoring, educational use, and notification. In the Proceedings of Human Computer Interfaces* (pp. 542–543). Minneapolis, MN: ACM.

Gerosa, M. A., Pimentel, M. G., Fuks, H., & Lucena, C. J. P. (2005). No need to read messages right now: Helping mediators to steer educational forums. In the *Proceedings of the 2005 Conference on Computer Support for Collaborative Learning* (pp. 160–169). Taipei, Taiwan: International Society of the Learning Sciences.

Hai-Jew, S. (2007). The trust factor in online instructor-led college courses. *Journal of Interactive Instruction Development*, *19*(3), 11–25.

Hiltz, S. R., & Turoff, M. (2002). What makes learning networks effective? *Communications of the ACM*, *45*(4), 56–59. doi:10.1145/505248.505273

Hmelo-Silver, C. E. (2002). Collaborative ways of knowing: Issues in facilitation. In the *Proceedings of the Computer Supported Collaborative Learning* (CSCL 2002), (pp. 199–208).

Hoadley, C. M., & Enyedy, N. (1999). Between information and communication: Middle spaces in computer media for learning. In the *Proceedings of the 1999 Conference on Computer Support for Collaborative Learning,* Palo Alto, California. Article 30.

Kilner, P. G., & Hoadley, C. M. (2005). Anonymity options and professional participation in an online community of practice. In the *Proceedings of the 2005 Conference on Computer Support for Collaborative Learning,* (pp. 272–280). Taipei, Taiwan: International Society of the Learning Sciences.

Kuhn, D., & Goh, W. (2005). Arguing on the computer. In the *Proceedings of the 2005 Conference on Computer Support for Collaborative Learning* (pp. 346–352). Taipei, Taiwan: International Society of the Learning Sciences.

Lamon, M. (2005). Information and communications technology and literacy development. In the *Proceedings of the 2005 Conference on Computer Support for Collaborative Learning,* (pp. 358–367). Taipei, Taiwan. International Society of the Learning Sciences.

O'Brien, A. J., Alfano, C., & Magnusson, E. (2007). *Improving cross-cultural communication through collaborative technologies, LCNS 4744* (pp. 125–131). Berlin/ Heidelberg, Germany: Springer-Verlag.

Sorensen, E. K. (1999). Intellectual amplification through reflection and didactic change in distributed collaborative learning. In the *Proceedings of the 1999 Conference on Computer Support for Collaborative Learning*. Palo Alto, California. International Society of the Learning Sciences. No. 71. Kolb, D. A., Boyatzis, R. E., & Mainemelis, C. (2001). Experiential learning theory: Previous research and new directions (Ed. R. J. Sternberg & L.-F. Zhang pp. 227–248). Mahwah, NJ: Lawrence Erlbaum Associates, Inc.

Wegerif, R. (2005). Towards a dialogic understanding of the relationship between CSCL and teaching thinking skills. In the *Proceedings of the 2005 Conference on Computer Support for Collaborative Learning* (pp. 707–716). Taipei, Taiwan: International Society of the Learning Sciences.

KEY TERMS AND DEFINITIONS

Access: The ability to locate information or data; the ability to contact another individual

Anonymity: The state of not being able to be identified individually

Archival: Storage over time

Cognition: Perception and knowing

Critique: A critical and analytical comment or essay

Data Repository: An electronic compilation of digital resources

Digital Library: An electronic repository of professionally vetted and archived resources

Discourse: Communication of thoughts

Forum: An asynchronous textual communication tool with threaded discussions; an online discussion space; an asynchronous message board

Heuristic: Based on experience for discovery

Interactivity: The transfer of information and communications between multiple individuals

Intercommunication: The sharing of messages between individuals

Intercultural Communications: Communications between individuals from different backgrounds or cultures

Intertexuality: The interplay between various texts to highlight new meanings in each of the works and beyond

Learning / Course Management System (L/CMS): An electronic system that combines various functions and tools of a "classroom" that enables online learning

Literacy: The quality of being literate or educated in a particular discipline or field

Peer Review: The employment of student peers to provide quality review and feedback on other students' works

Rubric: A grading method that uses a table of defined factors and grading standards

APPENDIX

OFFERING CRITIQUES TO PEERS

The Golden Rules

1. Show what you appreciate about the author's writing.
2. Personal attacks or personal comments should never be made. Discussions should remain on a professional, educational and intellectual levels.
3. Contextualize comments by offering examples and specifics. Cite the exact lines or paragraphs, for more precise feedback. Comments should be serious and well-thought-out and be based on the essay analysis vocabulary.
4. Consider the assignment given when making comments. Refer to the criteria there.
5. No excuses should be made for the work such as "I didn't have time to write, so this isn't very good." or "I didn't have the energy to read this very well."
6. Show the writer where there are gaps in clarity. Show where there are gaps in information offered.
7. People may hold their own opinions and values and not be attacked or slighted for those opinions.
8. Offer substantive comments. Avoid "sweet nothings".

General Questions to Ask about a Student Essay Draft

Note: Some points which need to be considered include the following:

Revising of Information and Organization and Tone

INFORMATION: Did the author include enough information? What parts involved too much information?

ORGANIZATION: Did the author follow directions for the essay format (rhetorical mode)? Did the author organize the information in a readable and logical way by strong paragraphing? Is there a clear thesis which is supported well?

TONE: Did the author use the appropriate tone (e.g. formal, informal, friendly, seriously, and satirical) for the material and the audience and purpose?

PURPOSE: Did the author seem to have a clear purpose in writing this essay? What is the apparent purpose? Does the essay have "social value"?

PACING: For the writer's purposes, did he/she pace or move the essay's action at a proper speed--not to dull or slow, not too fast for comprehension?

DETAILS: Are the details supportable, memorable, and well-described? Do these use all five senses?

INTEREST LEVEL: Does the author manage to keep up your level of interest from beginning to end? Is there a good catchy title and lead-in/introduction, tightly-edited middle without wordiness, and an end which clinches the essay with a powerful thought or image?

UNIQUENESS AND DEMONSTRATION OF STUDENT PERSONALITY: Does the writing show authorship?

Editing

Note: This is of secondary importance for this revising assignment.

SENTENCE STRUCTURE: Are the sentences correctly written?
MECHANICS: Are there any spelling or punctuation mistakes?
VOCABULARY/DICTION: Are the words chosen and used well? Are these words appropriate for the audience at hand (an assumed audience of peers)? Are these powerful university-level words?

Chapter 10
Metaphors in Meta-Communication

Mehmet Firat
Anadolu University, Turkey

Isil Kabakci Yurdakul
Anadolu University, Turkey

ABSTRACT

This chapter is based on the claim that the metaphors as a new and powerful tool in different sciences especially including Information Systems and a number of sociological disciplines such as linguistic, education, and sociology can be used for the implementation and sustainability of the components of meta-communication for distance education. The meta-communication aims to move the intercultural components of metaphors to the distance education and its applications. Thereby, metaphors serve to the basic mission of distance education creating cross-cultural educational environments. In order to use metaphors with the meaning put forward by this claim, restructuring of metaphors with the contemporary metaphor theory, use of metaphors in computer systems and user interfaces, the intersection of metaphors and meta-communication and finally the power of metaphors in digital meta-communication for distance education are discussed below.

INTRODUCTION

Metaphors are quite old Linguistic structures. Until 1980s, metaphors that we use in almost every area of our daily lives were considered as a technique of using the language effectively and were defined as an art of using words without reference to their real meanings. However, in their study named "Metaphors we live by", two cognitive scientists, George Lakoff and Mark Johnson, mentioned the importance of cognitive aspects of metaphors. According to this new theory, later called contemporary metaphor theory, metaphors are structures that we use not only in a language but also in our thoughts and actions. To Lakoff and Johnson (1980), if our conceptual system is

DOI: 10.4018/978-1-61350-071-2.ch010

largely metaphorical, then the way we think, our experience and what we do every day are very much a matter of metaphor.

The concept of guiding our thoughts and actions are not only mental. These concepts shape our everyday activities up to the most ordinary details and structure the things we perceive and the style of our communication. Therefore, our concept system has a central importance in the ordinary sense of reality. If we accept that our concept system is largely metaphorical, it is possible to say that metaphors are located naturally in almost every thought and action. Besides this, metaphors allow us to become aware of things that are otherwise left unseen and unfelt and thus enrich our experience of the natural world (Ashkenazi, 2006). Through the metaphors, we become aware of the meaning and structure of the complexity of the surrounding world.

Metaphors are affected by cultural differences. For example, the "discussion is war" metaphor could be translated as "discussion is dancing" in a different culture. However, the most prominent feature of metaphors is their potential to create an intercultural language. Use of visual and verbal metaphors in order to eliminate the need for the creation of common structures in computer systems is the best example of this situation. In the simplest term, the visuals and concepts related to the computer such as window, desktop, mouse, recycle bin, file, folder, page, document, loading, download, and memory are all old metaphors for new concepts (Firat and Kabakçı, 2010). Use of metaphors is one of the most appropriate ways of intuitively understanding computers. For this feature of metaphors, it is thought that appropriate metaphors can be used as a knowledge-creation tool for meta-communication applications in distance education. The reason is that the most important phase in building knowledge is using a meta-communicational element (Demiray, 2009). However, we need universal examples here rather than domestic ones like computer desktop metaphors.

METAPHORS IN META-COMMUNICATION FOR DISTANCE EDUCATION

It has not been easy for metaphors to gain their current meanings. In order to become active in the interdisciplinary area and in daily language, metaphors had to wait for ages. In this process, metaphor perceptions had to be interrogated by the human mind and reshaped with a new comprehensive structure. Therefore, it would be better to clarify this transformation before going on with the multifaceted up-to-date structures of metaphors.

From Rhetoric to Contemporary Theory of Metaphors

The concept of metaphor is commonly defined as elocution or citation of a thing for the purpose of pointing out a similarity that cannot be explained straightforwardly. According to Lakoff and Johnson (1980), metaphors allow understanding or experiencing a kind of thing with the help of another kind of thing. In other words, metaphors are used to establish a relationship between such two concepts as "the brain is a computer" and "human body is a machine" and to do effective transfer from the source concept (brain, human body) to the target concept (computer, machine). In order to do this transfer between the dimensions of the concepts, similes are used, but in similes, generally, "like" or "as" are used to emphasize the transfer. In other words, simile includes explicit comparison in contrast with the implicit comparison made by a metaphor. Another concept related to this subject is the analogy frequently confused with the metaphor. According to the dictionary of Webster, the concept of analogy is defined as "a functional relationship or harmony between totally different organs or components" (WordNet, 2010). The concepts of analogy and homology used in biology help understand the limits of analogy. Analog is used to define organs which have different origins yet the same functions, while homolog refers to organs which have the same origins yet different functions. For example, the wings of a bat and those of a bird are the same analog organs which have different origins.

For a long time, metaphors have been perceived as the use of such words with different meanings as "soil", "mother" and "darkness" - mostly used in poetic language. Since the time of Aristotales, metaphors have not been used in different ways by traditional theorists (Lakoff, 1993). In other words, since the time of Aristo, metaphors have been perceived as a rhetoric and poetic tool. Therefore, in traditional language theories, it could be stated that metaphors refer to the issue of language not to that of thought. According to Lakoff (1993), the following question can help deal with this thought, which does not go beyond the concept of "simile": what are the generalizations that direct linguistic statements known as traditional poetic metaphors? An appropriate answer to this question will certainly reveal that the generalizations directing metaphorical poetic explanations have to do with not only language but also with thought. The reason is that these generalizations are the maps of conceptual areas (Lakoff, 1993).

In his book named *Mode/s and metaphors*, Black (1962) reported that a metaphorical statement has two subjects as main and auxiliary. For example, in the metaphor of "human body is a machine", the phrase "human body" is the main subject, while the word "machine" is the auxiliary subject. Here, the function of the metaphor is to apply the common features of the auxiliary subject to the main subject. In other words, normally, the features of the main subject related to the auxiliary subject are chosen, organized and emphasized. Metaphors carry explanatory structures from a familiar domain of experiences into another domain in need of understanding or restructuring, require seeing some structural similarities between these two domains and have entailments for the target domain they thereby organize far beyond any initial structural similarity (Krippendroff, 1993; Lakoff and Johnson, 1980).

The Contemporary Metaphor Theory favored by Lakoff and Johnson has caused metaphors not only to be used as the rhetoric and poetic language but especially also to be considered as tools that influence almost all our actions and our way of thinking. Today, this approach, which allows using metaphors in different scientific areas, has changed the viewpoints regarding metaphors to a great extent. The benefits of metaphors especially in information and communication technologies have caused researchers to become interested in metaphors.

As mentioned above, metaphors, which we use almost in every area of our daily lives, were mostly regarded as a technique of using the rhetoric or language effectively up until 1980s and were defined as an art of using words with meanings different from their own. The traditional metaphor understanding was in use so much for ages that people used to forget this approach was just a theory (Ortony, 1993).

However, in 1980, two cognitive scientists, George Lakoff and Mark Johnson, in their study called "Metaphors We Live By", mentioned the importance of the cognitive aspects of metaphors stating "If our concept system is metaphorical to a great extent, then our way of thinking, all the facts that we experience and all the things that we everyday do are all metaphorical in a sense" (p. 104). Here, what is intended to be emphasized is the fact that metaphors are structures that we use in actions and thoughts, not just in language. In other words, metaphors are general map pings across conceptual domains. As a result, the word metaphor has come to mean a cross-domain mapping in the conceptual system. In addition, this approach, also known as Contemporary Metaphor Theory, has taken its place as an interdisciplinary approach studied especially in such different areas as computer sciences, cognitive science and communication sciences. As can be seen in Figure 1 below, based on the updated metaphor approach, known as the Contemporary Metaphor Theory, metaphors can be examined under three headings:

Figure 1. Metaphor types in contemporary metaphor theory

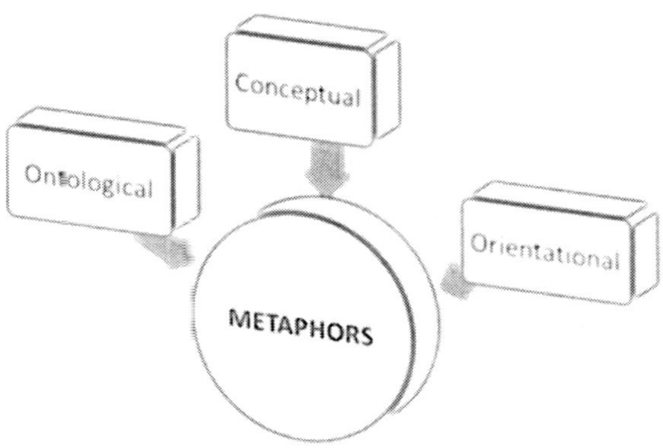

conceptual metaphor, ontological metaphor and orientational metaphor.

Conceptual metaphors, also known as structural metaphors, are mostly related to linguistics. In conceptual metaphors, there are meaningful transfers from the soource concept area to the target concept area (Lakoff, 1993). In ontological concepts, a non-physical concept is explained with an existing physical concept. Orientational metaphors are related to our physical life experiences. Starting from our childhood, we learn such concepts as gravitation, balance and symmetry, and we frequently use these concepts when we learn a new thing. For instance, up-down, back-front and inside-outside are all orientational metaphors.

Besides the classification in the contemporary metaphor theory, metaphors have two didactic dimensions: width and depth (Hron, 1998). The width of a metaphor is related to the number of concepts it includes. These two dimensions of metaphors can be used effectively in multimedia environments. For example, the metaphor of travel can use different destinations to explain a different subject matter, special trips to give better insight into the subject matter and special routs to cover a special matter. Width is related to the support provided at any level for the metaphor used. For example, the metaphor of book can be used to present the content like a book in a digital environment. The pages, as they are in a book, can be turned by clicking or dragging with a mouse.

Metaphors and Basic of Computer Systems

Today, computers that most people are supposed to use almost every day are quite complex and difficult devices to learn. One of the ways most commonly used to understand computers intuitively is the use of metaphors (Barr, 2003). The reason is that the comparisons that can be made via reasoning in a long time can help with the satisfaction and success in understanding the system by loading the first system-related comparison on the working memory (Carroll and Ihomas, 1982). To state this more clearly, in order to understand a thing that we have not been able to fully understood, that thing can be explained better with the use of another thing that we know well. Therefore, an old metaphor is used to explain a new concept at any level of interaction with computers (Barr, 2003). In its simplest term, all the concepts and visuals related to computers such as window, desktop, mouse, recycle bin, file, folder, page, document, loading, downloading and memory are old metaphors of new concepts.

On the desktop we use, the visual metaphors of files and folders are used instead of the traditional hierarchy of directories and sub-directories. In fact, directories and sub-directories are interrelated in hierarchical structure and are explained technically in this way. However, this structure is called "tree" in information and communication technologies (Figure 2). The reason is that as we know the structure of a tree, it would be easier to understand the structure of the system of directories by making use of this structure.

Most icons, symbols, buttons and signs convey a metaphorical meaning whether they are used in computer systems or in the web environment. Some examples regarding the metaphoric icons

Figure 2. Tree metaphor for file system

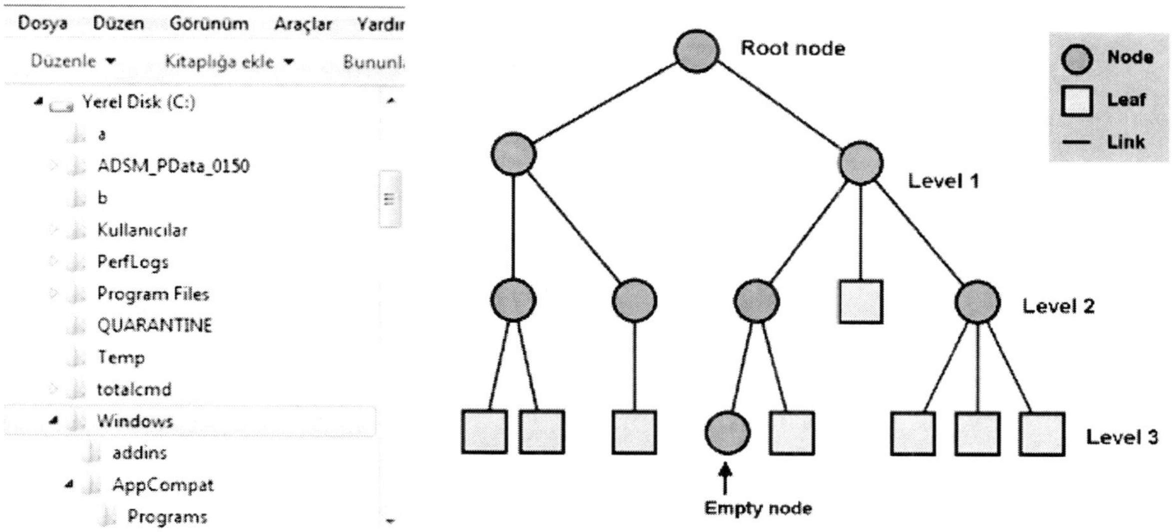

and buttons used in digital environment can be seen in Figure 3.

The recycle bin, the mouse used as an input tool that helps control the movements on the computer screen, and the interfaces of operating systems definded as desktop are all conceptual metaphors (Figure 4). Such phareses, concepts and structures as "Cleaning the memory", "Opening-closing a file" and "disc partition" used in computer sciences are examples for ontological metaphors.

One of the metaphors most frequently used in a computer environment is the orientational metaphor. Almost all kinds of moving or non-moving arrows used in a computer environment, the download used in data transfer and the processing that defines the stream of operations are all examples for the orientational metaphor.

In fact, the desktop metaphor constitutes the basis of early computer systems (see Figure 5). The "desktop" metaphor, which the present computer systems are still built upon, was widely used for the first time in 1980s. Around 30 years ago, designers created this successful metaphor – which constitutes the basis of computer systems and which is still in use today – on the basis of running, accessing and saving applications in indivisuals' traditional office environment (Kaptelinin & Czerwinski, 2007).

Use of Metaphors in Human-Computer Interaction

Metaphors that prevent users from writing down routine commands on the black screens of computer systems are now widely used with the help of the development and spread of computer technologies. Metaphors are also used in hypertext, hypermedia and multimedia environments to help users get accustomed to these new environments. According to Erikson (1990), because metaphors allow us to obtain information from familiar and reliable objects and because they act as natural models, their use in hypertexts and hypermedia is quite important.

The basic role of interfaces is to provide interaction between the user and the material. Functional and aesthetical interfaces that support interaction play an important role in helping students focus on learning activities. First of all, interesting, effective and productive interfaces can draw students' attention to learning and support the interaction

Figure 3. Metaphoric buttons and icons

between students and the learning material. These interfaces can also create a platform for students' skills regarding perception, organization, integration and recall (Cheon & Grant, 2008). Therefore, it is an important responsibility of instructional designers to develop effective, productive and aesthetical interfaces.

A metaphorical interface, which is a rather new concept, generally is designed with the use of content-related visual metaphors in a way that provides interaction with the environment. The pictures included in metaphoric interfaces and other multimedia components may be more meaningful than direct definitions, concepts or idioms. The reason is that metaphors enable users to internalize new information more easily for appropriate schemes (Ohl & Cates, 1997). Lee and Hsu (2004), in their experimental study conducted with 201 university students, aimed at determining the effects of visual metaphoric interfaces on the learning performances of university students. The researchers found out that metaphoric interfaces increased the learning performances of the students.

In their cross-cultural case study related to metaphors and web sites, Shaikh, Chaparro, Nelson and Joshi (2005) investigated the generalization of a home metaphor used in a web site. Based on the results of their study, care must be taken in website design when metaphors are used as the primary means of interaction. The reason is that population may reveal specific cultural difficulties with the metaphor. Therefore, it is possible to say that specific cultural differences should be eliminated if an intercultural metaphorical interface is to be created.

Figure 4. Trash metaphor

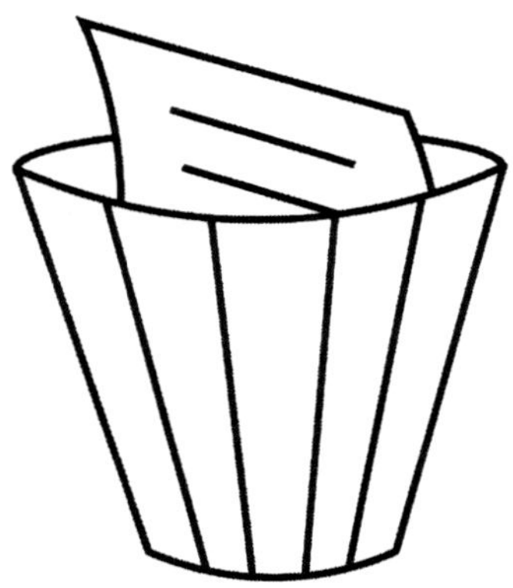

Castro Salgado, Souza and Leitao, (2009) proposed a set of conceptual metaphors for the design of multi-cultural systems. As a result, they proposed five multi-cultural design metaphors to guide different communicative strategies that affect both designer-to-user communication and user-system communication with the help of results from previous studies along with Semiotic Engineering concepts. In the study, it is emphasized that multi-cultural HCI designs focus on

Figure 5. Desktop metaphor

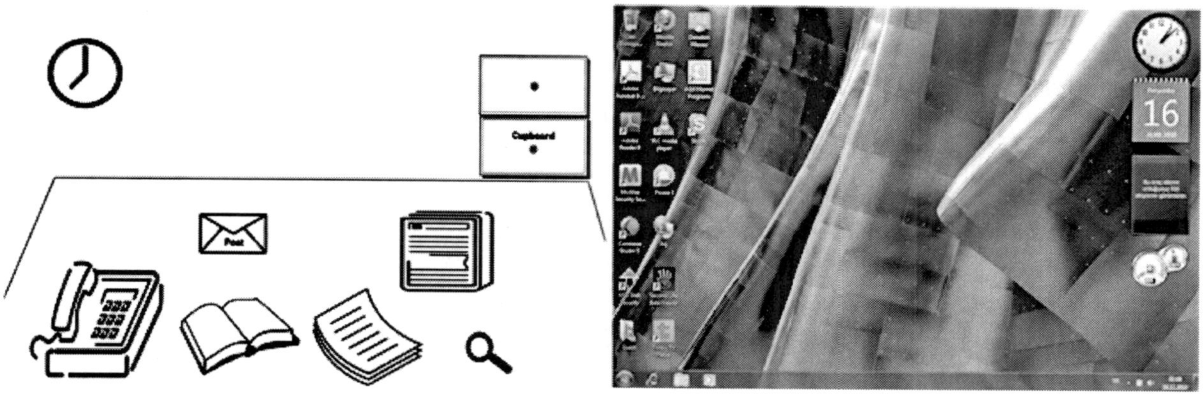

designer-to-user meta-communication and that this type of meta-communication is necessarily influenced by the designer's own cultural values and orientation.

With respect to the way of their use, metaphoric interfaces can be examined in two categories such as thematic and immersive (Cheon & Grant, 2008). Metaphors used in thematic metaphoric interfaces do not fully reflect the content but support it with such metaphors as home and book, which are familiar to users. On the other hand, authentic environments which reflect the scope of the content given with various signs and clues are created in immersive metaphoric interfaces. A scene of a play in theatre can be given as an example for the immersive metaphoric interface. While the components of a theatre scene provide various signs and clues, the environment as a whole may reflect a realistic environment.

Fırat and Kabakçı (2009), in their study, examined the effects of metaphors on the navigation performances of users in educational hypermedia. In the study conducted with 33 undergraduate students attending Anadolu University, two hypermedia environments were created with the same content. For navigation in one these environments, a visual metaphor was used, while for navigation in the other, a traditional text link was used. Three different performance measurements such as disorientation, time and the teacher candidates' self-evaluation of their performances were used. According to the results obtained, it was revealed that the teacher candidates showed higher-level performance in hypermedia in which a visual metaphor was used. In another study conducted by Hsu and Schwen (2003), the researchers tried to determine the effects of structural signs – that can be inferred from the metaphors used in hypermedia – on the search performance in hypermedia. A total of 54 university students were assigned a task of information search in the hypermedia designed. At the end of the study, the metaphorical signs given were found to help students reach more correct information in shorter time.

Intersection of Metaphors and Meta-Communication

A metaphor is a figure of speech. In a metaphor, a word or a phrase is applied to a thing to which it is not literally applicable. Metaphors are among the most frequently used figures of speech not only in poetry but also on universal basis. The term metaphor is from the Greek. *Metaphora* formed by combining *meta* (over) and *pherein* (to carry).

Since the time computers were first invented or the time they became a part of our daily lives, there has been an increasing interest in metaphors and thus a striking change in the frequency of metaphor use. According to Jacobs (1999), the use of metaphors is the most effective way of facilitating the understanding of computers and the cyberspace. This situation also shows how dependent cognitive processes are on background knowledge.

Researchers from different disciplines such as cognitive science, intercultural studies, linguistics, sociology, education, human-computer interaction and philosophy have focused on the importance of intercultural communication in virtual environments. This interdisciplinary issue is one of the most popular research areas. Today, in general, the Internet, the World Wide Web, cyberspace and virtual environments are used to denote overlapping different perspectives on the world of networked digital communications. In addition, these are elements of meta-communication that means communication about communication (Demiray, 2009). As can be seen, most of the meta-communication samples - such as World Wide Web, cyberspace, virtual environment, surfing the web and information superhighway – which are used to create a common language between people and cultures are metaphorical. This demonstrates that metaphors are quite strong tools for meta-communication.

Metaphors are affected by cultural differences. For example, the metaphor of "Discussion is war" may be translated as "Discussion is dancing" in a different culture. However, the most prominent feature of metaphors is their potential to create an intercultural or over-cultural language. Use of visual and verbal metaphors to eliminate the need for creating common structures in computer systems is the best example for this situation. In its simplest term, the visuals and concepts related to the computer such as window, desktop, mouse, recycle bin, file, folder, page, document, loading, download and memory are all old metaphors for new concepts (Firat and Kabakçı, 2010).

Use of metaphors is one of the most appropriate ways of intuitively understanding computers. For this feature of metaphors, it is thought that appropriate metaphors can be used as a knowledge creation tool for meta-communication applications (Figure 6). The reason is that the most important phase in building knowledge is using a meta-communicational element (Demiray, 2009). However, we need universal examples here rather than domestic ones like the desktop metaphor.

The purpose for creating metaphors is to make the meaning of a rather new thing clearer with a familiar thing. In other words, defining a thing - which one wants to explain – with a thing widely known helps everybody understand that thing better. In this way, as can be seen in Figure 6, a metaphor created becomes a meta-communication tool for individuals, societies, cultures and eventually for people. Therefore, it could be stated that metaphors are used to develop meta-communication. That is to say, metaphors, by their nature, are created for meta-communication. The reason is that the use of metaphors in communication provides a window into one's own understanding of someone else's understanding.

Power of Metaphors in Digital Meta Communication and Distance Education

The real power of metaphors lies under their potential to help understand concepts, ideas and forms. In general sense, the metaphor created to better a situation can be seen just as a noun; however, it has an indisputable effect on the perception of a situation difficult to understand. According to Taniguchi (2003), the most important and the strongest metaphors that we commonly use today are the technological metaphors we use for the Internet. "The Net", "cyberspace", "Netizens", "cyberpunks" "Information Highway" and "Virtual Reality" are some examples of electronic communication metaphors used in on-line communication as well as of those used by on-line people. This situation shows how important the need for metaphors is in line with the developing technology as well as shows how important meta-

Figure 6. Metaphors in rising of basic communication to meta-communication

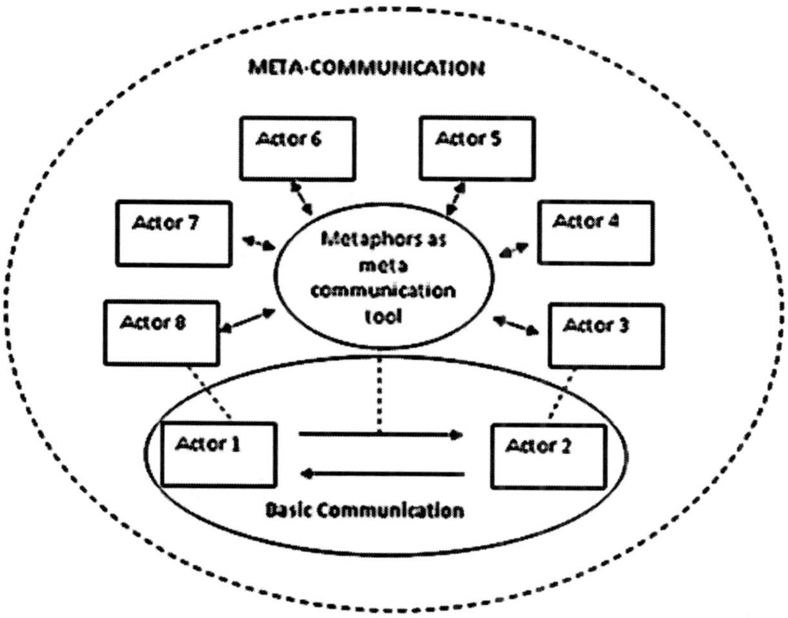

phors are for supporting the cognitive structures of individuals in renovations.

Especially visual metaphors are frequently used in today's digital media components. Similar to verbal metaphors, visual metaphors can be defined as the representation of a new system via visual images which serve the same purposes, which replace the system and which users are accustomed to. The use of visual notice codes in meta-communication cause metaphors – especially the visual metaphors used to explain meta-concepts by their nature - to become an important tool for meta-communication. The subject of meta-communication includes non-verbal visual notice codes related to the source and the receiver (Demiray, 1994).

The concept of Global Village is one of the concepts established by Mcluhan in 1960s and mentioned by the 21st century communication theorists as well. The metaphor of "the world is a global village" widely used to point out that today's communication facilities have spread throughout the world and that people from all over the world can establish communication in seconds with the help of developing information and communication technologies is a tool for meta-communication; in other words, it is a visual notice code.

It is obvious that actually, we intensely benefit from visual and verbal metaphors as a tool for meta-communication. Most icons and other structures used in information systems are built upon metaphors, and these components are used to represent the same procedure or concept with the same meaning in every part of the world. In this respect, as can be seen Figure 7 below, it is possible to establish a relationship for meta-communication in a digital environment with metaphors used to establish common communication or to create common perception.

As can be seen in Figure 7, metaphors can be used as an intercultural communication tool in a digital environment for meta-communication. Though not consciously, metaphors are frequently used as a meta-communication tool in today's information and communication technologies.

Figure 7. Metaphors stimulate meta-communication

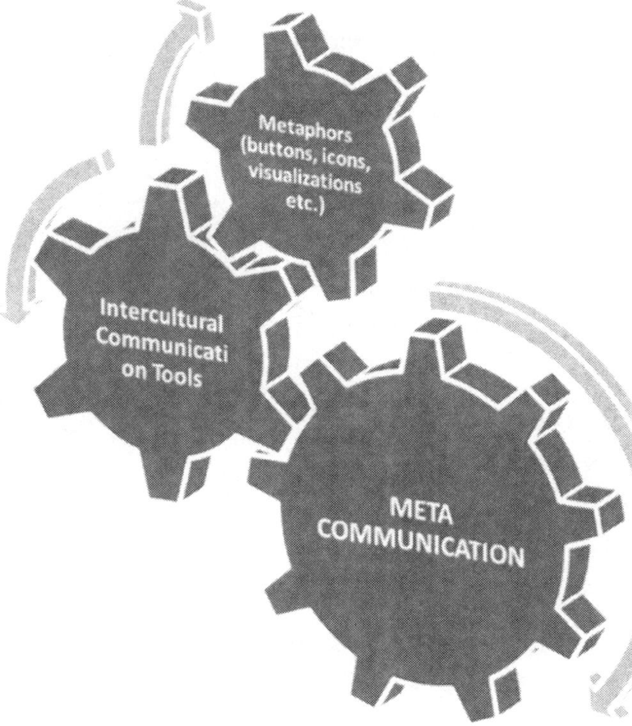

If the metaphor, probably one of the strongest meta-communication tools, were not used, computers and thus Information Technologies would not so rapidly develop or spread throughout the world. The reason is that the metaphor is a tool capable of transforming basic communication into intercultural meta-communication. If the metaphor were not used as a meta-communication tool in technological devices, it would not be so easy to use mobile phones, computers, cameras, mp3 players, navigation devices and a number of other current technological devices without knowing a foreign language. For a more specific example how do children use technological tools better than adults? If metaphors in technological devices were not used as in intercultural tool, children proficient in meta-communication would not adopt technology so easily.

The importance of metaphors for the distance education and e-learning applications is caused by forces of metaphors in digital meta-communication. The meta-communication aims to move the intercultural components of metaphors to the distance education and its applications. Thus, metaphors serve to the basic mission of distance education. This is because of the ultimate goal of distance education; which is to create easily understood, cross-cultural educational environments for its multi-cultural target groups.

In practice context, metaphors can be used in many e-learning tools for distance education. For example, the navigation components of Learning Management Systems can be designed with the help of appropriate metaphors. Thus, the understanding of the subject and the learner's navigation performance will be supported. Similarly, as shown in Figure 8, metaphors are effective

Figure 8. A simple interface metaphor for e-learning

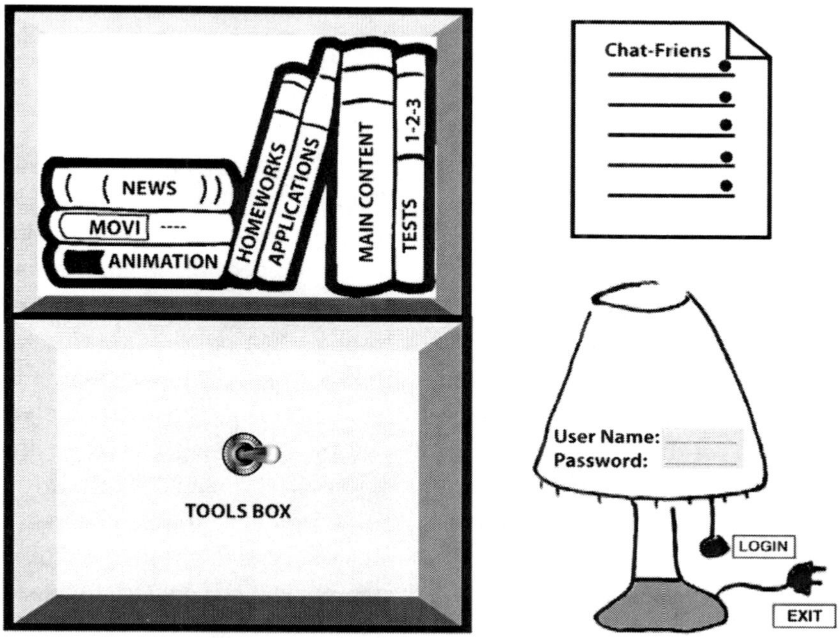

tools for Web site interfaces, educational videos and animations and visualization of educational contents.

CONCLUSION

This chapter is based on the claim that the metaphors as a new and powerful tool in different sciences especially including information systems and a number of sociological disciplines such as linguistic, education and sociology can be used for the implementation and sustainability of the components of meta-communication for distance education. However, in order to use metaphors with the meaning put forward by this claim, in the first place, the socio-psychological natures and the transformation of metaphors within the historical development process should be examined.

With the contemporary metaphor theory, metaphors used in almost every field of our daily lives have been more comprehensively taken into consideration since 1980s. In this process, the restructuring of metaphors was examined under the heading of "From Rhetoric to Contemporary Theory of Metaphors". The field that first benefited from the metaphor - which gained its real meaning with the contemporary metaphor theory – has been the field of computer and information systems. Metaphors such as "tree" and "desktop" that save people from writing routine commands on black and white screens have always interested researchers. These developments were examined under the heading of "Metaphors and Basic of Computer Systems".

The contribution of metaphors to computer and information systems was not limited to their use in basic structures; in contrast, this contribution of metaphors has increased with its spread at more practical interaction levels. The creation and spread of Web played a very important role for the Internet regarded as the biggest development of the last century throughout the world. Metaphors that became inevitable components of user interface designs have contributed much to the present situation of the world, which has thus become a "global village". This process was examined with examples under the heading of "Usage of Metaphors in Human-Computer Interaction". Under this heading, first, various studies were mentioned, and then the relationship between meta-communication and metaphors was examined. Finally, the use of metaphors as a meta-communication tool for distance education was discussed. It was argued that meta-communication and metaphors had a special importance for distance education and e-learning applications. E-learning tools are often used in today's distance education systems (Bates, 2005). And this situation has facilitated the use of metaphors for distance education. Because, easily creating and using metaphors in digital media is one of the most significant reasons for the popularity of metaphors today.

Today, disciplines such as cognitive science intercultural studies, linguistics, sociology, education, human-computer interaction and philosophy often emphasize the need for supra-cultural communication in virtual environments. Meta-communication as an up-to-date approach, which is also the focus of this book, is believed to meet this need. However, meta-communication, which can transfer the communication between traditional factors (source-target) into a supra-factor dimension (source-source), needs intercultural components to make this transfer constant by structuring it. Right at this point, metaphors that are mainly used for conveying meaning play an important role. In other words, it is believed that traditional communication can be transferred into sophisticated supra-cultural communication via metaphors. This intersection of metaphors and meta-communication was examined under the heading of "Intersection of Metaphors and Meta Communication".

When the idea of using metaphors for meta-communication is put into practice in a digital environment, the power of metaphors doubles. The reason is that metaphors are already used effectively at almost all levels from the basic structures of digital environments to the top practical applications. This power of metaphors for meta-communication in digital environments was examined under the heading of "Power of Metaphors in Digital Meta-Communication". In this situation, the question to be asked is as follows: are metaphors that led to the Internet revolution already used as a meta-communication tool by supporting the intercultural spread in a digital environment? Well, this is quite a good point. However, the claim here was that when the idea of creating a digital environment for meta-communication is taken into consideration alone, it can be used in a more conscious and stronger way.

REFERENCES

Ashkenazi, G. (2006). Metaphors in science and art: Enhancing human awareness and perception. *Electronic Journal of Science Education*, *11*(1), 3–9.

Barr, P. (2003). *User-interface metaphor in theory and practice*. MSc. Thesis, Victoria University of Wellington, Department of Mathematical and Computing Sciences.

Bates, A. W. (2005). *Technology, e-learning and distance education* (2nd ed.). London, UK: Routledge Falmer.

Black, M. (1962). *Models and metaphors*. Ithaca, NY: Cornell University Press.

Carroll, J. M., & Thomas, J. C. (1982). Metaphor and the cognitive representation of computing systems. *Trans Systems, Man, and Cybernetics*, *12*(2), 107–116. doi:10.1109/TSMC.1982.4308795

Castro Salgado, L. C. d., Souza, C. S. d., & Leitao, C. F. (2009). Conceptual metaphors for designing multi-cultural applications. *Proceedings of 4th Latin American Conference on Human-Computer Interaction*, Mexico: Yucatan.

Cheon, J., & Grant, M. (2008). A cognitive load approach to metaphorical interface design: Reconsidering theoretical frameworks. In K. McFerrin et al. (Eds.), *Proceedings of Society for Information Technology & Teacher Education International Conference 2008* (pp. 1054-1059). Chesapeake, VA: AACE.

Demiray, U. (1994). *İletişim Ötesi İletişim (Metacommunication)*. Eskişehir, Turkey: Turkuaz Yayınları.

Demiray, U. (May, 2009). *Meta communication for knowledge building process in distance education*. Paper presented at Communicative Revolution? Media and Social Change in Eastern Europe After 1989. Vilnius, Lithuania.

Erickson, T. D. (1990). Working with interface metaphors. In B. Laurel (Eds.), *The art of human-computer interface design* (pp. 65-73). Reading, MA: Addison-Wesley.

Firat, M., & Kabakçi, I. (2010). Use of visual metaphors for navigation in educational hypermedia: Effects on the navigational performance. [Chesapeake, VA: AACE.]. *Journal of Educational Multimedia and Hypermedia, 19*(1), 5–22.

Herrington, A., & Herrington, J. (2001). Web-based strategies for professional induction in rural, regional and remote areas. In P. L. Jeffery (Eds.), *Proceedings of the Australian Association for Research in Education (AARE) International Educational Research Conference*, Fremantle, Australia.

Hron, A. (1998). Metaphors as didactic means for multimedia learning environments. *Innovations in Education & Training International, 35*(1), 21–28.

Jacobs, J. Q. (1999). *Cyberspace is a parallel world*. Anthropology and Archaeology Pages. Retrieved from www.jqjacobs.net

Kaptelinin, V., & Czerwinski, M. (2007). Introduction: The Desktop metaphor and new uses of technology. In Kaptelinin, V., & Czerwinski, M. (Eds.), *Beyond the desktop metaphor - Designing integrated digital work environments* (pp. 1–13). MIT Press.

Krippendorff, K. (1993). Major metaphors of communication and some constructivist reflections on their use. *Cybernetics & Human Knowing, 2*(1), 3–25.

Lakoff, G. (1993). The contemporary theory of metaphor. In Ortony, A. (Ed.), *Metaphor and thought* (2nd ed., pp. 202–250). Cambridge, UK: Cambridge University Press.

Lakoff, G., & Johnson, M. (1980). *Metaphors we live by*. Chicago, IL: University of Chicago Press.

Ortony, A. (1993). Metaphor, language, and thought. In Ortony, A. (Ed.), *Metaphor and thought* (2nd ed., pp. 1–16). New York, NY: Cambridge University Press.

Shaikh, D. A., Chaparro, B. S., Nelson, T. W., & Joshi, A. (2005). Metaphors and website design: A cross-cultural case study of the Tide.com stain detective. *Usability News, 7*(1).

Taniguchi, M. I. (2003). Internet metaphors matter. *New Directions for Teaching and Learning, 94*, 13–21. doi:10.1002/tl.94

WordNet. (2010). *Webster's online dictionary with multilingual thesaurus translation*. Retrieved July 7, 2010, from http://www.websters-online-dictionary.org

Chapter 11
The Cultural Aspects of E-Learning and the Effects of Online Communication:
A Critical Overview

Amani Hamdan
University of Dammam, Saudi Arabia

ABSTRACT

The purpose of this chapter is to build on the insights of educators regarding the relationship between culture and online learning. In this chapter, I shed light on the ways in which culture has a significant influence on online education and vice versa. The chapter is based on primary data drawn from undergraduate female students' responses regarding how online education is changing their learning culture and how their culture is influencing online education. Sixty undergraduate Saudi female students participated in the survey in order to identify how using the Internet, online education and online discussion forums is challenging cultural norms. The literature in the field of online and distance education is also explored to help answer these questions. Students indicated that online education helped them to challenge some cultural norms, enhance their learning culture and improve their communication skills.

INTRODUCTION

Challenging traditional, face-to-face methods of teaching and moving towards innovative, student-centered approaches are crucial trends in contemporary education. Online education in particular is emerging as an important feature of higher education in all fields. Over the last decade, educational programs worldwide have begun employing online learning as an essential part of the delivery of courses and even of entire programs, to the extent that it is now part of higher-education mainstream

DOI: 10.4018/978-1-61350-071-2.ch011

in many countries. "Students are demanding more courses and programs to be offered online. Yet, in light of the growing population of learners from various cultural backgrounds engaged in online education…" (Wang & Reeves, 2007, p. 1) there is an urgent need to understand how culture affects online education and, conversely, how online education affects culture.

Culture is defined by Hofstede (2005) as "the collective programming of the mind that distinguishes the members of one group or category of people from others" (p. 4). These differences in programming largely account for differences across cultures. It is clear that cultures and cultural values around the globe are changing in unprecedented ways as a result of the exponential growth of communication exchange channels, an important aspect of which is the increasing ease of access to online courses, programs and information. The culture of learning is undergoing rapid transition, including in the Middle East. Saudi Arabian students, for example, have begun to participate in this communications exchange and, in consequence, their culture of learning is changing in ways that could not have been anticipated even two or three years ago. These students, both female and male, are now able to gain access to learning resources such as journals, magazines, periodicals and intercultural-communication forums that would not be available to them but for their connection to the Internet. The unprecedented openness to new educational resources and cultural perspectives is leading Saudi Arabia's younger generation to become less conservative. The implications of this process for the Saudi culture as whole are reinforced by the fact that the youth component of the Saudi population (*i.e.* those under age 35) currently stands at 65 percent.

This paper aims to explore the ways in which students' culture of learning is changing as a result of the introduction of various modes of online learning. This paper also aims to explore the ways in which culture and cultural values affect the application and success of online-learning strategies. Particular attention is directed to learners' perceptions of the advantages and disadvantages of online communication. My analysis is based on observations of two groups of Saudi female university students as they begin to integrate online-learning systems into their studies. My analysis also draws on the key literature relating to online learning.

The core conclusion of this paper is that online education and culture have a reciprocal and correlative relationship. This paper explores the emergence of online education globally and in Saudi Arabia; issues, controversies and problems; traditional education as the backdrop to Saudi online learning; and, finally, the findings of an empirical study on the same.

THE EMERGENCE OF ONLINE EDUCATION GLOBALLY AND IN SAUDI ARABIA

Rapid technological advances and the emergence of the global knowledge-oriented economy have not only encouraged governments to provide the infrastructure for web-based instruction but have also necessitated a significant increase of investment in Internet technologies for increasing access to educational resources. Online education and embedded online communication in higher-education courses and programs are no longer considered to be luxuries or mere supplements to learning but, rather, integral parts of higher education in many parts of the world. "Colleges and university students in the USA increasingly view online components of their courses as commonplace as textbooks and other traditional resources" (Wang and Reeves, 2007, p. 2) and this is true not only of North American students but also of students in Saudi Arabia.

Many educational programs in Saudi Arabia have integrated online education into almost every undergraduate program. Major universities in Saudi Arabia are in the process of implementing web-based instruction through Web CT or Blackboard as a companion to all their classroom study programs. According to Mirza, (N.D.), "MoHE has just recently established a national center for e-learning and distance learning which aims to support in the creation of electronic educational material, and provide an electronic venue for faculty members of any local university to utilize in creating e-courses through its own Learning Management System" (p. 4). Nevertheless, there is considerable reluctance to introduce entirely online degree programs, as is confirmed by the fact that the Saudi Ministry of Higher Education continues to oppose offering entirely online programs or courses. It furthermore remains unprepared to accept or qualify anyone with an online degree from any foreign institution, even from such renowned universities as MIT, Harvard and Stanford. The MoHE's concerns stem from the fact that the very nature of online program delivery raises doubts about whether students are in fact submitting their own work and, by implication, about the fairness of the evaluation of students' performance.

According to Tony Bates (2010), a consultant who runs many e-learning workshops and provides e-learning training across Saudi Arabia,

King Fahd University in Dhahran has been working closely with UBC in Canada since 2003, with staff from King Fahd University visiting UBC for workshops a few times over this period. The use of e-learning at King Fahd University for Oil and Petroleum, for instance, had became widespread, both to support classroom teaching and in a hybrid mode, with a mix of reduced classroom time and online learning. (para. 3)

These workshops were part of the plan of the Saudi Ministry of Higher Education to study the feasibility of offering online education blended and integrated with traditional methods of course delivery. Distance education by online means has been discussed as a way of increasing the accessibility of higher education. Online education offers access to many students who aspire to study but live in remote areas or are working to earn income and therefore are unable to attend school on a full-time basis. Distance education is an aspect of online education that continues to have great untapped potential. As AlKlaifa (2009) remarked, Saudi Arabia "has been slower than many nations to move into distance education and that it has had a very short history of using printed, electronic, or broadcast means for students who are not physically on site" (para. 1).

The need to expand access to higher education is one of the main factors driving the ongoing growth of online learning in the Kingdom. In addition to the desire to make university education available to students who are located in rural areas or who are currently employed, there are powerful demographic forces at work. According to the latest national statistics, by 2009 Saudi Arabia's youth population had reached 65 percent of the entire population. Many high school graduates were unable to find places at the national universities yet approximately 100,000 are currently studying abroad on scholarships at higher-education institutions in such countries as the United States, the United Kingdom and Canada. Another factor that encourages the implementation of online learning is the visual learning style of many Saudi students. Online approaches, which of course incorporate visual learning, can therefore enhance the traditional and relatively passive approaches to learning. Thanks to this new mode of teaching, students are becoming more self-directed and engaged.

Backdrop to Saudi Online Education: The Traditional Approach

Since the advent of public education in Saudi Arabia in 1960s, the Kingdom has adhered to traditional educational culture. This system is premised on the transmission of information from the professor or teacher ("the power") to the students ("the empty vessels" / "the disempowered"). Paulo Freire has developed a similar analogy to describe this approach, which he calls the "banking system of education" (1970; 2003). This is an approach to education that resembles "an act of depositing, in which the students are the depositories and the teacher is the depositor" (p. 53; p. 72). The banking system of education is the antithesis of what Freire advocates – an education that announces the importance of dialogue, engagement and equality, denounces silence, and deplores oppression.

The Saudi education system continues to manifest many aspects of the banking system. In accordance with Freire's model, Saudi professors and teachers do not usually engage in dialogue with students over the course of the learning process but instead they impose information that is often irrelevant to students. Indeed, critics of the Saudi curriculum and pedagogy point out that the Saudi education system does not reflect the experiences of the majority of students and that much of what they learn is largely irrelevant to their lives and careers (especially in the old curriculum since there has been a reformed curricula implemented in 2009). On standardized tests, Saudi students are expected to provide answers that may have no connection to their background or context. This is also the situation in most Arab Muslim universities and schools.

In my experience, as both a student and a teacher in the Saudi education system, critical-thinking is usually discouraged. By critical-thinking, I refer to two elements. The first element is gaining a deeper understanding of issues and problems and the second element is examining and evaluating arguments from multiple points of view (McPeck, 1981). My observation is that students continue to learn from a very young age that knowledge and "truth" are fixed – that these constitute "a static entity that is context and value free" (Abdi & Ghosh, 2004, p. 37) and that what is taught in school or university is therefore unquestionable. While the roots of this phenomenon fall outside the scope of this paper, it should be acknowledged that the Saudi approach of focusing Islamic school curricula on only one school of Islamic thought trains students to think rigidly and to exclude diversity. If on the other hand students were exposed to a range of Islamic perspectives, they would have an early opportunity to expand their critical-thinking skills.

Despite the continuing dominance of rote memorization and passive learning in the Saudi education system, there are also many reasons for optimism. There is great enthusiasm surrounding the emphasis of the new monarch – King Abdullah Bin Abdulaziz – on education as a tool of empowerment. This emphasis is exemplified by a drive to achieve a position of scientific leadership in the Arab world, participation in international scientific competitions and the foundation of King Abdulaziz and His Companions Foundation for the Gifted *(Mawhiba)*, which is a new centre to promote openness to different learning possibilities and innovation. A reformed curriculum is in the process of being implemented in schools and many innovative measures are being considered and implemented by both the Ministry of Education (which oversees K-12) and the Ministry of Higher Education (which oversees all colleges, universities and other post-secondary institutions). One of these innovative measures is the promotion of online learning. Indeed, online learning is opening teachers and students to look beyond the strictures of the banking system of education as described above. Online education is encouraging students to take greater responsibility of their learning and "...is offering more self-paced learning alternatives and providing a richer interactive learning environment than learning from text" (Newton, Hase and Ellis, 2002, p.162). Although many observers initially considered online learning to pose a threat to the concept of classroom-based instruction and its delivery of experiences, it is today generally considered to be a complement to classroom instruction.

Methodology

The methodology used for this study has two main parts. The first part involves an analysis of the discourse surrounding online integrative or blended education. This analysis emphasizes Saudi Arabia, a country in which this is a new strategy in education as well as a new area of research.

The second part of the study involves an analysis of both personal observations and a survey created by the author and distributed among Saudi female first- and second-year undergraduate students from various classes of two major universities. All 67 of the participating students had experienced the integrative approach to online education through the requirement to use online learning as part of their university studies as a companion to traditional methods of education. Prior to distribution, the survey was examined by an ethical committee and by outsider university professors. The survey was undertaken in person and was data-driven with a view to exploring how students' culture of learning had changed as a result of accessing and working with an integrative approach to online learning. The survey questions were supplemented with probes to steer the discussion in a direction that would shed more light on the reciprocal and correlative relationship between learning culture and online education. The survey data were coded, themed and analyzed according to their relevance to the research question. The results were read and re-read by the author to find similarities and differences in respondents' answers to the questions. As indicated below in the Students' Feedback and through the attached graph charts, the respondents for the most part agreed that online education had positively influenced their learning experiences and outcomes.

Literature on Online Learning

The literature on online learning has greatly expanded over the last decade. "Studies have indicated that online learning enables institutions and/or instructors to reach new learners at a distance, increase convenience, and expand educational opportunities." (Bourne, McMaster, Rieger & Campbell, 1997; Hara & Kling, 1999, 2001; Hill, 2002; Hofmann, 2002; Owston, 1997; Rourke, 2001; Schrum, 2000; Song *et al.*, 2004, p. 60) Studies have typically emphasized the successful characteristics of online learners. Ohara (2004) has summarized some of the work of researchers in this area. Ohara's main finding was that online learners, out of many characteristics such as the level of engagement, the ability to deal with uncertainty and the willingness to try new things, have most notably displayed internal locus of control – that is, the ability to exercise a degree of personal, internally driven control over key life decisions. (Cooper, 1990; Altman & Arambasich, 1982; Parker, 1999 as cited in Ohara, p. 51, 2004)

Despite the growth in literature about online learning, there has been little emphasis on the ways in which online learning and the unprecedented openness of online communication have been changing cultures around the world in general and the culture of Saudi Arabia in particular. Similarly, there has been little emphasis on the ways in which culture affects the application and success of online learning. "Although few would disagree that cultural factors are important in theory, there is surprisingly little published literature concerning the cultural aspects of online learning and teaching, and there are even fewer research based studies on the subject" (Gunwarandena, Wilson & Nolla, 2003 as cited in Wang & Reeves, 2007, p. 2). There remain many pertinent aspects of learning culture that have not yet been discussed in the higher-education literature. For example, inadequate attention has been thus far accorded to the effect of online learning on such aspects of students' learning culture as locus of control, empowerment and the inherent tensions between individualism and collectivism and between autonomy and agency.

One study by Tapanes, Smith and White (2009) focused on the cultural diversity of online learning and the perceived effects of dissonance on levels of individualism, collectivism and tolerance of ambiguity. This article, like many others, highlighted the differences between people from a variety of cultural backgrounds in terms of the extent to which they demonstrated individualism, collectivism and intolerance for ambiguity. However, the study did not discuss the extent to which – if at all – exposure to online education had enhanced students' actual learning. Another study by Pattison (2003) explored how students from diverse cultural backgrounds drawn together in a program to train counselors reflected their experience as online learners. Pattison's approach is based on an individual-centered orientation that makes the individual the primary user and beneficiary of online-learning technology.

Other studies have indicated that interaction with others is one of the keys to online success – more so than in traditional settings such as the lecture hall or the classroom. (Picciano, 2002 as cited in Kim, Lei and Bonk, 2005) However, that study does not identify the specific elements of online learning that enabled students to be successful nor did it outline the parameters governing their success. Kim, Lei and Bonk (2005) argued that, especially in asynchronous conferencing, online learning fosters rich interactions and in-depth thinking because it provides participants with a greater amount of time in which to process other participants' statements and to formulate their responses. The study by Kim, Lei and Bonk (2005), as well as a few others like that of Benbunan-Fich and Hiltz, (1999), suggest that online interaction helps improve students' skills in the sense that they are able to provide more detailed answers to cases and problems by means of online discussion; however, these studies offered no details regarding the skills that were improved and the specific ways in which online learning helped students to build their social-interaction skills as well as other skills.

Issues, Controversies, Problems

Some researchers have argued that "technology is culturally, morally, and politically neutral – that it provides tools independent of local value systems which can be used impartially to support quite different kinds of lifestyle." (Pacey, 1983, p. 2) However, a strong case can be made that this is a misconception, particularly of the Western world, towards what are typically identified in the literature as "developing" countries (and formerly as "Third World" countries). Part of the problem is that the West has adopted a set of beliefs or a world view whereby, as Tony Jackson says, "the Third World is portrayed as a vast refugee camp, with hungry people lining up for food from the global food aid soup kitchen." Yet, "this view is false" (as cited in Pacey, 1983, p. 57), simply because there are many countries in the eastern part of the world such as China and India that are no less technologically advanced than those of the Western world. Technological advancement is not neutral because it differentiates between powerful and less powerful nations in terms of access to sophisticated technology in such a way that the success of some countries often comes at the expense of other countries.

The lack of research into how online communication and other forms of technological advancement are influencing Eastern countries, their peoples and their cultures is partially a reflection of the lack of advancement in the field of online learning in many of these countries. This is why there seems to be a near absence of understanding of the ways in which online learning is influencing different countries of the Eastern world and this near absence is palpable given the fact that many countries are trying to adapt to new methods of learning. This type of understanding is not a luxury but a necessity as most societies around the world are becoming increasingly knowledge-based.

The Participants

The study participants are all female first-year undergraduate students at two Saudi English-language universities. They attend a variety of colleges: Interior Design, Business Administration, Nursing and Health Sciences, and Engineering. The majority of the students in this study had not intensively used technology for studying or for other educational processes in the past. This course was the students' first experience with online learning as a mandated part of their education; they were required to access the course material online, to engage in online discussion with classmates and professors in the discussion forum, to upload their assignments, to obtain their grades and professors' feedback online, to take their tests and exams online, and to communicate their feedback regarding every aspect of the course. In fact, one of the requirements of these students' university program is that they access their courses online and that they interact with their professors and student colleagues through online discussion forums. Over the past five years many universities and colleges in Saudi Arabia have established online communication forums to supplement and reinforce face-to-face teaching. But these particular institutions went further by mandating participation in online learning as a condition for graduation.

Results

As explained above, Saudi university students come from a school culture that teaches them to rely on the teacher as the sole source of and conduit for knowledge. The strong hold that the traditional approach to education has on the minds of many students leads some of them to resist approaches that place them at the centre of learning – and this is especially the case when they have to engage in discussions as a precondition for learning. Yet, despite these factors, many Saudi students are acquiring a new culture of learning as a result of being introduced to online communication and web-based instruction.

Thanks to the persistence and encouragement of the course professors, after the introduction of online interactive learning the students became much more familiar with the methods of navigating Internet sources and of interacting with classmates and professors in relation to their learning experiences. In fact, online learning offered students a multitude of opportunities to create learning experiences that have the effect of enhancing their critical-thinking skills, cognitive skills, and oral and written communication skills, as well as their general knowledge.

Some of the most salient aspects of online learning are its availability, efficiency and convenience to anyone with Internet access. Access to online sources offers many advantages to educators and students and one of these advantages is the positive impact of online integrative and blended learning on culture. Online learning influences culture, which the main phenomenon being explored in this study.

Some of the many advantages cited by researchers with regard to offering online learning opportunities to students are "[v]alidity, relevance, ease of editing and updating, use of visuals and minimal text and the potential for interaction both with the content and with peers or facilitator" (Newton, Hase and Ellis, 2002, p.163). However, as an educator one has to acknowledge the possible difficulties that some students associate with online learning. Although the group of students in this study did not single out any one major challenge that they might have faced, some research has indicated that some students

...doubt the technology and their ability to use it properly and take reassurance from their instructor before they begin to trust the technology. Some students never learn to trust and never reduce their uncertainty with the technology. (Ohara, 2004, p. 51)

Students' engagement in online communication cultivates new experiences and cultural interactions with their classmates and professors – experiences and interactions that not only enhance written and oral communication skills but that also expand their understanding of the various issues discussed. Students display personal control over their learning and an innovative approach to learning.

The Students' Feedback

When students were asked about how the integration of online communication affected and influenced their learning experience, one explained that:

It allows us to talk with the teacher directly and be able to be updated quicker.... Any question about an assignment is usually assigned faster. It also makes the learning experience much more rewarding as we are able interact with the teacher and get feedback regarding small segments of the assignment.

Another student noted that "Online education helped us connect with other students and instructors easily and spontaneously" which was echoed by the observation that

...online communication improves the process of learning. It enables students to be in touch with their colleagues and instructors other than saving their time when it's time for registrations and arranging schedules.

Yet another student commented that "Not being allowed to drive some days makes it hard to go to school and using online education and Blackboard allows me to post my assignment on time without having to worry about getting to school for that purpose." Indeed, several respondents were very pleased with the fact that they could access their courses any time and any place.

The majority of students emphasized that the accessibility offered by online education is one of its greatest advantages. They explained how the use of online technology affects their learning experience in a variety of positive ways, including sharpening their thinking and broadening their horizons. As one student explained, "When you meet new people through online learning... you will learn from their experience and share your ideas and thoughts with them." Another student elaborated that

It connects us with things that are not easily available in books.... The concept of learning through books and by going to the library is diminishing in face of online learning and online access to books and journals.

Many students were sensitive to the cultural impact of online learning. According to one student, "Online education is starting to change the culture.... It's now accepted that people study online and obtain their degrees and are able to continue with their education." Another observed that "...online education is changing the culture because we are now becoming increasingly dependent on the Internet and this is changing the culture of how we deal with one another." An especially perceptive student captured the reciprocity between online learning and culture:

Online education is expanding the culture which in turn influences education and how we view education... It is definitely changing our thinking in a positive way... Yet our culture is [also] influencing technology in that it is controlling it.

The vast majority of respondents agreed that this new approach to education "...is changing the culture by providing people with learning material that comes from different sources that present different perspectives and aspects of that material." One student emphasized that online education is opening up brand new opportunities for her as a female:

I believe that culture is influencing online education because it is not simple for us girls to travel abroad for higher education in our society. Therefore I think that it motivates the female to turn to studying online due to our limited options.

A few students noted possible negative cultural consequences. One suggested that "People can get addicted to technology if they over use it." Another argued that online learning has a negative side because it reduces the frequency of face-to-face interactions. Some other students agreed that online communications have the disadvantage of sometimes sending a different message than that which is intended. However, for the majority respondents, the major disadvantage of online learning was related to the unreliability of Internet connections, largely resulting from censorship aimed at blocking sexual and political websites. Some respondents also indicated that it is sometimes impossible or extremely time-consuming to log onto the Internet.

Discussion of Students' Culture

Important prior research about cultures has differentiated between high-context cultures and low-context cultures. According to Gupta (2010),

High context cultures are ones in which people tend to be indirect and formal communicators. People from low context cultures tend to be direct and informal communicators. Groups that have high context communication styles combine verbal and nonverbal messages to convey the entire meaning. A listener must read between the lines and add nonverbal nuances to fully understand the message. (para. 9)

Borisoff and Victor (1989) have found that

...high-context cultures include the Chinese, Korean, Japanese, Vietnamese, Arabian and Greek cultures as well as, to a lesser extent, the Spanish and Italian cultures (as cited in Corvette, 2007, p. 103). Saudi Arabia would be classified as having a high-context culture whereby context is of great significance to the discernment of meaning.

In online communication, context is central to the creation and discernment of meaning. Given the fact that online communication is effected by written means, it follows that the study participants were unable to offer any subtle, non-verbal cues which are critical aspects of face-to-face communication. Yet, when learners engage in online communication, the role of context is far less significant than in conventional communication and this, in turn, affects their locus of control. Saudi female students – the group from which the subjects of this study are drawn – usually display external locus of control and this impairs their ability to independently make major decisions in their lives. "In high context cultures, members rely heavily on inferred meaning while in low context cultures people strive hard to find a literal meaning" (Borisoff and Victor, 1989; as cited on Corvette, 2007, p. 104). In high-context cultures such as that of Saudi Arabia, people are more willing to use social power to accomplish their goals (Figure 1). It therefore follows that the students' engagement in online-learning experiences teaches them to become more independent and to take charge of their own decisions.

Although there were some limitations on access to online education as a result of poor or inadequate Internet infrastructure as well as technical difficulties, the Saudi students interviewed for this study found it indispensable to have unlimited access to the Internet. They also argued that their introduction to online sources enabled them to gain experience with different ways of thinking, different styles of writing and different approaches to improving their communication skills. They also learned to become more persis-

Figure 1. The majority of respondents answered with yes for the question if online affects culture, while minority denied any affect of online learning on culture

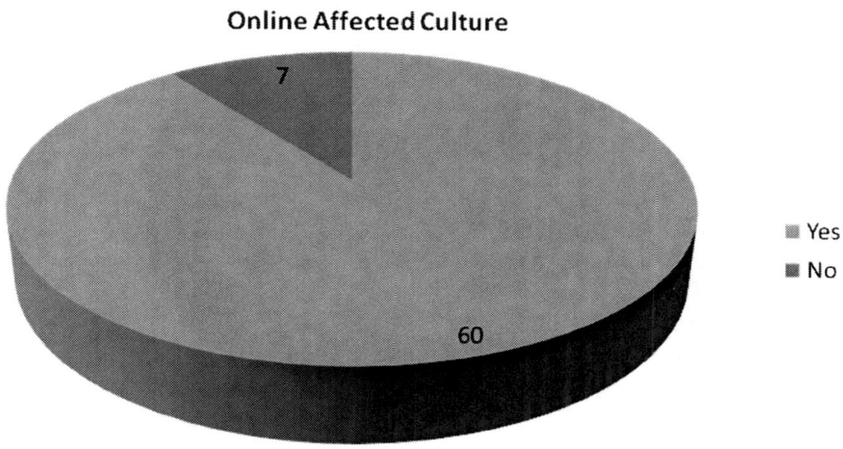

tent as a result of the slowness of Saudi Internet connections.

The students' participation in the online discussion forum involved learning about their own values, beliefs and attitudes. Before joining the online integrated discussion forums, the students did not realize the diversity of perspectives among them. It is therefore clear that online forums can serve as a platform for promoting greater understanding of diversity of cultures and opinions within the same society, as well as for developing greater appreciation for how cultural differences impact learning. These outcomes of online forums, as well as the internalization of locus of control, help to build students' communications abilities in the workplace and elsewhere (Figure 2).

Based on personal observations of the students' communication abilities throughout the courses, it was evident that the students' online discussions towards the end of the year displayed significant improvements in their abilities to present their perspectives (Figure 3).

Students not only increased their level of coherence but they also improved their ability to work with conflicting ideas, including within a group. They nurtured one another as they developed their individual points of view and built productive relationships and approaches that will benefit them going forward. Students' online communication towards the end of the semester encouraged and facilitated reflective thinking, cultural awareness, and awareness of prejudice and conflicting belief systems. They took a holistic approach to learning and development that "is suitable to the nature of the content and the outcomes that were intended of online integrative and blended learning" (Cameron & Limberger, 2004, p. 434). Clearly, online communication, which creates new learning experiences, is a catalyst for change in communication. As Moon (1999) suggests,

With emotions and attitudes expressed, there is an unusually good possibility of examination and modification... open communication in online forums is offering examination of beliefs systems and cultural assumptions which all requires the substance that drives the thinking—the experiences, beliefs, sociopolitical values and goals. (p. 60 as cited in Cameron & Limberger, 2004, p. 434)

Figure 2. The majority of respondents answered with yes for the question if our culture affects online learning, while minority denied any effect of culture on online learning

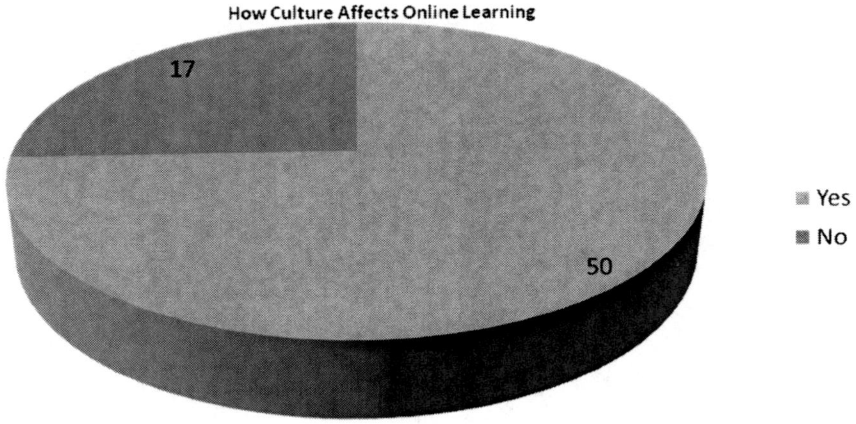

Figure 3. All respondents indicated that they would find their answers on Google

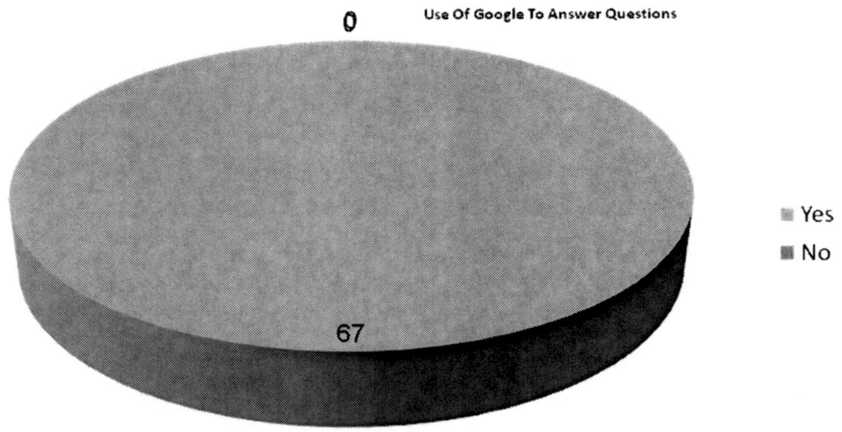

Online programs encourage students to learn at their own pace and to interact at their own level. In one of the discussion forums, students were asked to respond to some work relating to ethical concerns and cultural issues associated with cross-cultural communication. This discussion was enriching and may have challenged some of their existing deep-seated misunderstandings, judgments and assumptions about different cultures. Another quality that students embraced is self-discipline, which is a necessary condition for success in a globalised world. Throughout their engagement with online learning, the students displayed their ability to work independently (Figure 4).

This is particularly significant in that online education, in combination with traditional approaches to learning, enhances students' communication abilities, academic skills and level of self-motivation – especially with respect to topics that are relevant to their lives. After a semester of using online education the students demonstrated better personal management skills, including the ability to set achievable goals. Online education therefore helped students to be more successful and to have higher levels of satisfaction after an initial full-year engagement. Indeed,

Some studies indicated that student satisfaction – as identified through comments after the class ends – is generally higher for those higher for those students who have immersed themselves in the by participating in scheduled and informal online chats and maintaining a steady stream of comments in discussion forums. (Ohara, 2004, p. 51)

Discussion of Students' Empowerment and Online Learning

Students in this study showed a great deal of empowerment as a result of engaging in online learning. In discussing empowerment I am specifically acknowledging the fact that learning is both a personal and a social endeavour. According to Piaget (2000) and the school of constructivist theorists, learning is not a product transmitted from the more knowledgeable party (the teacher/instructor) to the less knowledgeable party (the students). Rather, from a constructivist point of view, learning is achieved in an environment in which the student is at the centre of the learning process and the role of the teacher is to act as a learning facilitator. Online learning provides an opportunity whereby students can construct their own understanding and their own knowledge. Furthermore, online education is geared to the fact that learning is intrinsically a social endeavour. According to Vyogtsky (1992), learning to a great extent occurs as a result of personal interaction, not just between instructors and students, but most importantly among students themselves. "Social constructivism is therefore a theory of learning empowerment within which students are conferred agency in the learning process, higher levels of responsibility over learning and choices about what where and how to learn." (Renner, 2006, p. 4) Renner (2006) continues by stating that,

Learning is both personal and social. It is personal to the extent that individual students must construct their own understandings. These understandings are subsequently regulated and tested through social interactions. (p. 4)

Figure 4. Majority of students are spending 1-10 hours daily and some are spending more than 20 hours online to learn and gain knowledge

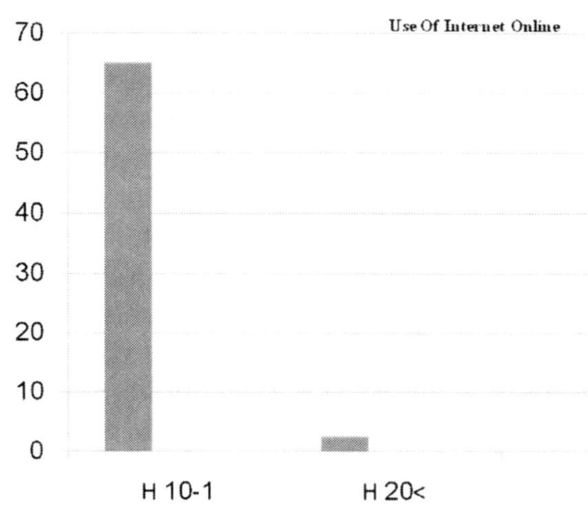

As discussed above, Saudi students usually are not directly engaged in the learning process but, rather, are educated through lectures alone. According to this traditional approach, students are required to abstain from discussions or other kinds of direct participation in learning and, in consequence, they do not contest, negotiate, discover or share their understandings. However, after employing the blended approach – including participating in online discussions – the students in the research sample demonstrated a keen interest in moving beyond the rote-learning tradition. Unlike under the old model of learning, students who engage in online learning display their autonomous identity – an identity that emerges through the acquisition of skills that serve as the scaffolding for the acquisition of knowledge. "Scaffolding" refers to the foundation of skills that enables students to reach new levels of educational and personal development.

SOLUTIONS AND RECOMMENDATIONS

"Although there was general consensus that online learning can play a role in providing the underlying knowledge for practical skills and competencies, there is a need for practical experience and assessment" (Newton, Hase and Ellis, 2002, p. 160) to assess students' abilities to engage in online communication. An understanding of the protocols and guidelines for using online communication is a requirement for students before they begin to engage in online communities. These protocols concern the ethical standards that are a necessary condition for students becoming responsible users of online resources. Some of these ethical standards include respecting privacy, maintaining security, and avoiding plagiarism and academic dishonesty. Despite the concerns that are being expressed by many educators over these serious issues, it appears that few concrete measures are being undertaken to address them.

"It was always thought that providing learning online from a centralized server could standardize procedures and practices improving competency standards compliance by maintaining quality and reducing the communication of unsafe or inconsistent procedures" (Newton, Hase, and Ellis, 2002, p. 160). Unfortunately, in the case of Saudi Arabia, the centralized server in many cases prevented or restricted access to important web sources because they touched on controversial issues of a political, sexual or religious nature. This centralized power structure limits the accessibility of many Internet resources that could be useful to students' development. Thinking should not be restricted or censored, regardless of the subject. This is a limitation that should be studied and discussed with a view to its eventual reform.

Another limitation in this study is that the research focused solely on female students' responses to and participation in online learning. In a future study it would be beneficial to include male students' input and analysis of online learning. Drawing comparisons between the male and female responses would allow critical analysis of the discourse that surrounds male and female education. Gender segregation is pervasive in Saudi Arabia. All education and schooling are completely separated from grade one up to and including higher education. The final years of medical school are the only exception were male are seated in rows in front of female students. Not having access to male students would be a great challenge if the researcher were to include males in the study, and thus the focus on female students, as males are only taught by males whereas the opposite is not true. Women, in many cases and when necessary, are taught by male professors.

Another recommendation for overcoming limitations is to enhance students' level of computer literacy in order to boost their confidence in participating in online integrated courses. In order to overcome the various challenges associated with online culture, students and instructors must be vigilant about students' disregard for or lack of knowledge about the privacy protocol. This protocol includes the requirement for students to respect both professors and classmates and to avoid the disclosure of personal information to each other and on the Internet except where to do so is absolutely necessary. Clear instructions must be provided. It cannot be expected that students who are first encountering a progressive education philosophy and who are the products of the traditional approach to learning would know what should and should not be done to protect their privacy so that they can reach their full potential while engaging in online discussions. Another protocol applies when students use other people's ideas in posts; specifically, they need to learn when and how to give credit to the author or the creator.

Learning styles differ widely among individuals (Kolb, 1984) and building an awareness of this is important in online-learning processes. In particular, the need for self-directed learning in the workplace, notwithstanding most employees' strictly traditional and passive educational experiences, calls for greater investigation. (Smith, 2000) In saying this, it must be acknowledged that students' ability to successfully use online education is also related to the fact that "distance education is inherently accommodating for a variety of learning styles" (Dille & Mezack, 1991 as cited in Dabbagh, 2007, p. 218). With various media such as video, audio materials and text being delivered via the Internet, students who tend towards visual, spatial, auditory or text-oriented learning styles are being accommodated through online learning.

FUTURE RESEARCH DIRECTIONS

The trend towards employing online learning in virtually every academic program worldwide is having a significant impact on learning cultures. Even though online learning is becoming integrated with traditional education, it is nevertheless the case that "The way learners acquire knowledge in on-line settings has not been extensively studied." (Bourne *et al.*, 1997, p.39) There is little research dealing with the factors that make online learning a significant part of undergraduate students' learning experiences. Some of the questions that remain to be tackled by future researchers relate to cultural values and the ways in which they are influenced by online learning and open online communication. Griffiths (2000) rightly argued that the "Internet is being overhyped but underestimated" and, furthermore, that

The widespread rhetoric of promises for more flexible access to training and the subsequent rapid adoption of these goals by government, educational institutions and industries have not been accompanied by an understanding of the factors and processes that contribute to effective implementation of online learning. (Newton, Hase, Ellis, 2002, p.157)

Another important unanswered question is whether the higher-education institutions that are offering courses to reach diverse learners around the world are paying enough attention to differences among cultures. There are many other questions that remain to be answered. Should online courses be designed to reflect the culture of the audience? How is access to sources of online learning influencing learners and their cultures? What are some of the critical challenges that instructors encounter when planning e-learning courses? To what extent is e-learning adaptable to non-Western students' needs and culture?

More research is needed to explore evidence of the importance of asynchronous group discussion in the online context. Some studies by Henri (1992) and Garrison (1992) experimented with the ways in which computer asynchronous classes are exhibited and affect students' learning. More research is needed to examine the difficulties associated with online learning culture. Relevant online learning strategies should be implemented to help students become more creative in using their various skills.

Future research should also examine the ways in which online education is affecting teachers and instructors – specifically whether it is affecting the teaching culture, the course management, the teaching strategies or some combination thereof. Detailed qualitative studies could provide great insight into blended online courses. One possible future research project would be to test the students enrolled in online learning to ascertain whether taking online courses empowers or disempowers them; this project could also measure students' level of self-confidence before and after they engage in online classes and then compare and analyze the data. Another possible project might be to identify students across various cultures who are taking the same online course and to interview them regarding the ways in which and the extent to which their cultural identity has been thereby influenced. Online communication is a tool for crossing geographical boundaries and thus it could be used to significantly connect cultures and build bridges of understanding.

CONCLUSION

This paper demonstrates that online learners' culture is influenced by online education and vice versa. This paper also provides ideas on how students' learning can be enhanced in the process of connecting to one another and to their professors. It furthermore provides insight into the ways in which the introduction of online learning can complement traditional teaching approaches and, in turn, impact students' learning cultures in positive ways. The evidence shows that students' cultural background influences their perception and performance in online learning environments in the sense that some students from some cultures require more help than some students from other cultures in order to become independent learners.

This study analyzed student-student and student-instructor interactions reflecting students' engagement in and benefits derived from open and online learning. Students revealed how their engagement in online discussion improved their thinking skills and allowed them to think deeply about various subjects in ways that would not be possible if it were not for online learning. Students engagement in online learning helps them to develop greater planning and time-management skills as well as greater self-discipline. Students in the study displayed an improvement in their abilities to set short- and long-term goals. These students' excitement for and involvement in every aspect of technology available to them made online education an outstanding vehicle for the improvement of their skills. Traditional learning approaches are still dominant in most Saudi classrooms. Nevertheless, online education is in the process of being introduced and many universities are employing blended learning strategies that are constructing new learning realities for students. Students' learning culture is clearly being positively influenced by online education – an approach that enables them to actively participate in discussions, to engage in self-directed learning and to construct their learning by drawing on and creating their own experiences.

REFERENCES

Al-Khalifa, H. S. (2009). The state of distance education in Saudi Arabia. *eLearn Magazine*.

Albalawi, M. S. (2007). *Critical factors related to the implementation of Web-based instruction by higher-education faculty at three universities in the Kingdom of Saudi Arabia.* Unpublished Dissertation, The University of West Florida, Florida.

Barnard, L., William, L., To, Y. T., Paton, P. V., & Lai, S. (2009). Measuring self-regulation in online and blended learning environments. *The Internet and Higher Education*, *12*, 1–6. doi:10.1016/j.iheduc.2008.10.005

Bates, T. (2009). *A personal view of e-learning in Saudi Arabia.* Retrieved October 7th, 2010, from http://www.tonybates.ca/2009/11/05/a-personal-view-of-e-learning -in-saudi-arabia/

Corvette, B. (2007). *Conflict management: A practical guide to developing negotiation strategies*. New York, NY: Pearson.

Dabbagh, N. (2007). The online learner: Characteristics and pedagogical implications. *Contemporary Issues in Technology & Teacher Education*, *7*(3), 217–226.

Devers, C. J. (2009). *Students. Perspectives and learning from a cross-cultural online course: The influence of a critical pedagogical approach.* Urbana-Champaign, IL: University of Illinois at Urbana-Champaign.

Esterhuysen, S., & Stanz, K. J. (2004). Locus of control and online learning SA. *Journal of Individual Psychology*, *30*(1), 63–71.

Garrison, D. R. (1992). Critical thinking and self-directed learning in adult education: An analysis of responsibility and control issues. *Adult Education Quarterly*, *42*(3), 136–148.

Henri, F. (1992). Computer conferencing and content analysis. In Kaye, A. R. (Ed.), *learning through computer conferencing: The Najaden papers* (pp. 115–136). New York, NY: Springer.

Kea, F., & Xieb, K. (2009). Toward deep learning for adult students in online courses. *The Internet and Higher Education*, *12*, 136–145. doi:10.1016/j.iheduc.2009.08.001

Kim, K., Liu, S., & Bonk, C. (2005). Online MBA students' perceptions of online learning: Benefits, challenges, and suggestions. *The Internet and Higher Education*, *8*, 335–344. doi:10.1016/j.iheduc.2005.09.005

McCord, L., & McCord, W. (2010). Online learning: Getting comfortable in the cyber class. *Teaching and Learning in Nursing*, *5*(1), 27–32. doi:10.1016/j.teln.2009.05.003

Mirza, A. A. (n.d.). *Is e-learning finally gaining legitimacy in Saudi Arabia*? Retrieved from http://www.faculty.ksu.edu.sa/.../Is%20e-learning%20finally%20gaining %20legitimacy%20in %20Saudi%20

Newton, D., Hase, S., & Ellis, A. (2002). Effective implementation of online learning: A case study of the Queensland mining industry. *Journal of Workplace Learning*, *14*(4), 156–165. doi:10.1108/13665620210427285

Ohara, M. (2004). Maximizing e-learning ROI: Identifying successful online learners. *Allied Academies International Conference*, *8*(1), 49-54.

Pacey, A. (1983). *The culture of technology*. Cambridge, MA: MIT Press.

Pattison, S. (2003). Cultural diversity: Mapping the experiences of students on an international counsellor training programme. *Counselling & Psychotherapy Research*, *3*(2), 107–113. doi:10.1080/14733140312331384472

Renner, W. (2006). *E-learning 2.0: New frontier for students empowerment.* Paper presented at the Edu-Com 2006: Engagement and Empowerment, Thailand.

Sendag, A., & Odabasi, H. F. (2009). Effects of an online problem based learning course on content knowledge acquisition and critical thinking skills. *Computers & Education*, *53*(1), 132–141. doi:10.1016/j.compedu.2009.01.008

Song, L., Singleton, E. S., Hill, J. R., & Koh, M. H. (2004). Improving online learning: Student perceptions of useful and challenging characteristics. *The Internet and Higher Education*, *7*, 59–70. doi:10.1016/j.iheduc.2003.11.003

Tapanes, M., Glenn, G., Smith, B., James, A., & White, B. (2009). Cultural diversity in online learning: A study of the perceived effects of dissonance in levels of individualism/ collectivism and tolerance of ambiguity. *The Internet and Higher Education*, *12*, 26–34. doi:10.1016/j.iheduc.2008.12.001

Wang, C., & Reeves, T. C. (2006). The meaning of culture in online education: Implications for teaching, learning, and design. In Edmundson, A. (Ed.), *Globalized e-learning cultural challenges* (pp. 1–17). Hershey, PA: Idea Group Inc. doi:10.4018/978-1-59904-301-2.ch001

ADDITIONAL READING

Arbaugh, J. B., & Hwang, A. (2006). Does "teaching presence" exist in online MBA courses? *The Internet and Higher Education, 9*(1), 9–21. doi:10.1016/j.iheduc.2005.12.001

Bentley, P. H., Tinney, M. V., & Chia, B. H. (2005). Intercultural internet-based learning: Know your audience and what it values. *Educational Technology Research and Development, 53*(2), 117–127. doi:10.1007/BF02504870

Bourne, J., McMaster, E., Rieger, J., & Campbell, J. (1997). Paradigms for On-Line Learning: A Case Study in the Design and Implementation of an Asynchronous Learning Networks (ALN) Course. *JALN, 1*(2)

Brahler, C, J., Quitadamo, I, J. & Johnson, E. C. (2002). Student critical thinking is enhanced by developing exercise prescriptions using online learning modules. *Advances in Physiology Education, 26*, 210–221.

Bullen, M., & Janes, D. (Eds.). (2007). *Making the Transition to E-learning: Strategies and Issues*. London: IGI Global.

Chitty, B., Ward, S., Noble, T., & Tiangsoongnern, L. (2009). *How locus of control influences students' e-satisfaction with self service technology in higher education*. ANZMAC.

Conrad, D. (2007). The Plain hard work of Teaching Online: strategies for Instructors. In Janes, D., & Bullen, M. (Eds.), *Making the Transition to E-Learning: Strategies and Issues* (pp. 191–207). London: Information Science Publishing.

Cram, B. and Morrison, D. (2004). University continuing education units: Agents for social change? *Canadian Journal of University Continuing Education*, (Special Issue),

de Corpo, S., Hewson, L., & Hughes, C. (2005). *Balancing tools and teachers: Can features of online software influence the effectiveness of the teaching that it supports?* Paper presented at the ascilite

Edmundson, A. (Ed.). (2007). *Globalized E-Learning Cultural Challenges*. London: Information Science Publishing.

Felix, U. (2000). A multivariate analysis of students' experience of Web-based learning. ASCILITE. Conference, Southern Cross University, Proceedings, 285-297.

Ferris, S. P., & Godar, S. (Eds.). (2006). *Teaching and Learning with Virtual Teams*. London: IGI.

Gupta, S. (2006). *A Quick Guide to Cultural Competency*. Available from: www.guptaconsulting.com

Hara, N., & Kling, R. (2000). *Students' Distress with a Web-based Distance Education Course: An Ethnographic Study of Participants' Experiences*. Bloomington: Center for Social Informatics.

Hara, N., & Kling, R. (2001). Students' Distress with a Web-based Distance Education Course. *Information Communication and Society, 3*(4), 557–579. doi:10.1080/13691180010002297

Hill, J. R. (2002). Strategies and techniques for community building in Web based learning environments. *Journal of Computing in Higher Education, 14*(1), 67–86. doi:10.1007/BF02940951

Hill, J. R., Song, L., & West, R. E. (2009). Social Learning Theory and Web-Based Learning Environments: A Review of Research and Discussion of Implications. *American Journal of Distance Education, 23*(2), 88–103. doi:10.1080/08923640902857713

Hiltz, S. R., & Turoff, M. (2005, October). Education goes digital: "The evolution of online learning and the revolution of higher education. *Communications of the ACM, 48*(10).

Howard, C., Schenk, K., & Discenza, R. (Eds.). (2004). *Distance Learning and University Effectiveness: Changing Educational Paradigms for online Learning*. London: Information Science Publishing.

Ice, P., Curtis, R., Phillips, P., & Wells, J. (2007). Using Asynchronous Audio Feedback to Enhance Teaching Presence and Students' Sense of Community. *Journal of Asynchronous Learning Networks*, *11*(2), 3–25.

Kember, D. (1991). Instructional design for meaningful learning. *Instructional Science*, *20*(4), 289–310. doi:10.1007/BF00043255

La Frenierre, J., & Szyliowicz, J. (2008). *When Appropriate Isn't Enough: The Risk of Ignoring the Social and Cultural Implications of Technology.* Paper presented at the INTS 4965: Technology and Sustainable Development.

Newman, D. R., Webb, B., & Cochran, C. (1995). *A content analysis method to measure critical thinking in face to face and computer supported groups learning.* Retrieved Dec 30, 2003, from listserv@guvm.georgtown.edu

Owston, R. D. (1997). The World Wide Web: A Technology to Enhance Teaching and Learning? *Educational Researcher*, *26*(2), 27–33.

Rourke, L., & Anderson, T. (2002). Using peer teams to lead online discussions. *Journal of Interactive Media in Education, 1.* Retrieved August 27, 2007, from http://www-jime.open.ac.uk/ 2002/ 1/

Rourke, L., & Kanuka, H. (2007). Barriers to online critical discourse. *International Journal of Computer-Supported Collaborative Learning, 2*(1), 105–126. Retrieved August 24, 2007, from http://www.springerlink. com/ content/ r3243740340t0847/

Schrum, L. (2000). Online teaching and learning: essential conditions for success. In Lau, L. (Ed.), *Distance Learning Technologies: Issues, Trends, and Opportunities* (pp. 91–106). Hershey, PA: Idea Group Publishing. doi:10.4018/9781878289803.ch008

Schrum, L. (2002). Oh, what wonders you will see: Distance education past, present and future. *Learning and Leading with Technology*, *30*(3), 6–9, 20–21.

Shea, P., Li, C. S., & Pickett, A. (2006). A study of teaching presence and student sense of learning community in fully online and web-enhanced college courses. *The Internet and Higher Education*, *9*(3), 175–190. doi:10.1016/j.iheduc.2006.06.005

Singh, D. K. (200(6*Effectiveness of Online Instruction.* Paper presented at the 29th annual conference of the Teacher Education Division of the Council for Exceptional Children and the second annual Technology and Media, San Diego, CA.

Song, L., & Hill, J., R. (2007). A Conceptual Model for Understanding Self-Directed Learning in Online Environments. *Journal of Interactive Online Learning*. *6*(1).

Turban, E., King, D., Viehland, D., & Lee, J. (2006). *Electronic commerce: A managerial perspective*. Upper Saddle River, NJ, USA: Prentice Hall.

Tyler-Smith, K. (2008). Early Attrition among First Time e Learners: A Review of Factors that Contribute to Drop-out, Withdrawal and Non-completion Rates of Adult Learners undertaking eLearning Programmes. *Journal of Online Learning and Teaching.*

Visser, J. (February 2001). *Distance Learning as Seen from the North and the West: Points to Ponder for the World at Large.* Paper presented at the UNESCO Learning Workshop on Distance Learning, LEARNTEC 2001.

Wang, H. 2005. Cultural challenges in online education. *CTELT Newsletter*, Spring. http://www.fhsu.edu/ctelt/newsletter/07S/article.htm (accessed September 30, 2007).

Weigel, V. (2002). *Deep learning for a digital age: Technology's untapped potential to enrich higher education*. San Francisco: Jossey-Bass Publishing.

Willging, P. (2003). A Model for the Development of Online Instruction. [Norfolk, VA: AACE.]. *International Journal on E-Learning*, *2*(2), 21–28.

KEY TERMS AND DEFINITIONS

Asynchronous: communication that does not occur at the same time.

Synchronous: communication that occur at the same time; coinciding in time; contemporaneous; simultaneous.

APPENDIX A

Letter of Information

Informed Consent Letter
Online Learning

Dear Participant:

My name is Dr. Amani Hamdan, Assistant Professor. This is an invitation for you to participate in our research in which I seek to explore your learning experience using online learning programs asynchronously and/or synchronous. The data from this project will be used for scholarly presentations and publications.

In this study, written surveys will be the primary methods for gathering data. If you agree to participate, you will provide short answers in the survey.

Your identity will be maintained confidential in the project and any write up. The original or raw data will be stored under lock and key, and only I as sole researchers will have access to the raw data. If you choose to provide your written reflections this will be kept confidential, all the data will be kept two years after the research is complete, after which the raw data will be destroyed.

Your participation is voluntary and you may withdraw from the study or refuse to answer any question at any time. As a participant in the study, you will at no time be judged, evaluated or be at risk of harm. Neither your name nor the institution's will be revealed in any written reports. Once I receive your permission, we will follow up to arrange a suitable time for the interview.

Sincerely,

APPENDIX B

Interview Questions

Name:
Institution:
Number of years using online learning:

1. How integrating online communication affecting and influencing your learning experience? (short answers) 6 line minimum
2. How online education is changing the culture or culture influencing online education?
3. How online education is changing you and how is online education influencing you?
4. How frequent do you use online for educational purposes?
5. How frequent do you use Web Ct or Blackboard to access your courses online?
   a. 1-10 hours
   b. 10-20 hours
   c. More than 20 hours
   d. More than 40 hours
6. How frequent do you engage in online discussion on Web Ct or Blackboard?
   a. 1-10 hours

   b. 10-20 hours
   c. More than 20 hours
   d. More than 40 hours
7. How many courses have you taken online
   a. 1-3
   b. 3-5
   c. 7-9
   d. More than 10
8. How frequent do you use online educational activity per week?
   a. 1-10 hours
   b. 10-20 hours
   c. More than 20 hours
   d. More than 40 hours
9. What web pages do you use most?
   a. Google
   b. Ask me.com
   c. Wikipedia. com
   d. Others (specify)
10. Do you benefit from learning online? How?
11. Do you feel safe to state your opinion in an online learning course more than how you feel in a traditional classroom?
12. Are you more motivated to engage in online discussion than in a traditional classroom?

Chapter 12
A Global Conversation on Effective Technology Integration in Education

Kay Kyeongju Seo
University of Cincinnati, USA

Aimee deNoyelles
University of Cincinnati, USA

ABSTRACT

This chapter explored the technology perceptions and preparedness of pre-service and in-service teachers from three different countries. Twenty-one students in the Republic of Korea, twelve students in the United Arab Emirates, and thirty students in the United States of America were virtually connected. They participated in weekly online discussion forums for six weeks and shared how well prepared they felt about using technology in their content areas and how they would effectively use technology in their future classrooms. This study can serve as a good model for facilitating a global conversation and supporting a reflective online conversation across geographic distances and cultural barriers.

INTRODUCTION

As the world has become more closely connected through the advance of technology, societies have become more heterogeneous with respect to different cultures and multiple perspectives. This diversity requires that students learn to learn about others and develop communication and social skills (De Lisi, 2002; Schmitt, 2001). Interacting with others and sharing experiences have now become important parts of the learning process. In recent years, studies have proposed the use of intercultural communication to promote understanding among students across geographic distances and foster students' global awareness and international experience. An increasing number of universities in the U.S. have established intercultural distance learning partnerships with

DOI: 10.4018/978-1-61350-071-2.ch012

other countries to promote multicultural understanding and diversified learning environments (see Cifuentes & Murphy, 2000; Freedman & Liu, 1996; Liang & McQueen, 2000; Nickel, 2001; Shih & Cifuentes, 2001). In light of this new learning paradigm, this study was designed to provide students with the valuable opportunity to expand their horizons by communicating across divides and differences about how best to integrate technology in education.

By 2005, the U.S. had spent over $38 billion to bring computer and Internet access to public schools, ensuring that 99% of schools and 94% of instructional rooms had access to the Internet (NCES, 2005). With the influx of technology in schools today, the 21st century vision of student-centered, inquiry-driven learning has the potential to be realized. However, simple access and use of technology in the classroom does not guarantee that this vision will be achieved. Students must be able to use technology "to learn content and skills, so that they know *how* to learn, think critically, solve problems, use information, communicate, innovate, and collaborate" (Partnership for 21st Century Skills, 2006, p. 11). Given this emphasis, those who choose teaching as a profession face a daunting challenge ahead. Not only must they be prepared to teach content to students and manage the classroom, they must also seamlessly integrate technology into the curriculum. To achieve this objective, teachers must be prepared to "facilitate and inspire student learning and creativity; design and develop digial-age learning experiences and assessments; model digital-age work and learning; promote and model digital citizenship and responsibility; and engage in professional growth and leadership" (ISTE, 2008).

However, only one-third of all public school teachers and 44% of teachers with three years of experience or less in the U.S. felt well prepared or very well prepared to use computers and the Internet for instruction (NCES, 2005). Pre-service teachers are typically born in the 1980s and are usually comfortable with technology use. However, according to the national statistics, this comfort does not necessarily translate to knowledge about effective use of technology in order to enhance teaching and learning. The 21st century vision of learning presents new objectives for current teacher education programs; "Preparation of tomorrow's teachers does not depend solely on how well emerging technologies are incorporated into college coursework; instead, it rests on how well incoming teachers are taught to *leverage* the technologies to help their students develop these same skills" (Lambert & Cuper, 2008, p. 265). This statement suggests that pre-service teachers be provided more opportunities to leverage technologies in education courses and field experiences for their preparation for future technology integration.

BACKGROUND

Factors Affecting Technology Use: In-Service Teachers' Perceptions

In order to assess pre-service teachers' needs, it is helpful to review the current state of technology use among in-service teachers. Cuban (2001) argues that computers are underused as instructional tools in part because school systems have not been restructured to fully support integration. Barriers to effective technology integration include lack of time during the day (Forgasz, 2006; Franklin, 2007; Lim & Chai, 2008; Russell, Bebell, O'Dwyer, & O'Connor, 2003), too much curriculum to cover (Franklin, 2007; Lim & Chai, 2008), high stakes testing (Franklin 2007; Lim & Chai, 2008), lack of access (Forgasz, 2006; Pasternak, 2007), technical problems/support (Forgasz, 2006), student behavior (Forgasz, 2006; Lim & Chai, 2008), and lack of professional development (Coffland & Strickland, 2004; Forgasz, 2006; Russell et al., 2003). Despite the fact that almost every public school in the U.S. is wired for technology, concerns about the digital divide remain. In a qualitative study comparing low-SES and high-SES schools, Warschauer, Knobel and Stone (2004) found that although "student computer ratios were similar, the social contexts of computer use differed, with low-SES schools affected by uneven human networks, irregular home access to computers, and pressure to raise test scores" (p. 562).

These contextual factors influence teachers' use of technology, even when teachers hold student-centered beliefs. For instance, in Lim and Chai's observations of in-service teachers in Singapore (2008), while teachers espoused constructivist pedagogical beliefs, their technological lessons mainly focused on objectivist principles. When asked about this contradiction, teachers claimed they had to keep students on a strict schedule due to performances on standard examinations. Warschauer et al. (2004) also found that teachers felt conflicted between wanting to use technology for innovative purposes and wanting to use it to prepare students for standardized testing. Levin and Wadmany (2008) call this an "incompatibility between goals of education and interactions, and curricular goals and materials" (p. 235).

In addition to contextual factors, personal factors also influence teachers' use of technology. Teachers must have the confidence and motivation to use the technology for new approaches, lest they use the technology to support traditional learning approaches (Garcia & Rose, 2007; Levin & Wadmany, 2008). Teacher beliefs about the usefulness of technology for learning were directly tied to technology use (Russell et al., 2003). Teo (2009) found that perceived usefulness, attitude towards computer use, and computer self-efficacy had direct effects on pre-service teachers' technology acceptance, while environmental conditions affected it indirectly. In a study on teachers' views of technology, Archambault and Crippen (2007) asked in-service teachers to select and share effective educational websites with other teachers. The majority of the sites concerned lesson planning and information gathering, suggesting that technology is still being utilized for teacher-centered purposes.

To address teacher skills and beliefs, extensive professional development plays a crucial role (Forgasz, 2006). However, most teachers in the U.S. participated in professional development for 32 hours or less over a 3-year period (NCES, 2000). In addition, concerning teachers in schools with 50% or more minority enrollments, 81% claimed that professional development was available, compared to 91% of teachers in schools with 20% or lower minority enrollments. These statistics strongly suggest that more consistent, up-to-date development is necessary in order for teachers to keep up with the emerging innovation of technology tools and uses.

Current Preparation of Pre-Service Teachers

Considering the many personal and institutional factors that influence teachers' use of technology in schools, it is important that pre-service teachers are not only given the opportunity to practice and reflect on technology integration in their methods courses, but also experience it through their field work.

Course Work

According to Kleiner, Thomas, and Lewis (2007), nearly all teacher education programs in the U.S. emphasized to pre-service teachers that the primary goal of using technology was to enhance classroom instruction, with sub-goals including accommodating students' differing learning styles and developing individualized instruction. However, several barriers exist to realize these goals, namely faculty members' lack of time, training, and interest; "Lack of interest was a barrier according to 73% of institutions, with 24% citing it as a barrier to a major or moderate extent" (p. 10). In contrast, only 5% of institutions cited pre-service teachers' lack of interest as a barrier.

Clearly, there is a mismatch between faculty and student regarding interest in the subject.

In addition, colleges generally require some type of technology course in their teacher education programs, but pre-service teachers rarely have the opportunity to apply the newly acquired skills to their education courses or field experiences (Pope, Hare, & Howard, 2002).

Past research suggests that integrating technology in methods courses helps prepare pre-service teachers to use technology in their current and future classrooms; "If technology is to be used as a practice, the data show that experimentation needs to start in the methods classes for it to move into the field experiences and beyond" (Pasternak, 2007, p. 154). Through a survey, Dexter and Riedel (2003) found that pre-service teachers tended to use technology in their field experiences when they also took coursework that specifically addressed technology integration in these environments.

Pope et al. (2002) examined whether integrating technology into an elementary method course would influence pre-service teachers' confidence levels of using technology in their own classrooms. The survey results showed that technical proficiency increased after the integration, including issues such as ethical use, adapting resources, use of hardware and software, and networking skills. Based on these findings, they asserted that "teacher education programs that provide the opportunities for pre-service teachers to meet the standards such as planning and designing successful technology experiences, implementing strategies and methods that integrate technology in the classroom to enhance student learning, and using technology to enhance their productivity and professional development will ensure that pre-service teachers become successful, confident users of technology who can integrate technology seamlessly throughout their curriculum" (p. 202). In 2007, while about half of all teacher education programs offered stand alone courses in educational technology, 93% also taught educational technology within methods courses (Kleiner et al., 2007). However, it is unclear if those institutions incorporated technology evenly among methods courses.

Field Experience

Proper field experience is also an important factor for pre-service preparation of technology use. Dexter and Riedel (2003) found that pre-service teachers tended to use technology in their field experiences when both the site and the education program expressed clear expectations concerning technology integration. Support from the field site was a significant predictor of technology integration in the pre-service classroom. In general, 79% of colleges reported that pre-service teachers learned how to use technology during their field experiences (Kleiner et al., 2007). However, only about a half of the colleges reported that pre-service teachers were able to integrate technology in their field classrooms to a moderate or major extent. Several barriers were given as reasons for this moderate to major deficit, some of which corroborated with in-service teachers' barriers: 74% cited competing priorities in the classroom, while 73% cited issues with technology access. Mentor teachers were also influential; 64% of colleges mentioned lack of mentor teacher technology skill, while 62% cited time issues, and 53% mentioning mentor teachers' willingness to integrate technology. Concerning pre-service teachers, only 17% of colleges reported that pre-service teachers' limited skills and knowledge was a substantial barrier. Again, there appears to a mismatch between pre-service teachers and those guiding them. Pre-service teachers may not be allowed the rich experiences they need to prepare for their own classrooms.

METHODS

Participants

To provide a global view on the issues discussed above, this study explored the technology perceptions and preparedness of pre-service and in-service teachers from three different countries; twenty-one in-service teachers from the Republic of Korea, twelve undergraduate pre-service teachers from the United Arab Emirates, and thirty undergraduate pre-service teachers from the United States of America. Two questions were pursued in this study: (a) How well prepared did these students feel about using technology in their content areas?; and (b) what were their perceptions of effective uses of technology in classrooms?

Data Collection and Analysis

The participants were divided into ten discussion groups of six or seven members. The students were assigned so that each group had at least one discussant representing each country in order to promote diverse opinions and multiple perspectives. The students participated in weekly online discussion forums for six weeks. Two questions were posed to the students: (a) How well prepared do you feel about using technology in your content area?; and (b) what are your perceptions of effective uses of technology in classrooms?

The discussion forums were moderated by five doctoral students majoring in instructional technology at another public research university in the U.S.. They were asked to perform the following six tasks geared toward building a social community and supporting the intellectual content of the community: (a) create a friendly environment; (b) encourage participation by reminding participants of the course expectations; (c) encourage sharing of ideas; (d) clarify the topic and discussion schedule; (e) prompt participants to pursue their ideas; and (f) conclude each week's discussion by summarizing the shared ideas. The moderators received one hour training covering what their tasks would be and how they could effectively perform the tasks. They were also provided a moderator's guide summarizing the content of the training.

Using qualitative research methods, we coded and constantly compared the content of student postings for emerging themes and patterns. First we looked for regularities in the data to identify some notable themes and patterns, which were then organized into categories. Next we revisited the data to define relationships among these categories to create and refine codes. Using these codes, the data was analyzed to elicit meaningful answers to the research questions.

RESULTS

Student Preparedness to Use Technology

Technology Requirements in the Education Program

All three countries required at least one technology course specifically dedicated to pre-service teachers' applying technology in the classroom. An American student states, "Technology is probably the thing I am least confident about .... Next semester, I will be taking a technology course and I really look forward to it. Learning more about instructional technology will make me a better teacher candidate." However, according to other American students, this technology course could be postponed. One student shares, "I do not feel prepared at all to teach using new technology. I have not had to take a technology class so I do not know the new technology that is available for teachers." It seems as if the curriculum introduces the technology course later on, as another student attests, "My area of concentration is middle school language arts and now that I am getting farther into my degree and taking a technology class, I feel a little more comfortable about it." In some cases, the technology course could be waived altogether. An American pre-service teacher claims, "I do not feel that I have gotten any specific help from the institution to better prepare me for the technology I will hopefully be seeing in my future. In fact, the technology course that is a requirement for an elementary education degree was waived for me, as well as for some of my peers." Another student laments this; "I was waived from the technology course which probably would have been helpful to me." This practice of postponing or waiving technical courses for pre-service teachers may inhibit their technology integration skills. In contrast, students in the UAE reported taking several technology courses. A UAE student writes, "I think that I am very good in using technology because my university provides students with many technological courses." Korean discussants did not comment on this, probably because they are in-service teachers.

Although the universities in the three countries offered technology courses, it was interesting to know whether the students felt these courses were sufficient to prepare them for future classrooms. The UAE students generally posted positive responses. For example, one said, "I believe that I am prepared to use technology in my classroom. I really have high expectations because I am already taking education technology courses in my university covering how to use technology for my teaching … making quizzes that are based on computers... and am learning how to use lots of programs that will help me in teaching such as Flash." Another UAE pre-service teacher adds, "In my next semester, I will take [the] course which will help me as a teacher a lot. I will be trained to involve technology in my teaching and to choose the best technological equipments or creating my own one." Another student taking this course says, "I feel that I am on the right track where I started to discover different programs and use them in my daily life." A UAE student writes that the technology course "helped me to learn how to use some of technological tools …. When I become a teacher I will use these tools because students will feel interest when I will apply some technological tools in the teaching process."

Interestingly, students from the U.S. were not as positive. Commenting on the technology course, one student says, "I think [my university] does a great job of requiring us to have a class on technology, but it only scratches the surface of what technology can do." A fellow student agrees, also commenting on the structure of the course, "I'm excited about learning the latest technology but feel very unprepared to use it to teach. In a technology course, we have been shown some very helpful tools. In [one] class we discussed Web 2.0. We looked over a dozen excellent sites for presentations, storage, [and] blogging, and I left the lecture determined to start putting them to use. Unfortunately, a week later, and I haven't got there yet." Based on these comments, technology courses must go beyond lectures. Students in these courses must not only be able to use the tools introduced, but understand how to incorporate them in future classrooms.

Beyond technology courses, mixed results were found when students discussed whether their methods courses integrated technology. Concerning the UAE, students commented on taking design classes and technology classes, and some mentioned methods experiences; "[In] the math class, we used to work in a program called 'Maple' which deals with graphing and equations. It was very interesting to have the opportunity to use technology in different classes and that motivated me and I think it will motivate my learners in the future too." An American discussant shares, "In my classes, at least one assignment a semester per class, I have had to do some kind of technology interactive project."

In order for a methods course to integrate technology, students must gain proficiency in tool use. One American student recalls a class experience; "I recently had a project due … we were to create an I-movie. My portion of the project consisted of me videotaping a professor and it took me forever to learn how to operate the mini DVD recorder." If this student had received more training on the use of the recorder, she may have concentrated more on the assignment at hand. Another American participant says, "The more classes I have taken at the University, the more comfortable I am becoming in using technology, especially in a science methods course that I am taking for teaching. In this course, we are making our own science websites where we will turn in all of our work and format all of our work to be used in the website." Another adds to this explanation, "In my science class, we are making our own website where we can put lesson plans, links to other sites, and summaries and reactions to science articles. I was very interested in this assignment because it helps me to prepare for having my own website as a teacher." However, there seems to be a lack of consistency across course experiences. Another American pre-service teacher has a different take; "I think it would be better if there was more commonality among all the courses. For instance, my science method course does not require a website and I wish it did."

Technology in Field Experiences

Students from all three countries agreed that using technology in field experiences was crucial for teacher preparation. As one American student puts it, "I feel like nothing prepares me more than actually being in the classroom and seeing how to use the technology. I can read about the different types of technologies and strategies but actually seeing it first hand and being able to experiment with what works best for my students has been what has prepared me the most." A UAE student agrees, "I will start doing my practicum during this semester, so I hope to learn more about what technology are used in schools and what I can use as a teacher, because I will see more technological tools than what I think and I will learn more."

Clearly the mentor teacher plays an important role in the field experience. A Korean in-service teacher recalls, "I saw many teachers making good lessons while using technology in school, and they input appropriate technology at the right time." Regarding her field experience, an American discussant says, "The teacher I am [working] with has her own website ... and she uses a smart board ... to make learning more interactive with technology when she does math investigations. I am going to try to learn as much as I can from her so that when I become a teacher, I create a better website." Another American participant agrees that modeling is important; "While I have been in the classroom, I have not used smart boards or taught any lessons using technology, but the teacher I observe has. She uses the smart board for several things: engaging the kids in math competitions, dissecting stories, and preparing for the map test.... I will feel comfortable using this much technology in my future classroom!"

However, the comments from the American students are still somewhat questionable since the students have not reported actually incorporating technology. It would be interesting to know whether they are as prepared to use technology in her classroom as they perceive. In addition, not all field sites encourage the highest level of technology integration. An American discussant indicates, "I personally find it difficult to teach with technology on a regular basis in my placement classroom. I could take the students to the computer lab and have them work there but I would have to sign up for a time and that is not always readily available."

Professional Development Opportunities

In order for pre-service teachers to feel prepared to use technology in their future classrooms, they must be continually provided the opportunity to develop their skills. This notion is supported by an American student's statement; "I am also concerned that technology changes so fast that we have to stay caught up or we will get left behind by our students." Another pre-service teacher predicts, "I think we will see more and more training offered for teachers as our careers progress. School districts will find themselves falling behind the times if they don't offer technological education to both teachers and students." Many participants said that technology workshops were available in their colleges, and some were available in their field districts For example, an American student says, "For some of my classes, I have to take digital pictures and video of my teaching reading lesson plans. Also, I have to scan pictures of the book I am using for the lesson plan and put its pictures into the above power point. I am not sure I know how to do all of this, but we have a technology and learning lab to help us figure out how to make this presentation." However no American students specifically stated they attended a lab or workshop for professional development in either the college setting or the school district setting.

Opportunities for teacher training seem to be high in the Republic of Korea. A Korean discussant shares, "I'm not prepared about using technology when I started teaching. So I make efforts to learn a new technology … going to the computer academy…." Another Korean student explains, "Teacher training was activated in Korea … training was concentrated in summer and winter vacation. The training courses contain the use of multi-media and the production of data. So teachers can use technology [easily] in lessons." Again, this is concerning in-service teachers, so their experience may differ. In the UAE, different schools appear to receive different training opportunities. For instance, the elite model schools "are having special training classes for teachers, and have a special trainer for new technologies." It would be interesting to know whether the government or private schools receive similar support.

Digital Divide

The digital divide issue caused concern for several American students. Some were concerned that the technology in their colleges and field sites would not adequately prepare them for the technology in their future classrooms. An American participant indicates, "I feel prepared to use the technology in the classroom. From what I have observed at the schools I am at, the extent of their technology is not greater than what I am around on a daily basis. The thing I worry about is getting into a school that is more advanced than what we have a chance to go to right now." An American student who claims she is not technologically savvy, agrees, "At the district I will be teaching at, I know for a fact that if the district can't afford text books, then they won't be able to afford Mac computers as well, so I am not too afraid about my lack of technological skills. However, it would be a scary thing for me to get placed in another district where technology is predominately used."

In other cases, the student feels prepared by the college or field experience, while the future school district may not require the preparation. An American discussant says, "I have seen technology integrated into many aspects of my observing classroom, yet feel that many schools lack not only the know-how but the finances as well." A UAE student says, "In the university, we use technology for mostly everything. Most of the schools in my district are having the basic technology. Everywhere I hear, in the community, that they support technology but what I see in reality is different. Many people are trying to make difference in this matter, but I think it needs a major step by supplying schools with equipments and training teachers to use them." Another UAE participant agrees, "What really makes me doubt my preparation for using technology in the classroom is the administration. I don't know in which school I am going to teach, and I really don't know if they will accept my technology ideas because there are those old-fashioned administrators. I should also prepare myself on how to solve those kinds of problems." An American student anticipates, "I think that if I wanted to make technology more prominent in my own classroom someday I would have to ask for it from my principal." Another issue is of time. According to a Korean student, "Because I can make and search software, I think I feel well prepared to use technology in study. But the purpose of using technology is not to concentration of study, but to teach students easily in many cases. Usually Korean elementary school teachers have to teach from 25 hours to 30 hours in a week. So we don't have much time to prepare study." These are interesting points. These comments suggest that we make sure that colleges of education prepare pre-service teachers to use technology, integrate technology, and also address real-life school district issues such as these.

Student Perception of Effective Technology Integration

Student Needs in the 21st Century

When this topic was posed, most of the answers considered student needs, rather than teacher needs. American discussants felt that technology use is effective in classrooms when it supported students in acquiring 21st century skills. An American pre-service teacher says, "I believe that it is important to use technology regularly because the students will learn what forms of information are available to them, how to become fluent with the use of technology, and they will be up to date with how the world works and what resources people use." Another participant agrees, "I also think it's important to teach technology because the students will be growing up familiar with the technology, and if you can make a connection to the students' learning is a good thing."

One American student indicates the importance of preparing students to transfer technological skills to other life arenas; "I want the students in my class to have the opportunity to work with technology that they will be presented with in the real world." Another discussant claims that exposing all children to 21st century resources will give them an advantage; "For those students who do not have access to technology at home, it allows them to learn important technological skills."

Addressing Students' Diverse Learning Styles and Abilities

Students from all three countries agreed that technology use is effective when it accommodates students' learning styles. An American pre-service teacher explains, "I think it is very important to use technology in the classroom because not all students learn best when the teacher lectures to them, I think using technology is a good way to teach the different kinds of learning styles." A UAE pre-service teacher agrees, "I think the effective of using technology depends on students' learning style. To illustrate that, if the students like and learn with presentation on the PowerPoint, it will be very effective technology. However, if they feel [bored] and they don't learn anything, it will [not be] effective technology." Another UAE discussant explains, "Some of the students are visual and some are auditory, so when the teacher uses technology, she will be able to satisfy students' needs." A Korean in-service teacher continues, "I think using technology is an effective way to teach the different kinds of learning styles. For example, some of the students want visual learning style."

When used effectively, technology can also help students of differing abilities and needs. A UAE student states, "When a teacher uses technology in the classroom, he/she can meet the needs of diverse learners." Technology can be used to help those with learning difficulties. Another UAE student shares, "For students who have difficulties in learning mathematics, I can let them love math through using technology which most of students want to go through, so I may introduce them to some software that will assist them to understand the basic mathematics." Considering those who need special assistance, an American pre-service teacher says. "I think that the more a teacher can do using technology, the better the chance that the teacher will reach all of the students. I have used technology in my classroom.... I had a student that could not write very well at all. The device allowed him to get his work done and for others to be able to read it." A Korean in-service teacher cautions that technology is not a 'one size fits all' resource; "In order to effectively use technology in my classroom, I have to make individual education lesson plans before having lecture because many students have different learning ability." A UAE pre-service teacher agrees, "For me, I see that when choosing the technology in class, it has to meet the students' needs and therefore, I have to study my students to know what they need and what technology works for them because what might work for a certain students might not work for others."

Enhancing Student Engagement and Interest Level

The discussants agreed that in order for technology use to be effective in the classroom, it must capture students' attention and be engaging. Two students in the U.S. specifically mentioned motivating students. An American participant states, "I believe that an effective way to use technology in classrooms is one where the students enjoy the lesson and are hooked in and interested the whole time the lesson is going on." Another agrees, "Incorporating technology so that it hooks your students is the key." A UAE student explains, "It's a great tactic to change the routine of the traditional lecturing by introducing the students into several types of technology. For instance, I may orchestrate some flash games that related to math and science, so students certainly may be engaged and they may feel more enthusiastic to learn and discover in modern and new methods." A Korean student adds, "Technology can give students many interests. If the contents of learning [are] interesting, and if they learn something with [the] computer, they are pleased to learn something by [the] computer. So I think it is great way to incorporate learning material with students' interests."

Fostering Student Social Interaction

Discussants agreed that technology is used effectively in the classroom when it not only considers cognitive development, but social development in students. An American discussant warns, "When we immerse ourselves fully in a digital world, forgetting to supplement the personal interaction, I think children will lose their ability to relate to other human beings." A Korean student shares, "Students in Korea play with computer games very much in their houses or PC rooms. So time for playing with friends is decreasing gradually. Therefore communication with friends is decreased in quantity and they pay no attention to relation with other human beings. If teachers emphasize uses of technology in the classrooms, students will not communicate each other. Students ultimately will lose their ability to relate to other human beings." An American pre-service teacher states, "I almost feel that the knowledge we can gain from good use of technology somewhat outweighs the potential for loss of human relation skills, but I think if done correctly, you can have the best of both worlds." Another American participant suggests maximizing the affordances of the technology; "If technology is used like we're using it, to hold meaningful discussions, or to make movies that are beneficial to the subject, or anything that is beneficial, then that is fine." Another American student agrees, "My perception of effective use of technology is anything that is used to be beneficial to the students. I've been doing some research on Smart Technology (Smart Boards) and hopefully can get one of these for my classroom. These things are great ways for interaction to take place in the classroom."

Design Considerations: Technology to Support Learning

Discussants agreed that technology was effective in classrooms if it supported student-centered learning objectives. A Korean in-service teacher explains, "I think that using technology is important but the lesson is supposed to be the focus. Technology should be used as an appropriate means to aid in the delivery of instruction. Technology should only be used if it enhances learning." Another Korean teacher agrees, "[The] most important thing is to design the flow of lesson. Technology is just [a] secondary mean to reach the goal of lesson." Another Korean participant asserts that "the effective uses of technology should start at a question 'what is the learning objectives of the class?' and at a concept of 'flow' which come from attention, curiosity, challenge, and control. I think it is possible that the technology can just 'help' effectively the relating both of them, not be wholly in charge of it." An American pre-service teacher states, "If using technology helps to stimulate learning, then it is being used correctly and effectively. However, if the use of technology is just being used as a time-filler, or if it is being used incorrectly, then it is just a waste of time." A UAE pre-service teacher shares that technology does not have to be used in every lesson simply because it is available; "I still want to do handy lessons that involve drawing and writing and other work. Yes, technology will help me explaining my lessons better, but sometimes it's good to go back to teach the students to use their skills. It's good to develop different kind of skills in the students."

Teacher Considerations: Facilitation and Skills

Technology use is ineffective if the teacher does not facilitate student-centered cognition and learning. An American student explains, "Inappropriately used in the classroom, technology can be used to perpetuate old models of teaching and learning. Students can be 'plugged into computers' to do drill and practice that is not so different from workbooks." Regarding software applications, she shares, "[Sometimes] professors speed up or go too fast when using computer enhanced technology (such as power-point presentations or internet resources). Technology use contributes to the process of faculty glossing over complex topics too quickly. For example, faculty members forget students need time to let the information sink in before they go on to the next slide." Other discussants agreed that teachers must facilitate along with the technology in order for it to be effective. An American pre-service teacher says, "[College teachers] will read the power point directly from the screen and really supplement it with nothing else. There is nothing enriching about it. I really think there needs to be a delicate balance between authentic teaching and the integration of technology. Both can be done successfully, but it will take a lot of thinking and a lot of work."

Another American discussant indicates, "If technology is used just as a different way to delivery lectures, the student will not perceive this any differently from an instructor lecturing to them." Another student agrees, "I have observed, and have experienced teachers who replace authentic teaching with technology .... Many times teachers will put on a movie relating to a subject and expect students to learn all of their materials from this source." A UAE student suggests, "I think if we use technology as video or internet, we need from the student to submit reflection and feedback about what they learn. I mean that we cannot play video to the students without asking them any question." An American student adds that "power points can be very helpful visual aids, but the students should never learn all of their information through them. They should be able to discuss everything with their teacher to make sure they understand the lesson." A Korean discussant agrees, "Even with the best technology, use of it can't be effective if students do not understand the lesson." An American pre-service teacher visualizes a situation in which technology use is facilitated by the teacher; "The idea is that if they could work at their own pace, at a computer, and be guided by the teacher, then each kid would be more successful."

Finally, discussants felt that in order for technology use to be effective in the classroom, the teacher must have the skills to use the technological equipment. A UAE student explains, "In order to use technology in the classroom in a good way, teachers have to know how to use technological tools and they have to be trained in using those tools in the classroom." An American participant agrees, "Proper instruction, coupled with innovative technology can open many doors to active learning, but if teachers are unfamiliar with the software it is unlikely they will present it in a positive light, and therefore have little hope of creating motivation in their students."

CONCLUSION

This chapter explored how well prepared in-service and pre-service teachers from the Republic of Korea, the United Arab Emirates, and the United States of America felt about using technology and what they perceived to be effective technology integration. We found that despite their differing cultural contexts, they all acknowledged and emphasized the importance of integrating technology properly into the teaching and learning process and desired consistent opportunities to develop and practice technology skills. The findings from this study suggest important implications for pre-service training. Several factors must be in place to support pre-service teachers in their future classrooms. Teacher educators should aim to provide more practice-centered training, effectively connecting theories with real-life tasks. In addition, technology training must address pre-service teachers' beliefs, skills, and knowledge. Reflecting on their past and current technology integration experiences could affect their perceptions of effective uses of technology. Doing this enables pre-service teachers to approach any learning environment with an existing instructional model, lessening the dependence on any one technology. In addition, pre-service teachers must have exposure not only using technology in their methods courses and field experiences, but also integrating technology into the curriculum. These strategies can help pre-service teachers adequately prepare themselves to handle the contextual factors of school, such as high stakes testing, time management, and the persisting digital divide.

This study is meaningful in many ways. It can serve as not only a good model for facilitating intercultural communications but also an exemplary case for supporting the value of reflective online conversations. More importantly, this study can encourage our students to participate in the global conversation about how to effectively integrate technology in education, thus eliciting more dynamic interactions across geographic distances and cultural barriers.

REFERENCES

Archambault, L., & Crippen, K. (2007). The sites teachers choose: A gauge of classroom Web use. *Contemporary Issues in Technology & Teacher Education*, *7*(2), 59–74.

Cifuentes, L., & Murphy, K. L. (2000). Promoting multicultural understanding and positive self-concept through a distance learning community: Cultural connections. *Educational Technology Research and Development*, *48*, 69–83. doi:10.1007/BF02313486

Coffland, D. A., & Strickland, A. W. (2004). Factors related to use of technology in secondary geometry instruction. *Journal of Computers in Mathematics and Science Teaching*, *23*, 347–365.

Cuban, L. (2001). *Oversold and underused: Computers in the classroom*. Cambridge, MA: Harvard University Press.

De Lisi, R. (2002). From marbles to Instant Messenger: Implications of Piaget's ideas about peer learning. *Theory into Practice*, *41*, 5–12. doi:10.1207/s15430421tip4101_2

Dexter, S., & Riedel, E. (2003). Why improving pre-service teacher educational technology preparation must go beyond the college's walls. *Journal of Teacher Education*, *54*, 334–346. doi:10.1177/0022487103255319

Forgasz, H. (2006). Factors that encourage or inhibit computer use for secondary mathematics teaching. *Journal of Computers in Mathematics and Science Teaching*, *25*, 77–93.

Franklin, C. (2007). Factors that influence elementary teachers' use of computers. *Journal of Technology and Teacher Education*, *15*(2), 267–293.

Freedman, K., & Liu, M. (1996). The importance of computer experience, learning processes, and communication patterns in multicultural networking. *Educational Technology Research and Development*, *44*, 43–59. doi:10.1007/BF02300325

Garcia, P., & Rose, S. (2007). The influence of technocentric collaboration on pre-service teachers' attitudes about technology's role in powerful learning and teaching. *Journal of Technology and Teacher Education*, *15*, 247–266.

International Society for Technology in Education. (2008). *National educational technology standards and performance indicators for teachers*. Retrieved on May 5, 2009, from http://www.iste.org/Content/NavigationMenu/NETS/ForTeachers/2008Standards/NETS_for_Teachers_2008.htm

Kleiner, B., Thomas, N., & Lewis, L. (2007). *Educational technology in teacher education programs for initial licensure* (NCES 2008-040). Washington, DC: National Center for Education Statistics, Institute of Education Sciences, U.S. Department of Education.

Lambert, J., & Cuper, P. (2008). Multimedia technologies and familiar spaces: 21st-century teaching for 21st-century learners. *Contemporary Issues in Technology & Teacher Education*, *8*, 264–276.

Levin, T., & Wadmany, R. (2007). Teachers' views on factors affecting effective integration of Information Technology in the classroom: Developmental scenery. *Journal of Technology and Teacher Education*, *16*, 233–263.

Liang, A., & McQueen, R. J. (2000). Computer-assisted adult interactive learning in a multicultural environment. *Adult Learning*, *11*, 26–29.

Lim, C. P., & Chai, C. S. (2008). Teachers' pedagogical beliefs and their planning and conduct of computer-mediated classroom lessons. *British Journal of Educational Technology*, *39*, 807–828. doi:10.1111/j.1467-8535.2007.00774.x

National Center for Education Statistics. (2000). *Teachers' tools for the 21st century. (NCES 2000-102)*. Washington, DC: U.S. Department of Education.

National Center for Education Statistics. (2005). *Internet access in U.S. public schools and classrooms: 1994-2003. (NCES 20005-15)*. Washington, DC: U.S. Department of Education.

Nickel, T. B. (2001). Getting a glimpse in Guangzhou. *TechTrends*, *45*, 32–34. doi:10.1007/BF02772019

Partnership for 21st Century Skills. (2006). *Results that matter: 21st century skills and high school reform*.

Partnership for 21st Century Skills, March 2006. Retrieved March 1, 2009, from http://www.21stcenturyskills.org/ index.php? option=com_content&task =view&id=204&Itemid=114

Pasternak, D. L. (2007). Is technology used as practice? A survey analysis of pre-service English teachers' perceptions and classroom practices. *Contemporary Issues in Technology & Teacher Education, 7*, 140–157.

Pope, M., Hare, D., & Howard, E. (2002). Technology integration: Closing the gap between what pre-service teachers are taught to do and what they can do. *Journal of Technology and Teacher Education, 10*, 191–203.

Russell, M., Bebell, D., O'Dwyer, L., & O'Connor, K. (2003). Examining teacher technology use: Implications for pre-service and in-service teacher preparation. *Journal of Teacher Education, 54*, 297–310. doi:10.1177/0022487103255985

Schmitt, E. (2001, March 23). Tally of students equals number at boomer peak: Hispanic and Asian percentage increase. *The New York Times*, p. A17.

Shih, Y. D., & Cifuentes, L. (2001). One tale of why and how to teach and learn online internationally. *TechTrends, 45*, 8–13. doi:10.1007/BF02772015

Teo, T. (2009). Modeling technology acceptance in education: A study of pre-service teachers. *Computers & Education, 52*, 302–312. doi:10.1016/j.compedu.2008.08.006

Warschauer, M., Knobel, M., & Stone, L. (2004). Technology and equity in schooling: Deconstructing the digital divide. *Educational Policy, 18*, 562–588. doi:10.1177/0895904804266469

Chapter 13
Knowledge is Infinity, Language is Limit!

Simber Atay
Dokuz Eylul University, Turkey

ABSTRACT

This chapter discusses some common points of Distance Education and Photography in the context of meta-communication. Distance Education is a system. Therefore, it has a peculiar structure like all other systems, it is composed for heterogeneous student masses, but is accounted as having an individualistic quality. Distance Education is an intact system.

No room for discrepancy, hesitation, disagreement, intellectual fantasies, et cetera. It perfectly represents the humanistic tradition in postmodern times. Distance Education is a meta-communication problematic. Everything can be taught by Distance Education because there are innumerous programs ranging from business administration to literature....

But to what extent can it be taught? There are the heteronyms of this problem such as Polanyi's "tacit knowledge" or Hegel's/Agamben's Eleusinian Mystery. In Distance Education publications there is a current use of photographical illustrations; Photography itself is also a Distance Education program. Distance Education culture and Photography culture have also same mythological origins like Kairos and Mnemosyne.

DOI: 10.4018/978-1-61350-071-2.ch013

INTRODUCTION

I lecture photography. The History of Photography, The Theories of Photography, Iconography and The Art of Photography, The Culture of Photography, Project in Photography etc. And sometimes, in fact very rarely I write essays about photography. Because no need that the already written things shall be rewritten by me. Besides, I believe in the ephemera nature and the originality of one single lesson. But still I feel suspicious about the situation. Is the manner I prefer emerging from a mindset of noodiness peculiar to the Third World or is it an ordinary idleness?

Two years ago, I got a proposal from the authorities of Anadolu University which is one of the universities I lecture in and which has a global achievement about the Open Education. The Faculty of Open Education was launching a new program: The Photography! Textbooks would be written for this. They also invited me with a great generosity. I was so glad. Eventually I was becoming someone. The author of a book from which hundreds of students will benefit! I immediately set to work. I attended exciting orientation and coordination meetings. I also began writing. But while I was still in the world of dreams the time was over. My dear colleagues from the Faculty of Open Education, kindly declared that my text was not conforming their standards. Thanks. My one more dream was ended.Just, I have been remained outside of the System, like a science-fiction antagonist... But still I couldn't help myself remembering this humor: What matters for me is the process, not the conclusion!

DISTANCE EDUCATION AS A SYSTEM

Challenging to identify a system as an individual, isn't it taking the risk of being paranoiac? Well then, if we change the context and if we want to be a manifest writer rather than an academician:

Because photography was not the problem, in fact there was no problem. Because Open Education was a system, any information within the scope of any program, was valid only if it was formulated within the sense of the Open Education system. No room for critical attitude within the communication of the information. But the direct transfer of the straight data the way that to enable the possibility of criticism was projected. The aforesaid global system had a transparent structure. Within the broadcasting frequency, there were no noise reasons such as censor, discrepancy, hesitation, disagreement. The information was distilled within the Open Education mechanisms for the heterogeneous student masses. These student masses, certainly, forms an extraordinary diversity in terms of age group, profession group, social class, ideological structure, geographical position. The genuine character of the Open Education makes the information directly functional. Besides, the Open Education enables material and moral development in positive terms for millions of people who could not trained during the university study or who wants to develop oneself. Considering the heterogeneous structure of the student mass, the academic mission of the Open Education, may be idealized as it was useful in realizing the postmodern but unfortunately kitsch utopias such as the intercultural alliance or inter-ideology reunification. But the Open Education represents a more classical tradition moreover in postmodern terms: Humanism! The information is preserved, and offered for the universal share of the humanity through the methodological regulations peculiar to the system. The operators of the system communicate with the students of the system by means of the books, television broadcasts, web sites and publications. This is a virtual communication. Again relevantly, the functions of the managers of the Faculty of Open Education, the white-collar workers of the Open Education, the authorities of the Open Education exams, the assisting training center elements relevant to the Open Education system, the publications, the authors do not alter this virtual feature. Correspondingly, the Open Education system has an intact structure. Only knowledge! For the knowledge! With the knowledge!

No room fantasy within the Open Education system:

- The epistemological argument concerning the possible crisis situation which the ones see the light may experience as Plato mentioned in the cave allegory (Plato, 1942) does not exist. It is enough to see and of course to show the light.
- The ignorant teacher theory of Joseph Jacotot which crystallizes the education as an experimental method and putting the intellectual emancipation against popular instruction (Ranciere, 2009), is now only a homage to the emancipation notion.
- In the preface written by Jorge Luis Borges for introducing the Cardinal Napellus of Gustav Meyrink: "*Through 1916, in Geneva, I read Goethe's Faust, Kant's Critique of Pure Reason, Heine's Lyrisches Intermezzo with little German knowledge and a very small English-German dictionary...Back then, I believed to know the German language which I don't know even now.*" (Meyrink, 2009). No room for the passionate attitude of Borges towards the texts which evens up intuition and knowledge within this context.

Within the Open Education book publications, the chapters are written generally by different individuals. This information processed in respect of the chapter is supported by the additional reading parts, photographs, related illustrations, and charts. In addition, the information is divided into sections along the chapters and at the end there are the questions. Again at the end of the chapter, the listed summary of the chapter, test questions containing mainly the chapters and the answers are located. Thus the information is repeated throughout the chapter in variations, and the logic of not only communicating the information but also acquiring the information is built. The books have a design pre-determined by the Open Education Center. This design was determined through pedagogical and aesthetical criteria. Accordingly, although the credits of the contributors are printed naturally, the anonymous character of the publication is preserved.

Within the communication of the information, there is no frustration emerging from the academic and epistemological distinctions, categories, construal differences. The textbook can be about photography, mathematics, business administration or literature. All kinds of information can be communicated. The Social Sciences can be transferred as plain as the Positive Sciences.

The Open Education also had impact on the university study. Many lecturers publish their lessons also through the Internet

In addition to the books, the national and global television broadcastings, internet publishing, enables concurrent access to the information through different means of communication. As well as the books, the TV broadcasts and internet publishing avail the students by ensuring the recurrence of the information similar to the structure of the books. Besides, these visual, virtual but still anonymous and neutral featured publications, create an egocentric communication atmosphere for the student despite these features (Lucido and Borabo, 1997), namely forms a working model illusion authentic to the individual. At this point, I will not stop myself remembering the verses of the famous Turkish poet Nazım Hikmet where he expressed the formula of life: Unique and independent as a tree and fraternal as a forest!

The solitude of the Open Education student is an advantage. As one of the characters in the television series called Rubicon (Bromell, 2010) says: The solitude is a gift!

Further we, are no more the prisoners of the Panopticon, the paragon of grief of Foucault, but the optimistic inhabitants of the Synopticon structure realist to the current political and cultural conjuncture of Bauman (Bauman, 2000). The people of postmodern times are free and can make anachronical choices. Accordingly, as Bauman did, one can reach to Bentham by overcoming the Foucault's metaphor. By discovering his reform qualified good will, the structure of Panopticon can be identified ironically and the up-to-date variation design called Synopticon can be proposed.

Within the Open Education System, only information is valid. Our thoughts are of no account. Since the foundation date, the Open Education always utilized the high technology. No matter how tragic and how disappointing the background of the technology was from the Concentration Camps to the Twin Towers, beyond the totalitarian and the terrorist manipulations can represent the "modernist evolution" notion within its body discretely. The related technological developments increase the quality of the Open Education directly proportional.

DISTANCE EDUCATION AS A META-COMMUNICATION PROBLEM

Using any activity with meta- prefix, it means that we have analyzing issues or analyzing needs in relation to that activity. Cause, unknown realms were occurred beyond our knowledge and experience. For instance, giving an example from the Photography, when the Ashes and Snow of Gregory Colbert (2005), the project displaying lost or utopic harmony between the human and the nature through a Renaissance splendor like re-discovering an extinct creature, was initially presented, was defined as a meta-photography event (Photo, 2005). Besides, nearly the entire projects of Hiroshi Sugimoto which imprisons us to verboclasm with photography perfectionism for the photography are within the same field. Further, paradoxically, Miroslav Tichy, the victim of a rough totalitarian regime, the homeless who manufactured his own camera and lenses with the materials he grabbed from the garbage, who wrote the poem of a male voyeurism with his pale, flu, spotted photographs, is again a hero of this realm.

Again, for example, can we define the Wikileaks of the transparency militant (Imbert, 2010) Julian Assange as a meta-communication phenomenon? Cause, those days where the New York Times represented the justice are over. Fear, auto-censor, vulgarity became the main parameters of the media dynamics. The media, lost its authority of agenda setting, and it was reduced to a detail of the agenda. The death of a journalist or a photo-journalist is being experienced as a tragedy still not vanished on earth. Even mentioning a press having a pure national identity is impossible. How in technologically new designs the common features of the photography, cinema and television are compiled to offer the "visual recording" functions as the main overall feature, Wikileaks represents the main overall feature of the whole variations of communication and media: Information! Moreover, Wikileaks makes the institutional and functional existence of the national and global media meaningless.

But still it is a pleasure to read the articles of Claude Imbert or Bernard-Henry Lévy from Le Point, Yılmaz Özdil from Hürriyet. A literal pleasure! A linguistic euphoria! I wonder if the newspapers would not be published any more in the near future. Will everything be done over internet publishing?

Beyond my esoteric inclinations, meta-communication has its peculiar meaning in communication context; in this point let me make a Gertrude Stein joke please: *Rose is a rose is a rose is a rose.....!*

"Meta-communication is the general term for communication about communication that in everyday life is often part and parcel of any conversation ...Meta-communication is an inherent part of the design process of any information and communication system... Whether in meta-communication truth of some element of language (for example,

the meaning of a word) can be questioned at all is already matter of debate. Can some word meaning be fundamentally true or not? Is it possible to identify a false illocutory act? Another question is whether reality has to be reduced to the objective-scientific abstraction of it?"(Hoppenbrouwers and Weigand, 2010)

Hoppenbrouwers and Weigand, for answers of their questions, appeal to Polanyi, as it has been expressed by themselves: For Polanyi, "*all knowledge has a tacit dimension*". Tacit is opposed to 'explicit' or 'conscious. We can know more than we can tell....Knowledge is something that resides within us, and manifest itself through our actions, and we therefore do not need to document it for our own sake. And in language context "*...the structure and order of (tacit) knowledge reflect structures and ordering in reality. In that sense definitions make a claim to truth*" (Hoppenbrouwers and Weigand, 2010)

The Polanyi's Tacit Knowledge is an equivalent of Hegel's Eleusian Mystery! The poetry is an important self-verification possibility for Giorgio Agamben's philosophy. Just as is his book, Language and Death, Place of Negativity. One of the poems chosen of this book is *Eleusis*.

Your sons, Oh Goddess, miserly with your honor did not

carry it through the streets and markets, but they cultivated it

in the breast's inner chambers

And so you did not live on their lips

Their life honored you. And you live still in their acts.

.....

Often the life of your children reveals you,

And I introduce you as the soul of their acts!...

This poem, dedicated by young Hegel to his friend Hölderlin in August, 1796, recounts the Eleusinian mystery...the philosopher of the dialectic and logos portrays himself here as a guardian of Eleusinian silence (Agamben, 1991).

And according again to Agamben, in his Phenomenology Hegel writes:

"We can tell those who assert the truth and certainty of the reality of sense-object that they should go back to the most elementary school of wisdom, viz. the ancient Eleusinian mysteries of Ceres and Bacchus and they have still to learn the mystery of eating bread and drinking wine. For the who initiated into these mysteries not only comes to doubt (zum Zweifel) the being of, but to despair (zur Verzweiflung) of it; in part he himself accomplishes their negativity, and in part he sees them accomplish it themselves."(Agamben, 1991)

For Agamben: The content of the Eleusian mystery is nothing more than this: experiencing the negativity that is always already inherent in any meaning, in any Meinung of sense-certainty..... The Eleusian mystery of the Phenomenology is thus the same mystery of the poem Eleusis, but now language has captured in itself the power of silence, and that which appeared earlier as unspeakable *profundity* can be guarded (in its negative capacity) in the very heard of the world (Agamben, 1991)

Therefore, Knowledge is infinity; Language is limit! I remember you Dear Wittgenstein,always! Voila! We are in front of an epistemological vanity painting or a distance education panorama!

DISTANCE EDUCATION OF PHOTOGRAPHY

In distance education of photography, the usage of photography as a visual material is identical with the publications of other disciplines in denotative way

About photography, there are lots of Internet publishing that are popular or intellectual, institutional or individual, non-profit or commercial, the websites of the photography associations, photo-agencies, museums, photographers, digital encyclopedic information, e-magazines, forums, blogs, non-profit training programs etc. Besides, in terms of photography, the cyber world houses photography reserves, archives and collections, databases. But within the context of Open University, Distance Education of The Photography differs from other through its systematic and institutional character. The aforementioned academic activity has an interactive nature: The question, "What is photography?" is being asked, answered and exams are being made through this. Here, not only the correct answer of the question but also the instruction logic is being confirmed.

Into the bargain, can the Photography be learned in the context of Distance Education? Is it possible to pass through the Mystery of Helios (The inventor of the photography Joseph Nicephore Niepce named the process of his invention the Heliography,1827) (!)? Can the information regarding to the evolution of the language competence of the photography as an art become totally explicit? Why not? Already there are programs and applications about this. Moreover we have the ekphrastic hope! (Mitchell, 1995). And also the question "What is Photography? is the result of an ontological desire, remembering Barthes: "*I was overcome by an 'ontological desire', I wanted to learn at all costs what Photography 'in itself' by what essential feature it was to be distinguished from the community of images*" (Barthes, 1992). Even the answers to this question are a mathesis singularis like personally Barthes's (Barthes, 1992), it will sure a contribution for mathesis universalis.

DISTANCE EDUCATION AND USE OF PHOTOGRAPHY

The iconographical adventure of the humankind began with the pictures carved on the cave walls by Homo Sapiens in the Paleolithic era, nearly 35.000 years ago. He/she expressed himself/herself by visualizing the surviving skill.

Again, the Classical Mythology, forms the keystones of our culture with its anthropomorphic notion representations: Mnemosyne for the universal memory records and the archives; Hermes for the communication, Metis for profundity of knowledge, Athena for intelligence and strategy, Apollo for light in its all meanings, Theseus came out the labyrinth safely and victoriously...

The root of the information technologies contains the formulation of the knowledge, building the question-answer dialectics. Abelard achieved this while lecturing theology and philosophy, rendered this metaphysical realm understandable for the students and built an eligible reputation as a teacher (Saettler, 2004).His policy of visualizing the information has an importance of determining even the most common course applications today. I wonder if can't we account Abelard, as the father of Power Point presentations in addition to his other merits?

The frescos/visual expressions carved on the church walls in Medieval and including scenes from the Bible thus mentioned as the Bible of the Poor, is a source of theological information for the illiterates.

Regarding the historical Faust and the Faust Legend, Assoc. Prof. Burhanettin Batıman, through a citation from Witkowski, tells that Faust lectured also in the universities: "Faust, attempted to lecture about Homer in the Erfurt University and even showed Helena arousingly to his students; -it is more likely that he carried out this magic either by virtue of lanterna magica or through suggestion).

The interesting detail in this myth in early 16th Century, is the usage of lanterna magica and the enrichment of the lesson through visual course material.(!) (Batıman, 1942)

Ars Magna Lucis et Umbrae (1671) of Athanasius Kircher, is sometimes adorned with esoteric qualified illustrations like his other numerous works. This is a typical sample for that period of publishing. But the visual quality of Kircher's book and the illustrations within is an inspiring wealth not only for the Optics at the time written but also for the History of Photography, Theory of Photography today.

The Encyclopedia of Diderot and D'Alembert also has an illustrative feature. Cause, visual confirmation of the information is necessary within the scope of Enlightment mentality (Newhall, 1984)

The usage of photography as an indicator is made through the qualifications of being icon and index. The photograph directly represents what is aimed to be told or points it out within the framework of common use.

In distance education publications, photographs effect the flow of information and quality of its transmission, determine its rhythm, develop empathy with source of knowledge, make the knowledge visible and easy perceptible by their transparent structure render the text credible and dependable, facilitate picturing and developing the subject in mind, bring visual richness and sometimes cuteness to the text.

The open education benefits from the representational systems such as the photography but does not allow the paranoia caused by the meaning manipulation potential of the representational systems.

Visuality makes the information known. Of course if it was aimed to be known. Cause the information which cannot be understood and sometimes accounted as this but in fact not existing, becomes a means of metaphysical constrain.

Through the inspiration taken from Deleuze and Guattari (Deleuze and Guattari, 1996), as Chestov already discovered, if we attempt to call History to account absurdly like Dostoyevsky's *The Idiot*, we face nowadays, this scene:

Equality = mediocrity authority
Liberty = Kitsch nihilism
Fraternity = utopic inanity

But if we do what is necessary just as what Cusanus's Idiot, the sensible spoon master did: The Open Education has the meaning of the words which emerged from the novel of Orhan Pamuk bearing the same name but which afterwards became a dictum beyond the name: The Museum of Innocence!-sure virtual and without wall!

THE KAIROS VIRTUE

As we know, the time concept has two notions: 1) Kronos is quantity of time; 2) Kairos is quality of time.

According to Hans Rämö: "In Greek Mythology, Kairos was the youngest son of Zeus (the son of Kronos) and God of the favorable moment… Hesiod, the 8th century BC contemporary poet to Homer, says in his hexametrical rules of practical conduct, The Works and Days (line 694): observe due measure and proportion is best in all things. "In this sentence, which become a proverb, the words" due measure and proportion are two of the English translations of Kairos that carry ideas of wisdom and judgment (phronesis). "This kairic" stem stands as central in many ancient Greek conceptions of a means respect to which extremes are balanced.

The notion of Kairos specifically referring to time, however, became apperent some 400 years later during the Classical Greek Period when authors such as Aristotle, Gorgias, Isocrates and Sophocles thought of Kairos as exact time, critical time, season, or opportunity.

In particular, Aristotle has several references to Kairos, including a general distinction that Cronos is dating time and Kairos is the time that gives value .. What happens at the right time (Kairos-season) is good." (Ramö.1991).

Rämö, within his article, remembers also the significance of Kairos in Archery by Orions, (1954) and he citied some distinctions of Smith about Kairos; "*First timing (the right time); second, a time of tension which calls for a decision; Third, an opportunity to accomplish some purpose.*" (Ramö,1991)

Rämö, explains also meta-communicative meanings of the kairochora term, as a synthesis of kairos concept with chora (abstract space) concept. "Kairochora, is a communication based on human "right moments" to act judiciously in "virtual spaces, e.g. in virtual networks and virtual organizations. ''(Ramö,1991).

The time-geographical line-diagrams developed by Torsten Hägerstrand; The Lingua Moo, hypertext developed by Texas University or virtual relationship system that connects Open University to Skandia AFSA (Assurance and Financial Services)... are some examples based on Kairochora communication (Ramö, 1991)

Photography is a visual record realized in a fraction of time. The speed of shutter builds the logic of photographical time analysis, in each time. The sublime level of this photography time/momentum is Decisive Moment / L'instant Decisive of Henri Cartier Bresson. One of the greatest photographers of History, Henri Cartier – Bresson, was a perfectionist and a passionate reader of Eugen Herrigel's The Zen Archery (1948).In fact, The Decisive Moment is the title of a Cartier-Bresson album published in 1952.It is at the same time, the principal character of his style.

Decisive moment is a fruit of long process: "At once an account of an apprenticeship in the acquisition of a skill, a questioning of the self, the search for inner improvement, an initiation into beauty and the achievement of a harmony with the world, it holds the some spiritual, material and artistic dimensions that had always constituted a whole in his own experience as a photographer." (Montier, 1995)

This notion of Henri Cartier – Bresson, besides being a feature of his style, became a strategy of creativity; the quality moment began representing the quality photograph. Also became a part of the perfectionist photography aesthetics than of the non-perfectionist photography aesthetics. Within this context, discussing the evolution of a "decisive moment" during the development of the photographic language competence, the initial evolution is identified by the Henri Cartier–Bresson's perfectionist approach and today for instance Antoine d'Agata's non-perfectionist comprehension identifies the aforementioned evolution. Despite being on the apart poles, both are each materially and morally a photo-instrument. Photography act reveals a total dedication and absolute identification by their personalities; *Decisive Moment is Kairos !* What matters, is the existence of a design within a subject archetypal or not, within the same or different context.

Kairos is an origin of an analytical time consciousness, then of photography and virtual time activity like mentioned above. On the other hand Kairos represents also an existentialist point of view. I am sure, you will remember suddenly that famous jazz song:

Some of these days

You will miss me honey! (Sartre, 1981)

Just as the Decisive Moment photographs are conducive for the passionate exchange of glances between the operator and the spectator (with Barthes denotation), similarly the good songs offer perfect and plural lives.

In Jean-Paul Sartre's la Nausee, 'some of these days' song realized a perfect encounter between the Black singer, the Jewish composer and the hero of the novel: Antoine Roquentin, who is researching the meaning of his own existence. "*The self-inflicted alienation of Roquentin from his world is illuminated and given meaning by the voluntary / involuntary alienation of Negro artist and the Jew-artist.*" (Zimmermann, 1970)

Some of these days symbolize "*the aesthetic solution*"[1]for Roquentin's souffrence-moche of his own existence." (Arnold, 1965).

Than, Decisive Moment, together its technical, aesthetical and philosophical meanings are formulating perfectly within a Kairochora/Anadolu University Distance Education Program of Photography(Bodur, 2009) ; Throughout the beautiful photos of Cartier-Bresson, I may access the Truth; I'm the victim of d'Agata's melancholy Rimbaudiana.....But the song continues and Sartre has still a question. " Can the human being justify his existence? Even a little? (Sartre, 1981)

THE MNEMOSYNE VIRTUE

Mnemosyne is daughter of Gaia and Uranus. She is the mother of nine Muses by Zeus. Mnemosyne represents Memory, the systematic struggle against Oblivion, power and creativity.

Books, libraries, collections, museums, archives, glossaries, lexicons, dictionaries, encyclopedias protect and build the cultural memory of the mankind through their scientific functions, visual features, illustrative dimensions and objective natures.

François Arago, on July 3 1839, while introducing the Daguerreotype within the French Chamber of Deputies, remarks the extraordinary mnemonic notion of the photography:

To copy the millions of hieroglyphics which cover even the exterior of the great monuments of Thebes, Memphis, Karnak, and others would require decades of time and legions of draughtsmen. By daguerreotype one person would suffice to accomplish this immense work successfully. Equip the Egyptian Institute with two or three of Daguerre's apparatus and before long on several of the large tablets of the celebrated work, which had its inception in the expedition to Egypt, innumerable hieroglyphics as they are in reality will replace those which now are invented or designed by approximation. These designs will excel the works of the most accomplished painters in fidelity of detail and true reproduction of the local atmosphere (Trachtenberg, 1980).

Thus photography, not only contributes to the memory institutions as a visual proof and research instrument, but also builds visual reserves in which itself is also protagonist.

On the other hand, there are differences between the memory counterparts of the mankind and the memory records of the photography. As Siegfried Kracauer explains:

"Memory encompasses neither the entire spatial appearance nor the entire temporal course of an event. Compared to photography memory's records are full of gaps. Memory does not pay much attention to dates; it ships years or stretches temporal distance. The selection may have been made this very rather than another because disposition and purposes required the repression, falsification, and emphasis of certain parts of the object; a virtually endless number of reasons determine the remains to be filtered... Memories are retained because of their significance for that person. Thus they are organized according to a principle that is essentially different from the organizing principle of photography. Photography grasps what is given as a spatial (or temporal) continuum; memory-images retain what is given only in so far as it has significance" (Kracauer, 1933).

As an infinite visual production and consuming mechanism, Photography of the XIXth Century and early XXth Century, was a new activity, a different vision, an eclectic and explicator view. The photographs are magic objects with their meanings and the photographer is new type of his time.

The cultural patent of the Ala Recherche du Temps Perdu/In Search of Lost Time phenomena of the Photography which has an authentic function belongs, as is known, to Marcel Proust.

Through these features, the photography also effected the different and traditional forms of expression. Within this context, literature has a special position. The depictions within the literary works sometimes turn into photographical, partial and plural impressions, the photographs become the crucial/ dramatic elements of a plotline. Dostoyevski's *The Idiot* and Marcel Proust's *The Guermantes Way* are the example novels for this.

But as stated above, the position of Proust in this term is privileged. Cause for him the name of the existence, namely the writing, namely the whole poetica is In Search of Lost Time.

'Proust's love of painting, sculpture and architecture was awakened very early in an obviously favorable family environment. And from the beginning, photography played an important role in the writer's artistic formation. As a child the search suggests, he discovered Giotto's frescos or the Works of the Venetians masters thanks to photographic reproductions. Proust unambiguously hails the advent of an invention-the camera-which permits a new vision of the world. Did he not write: "*The only true voyage the only Fountain of Youth, consist not in venturing to new worlds but in having new eyes, in seeing the world with someone else's eyes?*" With photography, Proust believes, it is such new eyes which open on the world, different from the human gaze, and which, guided by the photographer's mind and personality, preserve their specificity, something irreplaceable by any other art: "*objectivity in the face of reality, authenticity of the world*" (Brassai, 2001)

Commenting the "Grandfather and Granddaughter", one of the photographs of Roman Vishniac which he shot in 1938 while photographing the Jewish ghettos in Eastern Europe, John Szarkovski, quotes from Henri Cartier – Bresson: "*Photographers deal in things which are continually vanishing and which known contrivance on earth can bring back again. Not even photography can bring these things back except in the memory of those who knew, or in the imaginations of those who did not.*" (Szarkovski, 1971)

I already told you ! (!)… Taking photographs is an existentialist action which takes the crimes, responsibilities and requirements of the mankind as a personal problem and undertakes the material and moral obligations of this.

The mnemonic manipulations are the fantasias of the mnemonic mechanisms. This also prevails within the context of meta-communication discussions. It's hard to explain some of the formations on Internet and some databases, to explain why some people projected these. The jokes and definitions such as the disciple of the Mnemosyne or philanthropist are already inadequate. But Jimmy Wales is such a kind of person. A golden heart who cares about us all. Wikipedia perfectly carries out our classical encyclopedic habits and necessities. But as well, for criticizing the shallow information the critics like O My God, again Wikipedia! is also being made. Besides, because of the cultural mentality differences, same clauses in different languages can be in different volumes. But still the primary school students get full marks for the home works that they prepared throughout the information downloaded from the Wikipedia. ''A wiki (from wikiwiki, meaning 'fast' in Hawaian) is a set of linked web pages that enables documents to be autored collectively. The application was invented by Ward Cunningham in 1995 for the collection and development of software design pattern. Wikis are open, incremental, organic, tolerant, and observable. Thus, these principles elaborate how web creation, maintenance and access can operate as well as the features the technology has to provide, so as to enable this form of collaboration. The editing options include, significantly, the opportunity to change, add, delete and link material….. Wikis are susceptible to vandalism and disruptions…most of the wikis rely on the concept of 'soft security': damage is not prevented in the first place, but easy to undo. The Online Encyclopaedia Wikipedia, which is based on these principles, has evolued since it was launched in January 2001, to be not only the most successful wiki Project, but to become the largest encyclopedic companion ever known (Pentzold, 2009).

According to Christian Pentzold again, Wikipedia, as a global memory place

"is not a symbolic place of remembrance but a place where memorable elements are negotiated, a place of the discursive fabrication of memory... the mnemonic community (Rigney,2008) or community of memory (Irwin-Zarecka,1994) of the Wikipedia authors can be viewed as an imagined community spread over an extensive territory"(Pentzold, 2009).

Once upon a time this kind of imagined community was a disutopic fiction subject like the human book community of Ray Bradbury's *Fahrenheit 451* (1951).As we know in this science-fiction novel, mnemonic human instruments form an alive library. Maybe, after digital revolution we could be more optimistic because the virtual space offers us many epistemological possibilities!-sometimes so popular!- like Wikipedia.

IDENTITY CRISIS

Photography has many origins, for examples (Atay, 2004): Mummification tradition of Ancient Egypt; Mythological figures like Apollo, Mnemosyne, Kairos, Helios, Hermes Trismegistus etc. The Cave Allegory and Mimesis Theory of Plato; Eclipse observations of Aristotle; Optical constitutions of Alhazen (965-1039); Perspective principles of Leon Battista Alberti (1404-1472) ; Camera Obscura design of Daniele Barbaro (1513-1570); Camera obscura illusions of Giovanni Battista della Porta (1535-1615);The Lanterna Magica of Athanasius Kircher (1601-1680); Portable Camera Obscura of Johann Zahn; (1631-1707);The Giphantie of Tiphaigne de la Roche (1729-1774) ;The Camera Lucida of William Hyde Wollaston (1766-1828); Alchemic experiences of Christoph Adolph Balduin (1632-1682)to obtain Weltgeist; Physionotrace of Jean-LouisChretien (1754-1811) (Atay-Eskier,2009)

Photography, as a visual record method and as a medium has many different usages and functions: Studio photography, documentary photography, scientific photograph art photography, ethnographical photography, archeological photography, CSI photography, fashion photography, photojournalism, vernacular photograph etc.

And we use photos as document, souvenir, artefact, cultural icon, art work, art object, objet-trouve etc. Photography, idiosyncratically is a science, an art and a mass-media medium.etc. Photography has a multiple character; its capability of production and creation of images means a multiplication process. According to John Tagg:

"Photography as such has no identity. Its status as a technology varies with the power relations which invest is. Its nature as a practice depends on the institutions and agents which define it and set it to work.Its function as a mode of cultural production is tied to definite conditions of existence, and its products are meaningful and legible only within the particular currencies they have.Its history has no unity." (Batchen, 1999)

According to Geoffrey Batchen (1999): "*The meanings of any individual photograph are similarly contingent, being entirely dependent on the context in which that photograph finds itself at any given moment. A photograph can mean one thing in one context and something else entirely in another.*" (Batchen, 1999)

There are also many different ways and methods of learning, instruction and understanding for photography: from classical university programs to avangard distance education programs, from photo-associations courses to philanthropic effort programs of municipalities, from Wikipedia (certainly!) to JStor (for example!)... This kind of multiple identity/no identity is also a modernist strategy to exist, sometime to resist, as Fernando Pessoa said in 1915: "*...I feel myself multiple. I* *am like a chamber (built) by innumerous mirrors that distord in false reflections a unique reality anterior which is not in nobody and is in everybody"* (Pessoa, 1997)

THE POLYHYMNIA VIRTUE

Polyhymnia please it's your turn:

-EPIGRAPH (Atay, 2002)

I am me! Full brother of Apollon, cousin of Helios and Kairos' himself.

I am me! Atropos's lover, Narkissos's comrade and Mnemosyne's alter-ego.

I got fed by optics and chemistry and feed the history and geography.

I'm the idee fixe of philosophers, passion of the moralists, utopia of the aesthetes. I'm the victory of the scientists, pride of the merchants, joy of the collectors and the reason for being of the theorists.

I'm the master and the servant of my people. I'm the radical/liberal consciousness; The eternal witness of grace and misery. I'm the source of nostalgia, indicator of the decadence, the reason and the remedy for paranoia.

I'm the warrior of life, messenger of death. I'm the miracle and the ordinary reality. Irony and elegy is presented by me. The identity is defined by me, the crisis of identity is experienced by me.

I'm the pure joy of the apprentices and the dedication of the masters.

I'm the gaze. The truth comes under me. At any time, at any place on earth and at the accessible far points of the universe, my agents fulfill my verdicts.

Prolocutors honor me by mentioning me. Ideologists, artists, inventors, explorers build pantheons for the past, labyrinths for the future with me.

I am me: the Photography!

Alpha and Omega... Omega and Alpha...

ACKNOWLEDGMENT

I cordially thank Dr. Ugur Demiray who encouraged me to write this chapter.

REFERENCES

Agamben, G. (1991). *Language and death the place of negativity (trans K. E. Pinkus with M. Hardt)*. University of Minnesota.

Atay, S. (2002). *Yazıt, black and white in colors.*

Atay-Eskier, S. (2009). *Aydibi üniteleri: Fotoğrafı düşünüyorum gözlerim kapalı. Barthes, R. (1992). Camera lucida. (trans. R. Akçakaya)*. İstanbul, Turkey: Altıkırkbeş.

Batchen, G. (1999). *Burning with desire the conception of photography*. The MIT.

Batıman, B. (1942). *Goethe Faust birinci kısmın tahlil ve tefsiri*. İstanbul, Turkey: İstanbul Üniversitesi.

Bauman, Z. (2000). *Liquid modernity*. Malden, MA: Blackwell.

Bodur, F. (2009). *Fotoğraf ve hareketli görüntünün tarihi*. Eskişehir: Açıköğretim Fakültesi Yayını 1061.

Brassai. (1991). *Proust in the power of photography* (trans. R. Howard). London, UK: The University of Chicago.

Deleuze, G., & Guattari, F. (1996). *Felsefe Nedir? (trans. Turhan Ilgaz)*. İstanbul, Turkey: Yapı Kredi.

Hans, R. (1991). An Aristotelian human time-space manifold from Kairochora to Kairotopos. *Time & Society*, *8*(2-3), 309–328.

Hoppenbrouwers, S., & Weigand, H. (2000). *Meta-communication in the language action perspective.* V. International Workshop on the Language-Action Perspective on Communication Modelling (LA 2000), Aachen, Germany.

Imbert, C. (2010). La democratie (aussi) pourrit par la tete. *Le Point*, *9*, 3.

Jacques, R. (2009). *The emancipated spectator (Trans. G. Elliott)*. London, UK/New York, NY: Verso.

James, A. (1965). La Nausee revisited. *The French Review. American Association of Teachers of French*, *39*(2), 212.

Karacauer, S. (1933). Photography. (trans. T. Y. Levin). *Critical Inquiry*, *19*(3), 425.

Lucido, P. I., & Borabo, M. L. (1997). *Educational technology*. Quezon City, Philippines: Kahta.

Meyrink, G. (1999). *Kardinal Napellus. (trans. Z. A. Yılmazer)*. Ankara, Turkey: Dost.

Mitchell, W. J. T. (1995). *Picture theory*. Chicago, IL/London, UK: The University of Chicago.

Montier, J. P. (1995). *Henry Cartier-Bresson and the artless art (trans. R. Taylor)*. London, UK: Thames and Hudson.

Newhall, B. (1984). *Storia della Fotografia, (trans. L. Lovisetti Fua)*. Torino, Italy: Einaudi.

Pentzold, C. (2009). Fixing the floating gap: The online encyclopedia Wikipedia as a global memory place. *Memory Studies, 2*, 256. Retrieved from http://mss.sagepub.com/ cgi/ content/ 2/ 2/ 225

Pessoa, F. (1997). *Una sola moltitudine, a cura di Antonio Tabucchi con la collaborazione di Maria Jose de Lancastre*. Milano: Adelphy Edizioni.

Photo. (2005). *Mars, 417*, 24-39

Plato,. (1942). *The republic. Trans.A.D. Lindsay & J.M.* Cambridge: Dent. London.

Rubicon. (2010). *An AMC drama series*. Executıve produced by Henry Bromell.

Saettler, P. (2004). *The evolution of American educational technology*. New York, NY: Information Age.

Sartre, J. P. (1981). *Bulantı*. Türkçesi: Selahattin Hilav. İstanbul, Turkey: Can.

Szarkovski, J. (1973). *Looking at photographs, the Museum of Modern Art*. New York, NY.

Trachtenberg, A. (Ed.). (1981). *Classical essays on photography*. Stony Creek, CT: Leete's Island Books.

Zimmermann, E. N. (1970). Some of these days: Sartre's petite phrase. *Contemporary Literature*, *11*(3), 380. doi:10.2307/1207794

Section 4
Meta-Communicative Assessments and Reflective Communication Skills

Chapter 14
Technology Supported Assessment in Distance Education:
Promises, Pitfalls and Prospects

Pradeep Kumar Misra
M.J.P. Rohilkhand University, India

ABSTRACT

Distance educators at any stage of their career or dealing with any discipline of knowledge are required to engage into number of tasks like present and construct assessment tools, make valid judgments of the student progress in learning, facilitate the provision of feedback and support the production and delivery of mark/grade to assess their students. Assessing students in distance education is a cumbersome task and technology offers number of possibilities and opportunities for educators to make this task more enjoyable, feasible, meaningful, and reliable. In this backdrop, the present chapter focuses on defining assessment in the context of distance education; discusses about promises and on-going initiatives for using technology to assess students; underlines pitfalls of technology supported assessment in distance education; offers useful strategies for distance educators to use technology for assessment; and predicts the future of technology supported assessment in distance education.

INTRODUCTION

The word "assessment" has a variety of meanings within education system. Assessment describes the status of a phenomenon at a particular time. It describes without value judgment a prevailing situation; it attempts no explanation of underlying reasons and makes no recommendations for action. It may deal with prevailing opinion, knowledge, practices, or conditions. As it is ordinarily used in education, assessment describes the progress students have made toward educational goals at a

DOI: 10.4018/978-1-61350-071-2.ch014

particular time (Best and Khan, 2006, p. 118). In sum, we can say that assessment is an important way of providing feedback to students regarding their state of learning. Therefore, assessment needs to be part of any effective course to help us to know that whether the course itself is "working' for student learning, what is going well and what is not. Besides, assessment is central to the educational reform debate for at least two reasons. First, assessment results are relied upon to document the need for change. Second, assessments are seen as critical agents of reform (Linn, 2003).

Assessment plays a central role in the educational process as it helps students, teachers, parents and educational administrators to know and deal better with the learning gaps. Assessment is said to drive student learning as it provides the motivation for learning through the provision of feedback (e.g. awarding of marks and grades). The concept of assessment for learning emphasizes integrating assessment and instruction and requires a dynamic, continuous and performance-based assessment system that emphasizes progress in learning and in becoming increasingly sophisticated learners and knowers (Moallem, 2007). Educators use assessment for a variety of reasons that range from individual student assessment to program evaluation to system-wide educational accountability (Wiggins, 1993). Good assessment provides objective information that can assist in diagnosing problems and identifying curricular areas that need improvement (Anastasi, 1988). Assessments can help an individual find his or her way in the decision-making journey or help a school system travel the road to educational excellence (Janet E, 2000). The prominent assessment types to fulfill these promises in educational settings are Formative Assessment, Summative Assessment, Norm referenced Assessment, Criterion referenced Assessment, and Authentic Assessment.

Feedback given to students to help their learning, for example, questions at the end of lectures is termed as *formative assessment*. Formative assessment can be self-assessment or peer-assessment as well as teacher assessment. The results which are used to grade students at the end of a course are examples of *summative assessment*. An individual's performance in relation to the norms established by a peer group is termed as *norm referenced assessment*. *Criterion referenced assessment* takes place when a student is assessed on his or her ability to meet a required level of skill or competence. Whereas, *Authentic assessment* also called as performance assessment, appropriate assessment, alternative assessment, or direct assessment includes engaging and worthy problems or questions of importance, in which students must use knowledge to fashion performances effectively and creatively (Wiggins, 1993, p. 229). Authentic assessment includes a variety of techniques such as written products, portfolios, checklists, teacher observations, and group projects (Olfos and Zulantay, 2007).

Assessment of students in both face to face(f2f) and distance mode of education has always been a challenge before educational practitioners, as noted by Moallem (2007), "One of the most challenging issues facing educators in all levels of formal schooling particularly higher education is assessment of complex learning outcomes. The emergence of distance education in the form of online or Web-based delivery has taken this challenge further and has added to its complexity and its ambiguity." In comparison to f2f mode, assessment in distance education is expected to diagnose and to improve the learning, to increase the adaptability of the systems and the personalization of the education, to increase the motivation and reduce the evasion rate, and to increase the quality and productivity of the learning (Pimentel and Omar, 2007). The assessment process in distance education often lacks to achieve these objectives, as noted by Ramsden (1992) that owing to an emphasis on written submitted assessment in distance education, students expect meaningful comments on their assignments and projects, and are disappointed when their efforts are not rewarded by constructive feedback or their assignments are marked inconsistently.

The need of the hour is that educationists and policymakers should look for ways to offer authentic, interactive, and continuous assessment in distance education. Technology supported assessment seems a right approach to fulfill these promises. The term technology comprises the entire system of people and organizations, knowledge, processes, and devices that go into creating and operating technological artifacts, as well as the artifacts themselves (NAE, 2002). Technology offers number of possibilities and opportunities for educators to make assessment an enjoyable and meaningful task. The use of technology to support assessment practices has a long history. Yet the focus to date has largely been on developing online objective tests and simulations rather than on using technologies to address fundamental educational issues (Nicol and Milligan, 2006). Emerging technologies has potential to improve the pace and face of assessment in distance education. Before discussing further on these issues, it will be worthy to discuss about possibilities of using technology for assessment purposes.

TECHNOLOGY FOR ASSESSMENT PURPOSES: POSSIBILITIES

As working and learning begin to require technology competence of almost everyone, assessing these skills will become routine. Perhaps more important for assessment, however, is that technology is also becoming a medium for learning and work (Bennett, 2002).The CEO Forum on Education and Technology (2001) suggests, "... as schools...integrate technology into the curriculum, the method of assessment should reflect the tools employed in teaching and learning." However, as learning becomes more collaborative, situated and distributed in its context, conventional methods of assessment of learning outcomes become inadequate. These have to be replaced with tasks and assessment procedures that can be focused on the processes of learning, perception, and problem solving. Methods that can capture some of these processes are learning logs, critical reflections and portfolios (Naidu, 2006, p.30). While, Moallem (2007) suggests that available course management systems (e.g., WebCT/Blackboard), tools and resources seem to provide an easier and more effective system to conduct project-based assessment because of its emphasis on interactive, formative and continuous assessment.

Technology can support task design for assessment in a variety of ways. It can support the presentation of assessment tasks to students and it often enables more flexibility in the timing of assessments. Increased clarity of task goals and greater flexibility in timing both give students more control over their learning and assessment thus enhancing opportunities for self-regulation. Technology can make it easier for teachers to monitor and track learner progress (e.g. through the recording of student activities) and to tailor assessments to individual student needs (e.g. through adaptive testing). Also, using Web 2.0 formats such as wikis, blogs, online discussions, social software and virtual worlds (e.g. Second Life), it is possible to assess and support the development of a much wider range of knowledge, skills and attitudes than in the past (ALT Wiki, 2010).

The use of technology for assessment presents a wide range of benefits for students and teachers. Sheingold (1992) suggests that technology support in assessment allows students and teachers: to make work in many media accessible, portable, examinable, widely distributable; to make performance replayable and reviewable; and to address ownership issues. Tucker (2009, p.4) observes, "A number of promising research projects are beginning to explore the potential of technology to transform testing in more fundamental ways. They suggest that the technology-enabled assessment system is indeed possible—a system that's deeper and broader, able to test knowledge and skills more thoroughly and to test skills and concepts that haven't been measured in the past, and a system that reflects far more fully what we know about how students learn."

Overall, new technologies are not only leading to new ways of enhancing current assessment practices and offering new possibilities (e.g. assessing online discussion) but they are also leading to deeper thinking about how we conceptualize assessment in higher education (Nicol and Milligan, 2006). Online delivery of instruction suggests that there are several tools and resources within this technology that can be used for assessment purposes. The situation demands that educators at any stage of their career, dealing with any discipline of knowledge, and teaching in any mode of education (f2f or DE) must understand technologies supported assessment and apply it to improve the quality of learning. Tshibalo (2005) suggests, now that many institutions of higher learning in developed and developing countries are currently designing e-learning courses, it is equally crucial that they research how assessment should be planned and conducted in this regard.

TECHNOLOGY SUPPORTED ASSESSMENT: TOOLS AND TYPES

The use of technology to assess students revolves around many tools. The use of these tools helps to make assessment processes more efficient and less time consuming for academic staff. Tools to support self-assessment are available as are tools to support the delivery of teacher and peer feedback even though more research is required to determine the effectiveness of different types of teacher feedback (Nicol and Milligan, 2006). Technological tools like Virtual Learning Environments (e.g. Blackboard, Moodle) can make it easier to present assessment tasks to students (e.g. to publish task requirements, the criteria to be used in assessment and the timings for submissions) and to track and record student progress (e.g. automatic time logging of activities and assignment submissions). While, tools for objective testing, within virtual learning environments and within dedicated assessment engines (e.g. Question Mark Perception) allow teachers to orchestrate frequent assessment testing (e.g. online objective testing) which can be used both to offer flexibility in the time and place of assessment and/or to encourage students to spend more 'time on task' out of class (ALT Wiki, 2010). The use of these tools for assessment has been clubbed under different categories.

Computer Assisted Assessment

Computer Assisted Assessment (CAA) is described as "any instance in which some aspect of computer technology is deployed as part of the assessment process" (Atkinson and Davies, 2000). Computer Assisted Assessment is used to manage or support the assessment processes e.g. use of the optical mark reader to score Multiple Choice Questions (MCQ) or database programs used to record student marks. Computer Assisted Assessment is usually formative and criterion referenced as it helps students to discover whether they have learned what the educator intended and provide timely feedback on how best to teach a subject. Increasingly, it can be summative, with limited feedback typically being given at the end of a course and serving to grade and categorize the student's work. There are many benefits linked to CAA, some of which are objectivity and consistency of standards; automatic, immediate, and detailed feedback to all students; and time saving for staff during marking and allocating marks (Billings, 2004; McKenna and Bull, 2000; Musham, 2004).

Computer Managed Assessment

Computer Managed Assessment (CMA) enables students to complete formative or summative assessments and surveys online and in print by using computers. The benefits of CMA for students include immediate feedback for formative tests, easy to use web interface for online tests, assistance in exam preparation, and ability to submit results via print or web. While the benefits for lecturers/examiners are automatic marking of tests, automatic upload of student results, automatic feedback generation, ability to generate print and web tests as well as feedback, considerable saving in time required for administering assessment of large courses, and individual test analysis and other reports (USQ, 2010). Book of Talent (2009) observes, "Computer assisted assessment of higher order skills such as comprehension, application and reasoning is difficult. Recent research has produced an improvement in CAA's ability to test these skills, and allowed for its implementation of the tools on the Web. Areas for development include graphical hotspot questions, which involve selecting an area of the screen by moving a marker to the required position. Text assessment is also being developed."

Online Assessment

Online assessment is defined as the process used to measure certain aspects of information for a set purpose where the assessment is delivered via a computer connected to a network. Most often the assessment is some type of educational test. Online Assessment has existed for a long time in the form of Multiple Choice Questions (MCQ's). The different Forms of Online Assessment are (a) End of semester paper, (b) Weekly tests, (c) Group projects, (d) Case study analysis, (e) Reading responses, (f) Chatroom responses, and (g) Threaded discussions participation. Online assessment is used primarily to measure cognitive abilities, demonstrating what has been learned after a particular educational event has occurred, such as the end of an instructional unit or chapter. When assessing practical abilities or to demonstrate learning that has occurred over a longer period of time an online portfolio (or ePortfolio) is often used. Instant and detailed feedback, as well as flexibility of location and time, is some of the many benefits associated with online assessments. There are many resources available that provide online assessments, some free of charge and others that charge fees or require a membership (Wikipedia, 2010).

Offline Assessment

The term offline assessment (sometimes also called paper pen based assessment) includes number of testing techniques in face to face sitting mode. In simple terms, offline assessment is faculty mediated assessment without using Internet. The most popular forms of offline assessment are (a) constructed-response items, (b) writing/essays, (c) oral discourse, (d) exhibitions, (e), experiments, and (f) portfolios. Educators are now looking for newer initiatives to use computers for offline assessment, as expressed by Carpenter (2009), "Teaching IB where I will be grading so many mock exams/essays with no lead up for formative assessment makes me think I will need to team up with students to create a rubric to guide their preparation for their exams and to then give them feedback via the rubric. I also see the need to provide more detailed insights within the paragraphs of their exams. As the students will be using paper and pens, I could set up a numbered comment key system which the students could refer to as a way for me to efficiently give them feedback while not having them try to read my terrible handwriting."

USING TECHNOLOGY SUPPORTED ASSESSMENT IN DISTANCE EDUCATION: PROMISES AND INITIATVES

Now most of the distance education courses follow the approach of Technology Enhanced Learning (TEL). TFL is generally referred as technological support of any pedagogical approach that utilizes technology for teaching learning process. Two parallel processes take place in a technology enhanced learning environment: students become more active, reflective learners and students and teachers engage in learning through the use of technology and become more familiar with technology by using it. This technology orientation in distance education demands that institutions must come forward to use the potential of technologies for assessment purposes. Puspitasari (2010) suggests that since the 1990s, online text conferencing methods have also become a common feature of distance education courses, at least as an option for those with online access. Online methods also provide students with the useful option of exchanging assignments for critical comments and peer-assessment

With the growth of online education, there is naturally growing interest in online assessment tools. A quick search on the Internet will reveal a great deal of information. Moreover, most prominent learning management systems, such as Blackboard and WebCT come with built-in assessment tools which allow the development of questions and surveys with objective type as well as open-ended responses. These are useful in online education as they enable frequent testing and provision of feedback. However, they remain somewhat unsuited for assessing more complex learning activities such as group work and project work (Naidu, 2006, pp. 33-34). The use of technologies for assessment in distance education has also been seen in a broader perspective, as observed by American Psychological Association (2002), the issues of quality assessment in distance education are best addressed within the broader context of technology advances that can potentially enhance and change professional education regardless of context

Use of technology for assessment purposes in distance education offer number of possibilities, as observed by Tucker (2009, p.1), "Using multiple forms of media that allow for both visual and graphical representations, we can present complex, multi-step problems for students to solve, and we can collect detailed information about an individual student's approach to problem solving. This information may allow educators to better comprehend how students arrive at their answers and learn what those pathways reveal about students' grasp of underlying concepts, as well as to discover how they can alter their instruction to help move students forward." Similarly, Hickey, Kindfield, Horwitz and Christie (2003) observes that design-based methods seem ideal for refining the alignment of innovative curriculum, classroom assessments, and external assessments and for maximizing the impact of formative feedback at the various levels.

The use of online methods in distance education has a major impact on the quality of interaction between teachers and learners, and on the development of online assessment methods (e-assessment), both formative and summative. The main advantages include- ease of course delivery; tighter control of scheduling (assignment deadlines, etc.); timely marking and feedback; more in-depth individual feedback; tracking of participation in discussions; and increased teacher-student and student-student interaction (Puspitasari, 2010). The use of technologies for assessment in distance education also offers number of opportunities for self-regulated feedback, as suggested by Nicol and Milligan (2006), e-tools are effective when they are allied to assessment approaches that enhance the students' ability to generate internal feedback against standards and to self regulate their learning. Current technologies can support these processes

Keeping these promises in view, educators world over are feeling enthusiastic and motivated regarding technology usage for assessment purposes in distance education. There enthusiasm is based on several factors, as noted by Carpenter (2009), "As for my current process of giving summative assessment, I find that with so much going into providing my students guidance as they create their projects that I am able to check off the criteria on provided rubric score sheets, add up the points and type a few comments. I then email students the rubrics making for a pretty timely method of grading their project and presentation work. Technology especially when using collaborative tools really can support and enhance student learning while providing an efficient way to provide assessment." This enthusiasm and support from teachers and students, motivates distance education institutions and technology experts to carryout innovative efforts to assess students in technology enhanced learning environments. Some of these experiments/efforts, based on technology usage for assessment purposes in distance/on-line education are discussed below:

- University of Terbuka uses technologies for formative and summative assessment of students. As formative assessment, students are provided online-self test with immediate feedback before taking the final examination so that they can make decisions about how to proceed in their study of the course materials. In summative assessment, technologies are used for tutorial assignments, reports, practical work and final examination scores (Puspitasari, 2010).
- The Virtual University of Pakistan (VPU) uses e-assessment methods for all of its students, and campus labs to conduct the electronic examinations using a customized e-assessment system. VUP tutors conduct both formative and summative assessment via a robust e-assessment system (Sangi, 2010).
- USQ is using CMA for assessments of their students. Under this system, grades are calculated automatically and uploaded into Gradebook. The system uses single source XML to generate all deliverables, including print, online and interactive CDs of the tests, as well as student feedback which is automatically sent to the students when results are released. Over 100 courses use the CMA system for exams and assignments with over 25,000 submissions per semester (USQ, 2010).
- CASTLE toolkit, part of the Book of Talent, which has been developed so that Tutors and Course managers can create online interactive assessment tools quickly and easily without any prior knowledge of HTML, CGI, or scripting languages. Its aim is to provide a High Level Authoring Shell for online Interactive Tutorials and Assessment, by developing a comprehensive courseware authoring tool, which will enable tutors to produce and maintain online Web pages (Book of Talent, 2009).
- One of the largest efforts to pilot new forms of technology-based assessment is the Problem Solving in Technology-Rich Environments (TRE) project. TRE tested scientific inquiry skills such as the ability to find information about a given topic, judge what information is relevant, plan and conduct experiments, monitor one's efforts, organize and interpret results, and communicate a coherent interpretation (Tucker, 2009).
- The River City project, led by Harvard education professor Chris Dede, is a multi-user, virtual environment where middle-school students explore a mysterious illness in a turn-of-the-century town. Students learn by becoming scientists in River City's virtual world. With the project focused on inquiry practices, students make observations, "chat" with townspeople, develop hypotheses, and conduct experiments to determine the cause of the epidemic (Dede, 2007).
- State University of New York (SUNY) College at Oneonta uses a combination of Microsoft Excel and Word, along with some programming and database management to automatically create quantitative

problems in Word and answers in Excel by using random numbers with a click of a button. Students expressed satisfaction with the new system, and instructors found that they were allowed more time for teaching preparation and research (Ozkul, 2009)

- MarkIt', a PC-based application provides feedback on assessment items and incorporates features that provide students with information on the performance of their peers, plus the capacity for markers to enter detailed and consistent feedback at all stages of the marking process. Key features of the system permit generation of e-mail feedback, use of key feedback comments across different units, and retention of feedback on each student's assessment (Dingsdag, Armstrong and Doug, 2000).

These experiments showcase that technology supported practices are gaining momentum to improve the process and image of assessment in distance education. The distance educators are required to mark a large number of assignments submitted by students and these practices unveil number of possibilities and opportunities for them to make assessment an enjoyable, feasible, meaningful, and reliable task. Commenting on these aspects, (Bennett, 2002, p.15) writes, "The question is no longer whether assessment must incorporate technology. It is how to do it responsibly, not only to preserve the validity, fairness, utility, and credibility of the measurement enterprise but, even more so, to enhance it."

PRACTICING TECHNOLOGY SUPPORTED ASSESSMENT IN DISTANCE EDUCATION: MAIN PITFALLS

Clearly technology, used properly and creatively, can advance opportunities for individuals and guide them through a journey where they can flourish (Janet E, 2000). But this journey is not easy. There are lot of challenges in the path of technology usage for assessment purposes in distance education. Oraifige (2009) who investigated the planning, implementation and evaluation of using technology supported learning for formative assessment of students' observed that online systems for students' teaching, learning and evaluation can be reliably implemented but a number of questions, problems and anomalies need to be resolved before the potential benefits that were originally envisaged can be fully realized. The main challenges related to technology usage for assessment purposes are as follows:

Financial Issues

Although physical access to computers at school differs little by income and racial group, home-access disparities are still substantial (U.S. Department of Commerce, 2002). The early entrants into computerized testing bore the cost of creating a computer-based test-center infrastructure, electronic tools for writing items presentation software, and the large item pools needed to support continuous high-stakes testing(Bennett, 2002, p.12).A key issue for academic staff and their institutions is time and resources. Some software requires a large financial investment (simulation software, databanks of objective tests) and individual institutions will not have the resources to develop these (ALT Wiki, 2010). Moreover, concerns that technology-enabled assessment will disadvantage primarily low-income students that may have limited access to computers and other forms of technology must also be overcome (Tucker, 2009, p.11).

Technical Issues

There are number of technical glitches regarding technology usage for assessment. The first major concern is of comparability. Reflecting on this issue, Bennett, (2002, p.13) noted that, "Regardless of whether the test is delivered solely on computer, there is a second comparability concern. This concern is for "platform" comparability. From one school to the next (and even within the same school), monitor size, screen resolution, keyboard layout, connection speed, and other technical characteristics may vary, causing items to appear differently or to take more time to display." The second concern is about uncertainty of functioning of tools for required purposes. We can not assume that during assessment process technology will work in the same way as we programmed and predicted. A number of external and internal factors affect the functioning of tools and that makes it difficult to predict the success of assessment process. Mangan (2001) observes, "As we all know, and as the large, high-stakes testing programs have found, computers do not always work as intended." Similarly, Sangi (2010) is of the view that losses of service in automated systems through power, equipment, software or network failure may cause loss of time and mental composure for the students, as well as actual loss of data.

Security Issues

The other major concern is of security. There is possibility to come across hackers and plagiarist during on-line assessment. Bennett (2002, p.14) warns us on this regard, "High-stakes electronic testing entails security problems that are not very different from those of paper programs; in particular, items can be stolen or examinee data tampered with regardless of delivery mode." Sangi (2010) also observes that there is a danger that expert computer users could gain access to, manipulate, copy, and misuse the answer scripts. Citing the example of Virtual University of Pakistan, he states, "VUP tutors conduct both formative and summative assessments via a robust e-assessment system, which nonetheless faces the usual challenges of online security and cheating on an ongoing basis" (Sangi, 2010, p.74). In context of these observations, it can be said that success and sanity of technology supported testing will mainly depend upon the efforts to keep hackers and cheaters away from assessment process.

Training Issues

Success of technology for assessment mainly depends on teachers. Teachers need to understand how the technologies work, what they offer, and how to use them for assessment. Teachers need to apply technologies wisely for assessment, and to reflect and search for the deeper issues that the technologies raise, and to bring up and discuss these issues with their peers and students. Here a question arises that whether our teachers are prepared to do these tasks. Tucker (2009, p.10) writes, "Technology has enabled mass customization in a number of areas, but the challenge of creating high-quality assessments and simultaneously making them adaptable by teachers for easy classroom use is considerable." Considering that teachers are vital to support almost any stage of the assessment cycle (task design -assessment/interpretation and feedback/grading), it will be important to devise ways and offer special programmes to train teachers to make technology based educational testing a success in distance education.

MAKING TECHNOLOGY COUNTED FOR ASSESSMENT IN DISTANCE EDUCATION: USEFUL STRATEGIES

The application of technology for assessment purposes mainly depend on educators. Along with tools and techniques, the knowledge, skills and enthusiasm of educators are key ingredients to make technology supported assessment a success. The researchers have already given a number of suggestions to improve the assessment process. These suggestions are equally applicable and important in technologies supported assessment settings, e.g. the suggestions given by Olfos and

Zulantay (2007) for improving the design of the authentic assessment holds relevance for effective assessment by using technologies in distance education. The suggestions are: to reduce the number of specific objectives, to harmonize the individual component with the group component, if applicable, to include self-regulation procedures, to apply differentiated evaluation in accordance with the roles in the collaborative work and to the potentialities of the peer evaluators and/or experts, in order to favor a context of effectiveness and ecological validation. Besides, the following strategies may be useful for educators to design, develop and implement technologies supported assessment processes in distance education.

Learn About Technological Tools and Techniques

In the past five to ten years, we have seen the appearance of scores of new technologies that have strong potential uses in education. They include email, search, texting and instant messaging, blogs, wikis, podcasting, polling devices, peer-to peer (P2P), complex computer and video games, networking, augmented reality, social and community building tools, digital cameras/videocams, phone-based cameras/videocams, GPS speed enhancers, interactive whiteboards, DVDs, wireless technologies, mobile learning, wireless technologies, skype, moodle and instant Messaging (Prensky, 2005). Learning about these tools and techniques is essential component of technology supported assessment. Therefore, distance educators are supposed to keep them acquainted with these emerging technologies and be skilled to use these technologies for assessment purposes. Talking about the preparation process for technologies supported assessment, Ozkul (2009) suggests that the instructors not only have a good command of domain specific knowledge, but also proficiency with Excel and Word and some programming skills.

Match Modes of Learning and Assessment Tools

A major purpose of assessment in education is the improvement of learning. When focusing on the improvement of learning, it is essential to bear in mind the congruency between the learning outcomes of a course and the measures of learning achievement (Naidu, 2006, p.29). Any use of technology for assessment is required to be underpinned by clear objectives. Practitioners must ask themselves whether the technology being applied is intended to enhance student learning through feedback or to support marking and grading. The educators are also required to take care that assessment design and use of technology are not in opposition (ALT Wiki, 2010). The reason behind this precaution is that a mismatch between the modes of learning and assessment could cause achievement to be inaccurately estimated (Russell and Haney, 2000).

Make Multiple and Continuous Assessments

In assessing online learning, it is important to create a "mix" of assignments that cover the multiple dimensions of learning that online courses can employ. Multiple assessments will allow one to measure incremental progress towards the final learning goal, so one can measure what exactly a student scored well on and where they have fallen short (Poe and Stassen, 2006). Keeping this advice in sight, the practitioners must try to evolve a mechanism for technology supported multiple assessments of students. Besides, the other good practice will be to make formative assessment based continuous assessment of students by using technologies. Continuous assessment can improve the learning in distance learning system by providing adaptive and personalization of the education, increasing the motivation and reducing the evasion rate. Besides, it can help to minimize the problems of credibility lack on who effectively took the assessment, allowing monitoring the evolution of the learning instead of having only one measure at the end of the course (Pimentel and Omar, 2007).

Adopt Team Approach

Use of technologies for assessment of students is mainly based on three facts-selection and use of appropriate tools, immediate feedback and continuous dialogue. The team approach is instrumental to make these happen in real situations. Ozkul (2009) suggests that instructors might consider a team approach to use the new system by recruiting fellow instructors or even graduate students with advanced computer skills. This argument is based on the fact that team approach will ensure that educationists and technology expert will think and act together to choose and use the right kind of technologies for assessment purposes and ensure new kinds of dialogue and feedback possible. The team approach will also help educators to debate about new possibilities, to innovate new practices, and to apply new approaches for technologies supported assessment.

TECHNOLOGY SUPPORTED ASSESSMENT IN DISTANCE EDUCATION: FUTURE PROSPECTS

Educators are using technology for instructional purposes including assessment and it is clear that the testing process can be enhanced through the use of technology (Sampson, 2000). Looking further in the future there are many possibilities. Technology will provide enabling tools for educators and counselors in locating information on assessment, organizing and maintaining test information, building relationships between and among test results and counseling and guidance interventions, using alternative assessment techniques, assessing difficult areas and higher order skills, introducing efficiencies into the assessment situation, and reaching audiences that are not normally accessible without the availability of certain technologies (Janet E, 2000).

According to Love (2004, p.2), "ICT has two immediate benefits for evaluators: enhancing the use of familiar methods (surveys, interviews) to achieve better, less expensive evaluations, and accessing the wellspring of innovation (wireless handheld devices, cellphone camcorders, etc.) to fashion new tools and create new evaluative processes (such as real-time analysis and collaborative weblogs, or blogs)." Discussing about future benefits of technology for assessment, Ozkul (2009) writes, "With the new system, instructors do not have to meet nearly as often with students about exam problems, and questions with answer keys are prepared in minutes just a few days before the quiz. Not only does this system provide relief for instructors from a once exhausting task, but instructors reported that the time and mental effort saved is now used to focus on the enhancement of teaching and research."

Future developments in technology-supported assessment are likely to occur at a number of levels. Firstly, big steps forward might be realized by just making it easier to use existing technological tools so as to make them better suited for assessment purposes. Tools such as wikis and blogs are not seamlessly integrated into virtual learning environments or within other university systems. At the next level up, more work might be directed to the development of intelligent tools and simulations that model learning processes and that could provide intelligent feedback to students on their developing understanding. Some researchers are looking at ways of supporting formative assessment using mobile devices. Web 2.0 tools to support the student generation of content and social networking will be a focus for future development as well new methods of assessing student contributions and collaboration (ALT Wiki, 2010).

These observations clearly indicate that use of technology for assessment purposes will certainly increase in future. Keeping in view that technology offers number of opportunities for assessment, educators will be required to keep them ready to understand, learn and use technologies for assessment purposes on continuing basis. In all areas of assessment, progress will depend more on how we conceptualize learning and assessment processes rather than technology we use. Tucker (2009, p.2) warns us, "… technology alone cannot transform assessment. New approaches to assessment would have to be aligned with standards, curricula, professional development, and instruction to be successful. Still, the convergence of powerful new computer technologies and important new developments in cognitive science hold out the prospect of a new generation of student testing that could contribute to significant improvements in teaching and learning in the nation's classrooms."

CONCLUSION

Traditional forms of assessment used in face-to-face and distance learning education are insufficient to ascertain the learning progress of student and therefore do not provide enough information to detect the student learning gaps and to improve the learning (Pimentel and Omar, 2007). The inherent flexibility of electronic tools should encourage us not to fixate on the hardware and software but to direct our attention to improving the evaluation process: making it more inclusive and transparent, building truly collaborative evaluation efforts, removing the drudgery from data collection and focusing more on data analysis and use, and vastly increasing the reach and impact of evaluative information for the betterment of all (Love, 2004, p.3). The bottom line is that, as students come to do the majority of their learning with technology, asking them to express that learning in a medium different from the one in which they routinely work will become increasingly untenable, to the point that much of the paper testing we do today will be an anachronism (Bennett, 2001). The situation demands that distance education institutions must deploy and use technology to practice more effective, efficient and transparent assessment systems. Emergence of these technology supported assessment systems will ultimately help distance education providers to attain the goal of quality education and effective learning.

REFERENCES

American Psychological Association. (2002). *Principles of good practice in distance education and their application to professional education and training in psychology*. Report of the Task Force on Professional Distance Education and Training in Professional Psychology. Retrieved December 14, 2010, from http://www.apa.org/ed/ resources/ finalreport.doc

Anastasi, A. (1988). *Psychological testing* (6th ed.). USA: Macmillan Publishing.

Atkinson, T., & Davies, G. (2000). *ICT4LT module computer aided assessment (CAA) and language learning*. Retrieved July 13, 2010, from http://www.ict4lt.org/ en/ en_mod4-1.htm

Bennett, R. E. (2001). How the Internet will help large-scale assessment reinvent itself. *Education Policy Analysis Archives, 9*(5). Retrieved April 27, 2009, from http://www.epaa.asu.edu/ epaa/v9n5.html

Bennett, R. E. (2002). Inexorable and inevitable: The continuing story of technology and assessment. *Journal of Technology, Learning, and Assessment, 1* (1). Retrieved April 27, 2009, from http://www.jtla.org

Best, J. W., & Khan, J. V. (2006). *Research in Education* (5th ed.). Eaglewood Cliffs, NJ: Prentice-Hall.

Billings, K. (2004). Online assessment: Perspectives of developers. *School Executive*, January/ February. Retrieved June 18, 2010, from http:// www.schoolexec.com

Book of Talent. (2009). *What is computer assisted assessment*? Retrieved July 8, 2010, from http:// www2.le.ac.uk/ uol/ institution/lts/

Carpenter, D. (2009). *Using technology for assessment & learning*. Retrieved July 8, 2010, from http://www.utechtips.com/ 2009/ 04/ 18/ using-technology-for-assessment-learning/

CEO Forum on Education and Technology. (2001). *School technology and readiness—Key building blocks for student achievement in the 21st century: Assessment, alignment, accountability, access, analysis*. Retrieved June 26, 2009, from http:// www.ceoforum.org/ downloads/ report4.pdf

Dede, C. (2007). *Transforming education for the 21st century: New pedagogies that help all students attain sophisticated learning outcomes*. Commissioned by the NCSU Friday Institute. Retrieved June 26, 2009, from http://www.gse.harvard.edu/ ~dedech/ Dede_21stC-skills_semi-final.pdf

Dingsdag, D., Armstrong, B., & Doug, N. (2000.) Electronic assessment software for distance education students. *ASCILITE 2000 Conference Proceedings*. Retrieved December 14, 2010, from http://www.ascilite.org.au/ conferences/ coffs00/ papers/ don_dingsdag.pdf

Hickey, D. T., Kindfield, A. C. H., Horwitz, P., & Christie, M. A. T. (2003). Integrating curriculum, instruction, assessment, and evaluation in a technology-supported genetics learning environment. *American Educational Research Journal*, *40*(2), 495–538. doi:10.3102/00028312040002495

Janet, E. W. (2000). *Technology-delivered assessment: Guidelines for educators traveling the technology highway*. ERIC Clearinghouse on Counseling and Student Services Greensboro NC, ERIC/CASS Digest (ED446327). Retrieved July 8, 2010, from http://www.ericdigests.org/

Linn, R. L. (1993). *Educational assessment: Expanded expectations and challenges, CSE technical report 351*. Los Angeles, CA: CRESST/ University of Colorado at Boulder.

Love, A. (2004). Taking the next step: Harnessing the power of technology for evaluation. *The Evaluation Exchange, 10*(3). Retrieved July 5, 2010, from http://www.hfrp.org/ evaluation/ the-evaluation-exchange/ issue-archive/ harnessing-technology-for-evaluation

Mangan, K. S. (2001). Error message leads many who took GMAT to question their scores. *The Chronicle of Higher Education*. Retrieved July 14, 2010, from http://www.uh.edu/ admin/ media/ topstories/ che09250ıgmat.htm

McKenna, C., & Bull, J. (2000). Quality assurance of computer-assisted assessment: Practical and strategic issues. [from http:// proquest.umi.com]. *Quality Assurance in Education*, *8*(1), 24–31. Retrieved May 5, 2010. doi:10.1108/09684880010312659

Moallem, M. (2007). *Assessment of complex learning tasks: a design model.* Paper presented in IADIS International Conference on Cognition and Exploratory Learning in Digital Age (CELDA 2007). Retrieved December 14, 2010, from http://www.iadis.net/ dl/ final_uploads/ 200714C051.pdf

Musham, G. (2004). *Using computer technology to support student assessment. OET Assignment*. January-April. University of London.

NAE. (2002). *Technically speaking: Why all Americans need to know more about technology.* National Academy of Engineering, USA. Retrieved December 25, 2009, from http://www.nap.edu/ openbook.php?record_ id=10250&page=3

Naidu, S. (2006). *E-learning: A guidebook of principles, procedures and practices* (2nd rev. ed.). New Delhi: Commonwealth Educational Media Center for Asia. Retrieved June 20, 2009, from http://www.cemca.org

Nicol, D. J., & Milligan, C. (2006). Rethinking technology-supported assessment in terms of the seven principles of good feedback practice. In Bryan, C., & Clegg, K. (Eds.), *Innovative assessment in higher education*. London: Taylor and Francis.

Olfos, R., & Zulantay, H. (2007). Reliability and validity of authentic assessment in a Web based course. *Journal of Educational Technology & Society*, *10*(4), 156–173.

Oraifige, A. (2009). Technology supported learning (TSL) for formative assessment. *Engineering Education: Journal of the Higher Education Academy Engineering Subject Centre, 4*(1). Retrieved July 13, 2010, from http://www.engsc.ac.uk/ journal/ index.php/ ee/ article/ view/ 119/160

Ozkul, A. (2009). Using Information Technology to enhance assessment of learning: Automating preparation of course exam materials and student feedback. *Information Technology, Learning, and Performance Journal, 25*(1), 15-23. Retrieved July 13, 2010, from http://www.osra.org/ itlpj/ ozkulspring2009.pdf

Pimentel, E. P., & Omar, N. (2007). *Formative assessment in distance learning education with cognitive and metacognitive measurements*. Paper presented in IADIS International Conference e-Learning 2007. Retrieved December 14, 2010, from http://www.iadis.net/ dl/ final_uploads/ 200711L030.pdf

Poe, M., & Stassen, M. L. A. (Eds.). (2006). *Teaching and learning online communication, community, and assessment: A handbook for UMass faculty*. Office of Academic Planning and Assessment, University of Massachusetts Amherst, USA. Retrieved July 11, 2010, from http //www.umass.edu/ oapa/ oapa/ publications/ online_handbooks/ Teaching_and_Learning_ Online_Handbook.pdf

Prensky, M. (2005). *The future is now: Strategies for reaching today's students*. A presentation made at the WCET Conference, San Francisco, USA, November 2005.

Puspitasari, K. A. (2010). Student assessment. In Belawati, T., & Baggaley, J. (Eds.), *Policy and practice in Asian distance education* (pp. 60–67). New Delhi: Sage.

Ramsden, P. (1992). *Learning to teach in higher education*. New York, UK: Routledge. doi:10.4324/9780203413937

Russell, M., & Haney, W. (2000). Bridging the gap between testing and technology in schools. *Education Policy Analysis Archives, 8*(19). Retrieved June 26, 2009, from http://epaa.asu.edu/ epaa/ v8n19.html

Sampson, J. P. (2000). Using the Internet to enhance testing in counseling. *Journal of Counseling and Development*, *78*(3), 348–356.

Sangi, N. (2010). E-assessment. In Belawati, T., & Baggaley, J. (Eds.), *Policy and practice in Asian distance education* (pp. 68–76). New Delhi: Sage.

Sheingold, K. (1992). *Technology and assessment*. Paper presented at Technology & School Reform Conference, Dallas, TX, June 1992.

Tshibalo, A. E. (2005). *Computer aided assessment and its potential impact on teaching and learning in higher education.* Paper presented in making a Difference: 2005 Evaluations and Assessment Conference, Sydney, 30 November-1 December 2005.

Tucker, B. (2009). Beyond the bubble: Technology and the future of student assessment. *Education Sector Reports*. Retrieved April 7, 2009, from http://www.educationsector.org

U.S. Department of Commerce. (2002). *A nation online: How Americans are expanding their use of the Internet*. Washington, DC. Retrieved July 12, 2010, from http://www.ntia.doc.gov/ ntiahome/ dn/ nationonline_020502.htm

USQ. (2009). *Computer managed assessment (CMA)*. Retrieved July 13, 2010, from http://www.usq.edu.au/dec/tech

Wiggins, G. P. (1993). *Assessing student performance*. San Francisco, CA: Jossey-Bass Publishers.

Wiki, A. L. T. (2010). *Technology-supported assessment*. Retrieved December 14, 2010, from http://www.wiki.alt.ac.uk/ index.php/ Technology supported_assessment

Wikipedia. (2010). *Online assessment*. Retrieved July 13, 2010, from http://en.wikipedia.org/ wiki/ Online_assessment

ADDITIONAL READING

Adelman, C. (2000*). A parallel postsecondary universe: The certification system in information technology*. Retrieved June 26, 2009, from http:// www.ed.gov/ pubs/ ParallelUniverse.

Astin, A. (1993). *Assessment for Excellence: The Philosophy and Practice of Assessment and Evaluation in Higher education. Phoenix, Ariz.* W.: Oryx Press.

Bennett, R. (1998). *Reinventing Assessment: Speculations on the Future of Large-Scale Educational Testing*. Princeton, NJ: Educational Testing Service.

Bostock, S. J. (2004). Motivation and electronic assessment. In Alexander, S., & Irons, A. (Eds.), *Effective Learning and Teaching in Computing*. London: Routledge Falmer. doi:10.4324/9780203416037_chapter_9

Brill, J. M., & Galloway, C. (2007). Perils and promises: University instructors' integration of technology in classroom-based practices. *British Journal of Educational Technology*, *38*(1), 95–105. doi:10.1111/j.1467-8535.2006.00601.x

Bull, J. (1994). Computer based assessment: some issues for consideration. *Active Learning*, *1*(December), 18–21.

Bull, J., & McKenna, C. (2004). *Blueprint for computer-assisted assessment*. London: Routledge Falmer. doi:10.4324/9780203464687

Cuban, L. (2001). *Oversold and underused: Computers in classrooms*. Cambridge, MA: Harvard University Press.

Falchikov, N. (2005). *Improving assessment through student involvement*. Oxon: Routledge Falmer.

Fielding, A., & Bingham, E. (2003). Tools for Computer Aided Assessment. *Learning and Teaching in Action, 2* (1).

Gaytan, J. (2005). Effective assessment techniques for online instruction. *Information Technology, Learning and Performance Journal*, *23*(1), 25–33.

Grebenik, P., & Rust, C. (2002). IT to the rescue. In Schwartz, P., & Webb, G. (Eds.), *Assessment: case studies, experience and practice in Higher Education*. London: Kogan Page.

MacDonald, J. (2003). Assessing online collaborative learning: process and product. *Computers & Education*, *40*, 377–391. doi:10.1016/S0360-1315(02)00168-9

Rabinowitz, S., & Brandt, T. (2001). *Computer-based Assessment: Can it Deliver on its Promise?* San Francisco, CA: WestEd.

Russell, M., & Plati, T. (2001). *Effects of computer versus paper administration of a state-mandated writing assessment.* Retrieved June 26, 2009, from http://www.tcrecord.org/ Content.asp?ContentID=ı0709

Tennent, B., Becker, K., & Kehoe, J. (2005). *Technology-enabled delivery and assessment methods: Are we addressing student expectations and learning preferences*? ascilite 2005 Conference Proceedings, 649-659.

The Evaluation Exchange (2004). Special Issue on Harnessing Technology for Evaluation, *10*(3).

KEY TERMS AND DEFINITIONS

Assessment: Assessment is generally referred as testing/evaluating student performance and providing feedback to students for grading purposes. The process of assessment involves (i) devising learning tasks to sample the learning expected from participation in a course or programme of study (i.e. knowledge, skills and attitudes) (ii) assessing performance on these tasks and interpreting the results, and (iii) using the information acquired to enhance further learning (e.g. feedback) and/or to produce a grade.

Computer Assisted Assessment: Computer Assisted Assessment (CAA) is described as "any instance in which some aspect of computer technology is deployed as part of the assessment process" (Atkinson and Davies, 2000). Computer Assisted Assessment is used to manage or support the assessment processes e.g. use of the optical mark reader to score Multiple Choice Questions or database programs used to record student marks.

Computer Managed Assessment: Computer Managed Assessment (CMA) enables students to complete formative or summative assessments and surveys online and in print by using computers.

Distance Education: Distance education often referred as Distance Learning is simply defined as a field of education that aim to deliver education to students who are separated by time and distance or both, and uses educational media and technologies to enable the student to pursue their education without attending classes on a college or university campus.

Online Assessment: Online assessment is defined as the process used to measure certain aspects of information for a set purpose where the assessment is delivered via a computer connected to a network. Most often the assessment is some type of educational test.

Offline Assessment: Offline assessment (sometimes called paper pen based assessment) is faculty mediated assessment without using Internet.

Technology Supported Assessment: Technology supported assessment is generally referred as using multiple forms of technology to present complex, multi-step problems for students to solve, so that one can collect detailed information about an individual student's approach to problem solving.

Chapter 15
Meta Communication Concept and the Role of Mass Media in Knowledge Building Process for Distance Education

Ugur Demiray
Anadolu University, Turkey

Nurdan Oncel Taskiran
Kocaeli University, Turkey

Recep Yilmaz
Beykent University, Turkey

ABSTRACT

This chapter examines and focuses on some issues and questions relating to how the use of meta communication concept should be functional and how it could influence knowledge building process. In addition to this, the role of mass communication and the mass communication tools which can be regarded as vital for distance learning, primarily the Internet, television, printed materials, and the categories by which media tools interact are also investigated. The ways mass media interacts with imply the interaction taking place between communicational tools and human mind are quite similar; that's why mental building process of knowledge is dealt with likewise. Mind-tool interaction can be categorized into four sections: interaction through reading, interaction through listening, interaction through seeing-listening, and mutual interaction.

DOI: 10.4018/978-1-61350-071-2.ch015

INTRODUCTION

Verbal communication is supported by a raft of non-verbal signs and cues that reinforce what we are saying or clear up any ambiguities. For example, we may cross our arms when we feel threatened by what somebody else is saying, or we nod our heads when we agree with what they are saying.

"Meta Communication" is the process between message designers when they are talking about the learning process, as distinguished from their articulation of the "substantive" learning, itself. The hope is to increase the focus on the substantive knowledge and understanding being developed, by providing a separate channel for the support communication, and to do it in an easy, focused, and context aware manner. This may be particularly useful when the opportunity for face-to-face meta-communication is missing, as in much distance learning. (McLean, 2005)

To understand knowledge building it is essential to distinguish learning--"the process through which the cultural capital of a society is made available to successive generations" from knowledge building--the deliberate effort to increase the cultural capital. This, in turn, requires distinguishing knowledge building from a broad range of activities that share its constructivist underpinnings, but not its focus on the creation of new knowledge. These include collaborative learning, guided discovery, project-based learning, communities of learners, communities of practice, and anchored instruction.

Dynamics of knowledge building could be summarized as working on the creation and improvement of ideas. The dynamic is social, resulting in the creation of public knowledge. In contrast to knowledge situated within the individual mind (the traditional concern of education) and knowledge situated in the practice of groups (the concern of situated cognition and communities of practice), public knowledge has an out-in-the-world character. What makes knowledge building a realistic approach to education is the discovery that children as early as grade one can engage in it. Thus, there is a clear developmental link running from childhood education on into advanced education and adult knowledge work, in which the same process is carried out at increasingly high levels (http://www.ikit.org/kb.html).

Researchers from multiple disciplines (such as cultural studies, intercultural studies, linguistics, sociology, education, human-computer interaction, distance learning, learning technologies, philosophy and others) have initiated studies to examine virtual intercultural communication. The interdisciplinary of the field, however, offers distinct challenges: in addition to embracing different definitions of 'culture', investigators lack a common literature or vocabulary. Communicative encounters between groups and individuals from different cultures are variously described as cross-cultural, intercultural, multicultural or even transcultural. Researchers use terms such as the Internet, the World Wide Web, cyberspace, and virtual (learning) environments (VLE) to denote overlapping though slightly different perspectives on the world of networked digital communications. Others focus on CMC (computer-mediated communication), ICTs (Information and Communication Technologies), HCI (human computer interaction), CHI (computer-human interaction) or CSCW (computer-supported cooperative work) in explorations of technologies at the communicative interface.

NATURE OF KNOWLEDGE

The concept of knowledge has been comprehensively defined by some disciplines such as philosophy, sociology and psychology up to the present time. Philosophers agree in distinguishing between knowledge in the first of these senses, and belief. But they differ in their accounts of how they are to be distinguished:

- are they to be distinguished in terms of their objects, knowledge being exclusively of things that are necessarily true, such as that 2+2=4?
- are knowledge and belief mental processes (operation, acts), the difference between them being one that can only be known by introspection?
- does knowing some proposition, p, imply believing it and, if so, is the difference between knowledge and belief a matter of weather one's belief is caused in a certain way?

Locke described knowing and believing as 'operations' or 'actings' of our minds which we observe ourselves by reflection (Essay, I i 4), and Cambridge philosopher, G. E. Moore, said that the question 'How do you know that?' may be meant to ask 'What sort of a process goes on in your mind, when you know it? (*Some Main Problems of Phlilosophy*, London, 1953, p. 25). Bertrand Russell (*Problems of Philosophy*, Oxford, 1912, Ch. 5), have distinguished between 'knowledge by acquaintance' and 'knowledge by description', Russell defines 'acquaintance' in terms of the technical concept of 'direct awareness' so that we can be acquainted with 'sense-data' and with 'universals' (Vesey & Foulkes; 1990: 163-165).

Sociology of knowledge is explained as "the study of how styles of expression and the character of ideas or systems of thought are related to different social contexts". Karl Marx, from whom the contemporary impetus to the sociology of knowledge largely derives, sought to relate art and ideas to particular historical circumstances and the kinds of 'class' systems prevailing at the time. Karl Mannheim, who relativized Marx's ideas to all thought, including Marxism itself; Max Scheller, who divided the influences on thought into 'real factors' (different at different historical moments) and 'ideal factors' (a realm of timeless essences which constituted an absolute order of truth); and Émile Durkheim, who argued that the basic rhythms of social life experienced by a society - its sense of space and time -were a function of its kind of social organization". (Bullock, Stallybrass & Trombley; 1988: 457-458)

In psychology the most prevalent definition of knowledge is "the verified belief; dogmas and doctrines about the physical and social system (of human, society and culture); thoughts, hierarchy of principles; common things; whether it is innate or the experience gained, for the mental plane. In this sense, knowledge is close to what is meant by memory because; the memory is the place for storing information". (Budak, 2005: 129-130) However, all these definitions fail to provide us a full description within the circular frame of our study but beneficial on the way providing a full comprehension of what knowledge is and providing an advance information for the section dealing with the interaction between the mind and the mass communication tools in advance.

The first thing we should determine is to reveal the difference between the mind and the external world. This distinction is the meeting point of those who study on the subject matter. Therefore, dialectical relationship between human mind and external world takes place on the core of plane analyses of epistemology and ontology. In the opinion of western philosophers human mind and external world are irrelevant. The nature of the relationship between the external world being free from human mind and the mind trying to define it distinguishes the idealist, materialist and realist approaches. British philosopher Bertrand Russell studies these in his work titled 'Problems of Philosophy' and assesses an overall evaluation of the subject matter in chapter 'Appearance and Reality'. In his opinion, human being is just a thinking agent trying to interpret external reality in the light of his mental capability. He claims that reality is unknown to human mind and man could detect only some parts of reality with his limited perception. Thus, it infers that the knowledge acquired could be fallacious. Consequently, man's reality is nothing more than a pure image, in other words, image is the reality itself. (p.11-19)

In his work the relation manipulated between the external world and mind also exhibits the situation of reality and the direction of knowledge flow at the same time. However, it would be likely an incorrect behavior to reduce this information phenomenon into a simple relationship with the external world, which is unique to man only. Accordingly, it seems inevitable to clarify the structure of information.First of all, we should perceive the materials human mind interacted while producing information and the ways materials interact, as well. The key concept here is the ability that is called 'symbolization'.

Symbolization forms man in two ways: firstly, socialization of man as an individual; secondly ontological development of man. Becoming a man as an individual stage initiates with the progression of an infant from the world of images to the world of symbols. Jaques Lacan calls it 'mirror stage' and explains that "the mirror stage is a phenomenon to which I assign a twofold value. In the first place, it has historical value as it marks a decisive turning-point in the mental development of the child. In the second place, it typifies an essential libidinal relationship with the body-image". For the very first time an infant recognizes his/her image on the mirror as a whole the synthesis of this image produces a sense of contrast with the lack of co-ordination of the body which is perceived as a fragmented body. The child experiences this contrast initially as a rivalry with his or her own image; because the wholeness of the image threatens the child with fragmentation-thus the mirror stage gives rise to an aggressive tension between the subject and the image. Successively follows the language, which is the most authoritative form of symbolization. As a kind of organizer, language provides mental construction and positioning of the icons provided; consequently individual acquires the characteristic unique to man and is situated in the society.

Ontological progression of man is the major of philosophical anthropology and Jean Bruller Vercors provides a good example of it in his essay 'İnsan ve İnsanlar' (Man and the Man) (1988).In his opinion, human alone signifies nothing unless the participation of others. This could only be possible in case we accumulate our knowledge away from ourselves and employ symbols. By doing so, it would be possible to transfer a mental activity produced by a man to the next generation safely. It is the fact that underlines the basis of civilization and our ability for symbolization. Likewise, philosopher Ernst Cassirer, who is accepted as the founder of Neo-Kantian tradition, describes man as an 'animal symbolicum' in his work 'An essay on man' (1962). To Cassirer what makes man is, not his capacity for thinking but his ability for symbolizing basically.

Thanks to this ability, man gradually isolated himself away from all other creatures and has entered a completely different world of his own. Thus, his talent is the unique key to his evolution; therefore, man, who creates a reality in his mind with limited perceptions, could be able to destine himself new horizons.

Man's ability to symbolize is the basic component of being a human. Correspondingly, fundamentals of information also underlie this ability. Symbols have various functions in human mind; they enable external world to be permanent in mind because, man acquires knowledge through senses and decodes into images then transfers them to the mind. Among these inconstant images, mind can select the stable ones, which we call symbols. Symbols constitute the representations of external world in mind, barely consisting of morphemes and their compositions. We will name this kind of knowledge as 'perceptible'.

American philosopher Charles Sanders Peirce cites about that kind of knowledge in his work 'On a new list of categories' (1868:287-298) and clarifies man's ability to 'conceptualize' instead of what we propose as 'symbolize'. He also claims that

'... Universal conception which is nearest to sense is that of the present, in general. This is a conception, because it is universal. But as the act of attention has no connotation at all, but is the pure denotative power of the mind, that is to say, the power which directs the mind to an object, in contradistinction to the power of thinking any predicate of that object, -- so the conception of what is present in general, which is nothing but the general recognition of what is contained in attention, has no connotation, and therefore no proper unity. This conception of the present in general, of IT in general, is rendered in philosophical language by the word "substance" in one of its meanings. Before any comparison or discrimination can be made between what is present, what is present must have been recognized as such, as it, and subsequently the metaphysical parts which are recognized by abstraction are attributed to this it, but the it cannot itself be made a predicate. This it is thus neither predicated of a subject, nor in a subject, and accordingly is identical with the conception of substance'. - (Peirce, 'On a new list of categories', Proceedings of the American Academy of Arts and Sciences 7 (1868), 287-298 Sec3)

These conceptual configurations could only be provided through a relationship among object, representment and interpretant, which can be assumed as a sort of mechanism. Each concept may survive by the mediation of interpretants, being decoded into a sign. Let's take a duck in real life; it will be transformed into a representment of a duck depending on the willpower of interpretant.

This representment exists as a concrete concept in human mind. Interpretant could correlate a representment to another object so that s/he could get another sign such a process will provide mind more abstract knowledge and gradually it will construct itself a world of its own. On a plain basis, from a white duck image, a wide range of knowledge could be deductible: from environmental conditions ducks have to encounter after the civil war, to the increase in death rates, all mental activities should be considered within this structure. Peirce proposed a list of triadic relations which he made the most fundamental categories of all 'things' of any sort whatsoever the categories of 'Firstness', 'Secondness', and 'Thirdness' and he often described things as being 'firsts', or 'thirds'. His triadism constitutes the base of abstraction mechanism in general.

Hereby what we define about knowledge, implements us the facility of redefinition of knowledge. At present, we can redefine it as 'the act of rationalization of things'. New definition is now much more comprehensive and functional with respect to the ones in previous chapters. We deal with 'things' as obscurities which are already familiar to us and name other obscurities unknown to us as 'things'. We envisage the abstract but obscure ones in our minds similarly. On this point, we encounter '*corollarium*' (a logical and natural consequence obtained from a definition) by virtue of highlighting all sort of knowledge as a constituent of mind. The information acquired from mass media should be investigated on that platform.

DYNAMICS OF KNOWLEDGE BUILDING AND META-COMMUNICATION

There can be no doubt that most educators are focused on helping students learn and gain more knowledge about specific subject areas or skill areas. What is not always clear is how knowledge is developed in the sense that it becomes part of the specific and "useable" knowledge of the student rather than the general knowledge of multiple persons in a specific field of study or expertise. Students must not only understand what they hear, read, experience, or do in a class but must also incorporate that into their own structures of knowing so that it is recalled and applied in relevant situations. The Wiki tool can help facilitate this development process in several ways. We often test information recall in our courses, but we do not always evaluate knowledge development. The Wiki can help in this process of moving information towards useable knowledge.

The most well-known wiki is Wikipedia, the online user-created encyclopedia. Wikipedia reflects the philosophy that a community of site contributors and users will collectively ensure site accuracy. Instructional uses of wikis provide a benefit for the educational environment as a collaborative tool that wikis allow students to group author projects and papers, allow students to peer edited and review documents, and promote proofing skills with close reading, tracking, and revisions of drafts. As a participation tool wikis are an inexpensive collaboration and communication tool that promotes participation between students and students and the instructor.

When using a Wiki in an instructional setting, the context is essentially dynamic and moving. That is, the actual purpose of a Wiki is not to simply communicate information, but to invite participation at the level of input that will contribute to the understanding and application of the information shared. This can happen in a document or media project via a Wiki or a series of contributed knowledge "items" that can be collectively producing new knowledge. The Wiki, then, can "move" student work towards a collective goal (Reynard, 2009).

Although most of the above support is not available at present in the online learning environments of the course management systems widely in use, they are potentially useful. For instance, metaphorical designs like the following could be used to guide learners in the virtual space: a "student lounge" for social activities, postings of social events or personal information students would like to share with the class; a "virtual office" where students can have meetings with instructors; a "lecture hall" where students can listen and/or view content related information; and a "discussion forum" where students can annotate each other's work and conduct intensive discussions on course contents. Such design efforts would make the navigation intuitive and transplantation of roles easy in the virtual environment. All of these notification systems would enable students to coordinate their efforts in completing large projects.

To facilitate communication and knowledge construction, designers could build scaffold templates which instructors could later adopt to suit their needs in specific courses. Additionally, the capability of the system to simultaneously display artifacts and discussions would be beneficial to learners when the discussions are context-dependent. With improved designer support, more tools that address different aspects of online learning could be made available for instructors and learners to use in ways desirable for online collaboration and knowledge construction. Concerted efforts from designers, instructors, and learners could make computers function as "cognitive tools" in online learning environments. (Gao, et,al, 2005).

THE STRUCTURE OF MASS COMMUNICATIONAL INFORMATION AND LEARNING

It is possible to mention five basic characteristics of mass communication within the context of mental interaction. The first one is spatial independence. Unlike other communication forms, within their present communicational structures, mass communicational tools perform their interactivity by extending beyond contextually in spatial meaning. They can perform the communication simultaneously in an area of thousands of kilometers. As a secondary feature, this simultaneity, which can be designed, determines the strength of tools together with spatial independence.

The third characteristic of mass communication is that it can be directed from a center. The existence of a central area and simultaneous interaction that is independent of space gains them a capability of public control. As explained in previous sections, this is an instrumental capacity originating from their implemental (tool) aspect. Through mass communication, public opinion can be guided in a variety of ways. This guidance can be actualized on ideological dimension as well as learning dimension. Such public control constitutes the fourth dimension of mass communication within interaction.

The fifth feature is the cost efficiency. Installing a mass communication can be a real challenge. The installed communication may appear to be costly but once analyzed within the scope of mass context, it becomes clear that in the long run the cost of communication decreases significantly. For instance, the cost of an advertisement reaching the consumers through television is around 3 Dollars per thousand people. Indeed, media planners calculate the costs per thousand instead of per one person for the ease of calculation (Basal, 1998).

Those five elements also construct the structure of communicational information. All these elements emerge as an indirect element determining order for orientation. People are likely to imagine mass communication as a tool. Mass communication is indeed a tool for its beneficiaries rather than users. The pragmatism of interaction operates through logic of coverage. This logic has spread to all media systems. As for education, it shall emerge as a similar instrumentalization element. Particularly, the rise of distance education in Germany sets a good model. U. Winand, H. Kortzfleish and P. Wilferd in their joint article *Online Education: Virtualizing Data Transfer and Learning* (1998) state that the reason accounting for the rise of online education in Germany is related to the high-cost of face to face education (p. 881-891). Regardless of this objective, the instrumentalism that this orientation reaches also determines the structure of information construction. In order to investigate this matter elaborately, we should at first handle the topic of learning.

Learning is defined as the continual change occurring in behavior as a result of repetition and experience. People spend a great deal of their lives with learning hence a huge part of psychology is dedicated to learning as life goes on through learning. Learning mostly takes place in three forms which are classical conditioning, contingency conditioning and cognitive learning. People can learn through conditioning but they mostly learn through cognitive ways. Learning through cognition is usually an outcome of actual practices and element of cognizance is at the center. During this process the individual transfers the data of external world to his mind and this mental accumulation grows continually (Morgan, 1956; Ch. IV).

Principally the first element determining human learning is language aptitude. Thanks to language aptitude, a person can abstract the words and concepts and construct the interaction between them. Personal success is on the other hand determined by intelligence level, age, anxiety and stimulation and previous learning. The longevity of something learnt is set according to the positioning level in memory. The structure of learning material, way of learning, level of affinity and repetitions are determiners here (Morgan, 1956; Ch. V). It is obvious that after all, learning is a construction of information. If we handle information as raw information, processed information and reprocessed information, we can put learning through education to the third category. Information constructed through mass communication is also within this category.

Information constructed through mass communication is, above all else, a pragmatic information. People who consult to a mass communication tool for information perform a pragmatic act. The organizational structure conveying them the information becomes part of another type of pragmatism due to the relations outside its own realm. Hence the act of informing is also pragmaticized in a different dimension. The association among ad-giver, media channel and viewer sets a good example to this dimension. The orientation of viewer to media channel will be different from the orientation of media channel towards viewer. Media channel will be forced to discover the viewer while viewer shall be oriented to the channel hoping to have fun or catch the news. State of stimulated condition and affinity that emerge as a result of such anxiety become a personal external element determining the success of learning. The same holds true for distance education, too. A trainee, since s/he will be consciously oriented to learning, shall have high affinity level and the level of forming mental affectivity through mass communication will be higher.

The functionality of mass communicational information is conditioned by the materials used. As indicated previously, each tool operates the mind in different dimensions related to the media interacted, such as television or the internet. For that reason one of the points to focus on in act of learning is the outcomes of tool-mind interaction. For instance, while information on a newspaper allows the reader to make a comparison with previous learning, this is not the case on television. On the other hand, the power of visual imagination of television cannot possibly be compared to newspapers. Therefore, each tool shall be effective in different levels and competencies. As regards systematic learning however, it is necessary to apply a design that goes beyond daily information. Therefore, for a systematic learning via the internet and television, or shortly, distance learning it requires some course developing strategies of which range from students' characteristics to course assessment.

ROLE OF MASS MEDIA IN DISTANCE EDUCATION

At present mass communication is a significant online learning environment for distance learning. Primarily, the internet, television, printed materials can be included as major tools. Although having a vital essentiality, mass communication media have never formed up a bare affectively, because individual media have dissimilar capacities and therefore have a distinctive role on the mental process of knowledge building. Thus, the way that tools make human mind work is an inevitable case to deal with here. The word 'tool' is taken as Neil Postman employed in his work 'Amusing ourselves to death', that's, 'tool' stands for the integrity of technological equipment. Here what should be cared for is the recognition of textbooks as tools as well as television sets or printed media. Tool- mind interactions could be categorized into four sections. All sections form up an individual presentation, thus function as an external determiner of the message content. Mc Luhan explains it as 'medium is the message'. Meta communication has a similar impact indirectly, which is an essential participant determining the exactness of distance education. Likewise, distance learning acts in the same way: the way they interacted -mass media tools and mind is therefore vital here. We employ the ways mass media interacted with to imply the interaction taking place between communicational tools and human mind. As clearly indicated through its definition, such an interaction basically includes two parameters which are mass communicational tools and human mind. In that way the structure of dialectic shall find a meaning among variables since each of these tools has a specific character and unique interaction forms that come with this character. However once the mind is handled as a meaning production unit, it offers just one mechanical structure –This topic has already been analyzed in 'nature of knowledge' - Throughout the process, each tool operates the specific mechanism in a different dimension. Therefore the attempted interaction gains a new quality each time. For that reason in present study it seems plausible to continue on analyzing these forms.

Interaction through Reading

Interaction through seeing takes place between tools such as paper and ink and the mind. The visuals and linguistic indicators presented in a certain form determine the functioning of mind too.

Another determinant is the element of temporality. Indeed between concepts of present time and images formed with these concepts, temporality emerges as an element determining the nature of reception.

In the interaction through seeing the images uncovering iconic and symbolic indicators are perceived in a process which is totally dependent on the subject interacting. This form of reception provides various means to the mind in forming fantastic connections. In that way the mind can find an exit to exhibit its upper abstraction capacity. Let us discuss an advertisement text where there is a bunch with one flower, a bunch with a few flowers and a bunch with a dozen flowers. On top of the text suppose that such a statement is written: "How angry?" Under such condition the mind shall at first receive the elements. The mind shall identify the pictures on the paper with real world counterparts and imagine them as one and the same. Next the mind shall make sense of the text by establishing the context between words. Then it will form syntax between the elements. Since there is not an ordinary meaning in such a narrative form the mind will be forced to establish some kind of a context. Whether such a context can be formed or time of its formation is something completely related to personal competency. Still something is constant; the paper is there itself and unless the subject turns or closes the page it shall remain that way. Sooner or later, a person with normal temporal competencies shall make sense of it.

Since what is mentioned here is an implication, the mind shall be forced to consult mind linguistics pragmatics. Other meanings embedded within social reality shall be the determiner of meaning which is phenomenon commonly present in idioms. For instance while "Şekerleme yapmak" idiom in Turkish is the equivalent of producing sugar for an English person the same idiom means "sleeping" for a Turk.

In the advertisement text described above the person cannot solve the semantic structure between images of flower and linguistic message without knowing the element of discussion in man-woman relations and the role of flower in an apology ritual. Beyond that, once a subject that goes to upper abstractions is considered, this condition shall be carried to a far different level. For instance a person contemplating on the relation between flower sales and advertisement shall not only think about the analysis explained above but s/he also consider other parameters on a more abstract level. If s/he has an anti-system critical mind, based on this paradigm, this person can read the theorem on advertisement "buying flower in line with the level of anger" as "in capitalist system even love relations are materialized". A more competent mind can make sense of the same message as "reification". That is the way the mind functions on and on and what makes this possible is nothing but the stability feature of the tool. Interaction which is actualized through reception that is based on the stability of tool enables the functioning of mental mechanism in deeper dimensions.

Another significant point of the tool feature is *the style of the written text* written by which information is to be presented. Distance Education materials not only have to convey information to the students, but also they have to structure and control the process by which this information is presented to and assimilated by the students. Such materials need to be designed with much more care than the texts of formal systems. There is a need to develop an effective writing style in distance education is particularly significant. In writing styles some factors are very important for writing the distance education material. These are given as under by Yousuf, & et. al.:

Format of distance education material refers to the general appearance of the page and of the document as a whole. The placement of unit on the page, such as the headings, margins and number of columns, features of type, such as double or single spacing, paragraph indentation and type style. In many cases, a good illustration can replace the text and communicate the desired information more quickly and effectively. Any time writer can use a phone, line drawing, chart, graph, or table.

One of the main functions of any *visual and learning material* is to set in train the right kind and quantity of perceptions from which learning can take place. Now-a-days visual materials are being utilized to make the teaching more effective. As a matter of fact, it now appears obvious that properly designed visual material like pictures, photographs, maps, diagrams, graphs and symbols for distance education can be very useful for all open learners. Uses of pictures, use of comics, use of pictorial charts, diagrams in the text is very productive and creates stimulation in the students of open learning system (Yousuf, & et. al., 2008, p.129).

Interaction through Listening

In the interaction through listening the tool provides a verbal motion. This motion not only keeps the mind away from deep thoughts but it also operates the imagination intensely. A soccer match broadcast on radio is a good example. A subject listening to the match receives the story of speaker through verbal means. During this process the sound vibrating through air shall resonate in the ears of listener and turn into audio images in mind. Yet, unlike visual elements, these images are not presented in ready forms. The listener shall be obliged to imagine the narrated things in his/her mind. This condition pushes the imagination to operate intensely. The unique capacity of radio in creating a phantasm world is the determiner of its singularity as well. A mental world created through pure hearing is subjective to the same extent…

Mental interaction through hearing strengthens the emergence of subjective judgments as well. To illustrate, a verbal theorem "With the introduction of Post-Fordist production structure, surplus emerged" shall find a meaning within all mental designs that took place until the time theorem was presented. This meaning is a formation actualizing in an imaginary background. This formation does not take place in a form that is based on a personal graphics or gestures and mimics of a presenter. It is totally shaped within subjective semantic auras that are attributed to the historical transformation of the person's own production structure which adds a unique dimension to act of making sense. Among free associative semantic phrases any radio listener makes sense of the issue from a different aspect. This condition is a unique feature determining the quality of learning.

As a tool another feature the radio provides us is mobility. With the discovery of transistor technology in Bell Laboratories, this feature has forced us to take a new parameter into account about sense making. Indeed while the presented images are made sense in a phantasm world, the space we are in can also emerge as a determiner. The mental condition of a person travelling in his car and the person drinking tea in his yard and listening to the radio at the same time are not identical at all. The mind shall meet a different imaginary environment depending on the place radio is used. This stands before us as an element determining the success of reception so much as the level of reception.

The disadvantage of radio as a tool is that it offers a singular image. Ferdinand de Saussure in his work Course in General Linguistics (2006) presents an indicator as a combination of one concept and audial image. But an indicator is a combination of one concept and a good number of audial images. For instance, a piece of cube sugar is the expression of the unity of sweet, hard and white images. In society one or more than one of these images take prominence on pragmatic level and becomes the main image explaining the concept. For cube sugar, the dominant image here is the sense of tasting. Accordingly this definition presents us a fact: A thing can assume its real meaning through various images. Pure audial images are at the same a conceptualization that is deficient. This shows us the hardship that surfaces on the free associative level of conceptualization of radio.

Interaction through Seeing-Listening

The main components of tools that function according to the operating principles of television and radio are not only determined by visual and audial unity but element of motion as well. Arthur Asa Berger in his article "Television as a tool of Terrorism" (1991) reports that television as a tool attacks to us with a beam of light. During this process the mind is forced to continuously monitor light beams and the motion. Television captivates the mind involuntarily (pp 35-38). Such kind of a mental captivity impacts its reactance as well. In an interaction through television the share of phantasm is rather limited. Due to the tool characteristics it minimizes its imaging competencies. It is no doubt that this is a feature that comes with a pure concentration.

Another characteristic of television is its capability to present visual and audial elements together as a tool. That means while on one side semantic codes arriving through linguistics messages construct a discursive meaning, on the other side the semantic supplements that come with mobile audio indicators complete this discursive structure. Let us analyze the news narrating the operation of armed forces against illegal protestors. The images of the news shall be surrounded with chaos and combats. Simultaneously a speaker shall read a text that constructs a discursive structure on these images. In the presentation stage the viewer shall focus on the news text guided by the news transmitted from news reporter. Generally such type of information introduces question marks. While watching the news, a viewer finds answers to the questions in his/her mind at the same time. This reactionary model determines the act of making sense too. Here, the images assume a secondary quality. They go beyond observation and function as evidence. However in addition to this function, they also constitute the main component of making sense of the text. A person focusing on images gets away from imaginative competency and throughout act of watching, s/he moves away from abstract meaning auras which dwell on the upper dimensions of the mind. The main reason accounting for this fact is that verbal and visual motion operates quite fast. Similar to the example we have shown two parts earlier, the mind cannot read the text within a conceptual formation like "reification". This constitutes the weakest point of the mental interaction through seeing and listening.

The strong aspect of such interaction is that when a visual indicator is required, it can provide it on the spot. Some things are, regardless of their strong literary competency, hard to explain through linguistic means. Television and similar tools present such an image and they can also mobilize this image. The integrity of audial component is another element strengthening the competency of description. Hence such tools rise to a competent position not through imagination but the available capacity of presentation. Regarding unmediated description, there is nothing above television. This competency is present in narration as well. Narrative forms function as a primary element in assisting the individual to comprehend the world. Ludwig Wittgenstein in his work Philosophical Investigations (1953) explains it through metaphor of language games. According to him, our relationship with the world is totally determined within the metaphor of game. From this point of view, we can reasonably assume that television is quite a competent tool for us in internalizing the world.

Another point to consider in television broadcasts is meta-communication. On radio this element is possible only via sound tones but on television the dubbing and attitudes of portrayed characters shall be determiners. Referring to the previous example, if the news reporter made a face while narrating the news, we would perceive this act as a sign of discontent towards the protestors and their ideology as well. Unquestionably this would be an element that would affect us while reading the text. Again, the intonation of the speaker would be equally effective. That would be an element forming both its disadvantage and advantage. Pragmatic dimension of meta-communication is totally associated with its application.

Interaction

Interactivity stands before us as a communication form where mutual interaction is sustained. The difference of interactive communication tools from others is that they enable a reciprocal interaction. Teleconferences, live television links and internet use can primarily be given as examples. Interactivity is used mostly for situations where audio visual elements are reciprocally shared. Simultaneity is the main principle. Therefore mediated feedbacks cannot be included within this context.

Regarding their tool aspects, the tools that make interactivity possible are no different than the ones presented in the previous section. For instance in an interaction via internet the elements valid for television shall be the same. Additionally the windows enabling reciprocal chat shall be also included. This element shall be influential on communication course but it shall also act as a process determining the direction. Indeed a speaker shall form the direction of a speech according to the reactions and instead of a flat narration s/he will prefer a circular interaction.

One of the most critical aspects of interactivity is that the share of package forms is reduced. Communicational structures which are mostly based on reciprocal chat limit the existence of production elements. Consequently in an interactive communication environment, the tools are not as determinative as they are on television. However during the process the share of the domination of meta-communicational structures on meaning rises.

In interactive applications the low quality of the conditions enabling the interactive communication is another striking point. Since vision, sound and transmitting elements are actualized in relatively low quality, there is a definite decrease in their affectivity rates. In addition to all, interactive environments lack the level of interaction provided via face to face interaction. For instance, in a course presented on electronic environment the instructor is no more than a small image window for the viewers. For the instructor the viewers are simply a chat window on computer. That condition is determinant in the success of reciprocal interaction as well.

A suggestion made by Scandamalia argues the classroom conditions as a knowledge building environment. In her article (1994) Scandamalia focuses on the educational ideas for knowledge-building discourse - with some discussion, and she argues that the classroom needs to foster transformational thought, on the part of both students and teachers, and that the best way to do this is to replace classroom-bred discourse patterns with those having more immediate and natural extensions to the real world, patterns whereby ideas are conceived, responded to, reframed, and set in historical context. Her goal is to create communication systems in which the relations between what is said and what is written, between immediate and broader audiences, and between what is created in the here and now and archived are intimately related and natural extensions of school-based activities.

CONCLUSION AND RECOMMENDATIONS

An essential point to add is to assert that the basic reason accounting for the orientation towards distance education is, as explained in the text, its effectiveness and easy access which are the preliminary advantages of distance education. One disadvantage of such education is that it lacks the reflexivity presented in class environment (Harri-Augstein & Thomas, 1991, p. 51-69). Although through interactive education this can be compensated to a certain extent intra- class group interactions, environmental motivation and meta-communicational elements can in no way be filled. Besides face-to-face education offers a chance of melting pot for students and this is an element that determines anxiety and level of affinity. However, it is still possible to perform an effective learning program via distance education. Uğur Demiray, who was one of the leaders of e-learning in Türkiye working for Eskisehir Anadolu University distance learning teaching staff, proposes some methods and their outcomes for distance education in his book (ch.1, p.5). To achieve that, there are certain points which should be noted comprehensively as well.

The first point to pay attention is that while preparing a learning program an inter-instrumental structure should be used as a base. As analyzed in detail earlier, each tool has different capacity regarding mind operation. While preparing learning materials, this should be taken into account and concept construction, different characteristics of different tools in language and visualization should be employed coordinately. To that end, first of all the deficiencies of tools should be clarified.

The gaps which are likely to emerge in the act of learning should be filled by making use of other tools. These deficiencies can be given as below:

- For the interaction through listening, lack of visual image.
- For the interaction through reading, the stability or mechanical immobility of visual image.
- For the interaction through seeing-listening, shift of attention to visual images or lack of abstraction.
- For interactivity, motivational lacks caused by spatial distance and meta-communicational deficiencies.

However it should also be remembered that while preparing the program the strong sides of tools should also is taken into account. These strong sides have been explained in detail in the fourth chapter.

The second point deserving attention is that education is an activity that mostly takes place on conceptual level. In this level, the dialectic relation between language and thought should be paid heeds. Particularly in concept construction, printed materials should be focused on more audio-visual and audial tools should act as a pre-information provider and reinforcer. The level of applied language also emerges as a significant element at this point. In all acts, except act of reading, it should be ensured that the abstraction of the employed language and familiarity of the words are not beyond the comprehension of receiver. It should be kept in mind that the success of communicational transfer is usually determined by the success of reception.

The speed of contact in the attempted interaction is the third point we must note. This is directly proportional to the mechanism of employed tool. There is a connection between implemental (tool) mechanism and the way this mechanism operates mental mechanism. In particular, the mechanical structure of printed materials draws a favorable picture for concept construction. On the other hand, audio-visual tools can be more effective in context formation and reinforcement. Purely audial tools can be useful in reinforcing through repetitions.

To sum up, the final point to pay heeds is the role of individuality in the success of learning. Each receiver has a different mental structure which eventually determines the final success of education. For instance, for a person with high visual intelligence television or internet would be an effective channel while for a receiver with high verbal intelligence the opposite holds true. Also with respect to implemental (tool) interaction forms, different reactions are likely to emerge.

In order to prevent this, students enrolling in distance learning program should receive pre-tests and be offered different programs according to their intelligence types.

WEBLIOGRAPHY

http://www.anadolu.edu.tr/en/akademik/fakulteler.aspx retrieved March 1, 2009

http://campustechnology.com/Articles/2009/02/04/Why-Wikis.aspx April 28,, 2009

http://www.ikit.org/kb.html retrieved March 11, 2009

http://eogrenme.aof.edu.tr Retrieved March 8, 2009.

http://www.knowledgeforum.com/Kforum/InAction/resrch.htm retrieved March 20, 2009

http://www.ccl-cca.ca/CCL/Reports/LessonsInLearning/RSS/LinL20070906_Building-knowledge-building-the-future.htm retrieved on April 1, 2009,

http://tcbdevito.blogspot.com/2007/11/abcd-meta-communication.html retrieved on April 22, 2009

http://www.thefreelibrary.com/What+Is+Etiquette+for+Online+Business+Communication%3F-a01073799161, retrieved on April 8, 2009.

REFERENCES

Alexander, G. O. (1972). *Instructional meta-communication and self-directed learning.* Paper presented at the International Communication Association Annual Convention (Atlanta, Georgia, April 19–22, 1972). Retrieved April 5, 2009, from http://eric.ed.gov/ ERICWebPortal/ custom/ portlets/ recordDetails/ detailmini.jsp?_nfpb=true&_&ERICExtSearch_SearchValue _0=ED063737&ERICExtSearch_SearchType_0=no&accno=ED063737

Atac, E., & Mutlu, M. E. (2006, October). Very large scale e-learning practices in the open education system at Anadolu University. [Waikiki Beach, Honolulu, Hawaii.]. *E-Learn, 2006*, 13–17.

Basal, B. (1998). *Medya Planlaması* [Media planning]. Istanbul, Turkey: Cantay Kitabevi.

Bateson, G. (1955). A theory of play and fantasy. *Psychiatric Research Reports, 2*, 39–51. Reprinted in Bateson, 1972.

Beckham, K., & King, J. (2008). *Ohio State University fact sheet CDFS-6: Communication in coalitions*. Retrieved March 3, 2009, from http://ohioline.osu.edu/ bc-fact/ 0006.html

Berger, A. A. (1991). Bir Terör Aygıtı Olarak Televizyon [Television As A Terrorist Medium], *Enformasyon Devrimi Efsanesi: Modernleşme Kuram ve Uygulamalarının Eleştirisi*, der. Yusuf Kaplan, Kayseri: Rey Yayıncılık.

Budak, S. (2005). *Psikoloji Sözlüğü* [Dictionary of psychology]. Ankara, Turkey: Bilim ve Sanat Yayınları.

Bullock, A., Stallybrass, O., & Trombley, S. (Eds.). (1988). *The Fontana dictionary of modern thought* (2nd ed.). London, UK: Fontana Press, an imprint of HarperCollins Publishers.

Cassirer, E. (1962). *An essay on man: An introduction to a philosophy of human culture* (2nd ed.). London, UK: Yale University Press.

Chen, P., & Chen, H. (2007). Knowledge building and technology dynamics in an online project-based learning community. [from http://www.sicet.org/ijttl/specialIssue/chen.pdf]. *International Journal of Technology in Teaching and Learning, 3*(2), 1–16. Retrieved March 3, 2009.

Dainton, M. (2000). Maintenance behaviors, expectations for maintenance, and satisfaction: Linking comparison levels to relational maintenance strategies. *Journal of Social and Personal Relationships, 17*, 827–842. doi:10.1177/0265407500176007

Demiray, U. (2002). *Televizyonda Canlı yayın ve Açıköğretim* [Live Broadcast on TV and Open Education Faculty]. Konya, Turkey: Çizgi Kitabevi.

developing distance learning material. *Turkish Online Journal of Distance Education-TOJDE, 9*(2). ISSN 1302-6488

DeVito, J. (2000). *Human communication*. New York, NY: Longman.

DeVito, J. (2001). *The interpersonal communication book* (9th ed.). New York, NY: Addison Wesley Longman, Inc.

Dindia, K., & Baxter, L. (1987). Strategies for maintaining and repairing marital relationships. *Journal of Social and Personal Relationships, 4*, 143–158. doi:10.1177/0265407587042003

Ely, R., Gleason, J., Narasimhan, B., & McCabe, A. (1995). Family talk about talk: Mothers lead the way. *Discourse Processes, 19*, 201–218. doi:10.1080/01638539509544914

Gao, H., Baylor, A. L., & Shen, E. (2005). Designer support for online collaboration and knowledge construction. *Journal of Educational Technology & Society, 8*(1), 69–79.

Giler, J. H. (2009). *Kids with learning disabilities understand the language of friendship*. Retrieved April 28, 2009, from http://www.schwablearning.org/ articles.aspx?r=575

Hand, K. (2000). A picture or 1000 Words? *Turkish Online Journal of Distance Education- TOJDE, 1*(1). ISSN 1302-6488

Harri-Augustein, S., & Thomas, L. F. (1991). *Learning conversations: The self-organised learning way to personal and organizational growth*. London, UK & New York, NY: Routledge Publications.

Hatcher, S. L. (2003). Reading between the lines: Meta-communicative aspects of online education. A paper presented at the Annual Conference of the American Psychological Association Toronto Canada on 7-10 August 2003.

Kelman, C. A., & Branco, A. U. (2004). Deaf children in regular classrooms: A sociocultural approach to a Brazilian experience. *American Annals of the Deaf, 149*(3), 274-280. Retrieved April 12, 2009, from http://muse.jhu.edu/login?uri=/journals/american_annals_of_the_deaf/v149/149.3kelman.html

Lacan, J. (2007). *Ecrits: The first complete edition in English*. London, UK: W. W. Norton & Company.

Lyn, D. E., & James, J. W. (2004). Mathematical modelling with young children. *Proceedings of the 28th Conference of the International Group for the Psychology of Mathematics Education*, 2004 Vol 2 (pp. 335–342).

McLean, R. S. (1999). Communication widgets for knowledge building in distance education. computer support for collaborative learning. *Proceedings of the 1999 conference on Computer support for Collaborative Learning* 1999, Palo Alto, California December 12–15, 1999, Article No. 48. Retrieved 20th May, 2008, from http://portal.acm.org/ toc.cfm?id= 1150240&coll=GUIDE&dl=GUIDE&type=proceeding&idx=SERIES11363&part =series&WantType=Proceedings&title =CSCL&CFID=69778328&CFTOKEN=28671871

McLuhan, M., & Powers, B. R. (1989). *The global village: Transformation in world life and media in the 21st century*. USA: Oxford University Press.

Morgan, C. T. with L.T. Alexander. (1956). *Introduction to psychology*. New York, NY: McGraw-Hill.

Newman, H. (1981). Interpretation and explanation: Influences on communicative exchanges within intimate relationships. *Communication Quarterly, 29*, 123–131. doi:10.1080/01463378109369397

Patch, M. (1995). The effect of asymmetrical use of metacommunicative behavior on judgments of power. *The Journal of Social Psychology, 135*, 747–754. doi:10.1080/00224545.1995.9713977

Patch, M., & Hoang, V. (1997). The use of meta-communication in compliance: Door-in-the-face and single-request strategies. *The Journal of Social Psychology, 137*, 88–95. doi:10.1080/00224549709595416

Peirce, C. S. (1868). On a new list of categories. *Proceedings of the American Academy of Arts and Sciences, 7*, 287–298. doi:10.2307/20179567

Perlmutter, M., & Hatfield, E. (1980). Intimacy, intentional meta-communication, and second order change. *The American Journal of Family Therapy, 8*, 17–23. doi:10.1080/01926188008250344

Postman, N. (2006). *Amusing ourselves to death: Public discourse in the age of show business* (20th ed.). New York, NY: Penguin Books.

Rashid, M. (1999). *System of distance education: Study guide for non-formal education*. Islamabad, Pakistan: National Book Foundation.

Reynard, R. (2009). *Why wikis?* Retrieved April 28, 2009, from http://campustechnology.com/ Articles/ 2009/ 02/ 04/ Why-Wikis.aspx

Russell, B. (2008). *The problems of philosophy*. Canada: Bastian Books.

Saussure, F. (2006). *Course in general linguistics*, (16th ed, trans. Roy Haris). Chicago, IL: Open Court Publishing Company.

Scardamalia, M., & Bereiter, C. (1991). Higher levels of agency for children in knowledge building: A challenge for the design of new knowledge media. *Journal of the Learning Sciences, 1*, 37–68. doi:10.1207/s15327809jls0101_3

Scardamalia, M., & Bereiter, C. (1992). An architecture for collaborative knowledge-building. In De Corte, E., Linn, M., Mandl, H., & Verschaffel, L. (Eds.), *Computer-based learning environments and problem solving. NATO-ASI Series F: Computer and Systems Science*. Berlin, Germany: Springer-Verlag.

Scardamalia, M., & Bereiter, C. (1994). Computer support for knowledge-building communities. *Journal of the Learning Sciences, 3*(3), 265–283. doi:10.1207/s15327809jls0303_3

Steven, B. D., & Rita, L. (n.d.). The Internet's role in education. *Teaching Techniques Instructional Tools, 67*(1). Retrieved March 27, 2009, from http://www.asrt.org/ media/ pdf/ foreducators/ 3_instructionaltools/ 3.3internet.pdf

Vercors, J. B. (1998). *İnsan ve İnsanlar [Mankind and People]*, (trans. S. Eyüboğlu, A. Erhat, & V. Günyol). İstanbul, Turkey: Toplumsal Dönüşüm Yayınları.

Vesey, G., & Foulkes, P. (1990). *Collins dictionary of philosophy*. Glasgow, UK: Harper Collins Publishers.

Winand, U., Kortzfleish, H., & Wilferd, P.(1998). Online Eğitim: Bilgi Aktarımının ve Öğrenmenin Sanallaştırılması [Online Education and virtulationzing of learning and Knowledge Transfering]. *Yeni Türkiye Dergisi: 21. Yüzyıl Özel Sayısı*, trans. Nurhayat Yoloğlu, (sayı 19).

Wittgenstein, L. (1953). *Philosophical investigations*. United Kingdom: Blackwell.

Yousuf, M. I., et. al. (2008). Perceptions of course coordinators and course writers for

Chapter 16
Adding Self-Discovery Learning to Live Online Conferences:
Using Digital Poster Sessions in Higher Education

Shalin Hai-Jew
Kansas State University, USA

ABSTRACT

In recent years, pre-recorded digital poster sessions have become more widely used as parts of real-time face-to-face conferences and as complements to online conferences and colloquiums. The multimedia-enriched building of various types of digital poster sessions offers high potential for conference organizers to be more inclusive of a variety of topics, and it helps conference participants gain more value from the shared synchronous time and virtual experiences. This chapter examines the role of digital poster sessions in contemporary online conferences and highlights some basic production-quality issues in the creation of digital posters.

INTRODUCTION

Recent global economic pressures have pushed a number of academic conferences to move from real-space to virtual. Virtual conferences involve wholly online conference interactions: the live (and pre-recorded) presentation of papers, live-stream video-ed or simulated demonstrations, the sharing of multimedia, and the promotion of scholarly interchanges and networking among all the conference participants. There are small-group decision-making sessions. The real-world metaphor of a conference has offered a potent organizing structure for ways that people interact

DOI: 10.4018/978-1-61350-071-2.ch016

and share information in online virtual spaces, based on understood conventions. Many online conferences follow the chronology and flow of a real-world conference. Some even emulate a conference environment. According to Ball (2000), virtual conferencing refers to

a time-limited series of research presentations and discussions among academic practitioners within a discipline or on a specific topic. Virtual conferences take place over the public Internet, but participation may be restricted (pp. 147 – 148).

The harnessing of these virtual conferences may enhance authentic learning in higher education (Basque, Dao, & Contamines, 2005). These conferences offer ways for professionals to share their research and to learn from others; they also offer venues for students to acclimate into a domain field and advance their respective careers. Some early research has been done to understand how to promote social interactivity in online conferences, in terms of both enablers and inhibitors. Nyirenda and Seymour (2009) found that in one online cross-disciplinary research conference that it was important to consciously promote social communications:

Effective enablers were found to be the facilitation and the use of prescribed topics of discussion. Some major inhibitors of social interaction were found to be the lack of community amongst members, poor conference timing and notice period, lack of immediacy and unclear or not relevant topics (p. 93).

These connections and communications may be enhanced by year-round electronic interactions, collaborations, information sharing, and research. These online academic conferences (through desktop machines and laptops) have recently started adding digital poster sessions to their offerings. As such, it is important to examine these digital forms to consider some ways to more effectively use these.

A Review of the Literature

Conferences are a critical part of building virtual communities of professionals; in part, they serve to reaffirm membership connections, given that self- and group-identification works as an "organizational glue" that holds a community together (Wiesenfeld, Raghuram, & Garud, 1999, p. 788). These conferences enable those in communities of practice (Lave & Wenger, 1991, as cited in Lave & Wenger, 2002, pp. 111 - 126). to deepen their participation within these communities. These communities also enable the building of shared knowledge through social cognition, in which people's ideas spark off each other's different interpretations and world views. Virtual conferences offer a way to strengthen potential identities especially for "decoupled organization members" who are regionally dispersed.

In a live conference, the main focus is on the live presentations and speeches: at the top level of attention would be the keynote address, which features a main speaker in a one-to-many type of address. This dynamic is true even for panel discussions—with the few-to-the-many, in a formal setting. Poster sessions offer a mix of informational displays that focus on complementary topics to the main presentations. These offer more one-to-one and few-to-few channels for discussions and interactions. Historically, poster sessions consisted of static posters on physical A-frames with complementary handouts or short academic papers on a nearby table. Harris, Maricle, and Birkenholz (1990) describe a traditional poster used in a conference poster session in the following way:

A poster consists of a series of illustrations containing information mounted on various sizes of poster boards to describe innovative ideas or research results to interested parties on an informal basis (1990, p. 3).

Poster sessions, events in which people socialize around and learn from displayed posters in a defined space, are used across a wide variety of academic fields, but there is little research about their efficacy in the research literature (Aust & Kinnick, 1996). Presenters might have laptops as part of their presentations (Jones, 2006).

The value of poster sessions continues into the present-day in the form of digital ones. A reception with food and wine may be held in the poster session area in order to encourage conference participant attention (which may in turn enhance the quality of conference interactions: the keynote and plenary sessions, discussions, small-group work, and other interactions). The presenters of the posters would stand next to their posters to socialize, explain, and demonstrate. The charm of a poster session was the informality and chaos of people-to-people interactivity around shared issues of interest. For graduate students and young professors, these poster sessions were something to put on their resumes but also a chance to learn and also to share their work. During the rest of the conference, other conference-goers would wander through the room with the posters, read them, and pick up handouts, but they would not have the benefit of the presence of the originators of the original research and expressive posters.

Online Conferences and Colloquiums

In the same way that live conferences have now moved to wholly online formats, poster sessions have now evolved to digital forms. Human organization of these conferences has moved coherently online. They bring sophisticated facilitation of the various live sessions. Many now have added Communication Access Realtime Translation (CART) services for live human textual transcription of presenters' comments (accessed through the universal Closed Captioning symbol), and some have use live video with American Sign Language (ASL) translations. Other conference sponsors even bring on live professional illustrators to depict ideas visually in real-time and to spark conversations and thoughts as keynote speakers share their ideas. Figure 1, "Live Illustration of a Keynote at the International Online Conference (2010)," shows the evocative nature of a live illustrator's work using an electronic tablet.

Online sites used for live synchronous conferences have become more sophisticated. These manage human identities effectively, for administrators, presenters, facilitators, and participants. These sites convey both individual telepresence and group social presence (through images, biographical information, textual representations of names, and / or digital avatars—and other indicators). Some online conference sites enable small-group forums on unique topics of interest.

Many virtual conferences include clear organizational structures for the presentations, with searchable titles, abstracts, and presenter biographies. They integrate live web conferencing technologies for real-time voice, text, visual, whiteboard, and multi-media interchanges. There are formal and public channels for communications as well as informal and private channels. These sites enable widgets with live-running commentary through microblog feeds. They offer podcasting features that enable mobile device interactivity. They host text-based discussion forums on various topics related to the conference. They have live interactive polls that may be launched for more structured interactivity. There are spaces for conference sponsors to advertise and to reach out to the participants. At the end of the event, there is often a searchable knowledge repository of shared information.

Synchronous time—defined time that requires real-time presence and attention of a group of people--is comparatively expensive to asynchronous time (which is more convenient and less stringently defined). The nature of time enhances

Figure 1. Live illustration of a keynote at the International Online Conference (2010) (Used with permission of Susan Manning, Green Room)

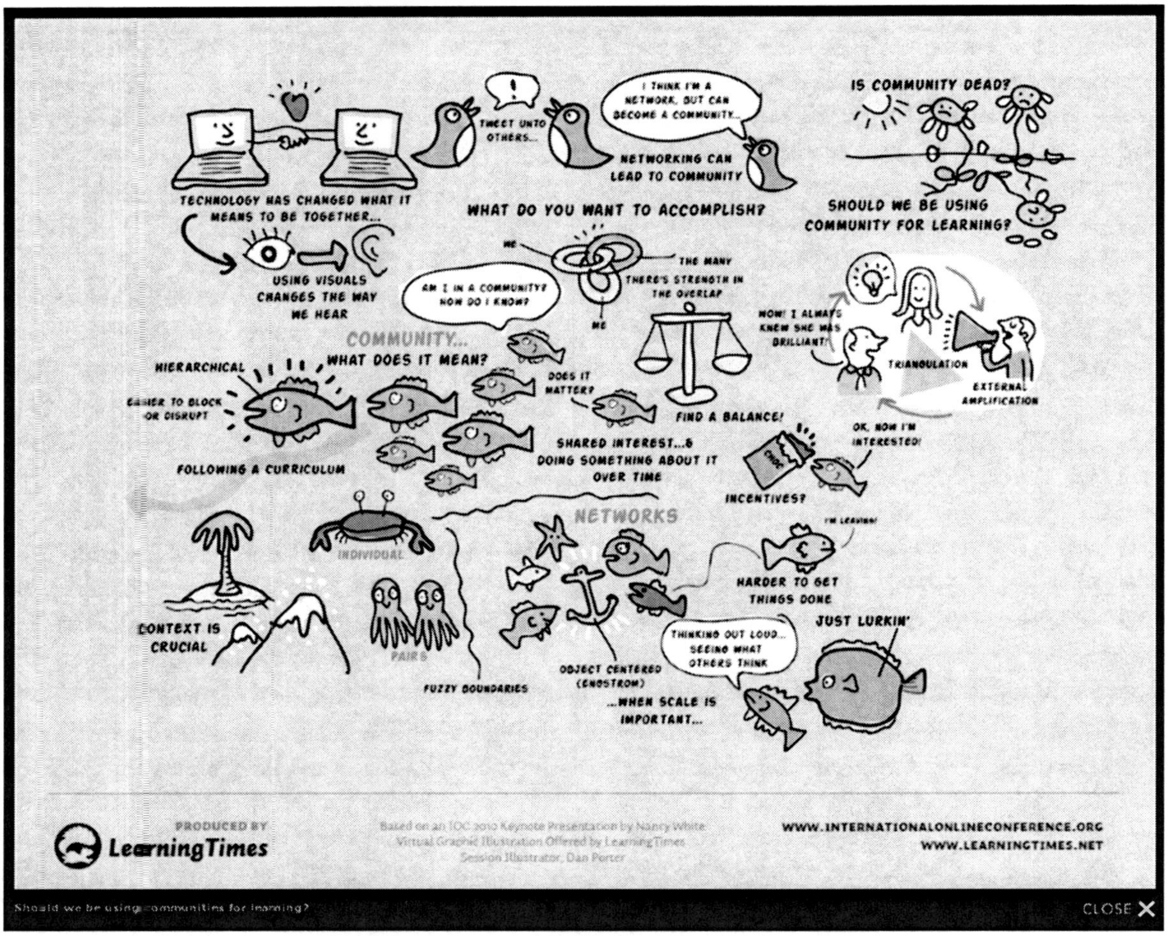

the complementary power of digital poster sessions, which require less expensive time for people to attend to them and to learn. The lower cost of attending a conference that is not space-bound or locative may also free up individuals to participate more broadly.

For example, Figure 2, "A Screenshot of the Landing Page for the International Online Conference 2010" shows a mix of design for channeling human attention and various conference-based functionalities. There is a keynote, features, registration, ways to sign up for an RSS feed for podcasts, and access to the conference program. There are also ways to access last year's conference with its recorded digital poster sessions. And this only captures the contents "above the fold." Below, there are additional resources like online discussion forums.

The multimedia and digital nature of digital poster sessions ensures that the contents are created and delivered online in many forms: lecture-capture lectures, videos, slideshows, short games, audio files, and "mash-ups" of various types of digital contents. Anything that may be created as a web-deliverable multimedia file or a web page may be made into a stand-alone digital poster session. These files fit easefully into the conventions of knowledge-based interactivity because

Figure 2. A screenshot of the landing page for the International Online Conference 2010 (Used with permission of Susan Manning, Green Room)

people do collaborate around digital information, such as distributed design review (Daily, Howard, Jerald, Lee, Martin, McInnes, Tinker, & Smith, 2000). In other words, people may experience and interact with a digital poster session and engage in conversations with other conference participants online about the contents. That is a comfortable mode of interaction around such digital contents.

Basic Elements of the Digital Poster Form

The essential limits of the digital poster form are few. A digital poster session should be experienced within a limited period of time (20 minutes to 30 minutes approximately). The topic of the digital poster session should be focused, not diffuse. Digital poster sessions all have titles, abstracts, and contents. Many poster sessions are sequential in presentation. Figure 3, "A Narrated Sequential

Figure 3. A narrated sequential presentation in time triptych (Used with permission of Susan Manning, Green Room, and Shalin Hai-Jew)

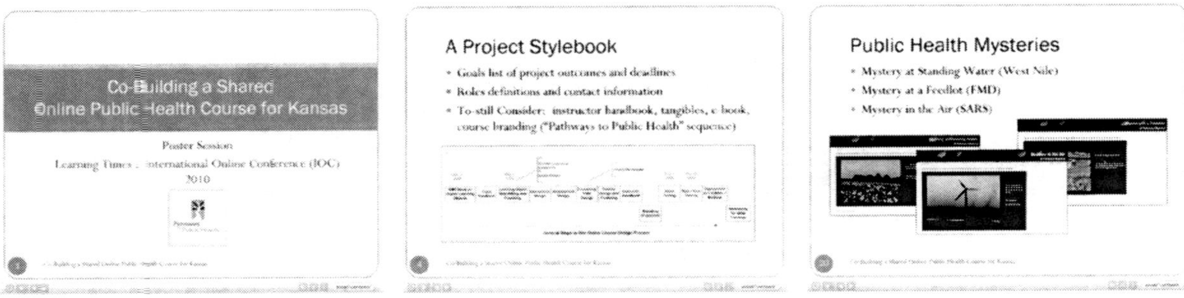

Presentation in Time Triptych," depicts a kind of developmental and logical structure to the information.

Others use spatial layouts, such as image maps. Or the Prezi method of presentation offers a large-context gestalt combined with specific information. So given the nature of web-delivered multimedia, what does that mean for the forms of such sessions?

Some Forms of Digital Poster Sessions

The ones currently used on the Web involve the following forms: audio files; desktop lecture captures (with voice narration, website demonstrations, software demonstrations, textual information, digital imagery, slides, and video snippets); slideshows (static and animated, non-narrated and narrated); photo albums (with captions); web pages and web sites; designed immersive spaces; videos and 3D *machinima* (machine + cinema); interactive multimedia; digital storytelling; light simulations, and light games (digital jigsaw puzzles, word finds, crossword puzzles, flashcard activities, mixes and matches, sorting, sequencing, and other games). In terms of more over-arching organizational structures, some digital poster sessions may be tours, mysteries, analytical cases, stories, and sequential experiences. They may be part of a simulated art show or professional studio environment or scenario. Finally, digital poster sessions may also come with related downloadable files like checklists or forms. Figure 4, "A Downloadable File accompanying a Digital Poster Session," shows an accompanying file being downloaded—in this case, a slideshow.

A recent add-on to many online colloquiums are pre-recorded digital poster sessions. Digital poster sessions currently do not involve real-time presentational aspects; rather, those reviewed by this author involved automated presentations—that had to be necessarily self-explanatory and stand-alone (without the give-and-take of the creator in attendance). The nature of digital multimedia means that such digital poster sessions do not have to be static; rather, they involve the full power of multi-sensory experiences—audio, video, and text, in various combinations. The relatively low-cost-of-entry for multimedia development means much higher access for a variety of subject matter experts (SMEs), even those without a high level of technological savvy.

Digital Poster Sessions in Immersive Virtual Worlds

Virtual conferences have moved to immersive virtual worlds, such as 3D metaverses. Virtual conference centers are built to emulate real-world spaces in some cases; in others, they are virtual-world only areas that are floating in gravity-free contortions. Figure 5, "Dell Corporation's Vir-

Figure 4. A downloadable file accompanying a digital poster session (Used with permission of Susan Manning, Green Room)

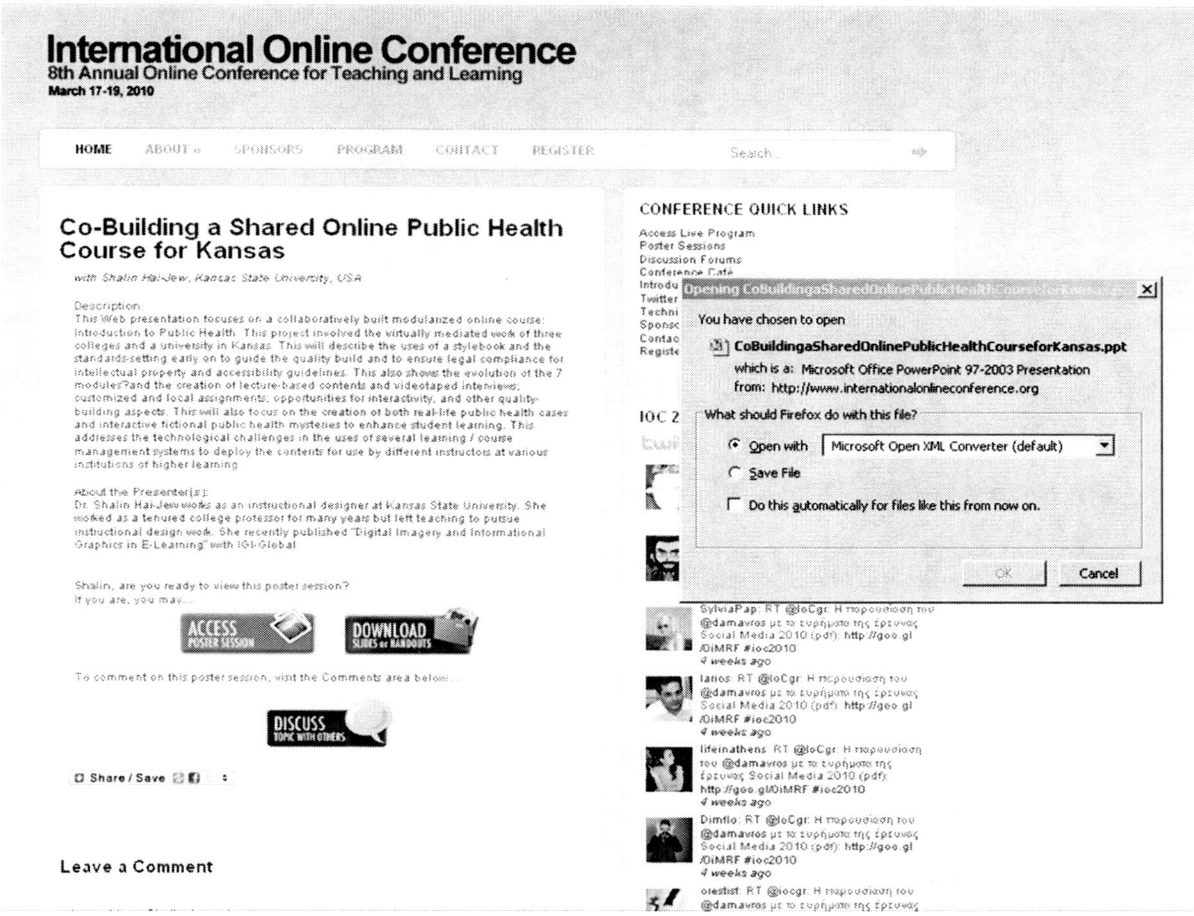

tual Conference Center on Dell Island in Second Life®," highlights spaces where humans may interact and collaborate through human-embodied digital avatars.

In Figure 6, the US's National Oceanic and Atmospheric Administration (NOAA's) virtual conference center includes an electronic billboard up front to welcome digital avatars. Inside are tasteful pieces of digital art on the walls. There are many virtual amenities.

For example, in Second Life®, generic digital kiosks may be set up to play audio or video or slides at the push of a button. Some fancier kiosks are animated, with the semblance of movement. There are some with creative lighting effects to draw attention. Figure 7, "A Virtual Space to Engage Pre-recorded Multimedia," shows the potential, with human-embodied avatars that may engage virtual contents and communicate and collaborate around those experiences.

In Figure 8, NOAA's virtual conference center includes endlessly looping multimedia as well as virtual seats and podiums. Here, a live speaker may present. Archived presentations may be run as digital poster sessions on the active screen. To access these, human-embodied avatars have to be in the virtual worlds and "present" in the defined

Figure 5. Dell Corporation's Virtual Conference Center on Dell Island in Second Life®

Figure 6. NOAA's Virtual Conference Center in Second Life®

Figure 7. A virtual space to engage pre-recorded multimedia (just push start to play)

Figure 8. NOAA's Virtual Conference Hall with endlessly looping multimedia slideshow

locale (with the specific latitude and longitude in terms of virtual spaces).

There are many collaborative virtual spaces on which to place static images, text, and other combinations of that. There are virtual A-frames, wall spaces, virtual screens, digital kiosks, virtual theatres, 3D simulation spaces, and even floating skyboxes which may be populated with contents. Figure 9, "Virtual 2D Images in a 3D Display Space," demonstrates the higher resolution of wall images even from a variety of angles.

The technological enablements from this feature have allowed various design and art shows to be held in virtual spaces, with live mediated presentations. A digital poster session would comprise pre-recorded contents that would be made available through the space. A sequence of slide or photographic images could be set up as part of a virtual display, for example.

Figure 10, "A Rotating Information Column in Front of a Virtual Conference Hall," takes advantage of 3D space to offer advertisements on all sides. The rotation helps online participants see all the messages. The resolution of such kiosks have improved over time for improved readability.

Figure 11, "The Presentation and Humanizing of Digital Poster Sessions," shows how poster session presenters are humanized with head-shots and how names and abstracts of the digital poster sessions are listed in a findable way.

The diversity of presenters of digital poster sessions enhances the learning by offering a range of points-of-view and insights. Poster sessions have value for conference participants throughout a virtual conference, as well as pre- and post-.

Figure 9. Virtual 2D images in a 3D display space

Figure 10. A rotating information column in front of a virtual conference hall

Affordances of Digital Poster Sessions for Online Conferences

Pre-, During, and Post-Conference Digital Poster Sessions

Digital poster sessions enable a much wider reach to an audience that is not often afforded in face-to-face conferences. Prior to a conference, digital poster sessions may pique interest. During a live and synchronous conference, they offer contextual information that may enhance the live experiences. After a conference, the poster sessions may be perused for deeper analysis and learning. Poster sessions have value as stand-alone self-exploratory learning, but they also have value as complementary parts of a larger conference—a contextualization of social and mediated learning.

Ball (2000) observes the greater innovation potential of online conferences, in part because of their fundamental nature, and in part because of the extensions of such virtual conference impacts over time with the archival of the virtual conference contents.

> *Innovations are made possible by the different ways that audiences can approach the material. In a virtual conference, one does not have to choose only one of several concurrent sessions or sit through a lengthy panel of loosely related papers to hear one of interest. Rather, the participant can view all of the material of the conference or just a single presentation of interest. This means, in turn, that concepts such as panel, roundtable, poster session, and discussant are much more fluid. Papers need not be grouped into panels, formal discussants and audience members can have equal opportunities to make informed comments and criticisms, and multiple paths can be defined through the conference material. Because a virtual conference can last longer than a traditional one and can leave its contents available for viewing indefinitely, the conference itself can be designed to serve as a more seamless springboard into continued collaboration among participants (p. 150).*

Figure 12, "A Live Online Presenter Pointing to How to Access Poster Sessions," shows how one presenter made a point to highlight the availability of digital poster sessions to participants in the live web presentation. The design of the site also drives traffic to these resources, as is highlighted by the prominent location of the links to the digital poster sessions.

Interactivity around Digital Poster Sessions

People who experience digital poster sessions are not just expected to be passive consumers of information and automated experience. They are expected to respond to the contents, spark multi-way conversations, participate in substantive discussions, and share new knowledge. Digital

Figure 11. The presentation and humanizing of digital poster sessions (Used with permission of Susan Manning, Green Room)

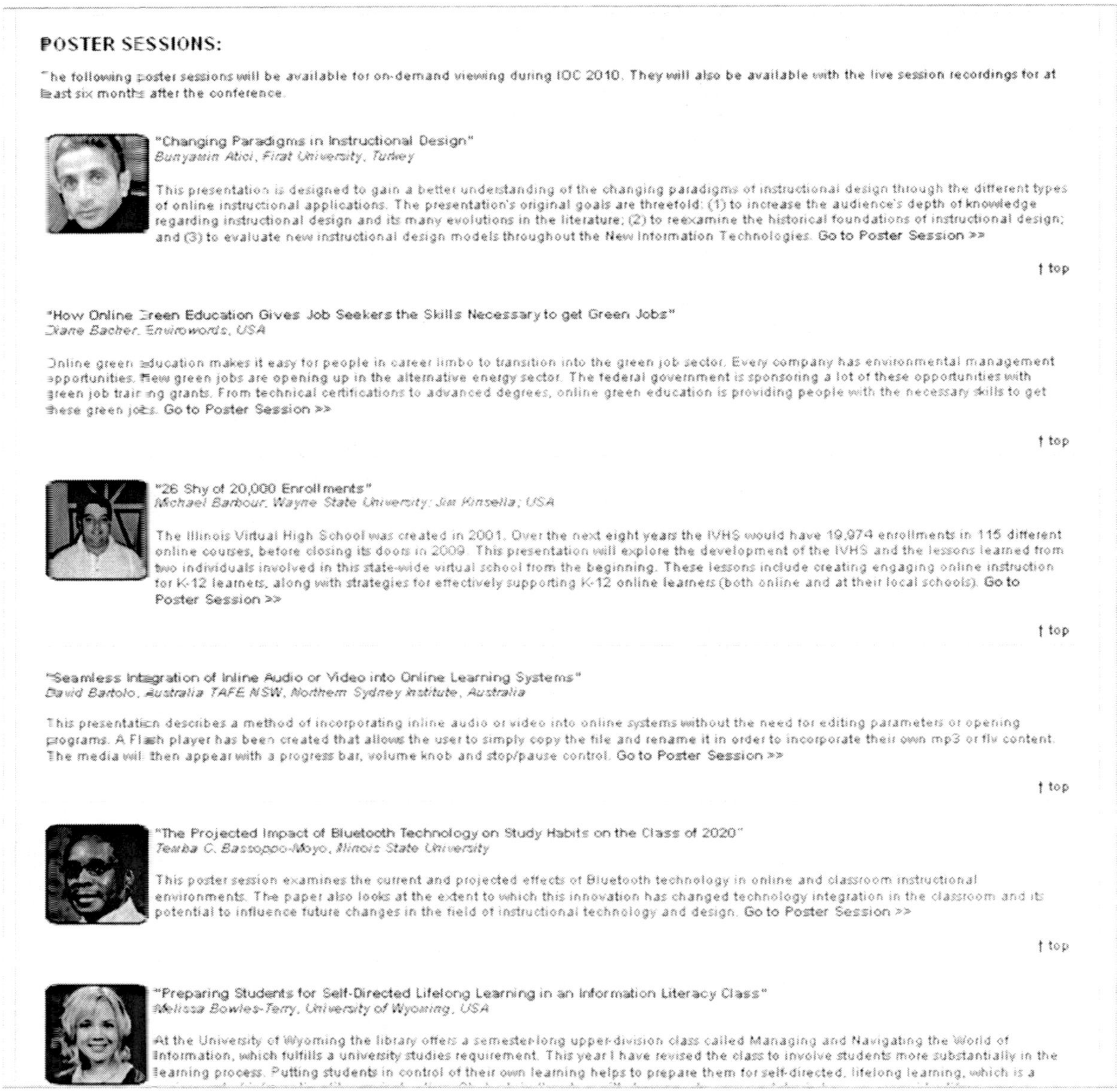

poster sessions may offer a body of digital work around which a community or network of practice may interact. Figure 13, "Discussion Tools around Digital Poster Sessions," highlights one text tool around a digital poster session.

People who start or continue conversations may also ask to be notified of follow-up comments. They may sign up for RSS (Really Simple Syndication) feeds to access related poster session contents.

Communications may be taken off-line and extended through emails, telephone calls, and other direct communications in cases where conversants want more privacy.

Figure 12. A live online presenter pointing to how to access poster sessions (Used with permission of Susan Manning, Green Room)

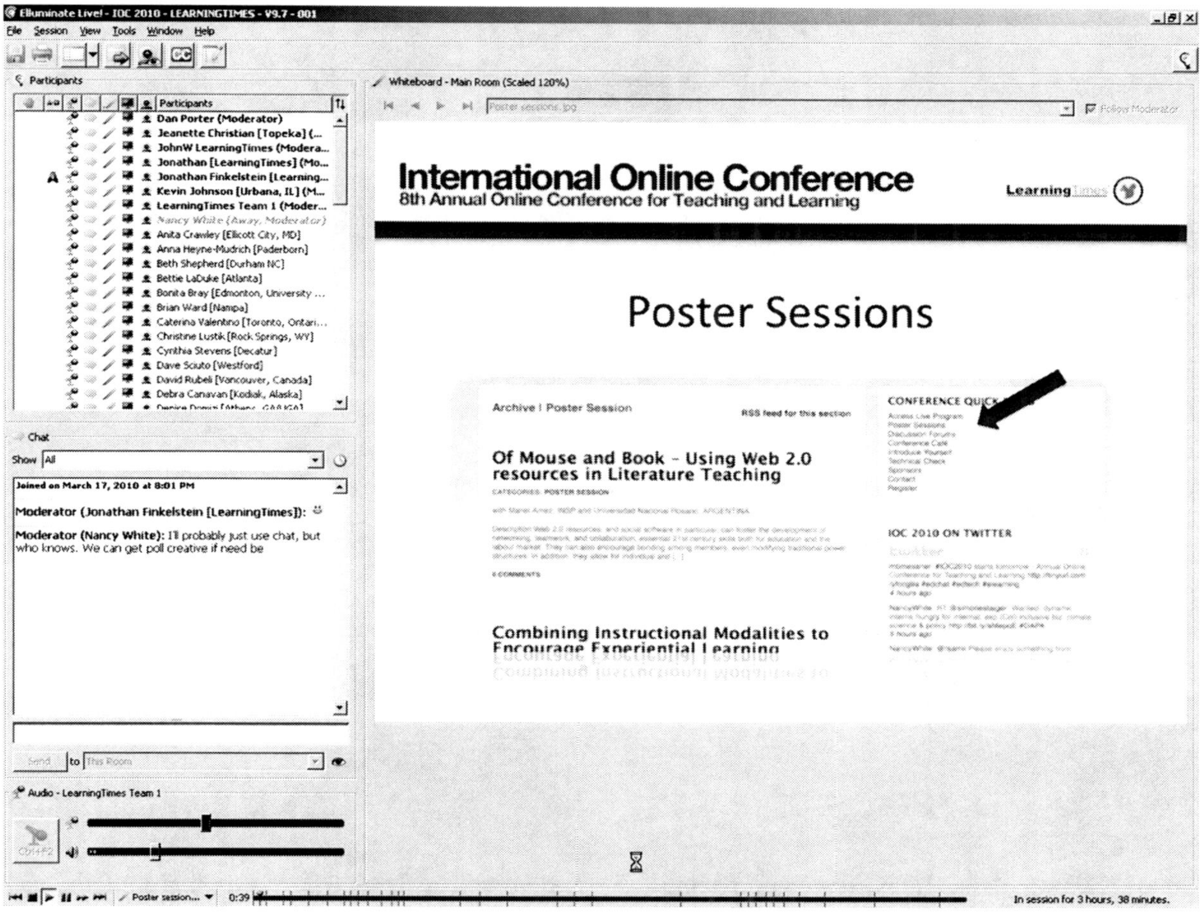

Other Pedagogical Uses of Poster Sessions

Poster sessions appear in the educational research literature as ways to enhance student learning and skills. Lowry (1992) describes the salutary effects of having students practice "visual reporting" in poster sessions to communicate their research results. Poster sessions have been used to help students summarize their research for easier grading by their professors in larger classes (Crowley-Long, Powell, & Christensen, 1997). Some faculty create learner assignments around digital posters sessions in order to promote discussions and even result in summative assessment of learner participation in such virtual symposiums (Basque, Dao, & Contamines, 2005).

Collaborative Builds of Digital Poster Sessions

While building digital poster sessions will involve learning value, collaborating with a team to co-build a poster session may add other layers of learning richness.

Virtual Professional Networking

A critical part of virtual professional conferences involves networking among professionals (Ball,

Figure 13. Discussion tools around digital poster sessions (Used with permission of Susan Manning, Green Room)

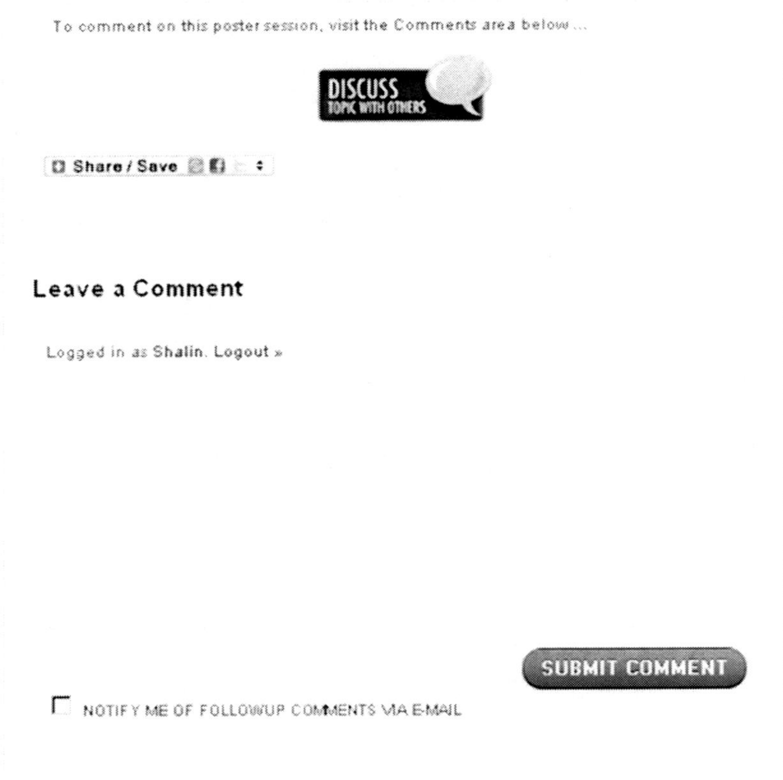

2000). Digital tools used for virtual conferencing—online profiles, email addresses, back-channel text connections, and narrow-casting capabilities (such as one-to-one connectivity)—enhances the possibilities of fellow professionals and students making professional ties and learning from each other. Even with something as "thin" as a name, people may find others' Internet profiles, social networking pages, emails, and other information to enhance connections.

High Production Values for Digital Poster Sessions

The efficacy of digital poster sessions will depend on a variety of factors. The more original and fresh the information, the more valuable the poster sessions will be. Digital poster session contents have to be designed to the extant knowledge base and interests of the potential audience members. (Ball (2000) notes that participants to online conferences may be the more advanced and technologically savvy participants, which may skew the membership. This skew may be noted in the design of digital poster session contents. Also, Brissenden (1983) suggests that posters must "provoke a desire to make contact and ask questions" (p. 26).) After all, these are objects used in an academic context. The higher the production values and the higher the innovative execution of the poster session, the more effective the digital poster will be. Designers of digital poster sessions may mix a variety of technologies and digital objects to communicate the information. They will also have to ensure that the contents are accessible, for the widest possible usage, particularly since such contents may be archived on websites, repositories, wikis, virtual worlds, or other spaces. Designers will need to be respectful of intellectual property. They will also have to design such poster sessions to be deployable on mobile devices.

Future Considerations

Future digital poster sessions may be hosted in synchronous events, and certainly, as technologies improve and connectivity becomes even faster, live web conferences may be able to handle such loads that live presentations of synchronous and multiple poster sessions may bring.

Currently, there is a dearth of research writing about digital poster sessions. In terms of research, there are many extant questions. In various domain fields, what are the most effective ways to create, design, and deploy digital poster sessions? What sorts of assignments are the most effective for exploiting digital poster sessions? What types of digital poster sessions are the most effective for conveying certain types of information? What are some strategies for collaborating effectively around the creation of digital poster sessions?

How may digital poster sessions further enhance face-to-face conferences? How may digital poster sessions enhance virtual conferences?

What are conference-level standards for digital poster sessions internationally? In various locales or for particular conferences? What are some design aesthetics for digital poster sessions? How may poster sessions be best archived and represented in repositories or on websites? Should such sessions be made available in the public domain for self-inquiry learning and direct "cold" exploration (without the "surround" of a virtual conference)?

If conference goers see a value in having live mediation of poster sessions, what sorts of technologies could be put into play to enable this? Should virtual participants "people" a digital poster session in immersive virtual spaces? Could they be scripted to add value and energy to digital poster sessions?

CONCLUSION

Digital poster sessions are a promising area for those engaged in computer mediated communication in higher education scholarly communication and collaboration. The occasion of a live virtual conference focuses the attention of professionals in a field around relevant and timely issues. The real-time events will enable the plenty of live interactivity that may spark new ideas. Having digital poster sessions archived and available will help carry the conversation from real-time into asynchronous time. The richness of enhanced textual interactivity around digital poster sessions enables further collaborations and discussions around the ideas in these digital posters.

Virtual conference attendees may be both consumers of information and creators. Exploring digital poster sessions through research will enable conference-goers to better exploit the learning from such sessions and may enhance their creation of digital posters.

ACKNOWLEDGMENT

The screenshots of the International Online Conference were used by permission of the conference organizers, the International Online Conference, which is based out of Chicago, Illinois. The conference was produced by LearningTimes, a leading producer of online conferences for education and training. The author participated in the conference as both a live presenter and a digital poster session participant in early 2010. Thanks to Susan Manning for making the screenshot images available for this chapter. I am grateful for the generous policies of Linden Lab in regards to Second Life® screenshots. Thanks to R. Max.

REFERENCES

Aust, C. F., & Kinnick, K. N. (1996). Communicating scholarly research via the poster session: The experience at a national convention. In the *Proceedings of the 1996 Annual Convention of the Speech Communication Association,* San Diego, California (pp. 1-16).

Ball, W. J. (2000). Political science: Academic virtual conferencing: The case of the teaching politics virtual conference. *Social Science Computer Review, 18,* 147–159. doi:10.1177/089443930001800204

Basque, J., Dao, K., & Contamines, J. (2005). Participating virtually in a scientific conference: A collaborative e-learning scenario for authentic learning in higher education. In P. Kommers & G. Richards (Eds.), *Proceedings of ED-MEDIA 2005,* Montreal, June 27 to July 2, 2005 (pp. 1953-1960). Association for the Advancement of Computing in Education (AACE).

Brissenden, T. H. F. (1983). Producing a poster: Some thoughts o the poster session at the 1982 conference. *Mathematics in School, 12*(1), 25–26.

Crowley-Long, K., Powell, J. L., & Christensen, C. (1997). Teaching students about research: Classroom poster sessions. *Clearing House (Menasha, Wis.), 70*(4), 202–204.

Daily, M., Howard, M., Jerald, J., Lee, C., Martin, K., & McInnes, D. … Smith, R. C. (2000). Distributed design review in virtual environments. In the *Proceedings of the Third International Conference on Collaborative Virtual Environments* (CVE 2000), San Francisco, California (pp. 57–63).

De Simone, R., Rodrian, J., Osswald, B., Sack, F.-U., De Simone, E., & Hagl, S. (2001). Initial experience with a new communication tool: The digital interactive poster presentation. *European Journal of Cardio-Thoracic Surgery, 19,* 953–955. doi:10.1016/S1010-7940(01)00694-7

Harris, C. R., Maricle, G. L., & Birkenholz, B. (1990). Poster presentation: The key to communication of ideas. In the *Proceedings of the Annual Meeting of the American Association for Agricultural Education / American Vocational Association,* Cincinnati, Ohio (pp. 1–6).

Jones, M. L. W. (2000). Collaborative virtual conferences: Using exemplars to shape future research questions. In the *Proceedings of CVE 2000,* San Francisco, California. Association for Computing Machinery, (pp. 19–27).

Jones, S. E. (2006, March 30). The significance of electronic poster sessions. Inside Higher Ed.

Lave, J., & Wenger, E. (2002). Legitimate peripheral participation in communities of practice. In Harrison, R. (Ed.), *Supporting lifelong learning: Perspectives on learning* (pp. 111–126).

Lowry, J. H. (1992). The poster session by undergraduate research methods students. *Teaching Sociology, 20*(4), 314–315. doi:10.2307/1318977

Nyirenda, T., & Seymour, L. F. (2009). Social interaction online: The case of a cross-disciplinary research conference. In the *Proceedings of the Southern African Computer Lecturers' Association* (SACLA '09), Mpekweni Beach Resort, South Africa (pp. 93–100).

Wiesenfeld, B. M., Raghuram, S., & Garud, R. (1999). Communication patterns as determinants of organizational identification in a virtual organization. *Organization Science, 10*(6), 777–790. doi:10.1287/orsc.10.6.777

KEY TERMS AND DEFINITIONS

Asynchronous: Not occurring at the same time.

Authoring Tool: A software tool used to create digital contents.

Digital Poster Session: A pre-recorded digital presentation.

Lecture Capture: A type of equipment and / or software that captures a person's demonstration into a video, slideshow, or animated format.

Online Conference or Colloquium: A meeting or seminar where subject matter experts and learners present professional papers and discuss relevant issues.

Synchronous: Occurring in real time, at the same time, simultaneously.

Wiki: An online editable database that contains user-created contents.

Chapter 17
Online Education:
Reflection on Communication Skills of Distance Learners

Satya Sundar Sethy
Indian Institute of Technology Madras, India

ABSTRACT

This chapter discusses and examines online learning in distance education (DE) context. It seeks to argue how learners cope with online education and become successful online learners. Further, while learning through the online mode how do communication skills assist them to prevent barriers in their learning activities? A critical reflection on communication skills of online learners is summarized and highlighted. The online learners' reactions and responses are also mentioned in this chapter, documented in a few case studies available at different journals and Web portals. Further, the significance of blogging as a communication tool of online platform is elucidated with reference to learners' engagement in social interaction and collaborative learning situations.

INTRODUCTION

With the advancement and upgradation in Information and Communication Technologies (ICTs) distance learning has shifted into another phase, which is quite exciting and enthralling for learners. Distance learners, in this situation, can continue their higher education by opting online learning and can do so from the comfort of their home. The expression 'online learning' is known by different titles include;

- E-Learning
- Web-based education
- Online education

DOI: 10.4018/978-1-61350-071-2.ch017

Distance education institutions across the globe offer a large number of online courses on different subjects encompassing humanities, social sciences, business administration, engineering, medical sciences, and professional courses. In order to acquaint with and adapting themselves to online courses, learners need some abilities/ characteristics include; self-motivation, time management skills, communication skills, and study skills. These skills assist learners to become familiar with the technological instructions designed for online courses and/or programmes. Thus, it is logically deducible that online learners are surrounded with three indubitable elements: technology, instructor, and curriculum.

The online environment offers unique challenges and opportunities for learners and instructors/tutors to establish successful online learning platforms. While instructors design the platform by keeping in mind the target group, their knowledge of technological usability and easy access to content, learners are also moving a step forward and try to do all sorts activities those asked by instructors to do on real time basis. But it is noticed that whatever flexible and convenient online education may be designed by the instructors, learners would take time to deal with an online course and/ or programme. They may save communicating time in an online course but spend much of their time dealing with technology concerns (Alford & Lawson, 2009). However, distance learners find online learning as very convenient and flexible for their studies. This kind of learning, therefore, matches with their learning goals and busy life style. Although online education allures many adult learners, but it is warranted with some challenges and problems when they deal with online courses. This is because of different instructional methods used in it and the prior requirement of communication skills involved in it.

Responsible Factors for Online Learning

Learning online requires a different preparation than in a physical classroom situation. It requires good reading and writing skills because it is largely based on text and organizes through computer and Internet. Further, the ability to navigate the Internet and search information quickly on Web pages will also be necessary.

Self-motivation is also a crucial factor in online learning. Strong independent learning skills including good time management are equally essential. Also, studying by using the Internet requires a strong sense of avoiding 'internet addiction' or time wastage as users follow interesting links that do not advance the original inquiry (Reid, 1997). In this context a student said, "A Web page has many links because of which I have been misguided and used to click on interesting topics rather than focusing on the study contents consistently" (Roper, 2007).

New users of online learning environment may do well, if they restrict themselves to courses of short time frames in order to evaluate quickly their ability to succeed in learning online. Again, new users are also required to familiarize themselves with the culture of communication on the Internet (Ryder and Wilson, 1995). Through online communication, the physical separation between learners-learners, learners-instructors, learners-institution would no longer remain as an obstacle for learning.

According to Dabbagh (2007) the curricular for online course should have the following features.

1. Encourage learners to work in teams
2. Assist them to think critically and independently
3. Instruct them to aware of the focused clients
4. Give space to work in a flexible atmosphere

For online course designers the issues are to look at how to provide maximum/optimum opportunities for interaction between and among instructors and learners (Anderson & Garrison, 1998). Instructors' training for managing this virtual environment should include an orientation to the appropriate technology and communication platform as well as training in the skills necessary to present content and facilitate synchronous (live) or asynchronous (time delayed) discussion (Whitworth, 1999).

It is admitted that instructors' role is the key factor for encouraging learners to schedule their time to participate in online discussion forum. In this regard, a student explained, "Weekly discussions were best when the teacher/ instructor encouraged it, especially by having pro versus con discussion, or asking 'why' or 'how' questions". Learners who plan for regular and frequent communication with their classmates through out the course schedule will achieve greater success in their online course (Roper, 2007).

Successful online learning ultimately depends on instructors, and learners being willing, and able to integrate appropriate skills with the networked resources and interactive communication power of the Internet / World Wide Web. When all participants respond actively to online resources and interaction opportunities, the potential of online learning to further both individual and organizational learning objectives can be realized (Smith & Benscoter, 1999). Online communication skills train learners to think critically, reflect analytically and correctly in their writings, and work effectively in teams (Gruba & Al- Mahmood, 2009).

Learners prefer their learning in the online mode both in synchronous and asynchronous environments because of easy access to information. It helps them remain update with the recent developments, establish contact to the concerned and desired persons in real-time basis, interact with their peer-groups and instructors, communicate in a quicker way, submit the assignment-responses in a click way, appear for the term end examination (TEE) online by taking comforts of their home, so on and so forth.

To do all sorts activities learners need communication skills. This is so because every activity is to be carried out only through communication. Hence, communication skills are very vital for online learners for their learning activities. Communication skills are those skills through which one communicates and interprets his/her thoughts to others. One can even share his/her feelings, beliefs, emotions with others. Communication is a way in which the information is transferred from sender to the receiver through a medium. Effective communication is the one where the receiver receives the correct message intended by the sender/ speaker. In this context, means of communication is broadly divided in two sorts.

1. Verbal communication
2. Non – verbal communication

The integration of these two types of communication is further observed as three kinds.

1. Oral communication (communicating through utterances, voices, sounds, etc.)
2. Written communication (communicating through written documents)
3. Sign language communication (communicating by using marks, spots, etc.)

In communication what one says and what doesn't say are equally important. To be a good communicator, one should be a patient listener. Communication skills thus include listening, feedback, and presentation skills. A research report (Chi, et al, 1989) expresses that learners (90%) learn better when they communicate their ideas/ thoughts with others either verbally or non-verbal means. Learning by communicating does not take place if it is one sided, thus it seeks interaction from both sides. Hence, it demands serious attention for the presentation on deliberations. To imbibe, acquire, and excel in communication skills, learners require constant effort and inquisitiveness for learning. Again, they must have ambition to be a successful communicator and therefore, keep on trying till they achieve the goal. Thus, it is stated that pursuing education through online mode requires communication skills as a basic ingredient to being a successful online learner.

There are three important points which learners need to concentrate upon for communicating effectively in an online platform. These are;

1. audience awareness
2. critical thinking
3. presentation skills

Further, they require the following strategies to do their study tasks in a better and effective way:

- Write clearly and purposefully
- Represent facts and/or events lucidly
- Be flexible to receive alternative views
- Respond early to queries
- Remain up to date with changes or modifications
- Adopt synchronous and asynchronous learning environments
- Build community resources centre

To write legibly and meaningfully, learners need to develop writing skills, and it can be acquired with regular practice, dedication, determination and commitment to write purposefully. Careful reading in this case supports learners to write clearly. Participating in discussions with peer-groups even helps the development of writing skills. Adding annotations to the writings make the writings much stronger. It is suggested that before posting or attaching any messages online, learners need to review their write up for cross verifications; whether proper communication takes place or not, whether intentions are clearly reflected or not, whether there are any grammatical errors and spelling mistakes? Online communication is thus much more challenging than any other communication. Therefore, it is advisable for the online learners to write clearly, precisely, and concisely for better communication without leaving space for ambiguities.

Communication skills have direct impact on learners' achievements/ goals. Learners in distance education settings while pursuing their study through online mode oriented towards their goals both in short and long term achievements. If learners do not set their goals for learning, then they may not know whether they have achieved something worthwhile or not. Relying on their goals they must communicate accordingly in an online platform. Communication in this sense plays a vital role in achieving learners' goals. Learners should have personal goals in mind, such as; goals for the programme of study and desired degrees, goals for the assignment grades, goals to achieve success in life, goals for higher studies, etc.. Goals in the mind of learners create a clear picture of what they need to do to achieve their ambitions. And, thus they possess a strong sense of motivation to do their tasks sincerely, intelligently, and purposefully. In this regard, a few suggestions may help online learners to produce clear and effective written documents in their course related activities.

1. Try to construct short and meaningful sentences. Be vigilant for run-on sentences that don't break / crack ideas.
2. Make the paragraphs possibly short and informative
3. Give required space between words and sentences for easy reading
4. Check grammar and spelling
5. In the end, revise to look for unwanted spots or marks for the final version.

Advantages of Effective Communication Skills

Effective communication skills have the following strengths/assets in an online distance education context.

1. Learners will be able to write effectively, make formal and informal presentations, and give constructive comments while discussing issues.
2. They will able to work in teams efficiently.
3. They will be able to present their ideas in precise and concise manner.
4. They will feel comfortable in presenting themselves and even their ideas in online platforms.
5. They will be able to act as efficient moderators and acquire the skills to conduct productive meetings.
6. They will be able to acquire multi personal skills, which can utilize effectively in modes of presentation depending on the requirement of tasks. For example; face-to-face /remote, written/spoken, public/private, group / individual discussions.
7. They will be able to construct reasonable, rational, logical arguments and arrange evidences coherently to support an argument.
8. They will be able to be self–evaluators and critique of their writings.
9. They will be able to ascertain what information needs to be conveyed in correspondence to what is required.
10. They will be able to develop patience for listening and reading others' communications comprehend and understand these messages.
11. They will be able to absorb a keen sense of audience awareness while giving technical presentations to their fellow learners, non-technical friends, and family members.
12. They will be able to write their ideas clearly, concisely, and lucidly.
13. They will be able to use appropriate vocabulary for the topic /content and for the target audience.

Research indicates that interpersonal and communication skills, and fluency in the use of collaborative online learning technologies are critical competencies for the online learner (Dabbagh & Bannan–Ritland, 2005). William (2003) found that interpersonal and communication related skills (which include writing skills) enhance some desired competencies that used across all roles in distance education programmes supported by the Internet. Powell (2000) described the online learner as someone who is comfortable with Web technologies and proficient with computers". Interpersonal and communication skills are among other characteristics of a successful online learner. Cheurprakobkit, et al. (2002) reported that learners in online learning environments must possess 'self-behaviors' that embraces self–discipline, self-monitoring, self–initiative, and self- management, which are characteristics of self-regulated and self–directed learning.

Online learning becomes more interesting, informative, interactive and hence, stronger than any other modes of learning when learners post their ideas in online discussion forums for peer commenting. Further, reading peers' comments and discussions may help learners to come up with some new ideas and/or understanding of an issue in many occasions. By adhering to this method, learners can even pose their queries for the instructors and receive the ideal and possible responses within the expected time.

In an online learning environment preparing assignment-responses and then submitting in a click way becomes much easier because of direct writing and editing facilities in MS Word and effectiveness of Internet. Learners can open the text document files consciously, efficiently with attention to a Word processing programme or text editor. On this platform they can summarize their readings. They can even prepare notes directly on it by reading their peer group discussions and/or comments. While doing these activities they need to give their attention for not doing any plagiarism and citing incorrect references.

Through the online mode learners send and receive messages in a quicker and easier way. They can even clarify their doubts by asking their instructors immediately in many contexts. They can easily upload their questions either in text, or audio, or video format, and request instructors to send the responses in whatever format they wish to receive. By using appropriate emoticons learners can even communicate more accurately and intensely. Some of the usability emoticons will be available at http://kb.indiana.edu/data/ablk.html.

Online communicators often send or /and attach their postings immediately and irresistibly without re-reading their typed documents. Here, it is suggested that since Web pages are globally accessible, learners should be conscious about their writings. Otherwise it will create bad impressions on them and their writings. It will turn into a bad habit if they do not give proper attention to their writings. Thus, it is suggested that while sending or responding to a query and being part of an online discussion forum one needs to review his/her writings on content organization, clarity, and grammatical correctness. Online communication is of two kinds; synchronous and asynchronous.

Communication: Synchronous and Asynchronous Environments

Synchronous and asynchronous are two different types of communication found in online education. The earlier one takes place in real–time basis whereas the later one takes place over time (delayed time). Examples of earlier communication are; chat, instant messaging, video conforming etc., and the examples of later communication are; e-mail, discussion forums, bulletin boards, etc.. Synchronous communication always creates a live atmosphere whereas asynchronous communication gives opportunities learners to browse, read, and respond to others' postings at their own pace.

Communicating online compels learners to rethink, reorganize and represent their ideas in a logical and coherent way. In a research study, when asked how learners made the most of their online interaction with other learners, learners mentioned some interesting techniques. Among those, one student commented, "Interacting with other learners was the fun part of my online classes. As much as possible, I would post a response, question, or comment to another student's posting. This built up an online relationship." Another student suggested, "Respond to several student postings but make sure you have something meaningful to add, don't just say 'good post'. Also, don't often interact with some new classmates. Look for something to say with various learners."(Powell, 2000)

Online Education: A Virtual Classroom

An online learning environment is always embedded with fellow learners, instructors and a few unknown friends. Whatever mode learners may prefer (either synchronous or asynchronous) they will develop a professional and personal relationship with their peer groups. Here, the expression 'group' may be treated as 'classmate'. Learning through online gives an opportunity to know others' skills, and their ideas on various issues/concepts. Reading others' ideas and arguments may help learners to develop their communication style. This is so because there may be situations where learners follow others' writings or try to improve their communication skills as a competitor to others/peers. Since learners reside in different geographical locations of the globe and they meet in online platforms for discussions on different issues, the ample information generated may be used for writing their assignment-responses, preparing for the term end examinations (TEE), and doing research in future, if any. By communicating regularly with their peer groups, they will avail themselves of the opportunity to evaluate their writings by contrasting and comparing their peers' responses, and sometimes receive instructors' guidance to develop their writings.

Online Education: Resource Centre for Research

An online learning environment provides a lot of e-resources. Group discussions and contributions on online platforms even generate plenty of resources for academic purposes. Hence, searching resources for research work online becomes easier now. In this context, a student says, "I may have access to some of the resources that I am searching for on physical campus. But I may get plenty of information available online through special service arrangements. Only precautions, I have to take is that, I need to be careful about the validity of the resources and the legal and ethical issues concerning research" (Roper, 2007). Accessing library resources through online is a remarkable contribution of Web search engines. Online users can download the relevant documents by visiting the online library, they can request for some scanning pages of the books (if these documents are not available on online), they can read and assess the study materials online, they can even send their comments or reviews for the consideration and publication without any delay.

Discussing online education necessarily includes blogging as it is a major part of online learning activities.

Blogging

"Weblogs or Blogs, as they are known, are easily created, easily updateable Web sites that allow authors (learners and/or tutors) to publish instantly to the Internet platforms from any Internet connection" (Richardson, 2006). It facilitates the interaction through communication between tutors and learners and among learners. Since it is an interactive platform, it allows tutors and learners to begin conversations by adding information, and is published right there. Thus, weblogs are considered as the most widely adopted tool for reading and writing on Web so far. The weblogs are one among the other social platforms, as part of the Web 2.0 to provide a new educational environment where learners and teachers can create the subject contents collectively by exchanging their opinions on an issue or an event. In this regard, Pilar (2008) stated that 'communication' and 'interaction' are thus the terms that best describe this new reality.

Blogging allows learners to work collectively, interact, produce materials, access and share information with others. The pedagogical implication of this platform is to break the hierarchical nature and unidirectional method of 'traditional' teaching and learning and instead favor collaborative learning where knowledge is built by multiple participants and moves beyond the boundaries of the traditional classroom.

In the DE context, communication is a fundamental part of learning. This is so because learners stay at a distance while pursuing their course in the DE institutions and communicate online with their peers and instructors for better and improved learning, clarifying doubts in subject contents, resolving the problems faced while doing the learning tasks, etc.. The blogs in this sense, as asynchronous tools, have contributed a lot in retaining learners' motivation in their courses of studies. By blogging, learners can keep on working and collaborating in their course even if they are at distance and are engaged in other work at their home or office.

Learning through Blogs as a Collaborative Process

One of the biggest potentials of weblogs is the ability to create space where learners can collaborate online. The Read/Write Web opens up all sorts of new possibilities for learners to learn from each other (Pilar, 2008). Richardson (2006) expresses that "blogs are made of reflections and conversations updated every day (if not a couple of times a day). Blogging engages readers with ideas, questions, and links. It compels the readers-cum-contributors to think and to respond. It demands interaction and collaboration from the group members". Blogging ceases the feeling of isolation and brings the notion of 'togetherness' or 'we-ness' among learners which is rarely noticed in the early age of DE settings. Through constant interaction, it gives a sense of community feeling and motivates them to study together in a better way.

Blogging: A Motivating and Independent Learning Tool

Learning through blogging motivates learners to read and write carefully and consciously because a large audience are going to view it and submit their comments, suggestions, remarks on it, if any. Thus, learners while publishing their ideas on blogs take so much care, concern and responsibility of their writings. They take utmost care of their writings in the linguistic standpoint. By reading and commenting on others' entries, they start to learn from each other and this motivates them to express their ideas clearly by writing and publishing those on the blogs. This practise helps them to be more critical and analytical in their communication. Thus, it is stated that bloggers are not just readers and writers; they are editors and collaborators as well.

The weblog is a democratic tool that supports different learning styles. It assists learners who are reluctant and shy to express their ideas in front of others (counsellor/ instructor/tutor). In this case, a blog may give them an opportunity to share their thoughts or ideas in writing and publish it on blogs by seeking comments, suggestions, and remarks if any, from others.

The use of blogs in online learning environment encourages the practice of reflexive writing, where learners are stimulated to reflect on their writings before posting it in the Web pages. The possibility to make contributions publicly through the blog also stimulates their motivation. Blogs offer important possibilities of follow up and tracking the learning process of learners (Blogs as portfolios). In this context, instructors can collect evidence of the learners' progress and have elements to access them either individually or in groups. Blogs even allow immediate publication of didactic material through different multimedia, such as; hypertext, images, video, and audio. This material can be used in new and innovative ways such as using videos or images as a source for debate, doing project work, etc. (Camacho, 2009). Thus, to accommodate, support, and promote the online learning effectively, learners and instructors should consider dialogical pedagogical models among other models.

Dialogical Pedagogical Models

In these models the idea is to emphasize social interaction through dialogue and conversation. This helps learners in constructing new knowledge primarily through dialogue as a form of interaction. The online learning platform which is constituted by Internet and Web based technologies provides various mechanisms for supporting dialogue both in formal and informal learning environments. Through the exchange of dialogue, learners feel a sense of community and reduce the isolation stigma. For example, a Web-based group forum (discussion board) can support a formal conversational exchange that occurs in support of specific instructional objectives or an informal conversational exchange based on content interest (Dabbagh & Bannan- Ritland, 2005). Examples of dialogical pedagogical models include learning communities, knowledge building communities, and communities of practice. These models emphasize discursive or dialogical skills such as articulation, reflection, collaboration, and social negotiation, as well as self and group evaluation skills, which support the characteristics of successful online learners (Dabbagh, 2007).

Online learning technologies support the implementation of dialogical pedagogical models include asynchronous and synchronous tools, such as; e-mail, bulletin boards or discussion forums, computer conferencing, groupware, document sharing, virtual chat, and video conferencing. In this model of instruction, learners can interact and meet with their peer-groups and instructors on online discussion forum. While communicating ideas and thoughts in a threaded discussion platform, they can understand an issue in multiple dimensions. This atmosphere enthralls learners to feel as the classroom scenario, which was invariantly missing in the distance education system.

A survey report was prepared by Roper (2007) which documented that out of 93 learners 59 were respondents on the questionnaire "development of learners' online learning skills". The surveyor mentioned that participating in threaded discussions helped 52.6 percent students benefit most from interaction with their classmates, 15.8 percent benefit most by reading their peer groups' responses and/or comments, and 21 percent found e-mailing outside of the course platform a useful way to interact with their fellows. Thus, learning becomes more interactive and live.

From the above analyses, it is asserted that the emerging online learners can be described as those who have a strong understanding of study content, who is competent in the use of online learning technologies- particularly communication and collaborative technologies, understand values of engaging in social interaction and collaborative learning, possess strong interpersonal and communication skills, and bear self-directed learning attitude towards study activities.

REFERENCES

Alford, P., & Lawson, A. (2009). *Distance education student primer: Skills for being a successful online learner.* Retrieved September 17, 2009, from http://ittraining.iu.edu/ online/ tutorials/ de_student_primer.pdf

Anderson, T. D., & Garrison, D. R. (1998). Learning in a networked world: New roles and responsibilities. In Gibson, C. (Ed.), *Distance learners in higher education* (pp. 97–112). Madison, WI: Atwood Publishing.

Camacho, M. (2009). *Blogging and podcasting: Enhancing student's learning through Web 2.0 tools.* Retrieved September 18, 2009, from http:// claweb.cla.unipd.it/ cla/ EUROCALL/ abstracts/ camacho.pdf

Cheurprakobkit, S. (2002). Technicians' perceptions about Web-based courses: The University of Texas system experience. *American Journal of Distance Education, 16*(4), 245–258. doi:10.1207/ S15389286AJDE1604_4

Chi, M. T. H. (1989). Self- explanations: How learners study and use examples in learning to solve problems. *Cognitive Science, 13*, 259–294. doi:10.1207/s15516709cog1302_1

Concheiro, P. (2008). *Learning through blogging: An experience with Business Spanish learners at Rekjavik University.* Retrieved October 09, 2009, from http://malfridur.ismennt.is/ haust2008/ pdf/ malfridur-24-02-08-10-Concheiro.pdf

Dabbagh, N., & Bannan- Ritland, B. (2005). *Online learning: Concepts, strategies, and applications.* Upper Saddle River, NJ: Prentice Hall.

Dabbagh, N. (2007). The online learner: Characteristics and pedagogical implications. *Contemporary Issues in Technology & Teacher Education, 7*(3), 217–226.

Gruba, P., & Al-Mahmood, R. (2009). *Strategies for communication skills development.* Retrieved August 23, 2009, from http://crpit.com/ confpapers/ CRPITV30Gruba1.pdf

Powell, G. C. (2000). *Are you ready for Web-based training (WBT)?* Retrieved September 12, 2009, from http://it.coe.uga.edu/ itforum/ paper39/ paper39.html

Reid, J. E. (1997). Preparing learners for the task of online learning. *Syllabus*, *10*(7), 38–41.

Richardson, W. (2006). *Blogs, wikis, podcasts, and other powerful Web tools for classrooms*. US: Corwing Press.

Roper, A. R. (2007). How learners develop online learning skills. *Educase Quarterly*, *30*(1), 62–64.

Ryder, M., & Wilson, B. (1995). *From local to virtual learning environments: Making the connection*. Retrieved May 7, 2009, from http://www.cudenver.edu/ ~mryder/ aera95.html

Smith, S., & Benscoter, A. (1999). Implementing an internet tutorial for Web-based courses. *American Journal of Distance Education*, *13*(2), 74–80. doi:10.1080/08923649909527026

Whitworth, J. M. (1999). Looking at distance learning through both ends of the camera. *American Journal of Distance Education*, *13*(2), 64–73. doi:10.1080/08923649909527025

Williams, P. E. (2003). Roles and competencies of distance education programmes in higher education institutions. *American Journal of Distance Education*, *17*(1), 45–57. doi:10.1207/S15389286AJDE1701_4

About the Contributors

Ugur Demiray is Professor of Communication Teaching in the School of Communication Sciences of Anadolu University, Eskisehir, Turkey. His researches are dealt with distance education application of Anadolu University, Ministry of Education and by other universities in Turkey. His researches are on communicational gaps of distance education students with their institution, also interest also lies towards the profile of DE students, and relationship of graduates and job market in Turkey. He is also interested about changing of ethical behaviors around the world by inserting technological developments to the educational field, especially for distance education applications, marketing of distance education programmes, and e-learning. He has an extensive experience publishing e-journal on distance education internationally under the patronage of Anadolu University for 10 years, named, TOJDE-Turkish Online Journal for Distance Education. TOJDE is a peer-reviewed quarterly e-journal. He is also an editor, consultant editor, and reviewer for more than 15 international journals that deal with distance education and educational technology. In addition, he has responsibilities on advisory boards and as referee for conferences, symposiums, and panels. He has co-authored and individually contributed chapters in some Turkish and international books. Up to now he has around 15 imprint or eBooks dealing with distance education, and many articles published in national and international journals.

Gulsun Kurubacak is an Associate Professor in Applied Communication at the College of Open Education of Anadolu University. She undertook graduate studies at Anadolu University, Turkey (MA. Educational Technology) and the University of Cincinnati, USA (Ed.D. Curriculum & Instruction), and also worked as a post-doctoral fellow at the College of Education at New Mexico State University, USA (2001-2002). She is currently a graduate student in the Department of Computer and Instructional Technologies, and also an undergraduate student in the Computer Engineering at the College of Informatics Technologies and Engineering of Hoca Ahmet Yesevi International Turk-Kazakhstani University. Dr. Kurubacak has over twenty-five years experience in focusing on the democratic and multicultural aspects of distance education; finding new answers, viewpoints, and explanations to online communication problems through critical pedagogy; and improving learner critical thinking skills through project-based online learning. She continues to manage and provide pedagogical support for distance learning programs.

T. Volkan Yuzer, Ph.D., is an Associate Professor in Applied Communication at the Department of Distance Education, College of Open Education, Anadolu University, Turkey. He undertook graduate studies at Anadolu University, Turkey. His research interests are new communication technologies, synchronous, asynchronous, and interactive communications, and transformative learning milieus in distance and online education. He has over fifteen years experience in exploring additional distance learning media and providing communication and technological support for distance learning programs as well as develop online learning courses. He has participated in projects related to distance learning, online synchronous learning, and the virtual classroom. He has been teaching courses in distance learning, communication, and Information Technologies.

* * *

Simber Atay was born in Gaziantep on July 09, 1958. She finished primary and secondary schools there, completed her high school education in İzmir Namık Kemal High School, and graduated from Ege University, Faculty of Fine Arts, Department of Cinema-TV (1980). The subject of her undergraduate thesis was: "Kemal Sunal Comedy." She began working as a Research Associate in the department of graduation in 1981. She earned the Master Degree and Doctorate in Dokuz Eylül University Institute of Social Sciences. The subject of her postgraduate thesis was: "The Early Period of Photography and Ottoman Photographers" (1983); the subject of doctoral thesis was: "Manners of Approach in Turkish Film Critics" (1990). She took her Associate Professorship in 1992, and Professorship in 2000. She currently lectures in Dokuz Eylül University, Faculty of Fine Arts, Department of Photography and Anadolu University, Faculty of Communication Sciences, Department of Journalism. She conducted professional researches and examinations; in Rome Centro Sperimentale di Cinematografia in 1985-1986 academic year through the scholarship of the Italian Government, in Friuli on the occasion of Milano University, Organization of International Communication Laboratory in July, 1989, in Madrid Complutense University, Faculty of Communication in 1992-1993 academic year through the scholarship of the Spanish Government, in Bremen Goethe Institute in August-September 1995 through the scholarship of the Goethe Institute, in Paris in July 1998 through the scholarship of the French Government. She knows French, English, Spanish, and Italian.

H. Prentice Baptiste, Jr. is a Professor in the College of Education at New Mexico State University, in Las Cruces, New Mexico, USA. His research interests include the conceptualization of multicultural education, the process of multiculturalizing educational entities, and culturally diversifying science and mathematics instruction. His most recent research interest is centered on the U.S. Presidents and social justice and the role of instructional technology and its effect on scientific literacy among students of color. He has authored or edited six books, as well as numerous articles, papers, and chapters on multicultural education and science education. He works extensively with urban and rural schools and school districts in designing and implementing comprehensive diverse and multicultural plans. He has presented papers and conducted workshops in Nigeria, Egypt, Germany, Jamaica, Morocco, and the Netherlands.

Gayle M. Cicero, Ed. D., LCPC, is currently the Coordinator of School Counseling for Anne Arundel County Public Schools in Maryland, supervising and providing leadership to approximately 225 professional school counselors. Dr. Cicero has worked in public education for more than 20 years as a teacher, school counselor, pupil personnel worker, school administrator, and central office school counseling supervisor. At the college level Dr. Cicero has taught for the TEACH Institute of Anne Arundel Community College, the Graduate Counseling Department of George Mason University and is currently on the faculty of McDaniel College, Johns Hopkins University, and Northcentral University. Her interests and specialty areas include: social justice issues in school counseling, leadership, qualitative research, online teaching/learning, and school reform. In particular transformational leadership and systems thinking are areas of expertise. Dr. Cicero has presented at numerous local, state, and national conferences regarding school counseling programs and issues. Dr. Cicero is passionate about the role of the school counselor as a leader in creating equitable opportunities for all students.

Christine Clark is Professor of Curriculum and Instruction, Senior Scholar for Multicultural Education, and Founding Vice President for Diversity and Inclusion at the University of Nevada, Las Vegas. Clark was a Fulbright Senior Scholar at La Universidad Autónoma de Ciudad Juárez in México, and at La Universidad Rafael Landivar in Quetzaltenango, Guatemala, where she conducted research with graduate students on the theme "Violencia en Espacios Escolares" (Violence in Schools). Clark has a three-tiered research agenda that focuses on: 1) white antiracist identity development and multicultural teacher education preparation; 2) the prison industrial complex and implications for urban educational leadership; and 3) multicultural curriculum transformation in P-12 and higher education across disciplines. Clark is on the editorial board of *Multicultural Perspectives* and the *Journal of the National Association for Multicultural Education* (NAME). Clark is also the Associate Editor for the Higher Education section of *Multicultural Education.*

Teresa Coffman is an Associate Professor of Education at the University of Mary Washington in Fredericksburg, Virginia where she teaches graduate courses in curriculum and instruction, educational theory and research, and technology integration to pre-service teachers as they work toward initial licensure and a Master's degree in Education. Her research interests are in the areas of educational technology, inquiry-based learning and collaboration, distance learning, and global education. She holds a Ph.D. and a Master of Arts in Education. Her professional background includes teaching at both the middle and high-school level, as well as serving as a technology coordinator and Director of Academic Technology in K-12 education. She has also consulted on technology issues to educators and previously worked in the telecommunications industry prior to academia.

Dave Cross has a varied background in education, including a B.S. in Engineering, a M.Ed., a MBA, a M.S. in Safety, and an Ed.D. in Curriculum and Instruction. He has been teaching in higher education for 16 years, both in the classroom and online. Most of his teaching has been with Embry-Riddle Aeronautical University. When not teaching, he is an international pilot on the Boeing 777, flying mostly in Asia. Living in Colorado affords him the opportunity to ski and hike all through the year.

Aimee deNoyelles received her M.A. in academic psychology from East Carolina University in North Carolina and is currently pursuing her doctoral degree in instructional design and technology at the University of Cincinnati, USA. Her research interests include computer-mediated communication, immersive technology, and virtual social identity.

Mehmet Firat is a Research Assistant working in the Department of Distance Education, Faculty of Open Education from Anadolu University, Eskişehir, Turkey. He continues his Ph.D. education at the Department of Computer Education and Instructional Technologies at Education Sciences Institution. He has articles published in international and national journals and papers presented at international and national meetings. His academic interests are cognitive science in educational technology, learning in educational hypermedia and multimedia, e-learning, virtual learning environments, 3D virtual worlds, instructional design, and personal learning environments. He is currently works on his Ph.D. dissertation related to use of metaphors in educational media and affects on learner performance.

Alexander G. Flor is Professor of Information and Communication Studies at the University of the Philippines - Open University. Formerly UPOU Vice Chancellor for research and development, he was the founding Dean of the Faculty of Information and Communication Studies serving two terms (2004 to 2010). He held the SEARCA-UP Centennial Professorial Chair in 2008-09 and the Metro Manila Professorial Chair in Development Communication in 1995-96. He served as Professor of Strategic Communication of the University of the Philippines Los Baños College of Development Communication. Dr. Flor completed his PhD in development communication, international relations, and policy studies at the University of the Philippines. He was a Fulbright-PAEF post-doctoral fellow at the East West Center Institute of Communication and Culture (Honolulu, 1989). Professor Flor has authored the following books: *eDevelopment and Knowledge Management* (SEAMEO-SEARCA, 2001); *Digital Tools for Process Documentation* (SEAMEO-SEARCA, 2002); *Ethnovideography* (SEAMEO-SEARCA, 2003); *Introduction to Development Communication* (UP Open University, 2003); *Environmental Communication* (UP Open University, 2004); *Development Communication Praxis* (UP Open University, 2007); and *Developing Societies in the Information Age* (UP Open University, 2009). Flor is a member of the East West Center Association, the New York Academy of Sciences, and the American Association for the Advancement of Science.

Shalin Hai-Jew works as an Instructional Designer at Kansas State University, and she teaches for WashingtonOnline. She has BAs in English and Psychology and an M.A. in English from the University of Washington, which she entered at age 15. She has an Ed.D. in Educational Leadership from Seattle University (2005), where she was a Morford Scholar. She recently wrote and published "Digital Imagery and Informational Graphics in E-Learning: Maximizing Visual Technologies" (2010). She recently edited and published "Virtual Immersive and 3D Learning Spaces: Emerging Technologies and Trends" (2011). She is working on a text titled "Constructing Self-Discovery Learning Spaces Online: Scaffolding and Decision Making Technologies," slated for release in 2011 by IGI-Global.

Amani Hamdan is an award winning scholar. Her doctoral research which came out later in a book: *Muslim Women Speak: A Tapestry of Lives and Dreams* won the first Canadian Society for the Study of Women in Education CASWE award in 2006. She obtained her PhD in Educational Studies at the Faculty of Education at the University of Western Ontario in 2006. Her research interests include education and curricula in Saudi Arabia, online education and cultural manifestation, higher education, narrative research, critical multicultural education, Muslim representation in Canadian schools and curriculum, equity and social justice, and Saudi women's education. Amani extensively researched global education in Canadian schools. In 2002 she obtained her M.A. of education from Mount Saint Vincent University in Halifax. Amani has over 15 years of teaching experience in Canada and Saudi Arabia. She taught Multicultural Education courses for pre-service teachers at the University of Western Ontario. She worked and taught at Ottawa University in Canada as an Adjunct Professor. She can be reached at amanihamdan2004@yahoo.ca

Murat Hismanoglu is the head of the English Language Teaching Department in the European University of Lefke, Faculty of Arts and Sciences, Gemikonagi, Mersin 10, Turkey. He teaches phonetics, phonology, language acquisition, and ELT methodology to BA students in the ELT Department. He is interested in educational phonetics, applied semiotics, and Web-based language instruction.

Sibel Hismanoglu is an English instructor in the European University of Lefke, English Preparatory School, Gemikonagi, Mersin 10, and Turkey. She teaches general English and academic English to BA students in Faculties of Arts and Sciences and Engineering. She is interested in language testing, vocabulary teaching, and Web-based language instruction.

Isıl Kabakci Yurdakul is Assistant Professor in Computer and Instructional Technologies Education Department of Education Faculty, Anadolu University, Eskişehir, Turkey. She received her Ph.D. in Computer and Instructional Technologies Education from Anadolu University, Turkey in 2005. She has articles published in international and national journals, papers presented to international and national meetings, and published national books and chapters in international and national books about her academic interest area. She served various projects as executive and researcher. Her academic interest areas are professional development, information and communication technologies integration, instructional design, internet, and children.

Mary Beth Klinger is a Professor of business and management at the College of Southern Maryland in La Plata, Maryland where she teaches undergraduate courses in business, management, leadership, organizational behavior, small business and entrepreneurship, and marketing. Her research interests are in the areas of knowledge management, leadership, innovation, and global education. She holds a Ph.D. in Organization and Management, a Master's in Business Administration, and a Master's in International Management. Her professional background includes educational consulting, employment in private industry in logistics and supply chain management, as well as several federal government agencies, to include the Office of Personnel Management, the U.S. Department of Labor, and the Federal Trade Commission.

Dennis Lessard is the Dean of the School of Education at Northcentral University, a totally online university with worldwide scope. He has served as Adjunct, Lecturer, Professor, Department Chair and Dean on five different University or Industrial faculties including Northcentral, Embry-Riddle Aeronautical University, Los Angeles City College, The George Washington University, and The Boeing Educational Institute. He has extensive experience in online and in-residence education in teaching, managing, and producing innovative methodologies for delivering interactive based academic courses. Dr. Lessard holds four educational degrees including a BA in Education, MA in Management, and PhD in Business Administration. He is also a graduate of two industry management programs. He is a member of the International Society of Air Safety Investigators (ISASI); the Daedalians - The National Fraternity of Military Pilots, Delta Mu Delta, the International Honor Society of Business Administration and Kappa Delta PI, the International Honor Society in Education.

Pradeep Kumar Misra is an Associate Professor (Educational Technology) in the Faculty of Education and Allied Sciences of M.J.P. Rohilkhand University, India. His research specializations are Educational Technology, Media for Societal Development and Lifelong Learning. Dr. Misra has received the prestigious DAAD Doctoral Scholarship, DAAD Senior Researcher Scholarship, and European Commission's Erasmus Mundus Visiting Scholar Scholarship. Dr. Misra was visiting scholar in Danish School of Education, Arhus University, Copenhagen in year 2009 for International Master's in Lifelong Learning: Policy and Management Programme. He has to his credit more than 30 publications in these areas, authored a book 'Educational Television in Germany', completed R&D Projects, presented papers in various International Forums and visited number of countries for academic purposes. Dr. Misra is also a founder member and Secretary of Society for Professional Development of Indian Teachers.

Vardan Mkrttchian is Professor and Chief Execute – Rector at the All Armenian Internet University of HHH Technology Incorporation at Sydney, Australia. He is on-line Professor in Faculty of Professional Education of Astrakhan State University (Russian Federation). He has authored over 250 refereed publications including 6 books and 27 patents. Dr. of Sciences Mkrttchian is a recipient of the Award of Pioneering and Innovation in Internet Education system, and he received the USSR Award for Innovation. Her current interest is in discourse theory; meta-communication model design, reflective practice, intercultural communication; Information Systems development; discourse ethics; avatar manager and student reflective conversations pedagogy theory; virtual teaching system; web-based courses and sliding mode control system theory and practices

Jennifer J. Neakrase finished her doctorate degree in Science Education under Dr. Julie A. Luft at Arizona State University-Tempe in 2010. Prior to working on her doctorate, she received a Master of Science degree in Physics from Arizona State University-Tempe, and a Bachelor of Science degree with honors in Astrophysics from Indiana University, Bloomington, IN. Most recently she has worked with Dr. Luft on a National Science Foundation study of beginning science teachers, where she focused on the pedagogical content knowledge and practices of in-field and out-of-field Physics teachers. She has presented her research at national conferences, including the American Association of Physics Teachers, the National Association for Research in Science Teaching, and the American Educational Research Association. Recently she accepted a shared assistant faculty position with New Mexico State University in the departments of Curriculum and Instruction and Physics.

Ashley N. Ryan is currently working on her doctorate degree in Critical Pedagogy with a minor in Higher Education under Dr. H. Prentice Baptiste at New Mexico State University, Las Cruces, NM. Prior to working on her doctorate, she received a Master of Arts degree with honors in Communication Studies from New Mexico State University, and a Bachelor of Arts in Communication Studies from New Mexico State University. Ashley has been involved in ESL/ELL education as a College Instructor, where she worked with students from around the world. Most recently she has worked with Dr. Eric L. Morgan on a study of interethnic couples and the revelation of their relationship to family.

Kay Kyeongju Seo is an Assistant Professor of Instructional Design and Technology at the University of Cincinnati, USA. Her research interests revolve around socio-cognitive development in online immersive virtual environments, constructivist approaches to educational simulations and microworlds, and student interaction in computer-mediated communication.

Satya Sundar Sethy, PhD is working as an Assistant Professor of Philosophy in the Department of Humanities and Social Sciences, Indian Institute of Technology Madras, Chennai, India. Prior to this engagement, he was serving to Indira Gandhi National Open University (IGNOU), New Delhi, India for quite a few years. On his account there is a book entitled "Meaning Atomism vs. Meaning Holism: An Approach to Philosophy of Language." He is an active researcher and believes in intra and inter-disciplinary research credited with a few chapters in edited books, papers in international and national journals followed by units and blocks in the Distance Education disciplines.

Melanie Shaw has over ten years of educational experience ranging from classroom and graduate level teaching to counseling and administration. Melanie received a Ph.D. in Education with a specialization in Curriculum and Teaching from Northcentral University, a Master's degree in Education Administration from Grand Canyon University, and a second Master's degree in School Counseling for the University of West Alabama. She received her Bachelor's degree in Liberal Studies and Music from Excelsior College. She holds teaching certificates in online teaching, elementary education, and guidance counseling. She is currently an Associate Professor of Curriculum at Northcentral University. In addition, Melanie is an Education Consultant for the national healthcare staffing organization, Temps Inc., President of Innovative eLearning Solutions, and the Executive Editor for the eLearning Institute.

Narong Sompong is Associate Professor of Educational Technology, Faculty of Education, Kasetsart University, Thailand. He earned his Doctor of Philosophy in Development Communication at the University of the Philippines Los Baños. In 1997, he served as Visiting Professor of Information Technology and Extension at the University of Queensland, Australia. Dr. Narong has published four books and authored fourteen research articles on educational technology.

Susan Stillman, Ed.D., a former K-8 school counselor and a National Certified Counselor, is on the graduate faculties of Northcentral University, Fielding Graduate University, and Northern Arizona University. She is Chair of the Social Emotional Learning Special Interest Group for AERA, past President of the CT School Counselor Association, a member of the AZ School Counselor Association Research Committee, and co-editor of the *School Counseling Research and Practice Journal*. She has co-authored a book chapter on emotional intelligence and school counseling, and has written articles for *ASCA School Counselor, School Counseling Research and Practice,* and *the World Futures Journal*. Dr. Stillman is developing a practice coaching youth and adults with the SEI and SEI-YV emotional intelligence assessments, and uses social emotional learning in all her work with graduate students, teachers, and school counselors. Research and praxis interests include grounded theory, emotional intelligence, school counselor outcome research, and systems thinking.

Gwen Stowers is Professor of Teacher Education and Program Lead for the Teaching and Learning in a Global Society concentration in the School of Education and National University in San Diego, California. Stowers began her tenure with National University in 2000, just as the University was beginning its foray into online education. Today, most of Stowers work with National is online. Stowers lives with her husband in rural, working class border town in Southern New Mexico. Together they promote border rights (taking pride in being called "border rats" and "horse traders"), teach English on both sides of the border, work as real estate agents for new immigrants, publish the bilingual newspaper, *Las Fronteras*, and continue to make aesthetic improvements on their hand sculptured adobe house.

Nurdan Oncel Taskiran has been working for Kocaeli University, Kocaeli, Faculty of Communication, Radio Cinema & Television Department since 2001. She has been an Associate Professor in Applied Communication Sciences since 2007 December. She has written two books, one of which is on Media Literacy researches in Turkey, and the other, which proposes some scriptwriting methodologies for television serials, is titled "Aliye, the new image of contemporary female minds." Her researches are primarily on popular culture products and Media Literacy. She also has researches on Semiology as a means of communication and advertising communication and decoding visual arts via Iconography. She is interested in distance learning as well, as a way of communication related with semiotics, as a part of human perception and signification. She has a keen interest on animal communication. She has papers, articles, and translations published in national and international journals. She has been giving courses on graduate and post graduate levels at Kocaeli University.

Elsa Q. Villa received her doctorate in 2010 in Curriculum and Instruction from New Mexico State University where she currently serves as a Research Associate. Dr. Villa was a full-time lecturer at The University of Texas at El Paso where she taught elementary mathematics and science methods courses. She has served as a principal and co-principal investigator of numerous federal, state, and corporate grants focusing on research communities, inquiry mathematics/science, and engineering education. Her research interests are learning communities, teacher identity, and inquiry teaching and learning. She has published several articles in refereed journals and a refereed book chapter.

Recep Yilmaz is a lecturer in Vocational High School of Beykent University, Istanbul, Turkey. He is a graduate of PR and Publicity Department of Konya Selcuk University and got his MA degree from Journalism in Kocaeli University with his thesis titled "Illocutionary Impacts of the Newspapers in Construction of Social Reality" in 2008 and now has been studying for his doctoral thesis in Communication Sciences at Kocaeli University.His studies are primarily on communication philosophy, advertising communication, public journalism, visual culture and discourse analysis methodologies. He has given courses on Decoding Advertisments, Advertising Language, Discourse Analysis, Media and Media Strategies, Scriptwriting for Advertising and film production, Public Relations, Scriptwring for Public Relations, Photography and Basic Optics, Visual Graphic Design and Visual Communication applications. He aims to bring up fellows to be employed in communication related fields.

Index

D

E

F

G

H

I

P

R

S

T

U

V

W

CPSIA information can be obtained at www.ICGtesting.com
Printed in the USA
BVOW060434230911

271894BV00004B/127-188/P